Improving Tax Administration In Developing Countries

Edited by

Richard M. Bird and Milka Casanegra de Jantscher

International Monetary Fund
1992

Cover and interior design by IMF Graphics Section

Library of Congress Cataloging-in-Publication Data

Improving tax administration in developing countries / Richard M. Bird and Milka Casanegra de Jantscher, editors.
p. cm.
Book is based on a conference held in Segovia, Spain, June 6–7, 1991.
Includes bibliographical references.
ISBN 1-55775-317-2
1. Tax administration and procedure—Latin America—Case studies—Congresses. 2. Taxation—Latin America—Case studies—Congresses. I. Bird, Richard Miller, 1938– . II. Casanegra de Jantscher, Milka. III. International Monetary Fund.
HJ3374.5.I48 1992
351.72'4'098—dc20 92-34718
CIP

Price: US$23.00

Address orders to:
International Monetary Fund, Publication Services
700 19th Street, N.W., Washington, D.C. 20431, U.S.A.
Telephone: (202) 623-7430
Telefax: (202) 623-7491
Cable: Interfund

Foreword

It has always been a source of amazement for me to realize how many books and articles in professional journals deal with taxation. Most of these discuss various aspects of tax policy or tax law. Some of them are theoretical, others practical. For the most part they are concerned with the impact of changes in tax laws on the economy or on the income of taxpayers. Economists have developed theories that provide guidance for assessing just how good a tax system is. Somewhat surprising is how little of this writing deals specifically with ways in which taxes are administered. In fact, most public finance textbooks allocate practically no space to tax administration, assuming implicitly that the administration of tax systems is a trivial problem. Most journal articles on taxation also largely ignore issues of tax administration, and only infrequently does one find specialized writing focusing exclusively on administration problems. Yet, taxation is the art of the possible. A tax system that is not administrable is not worth much. The theoretically most perfect tax system in the world may become a bad system if the intention expressed in the law is distorted by the practice.

There may be various explanations for this lack of attention to tax administration, but probably it has much to do with the fact that an intimate knowledge of how an administration works is necessary to write about tax administration. This knowledge is only acquired by years of practical experience. Perhaps, because of training, or because of what they do, tax administrators are not inclined to generalizing from the problems they face.

In recent years organizations such as the Inter-American Center of Tax Administrators (CIAT) and the Centre de Rencontres et d'Études des Dirigeants des Administrations Fiscales (CREDAF) have started changing the situation. CIAT conferences, for example, have been addressing general administrative problems. Still, the relative balance between writing on tax policy and writing on tax administration has not yet been corrected, so that when a new book, and especially an important new book, appears, which deals exclusively with administrative issues, it should be a cause for considerable satisfaction.

The Fiscal Affairs Department of the International Monetary Fund is one of the major centers in which tax policy and tax administration problems are discussed. The department assists many countries with advice on how to improve their administrations. Therefore, when Richard Bird and Milka Casanegra de Jantscher approached me about the project on which this book is based, I was particularly enthusiastic.

I felt that a book of this kind would be extremely valuable for our work, as well as for the work of tax administrators around the world.

I am hopeful that the current book will succeed in raising the quality of the discussion on tax administration to a much higher level than in the past. The book shows that techniques that have been successful in one country can be successful in other countries provided that they take full account of the local environment. The use of new computer technology has created new possibilities for filing, for identifying, and for auditing taxpayers. These possibilities are not necessarily country-specific. But the mechanical transplanting of techniques from one country to another is unlikely to generate good results. I hope that the book will make a substantial contribution to the field of tax administration and that it will become an essential reference for tax experts everywhere.

VITO TANZI
Director
Fiscal Affairs Department

Preface

This book originated in a request from Miguel Angel Lasheras, Director of the Instituto de Estudios Fiscales of the Ministry of Finance of Spain, to Richard Bird to help put together a book on the subject of tax administration in the member countries of the Inter-American Center of Tax Administrators (CIAT), as part of the Instituto's contribution to the five hundreth anniversary of Columbus's voyage to America. When Milka Casanegra de Jantscher, Assistant Director of the Fiscal Affairs Department of the International Monetary Fund, agreed to serve as co-editor, the project became feasible, and with the collaboration of the Fiscal Affairs Department and the unstinting support of the Instituto de Estudios Fiscales a conference on tax administration and tax policy in CIAT countries was held at Segovia, Spain, on June 6–7, 1991. The present book is based on the papers and discussion at this conference, as revised by the authors in light of the conference discussion and, to a limited extent, by the editors in order to produce a more integrated book than the usual conference proceedings.

The book has two principal parts, in addition to a brief introductory chapter intended to introduce the volume as a whole. In the first part, some of the more interesting recent country experiences with tax administration reform are summarized and evaluated. Different chapters deal with the major simplifications of tax structure and attendant administrative reforms in Bolivia and Uruguay, the important reform of income tax administration in Colombia, the development of a new system of information management in the Spanish tax administration, the introduction of a value-added tax in Trinidad and Tobago, and the on-going efforts to reform both tax structure and tax administration in Jamaica and Guatemala. Each of the chapters is written by people who were not only closely involved with what they discuss but who can also bring to bear a wider perspective on the reasons for the success (or failure) of the efforts they describe. In addition, in every case at least one comment on the chapter has been prepared by someone with substantial local knowledge—often an active participant in the experience discussed. Together, these five case studies provide an invaluable set of papers on specific country experiences with tax administration reform and its links to tax policy reform.

In contrast, the second part of the book stands back from specific country experiences and considers instead a number of important issues and aspects of tax administration reform more generally. One chapter, for example, focuses on the effects of inflation on tax administration.

Three chapters discuss three of the basic elements of tax administration: improving the organization and performance of the administration itself, improving the services and assistance provided to taxpayers, and improving taxpayer compliance. Finally, the last chapter of the book considers the extent to which tax administration can be "privatized" by turning over to the private sector some functions traditionally carried out by public employees. Both the authors of these papers and the commentators have had wide experience in the areas they discuss. Indeed, although the focus of this book is on the Latin American and Caribbean region, since many of the authors and discussants have worked on similar problems in other parts of the world, many of the lessons they draw are obviously of wider relevance.

The task of turning a set of papers and discussions originally delivered in two languages—Spanish and English—in a relatively short time into a book that reads well in both languages was by no means easy. The editors are most grateful to both the Instituto de Estudios Fiscales and the International Monetary Fund for their indispensable assistance in making this feasible. In particular, we are most indebted to Carlos Silvani of the Fiscal Affairs Department for editorial and other assistance well beyond the call of duty, in addition to his own impressive contributions to this volume. Isabel Menendez Ros and her colleagues at the Instituto de Estudios Fiscales were also of invaluable assistance both in organizing the complex logistics of a conference involving participants from 16 countries and in helping to bring the finished product to the publication stage. Vito Tanzi, Director of the Fiscal Affairs Department, was most gracious both in permitting his hard-pressed staff to make such a substantial contribution to this volume and in supporting the publication of the book. Similarly, Miguel Angel Lasheras, Director of the Instituto de Estudios Fiscales, whose idea this book originally was, provided unwavering support throughout the long process of its gestation. Esha Ray of the Fund's External Relations Department deserves special mention for editing the English version of the book for publication.

In the end, however, our main debt is of course to the contributors to this volume. We were exceptionally fortunate in being able to attract such a distinguished and expert group to the conference in the first place, and we were doubly lucky in the extent to which their papers complemented and reinforced each other. The contributors come not only from a variety of countries but also a variety of backgrounds, including administration, economics, and law. This diverse mix both produced some lively discussion at the original conference, as evidenced in this book, and gave rise to some of the more valuable insights that emerged from this discussion.

How to improve tax administration is one of the most important, and least studied, aspects of fiscal reform in developing countries. The present volume constitutes a major contribution to the relatively undeveloped literature in this field. It should be of interest to all those concerned with the important question of mobilizing resources for development. In particular, we hope that it will prove to be of use to those to whom we dedicate it: the many tax officials throughout the world who try, often under very adverse circumstances, to carry out the difficult but essential task of gathering the taxes that, in the words of U.S. Supreme Court Justice Oliver Wendell Holmes, are necessary to pay for civilization.

RICHARD M. BIRD
MILKA CASANEGRA DE JANTSCHER
Editors

Contributors

MARÍA CORINA AROCHA, Ministry of Finance, Venezuela
ROY BAHL, Georgia State University
RICHARD M. BIRD, University of Toronto
RENATO BOTARO, Deputy Director of Taxes, Brazil
RAMIRO CABEZAS M., Consultant, Bolivia
MILKA CASANEGRA DE JANTSCHER, International Monetary Fund
MICHAL Y. CHRISTIAN, VAT Office, Trinidad and Tobago
ISAIAS COELHO, International Monetary Fund
JOHN F. DUE, University of Illinois
JAVIER ETCHEBERRY, Director of Taxes, Chile
ARTURO FERNANDEZ, Instituto Tecnológico de Mexico
RICHARD GORDON, International Tax Program, Harvard University
FRANCIS P. GREANEY, KPMG Peat Marwick
EDGAR GUTIÉRREZ, Consultant, Costa Rica
MALCOLM G. LANE, KPMG Peat Marwick
ROBERT A. LEBAUBE, Consultant, Washington, D.C.
JORGE MARTINEZ-VAZQUEZ, Georgia State University
CHARLES E. MCLURE, JR., Hoover Institution
RAFAEL MOYA, Ministry of Finance, Spain
OLIVER OLDMAN, Harvard Law School
SANTIAGO PARDO M., Consultant, Colombia
JAIME F. PINEDA S., Ministry of Finance, Guatemala
ALBERTO H.J. RADANO, Consultant, Argentina
LUIS FERNANDO RAMÍREZ ACUÑA, Embassy of Colombia, Washington, D.C.
JOSÉ-DAMIÁN SANTIAGO, Ministry of Finance, Spain
ALDO SCHLEMENSON, Consultant, Argentina
CARLOS A. SILVANI, International Monetary Fund
EDWIN TULLOCH-REID, Board of Revenue, Jamaica
JAIME VÁZQUEZ-CARO, World Bank
CHARLES L. VEHORN, International Monetary Fund

Affiliations listed are those at the time of the conference.

Contents

1

The Reform of Tax Administration

Milka Casanegra de Jantscher and Richard M. Bird

The subject of tax administration is extremely important both to those concerned with the key role increased tax yields can play in restoring macroeconomic balance and to those concerned with tax policy and its effects on the economy in general. As Tanzi (1987) has pointed out, tax administration plays a crucial role in determining the real (or effective) tax system, as opposed to the statutory tax system. Indeed, there is a growing conviction among tax policy specialists in developing countries that "policy change without administrative change is nothing" (Bird (1991, p. 39)) and that it is critical to ensure that "changes in tax policy are compatible with administrative capacity" (World Bank (1991, p. 51)). In a very real sense, "tax administration *is* tax policy" in developing countries (Casanegra de Jantscher (1990, p. 179)).

The "best" tax administration is not simply one that collects the most revenue. *How* that revenue is raised—that is, the effect of the revenue-generation effort on equity, on the political fortunes of governments, and on the level of economic welfare—may be equally important. A poor-quality tax administration may collect large amounts from easy-to-tax sectors such as wage earners, while being unable to enforce taxes on business enterprises and professionals. The level of collection is therefore a somewhat unsophisticated measure of the effectiveness of tax administration. A more accurate measure is the size of the "compliance gap"—that is, the gap between actual and potential tax revenues—and how that gap varies among the different sectors of the taxpaying population.

Over the last three decades the governments of many Latin American and Caribbean countries, as well as those of the Iberian peninsula, have made considerable efforts to improve the effectiveness of their tax administrations. These efforts frequently took place under unfavorable macroeconomic circumstances. Tax administrators often had to cope with a barrage of tax reforms, interspersed with numerous ad hoc

We are grateful to Amaresh Bagchi and, especially, to Carlos Silvani for helpful comments on this chapter.

changes in tax rates, exemptions, and payment periods introduced largely for revenue reasons. As discussed in Casanegra de Jantscher, Coelho, and Fernandez (Chapter 7 in this volume), bouts of high inflation further complicated tax administration in a number of countries, both because of the adjustments needed to offset the impact of inflation and because of the negative effects inflation has on tax compliance.

In spite of these difficulties, several member countries of the Centro Interamericano de Administradores Tributarios (CIAT)[1] considerably improved the quality of their tax administration, particularly in the 1980s. In broad terms, the 1960s were a decade of hope, when some thought that the introduction of the then new computer technology would solve the problems of tax administration. In contrast, the 1970s were for many countries a decade of frustration, as it became increasingly clear that technology alone could not do the job. Finally, the 1980s—in so many ways a lost decade for a Latin America burdened with external indebtedness and characterized by macroeconomic instability—turned out to be a decade of achievement for the reform of tax administration. In South America, particularly solid achievements were recorded in Bolivia, Chile, Colombia, and Uruguay. Portugal and Spain also made considerable progress during the 1980s. Such successes show that, under the right conditions, the efficiency of tax administration *can* be increased significantly in a relatively short time. Moreover, as these countries have demonstrated, when administration is improved, revenues can be maintained and even increased while at the same time reducing excessively high tax rates and diminishing inequities through more adequate enforcement of taxes across different taxpaying groups (Silvani (1991)).

The progress made during the 1980s in these countries provides an encouraging example to other countries that are now undertaking major tax administration reforms. For example, Argentina, having reformed its tax structure significantly, has turned to overhauling its tax administration, with initially high returns in the form of increased tax collections.[2] Peru is also engaged in major reforms of both its tax structure and its tax administration. Important structural changes in administration are taking place in Mexico. El Salvador, Jamaica, Paraguay, and

[1]The headquarters of CIAT—the Inter-American Center of Tax Administrators—is in Panama. Its members include Latin American and Caribbean countries, as well as the United States, Canada, Spain, and a number of other nonregional countries.

[2]In Argentina the ratio of tax to GDP rose from 13 percent in 1989 to 20 percent in 1990, with at least one third of this increase being attributable to improved administration, particularly of the value-added tax (VAT). (The remainder is attributable to broadening the tax base and the beneficial effect on collections of the marked decline in the rate of inflation over this period.)

Venezuela are all planning to introduce a VAT and to implement major tax administration reforms. Brazil is also studying the possibility of undertaking reforms in its federal tax administration.

This book discusses which solutions have worked and which have not worked in the field of tax administration reform. Why have some countries been successful in their efforts to improve their tax administration and others have not? The five chapters in Part I of the book outline and assess in detail recent major administrative and policy changes in Bolivia, Colombia, Guatemala, Jamaica, Spain, Trinidad and Tobago, and Uruguay. Part II of the book then considers specific aspects of tax administration reform, drawing both on these country case studies and on the experiences of other countries such as Argentina, Chile, Mexico, and the United States. The commentators on each chapter also draw on experiences in each of these countries, as well as in Brazil, Costa Rica, Peru, Venezuela and, indeed, in most other countries of the Latin American and Caribbean region and in a wide variety of other developing and developed countries.

I. Lessons from Experience

One of the most important lessons emerging from the experiences set out in this book is that, as a rule, an essential precondition for the reform of tax administration is the *simplification* of the tax system to ensure that it can be applied effectively in the generally "low-compliance" contexts of developing countries. The experience of Bolivia, which introduced a major simplification of its tax system in 1986, is instructive in this respect. As Silvani and Radano (Chapter 2 in this volume) show, much of the success achieved in reforming the tax administration in Bolivia can be attributed clearly to the extensive simplifications made in the tax system. Indeed, as Bahl and Martinez-Vazquez (Chapter 3 in this volume) argue in the case of Jamaica, it seldom makes sense to try to reform tax administration without simultaneously reforming the tax structure so that it is both sensible and easy to administer. Of course, as experience in both Chile (Harberger (1989)) and Colombia (McLure and Pardo (Chapter 4 in this volume)) demonstrates, it is possible to improve administration with less drastic but nonetheless effective simplifications in tax policy. The reduction in the number of income tax deductions, for instance, permitted these countries to eliminate filing requirements for most wage earners, thus greatly reducing the administrative burden since withholding alone then sufficed to enable most income tax payers to fulfill their obligations.

Another important lesson suggested by experience is the need for a *strategy* for the successful reform of tax administration. "Strategy" in this context simply means a comprehensive plan that assigns clear priorities to the tasks that must be performed, tailored to the available resources. As the case studies show, no single strategy is appropriate for all countries and under all circumstances. In Bolivia, for example, where huge macroeconomic imbalances had practically destroyed the tax system and its administration, shock treatment was called for.[3] In other countries, such as Colombia and Uruguay, a more gradual approach to reform has been successful.[4] In still other countries, such as Trinidad and Tobago (Due and Greaney (Chapter 5 in this volume)), the introduction of a major new tax—generally the VAT—has required meticulous planning and implementation in order to ensure success.[5]

The third ingredient for successful reform of tax administration is a strong *commitment* to reform at both the policymaking and managerial levels, as well as a certain degree of technical competence. The best reform strategy applied to the most simplified system will fail if there is a lack of political will to implement it. While some crucial initial technical support can sometimes be obtained from foreign experts, a critical core of local expertise is needed to take full advantage of such assistance. Even more important is the presence of a managerial team fully committed to taking the steps necessary to improve the quality of tax administration, with the full political support of the highest authorities. Without such commitment and support, even the best-designed reform efforts will not be successful in the end.

Successful tax administration reforms thus have these three main ingredients in common—simplification, strategy, and commitment. There is, however, no single set of prescriptions—no secret recipe—that, once introduced, will ensure improved tax administration in any country. Developing countries exhibit a wide variety of tax compliance levels, reflecting not only the effectiveness of their tax administrations but also taxpayer attitudes toward taxation and toward government in general as well as many other factors. Attitudes affect intentions and

[3]For another example of a country in which similar shocks eventually induced major changes, see the discussion of Argentina in World Bank (1990) and Bird (1992).

[4]The case of Uruguay is discussed in Silvani and Radano (Chapter 2 in this volume) and Harberger (1989); the Colombian case is discussed in McLure and Pardo (Chapter 4 in this volume) and Bird (1992).

[5]The planning and strategy required to introduce a VAT successfully is discussed further in Casanegra de Jantscher (1990) and Tait (1988, 1991).

intentions affect behavior.[6] Attitudes are formed in a social context by such factors as the perceived level of evasion, the perceived fairness of the tax structure, its complexity and stability, how it is administered, the value attached to government activities, and the legitimacy of government. Government policies affecting any of these factors may thus influence taxpayer attitudes and hence the observed level of taxpayer compliance. Measures sometimes recommended for countries with low compliance levels—for example, massive application of such administrative penalties as temporary closures of businesses that fail to issue VAT receipts[7]—may be inappropriate for countries with higher compliance levels, in which a targeted application of stricter penalties may be more effective in enhancing voluntary compliance.[8]

Finally, it should be emphasized that "gimmicks" or "quick fixes" are not of much use in resolving tax administration problems. Some such approaches—for example, lotteries in which tax invoices constitute lottery numbers and tax amnesties—have long (and properly) been derided by experienced tax administrators as being costly and of dubious effectiveness (Goode (1981); Casanegra de Jantscher (1990)). Even the more appropriate approach of widespread withholding—covering not only traditional items such as wages, interest, and dividends but also extending to professional fees, rents, and, in some instances, to practically all business transactions—is not without dangers.[9] Although undeniably useful in immediately strengthening collections, such widespread withholding does not obviate the need to strengthen the tax administration itself. The tax administration must, for example, be able to control withholders to make sure they hand over to the treasury the amounts withheld, and it must also be able to check whether the amounts taxpayers credit against their liabilities as taxes withheld have

[6]Although this proposition cannot be demonstrated very satisfactorily, there is some evidence in support of it: for a recent example—which appears to be the only published survey of taxpayer attitudes in a developing country—see Mann and Smith (1988) on Puerto Rico.

[7]In Argentina, for instance, such closures rose from almost none in 1989 to 750 in 1990 and to over 5,000 in the first nine months of 1991.

[8]Unfortunately, little real advance has apparently been made with respect to the analysis of penalties since Oldman (1965). Despite the huge economic literature on tax evasion, which fundamentally focuses on the appropriate role and implementation of penalties (Cowell (1990)), there seems to be no empirical study of penalty design and effectiveness in developing countries. What studies do exist, mostly for the United States, appear to be both model- and country-specific (Slemrod (1990)) and cannot easily be generalized to the quite different circumstances of developing countries.

[9]Some countries have gone so far as to introduce what may be called "reverse withholding" (Soos (1990)) in which purchasers (government agencies or large enterprises) "withhold" tax from sellers (small enterprises).

in fact been withheld. As the earlier Colombian experience (see McLure and Pardo (Chapter 4 in this volume)) suggests, although withholding constitutes an important element in a successful income tax, withholding alone will be insufficient unless the administration is able to control both withholders and taxpayers subject to withholding.

II. Paths to Reform

Reform strategies vary from country to country, but one constraint is usually common: the scarcity of resources for tax administration. Despite the high potential payoff in terms of increased revenue, it is usually difficult, and often impossible, for tax departments to obtain more staff, to raise wages to attract (and retain) highly qualified staff, or even to meet such basic material needs as office space and computers. Since tax administrators are civil servants, they are subject to all the constraints affecting civil services in developing countries. Reform strategies that require substantial additional administrative resources—particularly staff—are hence usually doomed to failure, because the resources needed are unlikely to materialize fully or in a timely fashion. Successful administrative reform strategies have therefore generally been based on better allocation of available resources rather than on accretions of major additional resources. Examples are cutting down unproductive tasks such as processing the returns of wage earners and devoting the resources thus freed to more productive work, as in Chile and Colombia. Other examples of more productive ways to use existing resources are set out in Schlemenson (Chapter 10 in this volume) and Silvani (Chapter 8 in this volume).[10]

An interesting example of internal reorganization that has been successful in some countries (for instance, Uruguay) in recent years has been the creation of special units to monitor the compliance of large taxpayers with filing and payment requirements. Since it is not uncommon for as much as 60 percent or 70 percent of collections to come from the top 1 percent of taxpayers (that is, a few hundred or at most a few thousand firms, with the number depending largely on the size of the country), it is critically important to ensure that these taxpayers file and pay on time.[11]

In addition, in some instances it may make sense also first to introduce, for example, modern techniques of information management in

[10]See also the classic, and still largely valid, recommendations in Surrey (1958), as well as many of the papers in Joint Tax Program (1965).

[11]See, for example, Casanegra de Jantscher and Silvani (1990).

such special "large taxpayer" units, which are usually well managed and relatively efficient to, as it were, work out the bugs before extending such procedures to taxpayers more generally. On the other hand, it is important not to use the existence, and success, of such units as an excuse for neglecting other taxpayers. For instance, if auditing resources are unduly concentrated on large taxpayers, compliance levels among small and medium-sized firms may actually decline, with the result that total revenue from all taxpayers may be lower.[12]

Some countries have introduced measures designed to "privatize" certain tax administration activities traditionally performed by government (Ramírez Acuña (Chapter 11 in this volume)). Countries such as Bolivia, Brazil, Chile, Colombia, Ecuador, and Uruguay have assigned a major role to banks in tax collection. This decision has generally been taken both because of insufficient resources in the tax administration and because these countries recognize that banks are already specialized in the handling and control of payments. Here again, however, the mere fact that banks are entrusted with the tasks of receiving payments, returns or even, in some countries, processing returns, does not assure success. For the collection function to work well, proper systems must be designed, the tax department must exercise adequate supervision, and the remuneration paid to the banks must be appropriate.[13] Much time and effort has been spent on these matters in those countries in which collection through the banking system operates successfully.

As emphasized earlier, simplicity is an important element in any successful administrative reform. The administration must be provided with simpler and, hence, potentially enforceable laws to administer. In addition, it is equally important to simplify procedures, for example, by eliminating demands for superfluous information in tax returns and perhaps consolidating return and payment invoices. Once procedures are simplified, the tax administration can then concentrate on its main

[12]A quite different example of the application of special rules to particular groups is the use of presumptive techniques of assessment to reach such hard-to-tax groups as the self-employed (Bird (1983); Tanzi and Casanegra de Jantscher (1987)). Such techniques may, if carefully developed and applied, be useful in extending the reach of the tax system into the less formally organized sector of the economy and indeed may be essential in many countries if widespread application of direct taxes is desired. A good presumptive system, however, is one that does not remain a permanent part of the tax system but rather withers away over time as taxpayers "graduate" to the normal tax system.

[13]There is considerable divergence in how banks are paid for their services. In Bolivia, for example, banks are allowed to keep 0.8 percent of the revenues they collect; in Mexico, in contrast, they are paid a fixed amount for each tax return processed. As noted below, this is one of a number of areas where further research in "tax technology" (Bird (1991)) seems necessary.

tasks: facilitating compliance, monitoring compliance, and dealing with noncompliance.

Facilitating compliance involves such elements as improving services to taxpayers by providing them clear instructions, understandable forms, and assistance and information as necessary (LeBaube and Vehorn (Chapter 9 in this volume)). Monitoring compliance requires establishing and maintaining current accounts of taxpayers and management information systems covering both ultimate taxpayers and third-party agents, such as banks, involved in the tax system (Vázquez-Caro, Reid, and Bird (1992)), as well as appropriate and prompt procedures to detect and follow up on nonfilers and delayed payments. Deterring noncompliance requires both establishing a reasonable risk of detection and applying penalties effectively (Silvani (Chapter 8 in this volume)).[14] The ideal approach is to combine these measures so as to maximize their effect on compliance—as it were, to move a country from a "low-compliance" to a "high-compliance" environment. For example, when introducing a VAT or other new tax, emphasis should first be given to assisting taxpayers to comply with the new tax—see, for example, the Trinidad and Tobago case discussed by Due and Greaney (Chapter 5 in this volume)—then to detecting noncompliance, and finally to applying penalties. As a rule, successful reform strategies require an appropriate mix of all these approaches.

The taxpayer's decision to comply, or not to comply, with his fiscal obligations is of course the subject of the large formal theoretical literature on the economics of tax evasion (Cowell (1990)). While some progress has been made both in incorporating the "strategic" aspects of the evasion decision in a game-theoretic framework and in modeling it in principal-agent terms, much remains to be done before the results of such analysis are likely to have much to say about the real world "game" in developing countries.[15] For example, apart from a pioneering paper by Virmani (1987), virtually the entire economic literature on tax evasion assumes that tax officials are completely honest. If not all officials are honest (and in the expected utility framework used in most of the theoretical literature it is not clear why they should be expected to be), the game is very different than that usually modeled. "Leakage costs," as Shaw (1981) calls that portion of tax revenues that flows into the pockets of officials rather than into the coffers of government, may simply be transfers in economic terms but they may nonetheless

[14]Of course, it is also important to ensure that judicial procedures and institutions are such as to facilitate the proper application of tax laws and penalties.

[15]See Graetz, Reinganum, and Wilde (1986) and Reinganum and Wilde (1985).

result in significant distortions as new taxes are introduced and tax rates are increased in attempting to make up for the revenue loss.

In addition to this serious gap in the existing formal analysis, the literature has not as yet managed to model very well either the long-term, repetitive nature of the tax game or the role of "norms" in determining how people play the game. Consideration of the temporal dimension of tax administration stresses the importance both of the interaction of officials and taxpayers and of changes in "tax technology" and taxpayer attitudes to government.[16] This dimension is especially important in the context of the present book since the problem of tax administration reform is essentially how to alter the outcomes of administrative effort by appropriate investment in developing new legal and organizational frameworks, adopting new technology (such as computerization), and changing the allocation of administrative resources.

Finally, in recent years virtually all attempts to reform tax administration have centered around some form of computerization. Certainly, it is difficult to conceive of a tax administration that can perform its tasks efficiently without using some form of computer technology. In too many instances, however, the expectation of greater effectiveness from computerization has not materialized. Evidence indicates that the more successful reforms did not merely involve computerizing antiquated processes but also the redesign and streamlining of systems and procedures—such as consolidating return and payment forms and eliminating unnecessary and unused information required from taxpayers. As Corfmat (1985) emphasizes and the study of Spain by Moya and Santiago (Chapter 6 in this volume) shows, successful computerization must be accompanied by a fundamental reorganization of both systems and procedures and cannot be used by itself to side-step such needed reforms.

III. Agenda for Further Research

As mentioned above, in recent years there has been considerable research on the theory and, to a limited extent, the facts with respect to tax evasion and tax compliance. Because of such work, much has been learned about taxpayers: why and when they comply and do not comply, what effects various penalties and inducements have on their

[16]See, for example, the historical discussion in Webber and Wildavsky (1986), the "predator-prey" analogy in Boyd (1986), and the "Darwinian" analogy in Mayshar (1991).

behavior, and so on (Elffers (1991)). Sociologists, psychologists, economists, and administrators have all contributed to this literature and are likely to continue to do so given the theoretical attractiveness and practical importance of the subject. Unfortunately, interesting and to some extent useful as this work has been, much of it has proved to be of only limited direct relevance to the on-going task of tax administration in developing countries.

One reason for this lack of relevance is the very different environment of tax administration in developing countries than in the developed countries in which this research has been carried out. Another important reason, however, is that there have been almost no studies in any country of tax officials, of why and how they do what they do. Tax administration can be thought of as encompassing both mass (routine) and individual (discretionary) tasks. The former includes functions carried out across a wide range of transactions such as withholding, the maintenance of taxpayer current accounts, and collection; the latter includes audit, investigation of suspected fraud, and so on. As Slemrod (1989) has pointed out, even in developed countries the most neglected aspect of tax analysis is how tax officials act: What are the decision rules they use? What is the evidence on which such rules are based? What is the reliability and validity of such rules? Almost nothing is known about such matters in any country.[17] Governments in some developing countries have little day-to-day control over tax officials, little knowledge of what they do, and, furthermore, no easy way to obtain such knowledge. For centuries, governments in the now developed countries had to spend almost as much time and effort trying to control the peculations and extortions of revenue officials as trying to squeeze more revenue out of an unwilling populace (Webber and Wildavsky (1986)). The circumstances in some developing countries today are not all that different: the need to keep tight control over the handling of cash and to monitor closely the gathering and use of information by tax officials is thus a high-priority task.

As shown in some of the cases discussed in this book, the accountability of officials can be improved both by separating various functions (for example, using controllable third parties such as banks and withholding

[17]For a good example, see Hessing and others (1990) who report that Dutch tax officials examine all income tax returns and select some for further investigation, but that there appear to be no formal selection criteria employed and no system of monitoring and evaluating the performance of different officials except the subjective judgment of their superiors. Such a system may work satisfactorily in the circumstances of the Netherlands. When transplanted to Indonesia, this system left much to be desired, as Gillis (1990) notes.

agents, which facilitates checking and verification) and by instituting systematic internal consistency and security checks (for example, maintaining tight internal security on computerized data bases) to ensure that no improper activities occur in these routine tasks. While much remains to be done along these lines in some countries, what needs to be done is not a mystery. The problem of ensuring accountability is much more difficult, however, with respect to such inevitably selective and discretionary tasks as audit. While there is much still to be learned about this subject, there appears to be no substitute for establishing a group of well-trained and adequately compensated officials, whose work is subject to regular monitoring and review.

Too often when the director of taxes in a developing country is asked for data, it transpires that the only number readily available is the amount of money collected yesterday, last week, or last month. Of course, collection data are highly important, but they are not enough. To run a good tax administration, one must know where the money came from and what the costs and benefits of various possible changes in legal framework and institutional infrastructure might be.

In the absence of such knowledge, it is difficult to develop an appropriate strategy for the reform of tax administration. The key information missing in most countries includes (1) a detailed breakdown of the uses of administrative resources; (2) information on the results of such uses with respect to the various outputs—revenues, numbers of cases handled, and so on—of interest; and (3) information on tax bases, both actual and potential. The first two of these items are needed for a good management information system in any case; the third is needed both for sound tax policy and sound tax administration policy. As tax administrations throughout the world move into the twenty-first century with computerized data bases, more and more information will be generated. To ensure that this information is both usable and is actually used, however, it is critical that it be both timely and reliable and that both operating administrators and researchers be closely involved in the development of tax management information systems. Computerized information is too important to both tax administration and tax policy to be left to computer specialists alone!

Although, as this book demonstrates, knowledge is gradually being acquired in many countries on many important matters related to the reform of tax administration and tax policy, much remains to be done to systematize and evaluate this knowledge. Some of the topics on which more systematic research seems needed are listed below.

- The measurement of tax "gaps" (between potential and declared taxes, between declared taxes and taxes paid, and between taxes paid and those that reach the treasury).

- The real resource costs (administrative, compliance, efficiency, evasion) of alternative tax structures and administrative procedures.
- The relative effects of penalties, information systems (reporting), simplicity (of laws), and publicity on compliance.
- The use of presumptive techniques to tax "hard-to-tax" sectors.
- The efficiency with which audit resources are allocated, and possible analytical bases for the administrative rules of thumb and decision rules used to select returns for examination.
- The pros and cons of the "large taxpayer" approach discussed earlier.
- The appropriate compensation system for third-party collection agents (for example, banks).
- The costs and benefits of tax amnesties (see, for example, Stella (1989)).
- The administrative implications of rate differentiation and exemptions (for example, in a VAT; see Tait (1991)).
- The incidence and allocative effects of judicial appeal procedures.
- Possible systems for linking administrative rewards to administrative effort.
- The costs and benefits of alternative refunding procedures.
- The costs and benefits of different degrees of administrative decentralization.
- The role of specialist tax preparers (for example, accountants) in developing countries.

With respect to these and many other possible topics, different results may be expected in different countries for various reasons. For example, different macroeconomic environments (inflation); differences in market structures, risk and time preferences, social welfare functions, information costs and availability, and reaction functions; and different "environments" with respect to relations with government, the nature of government expenditure, "morale," and so on. While many of these terms are rather nebulous and subject to varying interpretations, one cannot form adequate judgments on the many policy issues explicit and implicit in the preceding list without much more careful and systematic analysis than is now available of the relation between such different contexts and the questions raised in the list.

IV. Conclusion

Thus, while much remains to be learned about tax administration reform in developing countries, as this book shows, a great deal is already known about the subject and much has been achieved in practice in a number of countries to improve their tax administration. As noted earlier, more could be done to improve tax administration if more people, in both the tax administration and research communities, were interested in it. In effect, the task is to find ways in which to codify the present "expert diagnosis" system of coping with tax administration reform by freeing it as much as possible from the country-specific and time-specific biases we all have. The task is not easy; but it is important, and worthy of much more effort and resources than have so far been devoted to it. Moreover, since governments and taxes seem more likely to grow in importance in most developing countries in the future than to shrink, the problem is not going to go away. The problems are there; the methods and the information needed to tackle them are in their formative stages; what needs to be done is to seize the opportunity to make a more systematic inroad into this important area.

The experiences discussed in this book provide useful lessons regarding tax administration reform. While there is no consensus on a number of issues, it is fair to conclude that most authors and commentators agree that three main ingredients are necessary for a successful tax administration reform in developing countries. First, the tax structure usually needs to be simplified for ease of compliance and administration. Second, a reform strategy suitable to the specific circumstances of each country must be developed; gimmicks or quick fixes are no substitute for a comprehensive strategy. Finally, and above all, there must be a strong political commitment to the improvement of tax administration; otherwise, even the best intentioned and best designed efforts will fail.

REFERENCES

Bird, Richard M., "Income Tax Reform in Developing Countries: The Administrative Dimension," *Bulletin for International Fiscal Documentation,* Vol. 37, No. 1 (1983), pp. 3–14.

———, "The Administrative Dimension of Tax Reform in Developing Countries," in *Tax Reform in Developing Countries,* ed. by Malcolm Gillis (Durham, North Carolina: Duke University Press, 1989).

———, "Tax Administration and Tax Reform: Reflections on Experience," in *Tax Policy in Developing Countries,* ed. by Javad Khalilzadeh-Shirazi and Anwar Shah (Washington: World Bank, 1991).

———, "Tax Reform in Latin America: A Review of Some Recent Experiences," *Latin American Research Review,* Vol. 27, No. 1 (1992), pp. 7–36.

Boyd, Colin, "The Enforcement of Tax Compliance: Some Theoretical Issues," *Canadian Tax Journal,* Vol. 34 (May/June 1986), pp. 588–99.

Casanegra de Jantscher, Milka, "Administering the VAT," in *Value Added Taxation in Developing Countries,* ed. by Malcolm Gillis, Carl S. Shoup, and Gerardo P. Sicat (Washington: World Bank, 1990).

______, and Carlos Silvani, "Guidelines for Administering a VAT," *International VAT Monitor* (December 1990), pp. 2–19.

Corfmat, François, "Computerizing Revenue Administration in LDCs," *Finance & Development,* Vol. 22 (September 1985), pp. 45–47.

Cowell, Frank, *Cheating the Government: The Economics of Evasion* (Cambridge, Massachusetts: MIT Press, 1990).

Elffers, Henk, *Income Tax Evasion: Theory and Measurement* (Deventer, Netherlands: Kluwer, 1991).

Gillis, Malcolm, "The Indonesian Tax Reform After Five Years," Conference on Tax Policy and Economic Development Among Pacific Asian Countries (Taipei, 1990).

Goode, Richard, "Some Economic Aspects of Tax Administration," *Staff Papers,* International Monetary Fund, Vol. 28 (June 1981), pp. 249–74.

Graetz, Michael, Jennifer F. Reinganum, and Louis L. Wilde, "The Tax Compliance Game: Toward an Interactive Theory of Law Enforcement," *Journal of Law, Economics, and Organization,* Vol. 2, No. 1 (1986), pp. 1–32.

Harberger, Arnold, "Lessons of Tax Reform from the Experiences of Uruguay, Indonesia and Chile," in *Tax Reform in Developing Countries,* ed. by Malcolm Gillis (Durham, North Carolina: Duke University Press, 1989).

Hessing, Dirk, and others, "Does Deterrence Deter? Measuring the Effect of Deterrence on Tax Compliance in Field Studies and Experimental Studies," in *Tax Compliance and Tax Law Enforcement,* ed. by Joel Slemrod (unpublished; Office of Tax Policy Research, School of Business Administration, University of Michigan, 1990).

Joint Tax Program: Organization of American States, Inter-American Development Bank, and Economic Commission for Latin America, *Problems of Tax Administration in Latin America* (Baltimore: Johns Hopkins Press, 1965).

Mann, Arthur J., and Robert Smith, " Tax Attitudes and Tax Evasion in Puerto Rico: A Survey of Upper Income Professionals," *Journal of Economic Development,* Vol. 13 (June 1988), pp. 121–41.

Mayshar, Joram, "Taxation with Costly Administration," *Scandinavian Journal of Economics,* Vol. 93, No. 1 (1991), pp. 75–88.

Oldman, Oliver, "Controlling Income Tax Evasion," in Joint Tax Program: Organization of American States, Inter-American Development Bank, and Economic Commission for Latin America, *Problems of Tax Administration in Latin America* (Baltimore: Johns Hopkins Press, 1965).

Reinganum, Jennifer F., and Louis L. Wilde, "Income Tax Compliance in a Principal-Agent Framework," *Journal of Public Economics,* Vol. 26 (February 1985), pp. 1–18.

Shaw, Graham K., "Leading Issues of Tax Policy in Developing Countries: The Economic Problems," in *The Political Economy of Taxation,* ed. by Alan T. Peacock and Francesco Forte (Oxford: Basil Blackwell, 1981).

Silvani, Carlos, "Informe del Relator General," in Centro Interamericano de Administradores Tributarios and Instituto de Estudios Fiscales, *Innovación tecnológica y gestión tributaria* (Madrid: Ministerio de Economía y Hacienda, 1991).

Slemrod, Joel, "Complexity, Compliance Costs, and Tax Evasion," in *Taxpayer Compliance: Social Science Perspectives*, ed. by Jeffrey A. Roth and John T. Scholz (Philadelphia: University of Pennsylvania Press, 1989).

———, ed., *Tax Compliance and Tax Law Enforcement* (unpublished; Office of Tax Policy Research, School of Business Administration, University of Michigan, 1990).

Soos, Piroska, "Self-Employed Evasion and Tax Withholding: A Comparative Study and Analysis of the Issues," *U.C. Davis Law Review*, Vol. 24, No. 1 (Fall 1990), pp. 107–93.

Stella, Peter, "An Economic Analysis of Tax Amnesties," IMF Working Paper No. 89/42 (Washington: International Monetary Fund, June 1989).

Surrey, Stanley S., "Tax Administration in Underdeveloped Countries," *University of Miami Law Review*, Vol. 12 (1958), pp. 158–88.

Tait, Alan A., *Value-Added Tax: International Practice and Problems* (Washington: International Monetary Fund, 1988).

———, ed., *Value-Added Tax: Administrative and Policy Issues*, IMF Occasional Paper No. 88 (Washington: International Monetary Fund, 1991).

Tanzi, Vito, "Quantitative Characteristics of the Tax Systems of Developing Countries," in *The Theory of Taxation in Developing Countries*, ed. by David Newbery and Nicholas Stern (New York: Oxford University Press, 1987).

———, and Milka Casanegra de Jantscher, "Presumptive Income Taxation: Administrative, Efficiency, and Equity Aspects," IMF Working Paper No. 87/54 (Washington: International Monetary Fund, August 1987).

Vázquez-Caro, Jaime, Gary Reid, and Richard Bird, "Tax Administration Assessment in Latin America," Latin America and the Caribbean Technical Department, Regional Studies Program, Report No. 13 (Washington: World Bank, January 1992).

Virmani, Arvind, "Tax Evasion, Corruption and Administration: Monitoring the People's Agents Under Symmetric Dishonesty," Development Research Department, Discussion Paper DRD271 (Washington: World Bank, May 1987).

Webber, Carolyn, and Aaron Wildavsky, *A History of Taxation and Expenditure in the Western World* (New York: Simon and Schuster, 1986).

World Bank, *Argentina: Tax Policy for Stabilization and Economic Recovery* (Washington, 1990).

———, *Lessons of Tax Reform* (Washington, 1991).

PART I

Tax Administration and Tax Policy: Case Studies

2

Tax Administration Reform in Bolivia and Uruguay

Carlos A. Silvani and Alberto H.J. Radano

This study describes two different experiences in the area of tax administration. Each was successful: each brought about a significant increase in the effectiveness of tax administration and, consequently, a rise in the collection of internal revenue.

I. Background

In Bolivia the increase in tax receipts was spectacular: it rose from approximately 1 percent of GDP in 1985 to 7.4 percent in 1990. For Uruguay the increase was more modest, climbing from approximately 11 percent of GDP in 1984 to 13.5 percent in 1990. Nevertheless, in real terms, collection grew by 40 percent during the period. This difference in results may be explained by several factors. The heavier the tax burden, the harder it is to increase the effectiveness of tax administration. Likewise, the higher the tax rate, the greater the enforcement difficulties faced by the tax administration. The value-added tax (VAT) rate is 10 percent in Bolivia and 21 percent in Uruguay.[1] Further, it is particularly difficult to evaluate the Uruguayan experience in terms of collection results because, during the period under review, there were not only changes in the tax system but important variations in the rate of inflation and economic growth as well.

No single set of prescriptions for improving tax administration applies universally. The most appropriate strategy depends on the particular circumstances of each case. In Bolivia, the change was drastic, both in the tax system and in the tax administration. In Uruguay, the change was gradual and focused only on the tax administration. The choice of strategy could perhaps be explained by the fact that in 1985 Bolivia

---

The authors are particularly grateful to Paulo Sergio dos Santos for his help in the preparation of this study. Mr. dos Santos was in charge of implementing the Uruguay project between November 1987 and November 1989 on behalf of CIAT.

[1]In March 1990, on a temporary basis, it was raised to 22 percent.

was in a critical situation in which tax receipts had fallen to about 1 percent of GDP. In Uruguay, on the other hand, an attitude of extreme opposition to change, coupled with a state of affairs that was not too critical, may explain why a strategy of gradual change was selected.

Elements Common to Both Countries

Designing a General Strategy

In both countries, the reforms were carried out within the same time frame (1985–90). In both cases, the first step was to design a general strategy that specified with precision the goals to be attained and the means to be employed. In addition, the overall strategy was reflected in a work program: general guidelines for developing information systems were defined and a timetable for the key stages was planned.

Another common feature was that several international organizations supported the projects. In Uruguay, the participating agencies were the IMF, the Inter-American Development Bank (IDB), and the Centro Interamericano de Administradores Tributarios (CIAT). In Bolivia, the supporting organizations included the IMF, the IDB, the World Bank, and the United Nations Development Program. Although the assistance of these agencies was essential, it is important to stress that these efforts would never have been successful if the authorities in each country had not displayed the strongest will to see the changes through.

Simplicity of Procedures

In both countries, simplicity was the guiding principle in the design of procedures. In Bolivia, administrative reform was preceded by a drastic simplification of the tax system. A near-obsession with simplicity resulted in very simple tax returns that called for only essential data. Furthermore, tax return forms were designed to be used also as payment forms. Since the same form was used to record the debit (resulting from the tax return) and the credit (the amount actually paid), the processing burden was lightened because certain data, such as those identifying the taxpayer and the tax period, did not need to be entered twice (once to record the debit and again to record the credit). The quality of the information was also improved because using a single form simultaneously as a tax return and as a payment form eliminated the typical problems of charging credits against debits.

Records Storage

Another feature common to both countries was the method used to store the returns filed by taxpayers. Traditionally, tax administrations in Bolivia and Uruguay had kept all tax returns received from each taxpayer in a separate folder. This system required substantial use of staff resources and, worse, meant that the quality of the work was not (nor could ever be) good, because the number of returns to be placed in the files was so large. Consequently, when it came to reviewing the file of a taxpayer, the absence of a return could mean one of three things: (1) the taxpayer had not filed a return; (2) the taxpayer had filed a return but the return had not yet found its way into the folder; and (3) the taxpayer had filed a return but the return had been erroneously placed in the folder of another taxpayer or had been mislaid in some other way. The tax administration was thus unable to determine by checking the contents of a file whether a taxpayer had, for instance, failed to file a return or was delinquent. Thus, the administration was compelled to rely on documents in the hands of taxpayers to establish whether they had discharged such elementary obligations as filing a tax return and paying the reported tax.

Priorities

The highest priority under the work program was accorded to activities related to taxpayer registration and the processing of data recorded on the tax return/tax payment form. Special attention was paid to the validation of the data, to ensure that the information entered in the computer accurately reflected the information reported by taxpayers. This made it possible, as a first step, to exercise a reasonable measure of control over nonfiling and delinquent taxpayers.

Auditing

Auditing was a second priority in both countries. More therefore remains to be done in that area than in any other, because its development has only just begun. Basically, the proposed audit strategy consisted of the following: (1) Selecting the taxpayers to be audited according to objective criteria; computer analysis of the markup (that is, the ratio of sales to purchases) reported by taxpayers played a fundamental role in this respect. (2) Cross-checking information in order to detect unreported sales and purchases improperly deducted from the VAT. (3) Making quick checks (covering only a few items) designed to encompass a large number of taxpayers. (4) Applying extensively the penalty of temporary closure of establishments for failure to comply with certain provisions of the VAT or the tax code.

Time Required for Change

Both experiences clearly show that for any significant change to take place, a reasonable length of time is required to come up with ideas, to develop them, and to put them into practice. The Governments of both countries must be credited with knowing that this length of time was needed, because attempts to hasten matters might have led to failure.

Data Bank

In each case, it was possible to gather high-quality and timely data, resulting in the establishment of a data bank that permits simulations, economic and financial analysis, more accurate diagnoses, and better decision making.

Differences Between the Two Countries

Scope of the Project

As mentioned above, in Bolivia, a total structural change was made, ranging from reform of the tax system to changes in its administration. In addition, when new procedures were introduced they were made applicable to all taxpayers. In Uruguay, the changes in procedures were gradual. In the beginning the new procedures applied only to the VAT and to the 2,700 largest taxpayers who accounted for 70 percent of total tax receipts. Once the system was operating adequately, other taxes were included, and the number of taxpayers required to report and pay their taxes under the new procedures rose. The system will continue to expand until it covers some 15,000 taxpayers, who together account for over 95 percent of all tax revenues.

Features of the Project

In Bolivia, all tax collection takes place through banks and all data are batch-processed. In Uruguay, payments from taxpayers covered by the new system are received by tellers at the Dirección General Impositiva—DGI (Internal Revenue Service) and the information is processed on-line when the tax return is filed. Taxpayers who are not covered by the new system pay their taxes at the Banco de la República Oriental del Uruguay (BROU) and their tax returns are batch-processed.

Conclusion

Even leaving aside the increase in tax receipts mentioned at the beginning of this paper, these two experiences may be considered successful because they laid the foundation for deep structural changes in tax administration. In neither case is the work finished. Nevertheless, the changes made to date clearly constitute steps in the right direction, and these two tax administrations will increasingly have available more and better information to improve their effectiveness.

II. Bolivia

Introduction

The Situation at the Outset

In 1985, the President of Bolivia, Hernan Siles Suazo, decided to cut short his term of office because of the serious political and economic situation facing the country. After an early presidential election, he turned the government over to his successor, Victor Paz Estenssoro, one year ahead of time, in August 1985. On an annual basis, the inflation rate was then about 23,500 percent.

The enactment of Supreme Decree No. 21060 in August 1985 launched what is known as the new economic policy. This decree freed most economic variables from official controls, with the exception of the prices of fuel, public services, and pharmaceutical products. In addition, public sector salaries were frozen until December 31, 1985.

The tax system was chaotic, with more than 400 separate national, departmental, and municipal taxes. Tax administration was largely ineffective. Taxpayer registers were completely out of date, and tax collection record keeping was extremely delayed—in some departments the time lag was as long as 16 months. Data processing was virtually nonexistent. As mentioned earlier, the tax burden in 1985 had dropped to the very low level of 1 percent of GDP. It was in this situation that the tax reform described below was introduced.

General Strategy

Once the reform was enacted, the great challenge lay in reorganizing tax administration. A comprehensive plan was drawn up for this purpose. The plan included restructuring the tax administration; the design, development, and implementation of its principal systems; and the training of personnel to operate those systems. To attain these ends, the Government relied mainly on the following:

(1) A temporary Ministry of Tax Collection was established. This ministry was charged both with drafting regulations to cover all taxes enacted under the Tax Reform Law and with leading the whole process of change in tax administration. Under this ministry were placed the Tax Collection Undersecretariat and, through the latter, the General Bureau of Internal Revenue (DGRI) and the General Bureau of Customs (DGA).

(2) A team of international consultants, some specialized in tax administration and others in computer systems, was hired to design, develop, and put in place new systems to be operated by the DGRI. This team, which at one point was made up of 25 persons, worked in a very close and fluid manner with the new ministry. The project was financed by the UNDP, the IDB, and the World Bank. The IMF also participated in the technical assistance side of the project.

(3) The Government adopted political decisions with firmness and abided by the deadlines set for developing the systems and making them operational. Wisely, it waited out the allotted time without becoming impatient or resorting to quick-fix solutions that could have set back progress with the reform of the basic structure of tax administration.

(4) The Government ensured that the resources needed for the team of consultants to do their job effectively were delivered on time.

The task at hand was not simple. Aside from the complexity of the work, it was necessary to fight against the proposals of some government officials. It had to be demonstrated, for instance, that the proposal to establish a new tax administration with completely new personnel, while gradually phasing out the old administration, was not advisable. Under that proposal, the salaries of the staff of the old administration would have continued to be paid for a specified length of time, while they did no work at all.[2]

[2]About 25 percent of the staff of the old tax administration were fired. They were replaced by better qualified staff, and the total number of staff was kept at roughly the same level. In 1986 the DGRI had 1,120 employees, compared with 1,130 employees in 1990.

The arguments that led to dismissal of the idea of establishing a new tax administration and dissolving the old one were as follows:

(1) In an agency with approximately 1,000 employees not all were inefficient and unreliable. Waiting a reasonable length of time would make it possible to detect the good employees—and this in fact is what happened.

(2) A new agency would require new buildings and these were not available; nor were there any resources available to construct new buildings.

(3) Paying salaries to employees who were assigned no work would cause political and labor union problems.

(4) Searching for and hiring such a large number of new staff would prove very difficult; in addition, such recruitment would take a long time, and essential tasks had to be carried out without interruption.

Increase in Collection

In 1987, the first calendar year after the reform went into effect, tax collection rose from the previous year by 111 percent in constant values.[3] The tax burden increased from 1 percent of GDP in 1985 to 7.4 percent in 1990, including only the taxes administered by the DGRI.

Tax Structure Reform

General Characteristics of the New Taxes

After the new economic policy was launched, the focus shifted to devising a tax system capable of replenishing government coffers. The choice fell on a simple system, with moderate rates, that would not distort the allocation of resources within the economy. It was decided to introduce seven new taxes, repealing at the same time all previous tax legislation except for taxes established in the General Law on Hydrocarbons, those in the mining code, and those levied on the production and marketing of rubber and wood.

A basic feature of the new legislation is that it does not include income taxes in their traditional form. The seven new taxes are as follows:

[3]See Table 4 in Annex III.

Taxes on income and assets

(1) Special tax on tax regularization (tax amnesty).
(2) Tax on presumed corporate income.
(3) Tax on presumed income of property owners, which includes tax on motor vehicles, motor boats, and aircraft; tax on urban real property; and tax on rural property.

Taxes on transfers of goods and services

(4) VAT.
(5) Tax on transactions.
(6) Tax on specific consumption.

Income tax

(7) VAT supplementary system.

The tax reform was enacted on May 20, 1986; it is described more fully in Annex I. Subsequent to this reform, two new taxes of minor significance were introduced: the gift tax and the tax on foreign travel.

In relation to GDP, the contribution from each tax in 1990 is illustrated in Table 1.

Table 1. Bolivia: Revenues from the Main Taxes, 1990[1]

	Collection as a Percentage of GDP
Tax	
Value-added tax	3.72
Tax on transactions	1.28
Tax on specific consumption	0.89
VAT supplementary system	0.46
Tax on presumed corporate income	0.54
Tax on presumed income of property owners	0.46
Total	7.35

Source: Statistics Section of the DGRI.
[1]Changes in total tax receipts over time are shown in Tables 3 and 4 in Annex III.

Amendment of the Tax Code

The Tax Reform Law also amended the tax code. The most important changes were the following:

(1) Introduction of a fine ranging from 50 percent to 100 percent of the unpaid taxes when tax fraud is committed.

(2) Provision of jail terms for tax fraud.

(3) Cancellation of registration in public registers when tax fraud is committed.

(4) Introduction of the penalty of temporary closure of establishments where tax fraud has been committed.

(5) Provision for automatic indexing, in line with changes in the official exchange rate of the U.S. dollar, of outstanding tax debts as well as of credits in favor of the taxpayer. (Fines for failure to comply with formal tax obligations are indexed in the same manner.)

(6) Provision for interest on delinquent amounts to accrue automatically from the moment the unpaid tax is due, without any need for proceedings of any kind on the part of the tax administration.

Special Systems

Much of the population in Bolivia is engaged in small commercial and service activities at the retail level (that is, the informal economy). As a rule, these people have no shops of their own; they carry out their activities on sidewalks or by means of makeshift stands that are put up and taken down daily. In addition, there is a high level of illiteracy.

In order to bring this part of the population into the tax system, decrees were issued establishing three special systems, each providing for several categories or levels of taxpayers.

A taxpayer who opts for one of these systems complies with a set of taxes (VAT, VAT supplementary system, tax on transactions, and tax on presumed corporate income) in a very simple manner. He must go to any bank, show his taxpayer card, and purchase the proper tax form bearing the pre-established value applicable to the category under which he is registered. He does not need to fill out any forms.[4]

Reform of the Tax Administration

After enacting the Tax Reform Law, the Government turned its attention to two fundamental tasks: (1) regulating the new taxes by issuing decrees and administrative resolutions; and (2) the comprehensive reform of the tax administration.

---

[4]Table 5 in Annex III shows the changes over time in taxpayer registration under the various systems.

With these ends in mind, as mentioned earlier, a Ministry of Tax Collection was established and a team of experts in tax administration and computer systems was hired. One main reason for the success of this process was that the team was made up of like-minded specialists, selected by the people in charge of the programs to revamp the tax administration without any interference from the Government or from the international agencies financing the programs.

Each consultant was aware that his assignment included the installation and start-up of the systems to be designed, and that, consequently, the scope of his work went well beyond simply defining systems and submitting the plans to the Government for approval and implementation. For example, if a new form was to be designed, the consultant had to make sure that he had defined with precision every characteristic of that form (size, copies, weight of the paper, color, quantity, delivery deadlines, and so on) before the purchase order could be processed. In addition, the consultant had to take part in the national or international search for companies capable of manufacturing the form, visit local companies to make sure that their machinery could produce the form in the required manner and time, check the galley proofs of the form, and so forth. This style of work, illustrated here by reference to one form, was also applied to all procurement, whether office space, special equipment, or software. The attitude of the consultant at all times was that he had to be the driving force behind the procurement of the required resources, because his mission ended only when the system was in place and the personnel had been trained.

This frame of mind, coupled with total dedication to the work in hand by all concerned—for instance, during the first two years work continued through Saturdays and nearly all holidays—was one of the keys to obtaining within a short length of time the results discussed here.

Basic Systems and Procedures

Single national register of taxpayers

Because the Padrón de Contribuyentes (taxpayer register) was so out of date it was decided to launch a general registration of taxpayers. The initial goal was to register 190,000 taxpayers. When the job of checking addresses was finished in April 1987, registered taxpayers totaled about 240,000. By December 1990 registered taxpayers numbered 365,559.[5]

[5]See Table 5 in Annex III.

Collection through banks

Since May 1987 taxpayers file their returns and make their payments only at banks that are part of the system. Simple returns have been designed for each tax, with the size of each form never exceeding one sheet of paper (two pages). Tax returns serve as payment forms as well. Banks receive them, distribute the money collected, enter and validate the data set out in each return, and deliver the supporting disks and relevant documents to the DGRI. All these activities are governed by an agreement between banks and the Tax Collection Undersecretariat.

This procedure constituted an important step forward in tax administration. It freed the DGRI from the heavy work load of receiving payments and tax returns and solved the problem of processing them. The monthly average of tax returns and payments processed by this system is about 190,000.[6]

Using securities to pay taxes

The system keeps a record of and controls all documents issued by the Government that may be used for paying taxes, such as customs rebate certificates, treasury credit notes, redeemable tax bonds, and negotiable credit notes. It also keeps a record of documents issued by the DGRI or by the Central Bank and controls the proper use of these documents by the taxpayer.

Control of tax returns filed

This system detects taxpayers who have not discharged their obligation to file returns and enables the tax administration to make a selection among them according to various criteria (by region, tax, taxable period, presumed tax importance, and so on). In this way, any action by the DGRI can be concentrated on taxpayers who will supposedly yield higher tax revenues. The system issues the orders to file the missing tax returns, each supplied with a return stub for notice of delivery, so that the post office can return evidence of delivery to the DGRI.

This system began operating in December 1987. At that time, 109,885 orders were issued (45,222 for La Paz and 64,663 for the rest of the country). One of the factors limiting the effectiveness of this system is the mail service, with which a special arrangement was made to

[6]See Annex II.

distribute letters from the DGRI. Although the postal system undertook to add vehicles and mailmen in order to do this work, the service is not yet efficient.

Demand for partial payment when no tax return has been filed

Taxpayers who persist in not filing a return, after being ordered to do so in the manner described above, may be compelled by law to make a partial payment in an amount similar to the largest tax reported or determined in the immediately preceding 12 months. This system makes the necessary checks and issues through its computers a form showing the amount that the taxpayer must pay as partial payment if he wishes to avoid enforced collection of the debt.

Review of tax returns

This system reviews each tax return and determines whether the arithmetical calculations of the taxpayer are correct and whether any applicable fines have been included in the event of a late filing. If there is a computation error or if the appropriate fine has been omitted, the system's computers issue the proper demand for payment with its payment form. Later, the system checks to make sure that payment has been made. In the first processing of tax returns for the whole country, in January 1989, errors were detected in 22.6 percent of all tax returns filed. By March 1991 this percentage had dropped to about 9 percent.

Control of taxes paid in installments

The only tax that may be paid in installments is the tax on presumed corporate income. The supreme decree that regulates this tax provides that 30 percent of it may be paid as a down payment and the balance would be due in up to ten equal consecutive monthly installments. These regulations were later supplemented by an administrative ruling regulating the reasons that would void the payment plan. The system watches over the strict observance of this administrative ruling, reporting which plans are behind in their payments, which should be voided, and supplying the information needed to obtain payment through enforced collection.

Control of partial tax payments deducted on tax returns

The system verifies that credits deducted by taxpayers on their tax returns (carryovers from the preceding tax period, payments on account, negotiable credit notes, payments made with securities, and so on) have been actually collected.

Control of large taxpayers

The system makes it possible to monitor tax compliance by the largest taxpayers almost immediately after their taxes are due. All systems and procedures needed to obtain quick results have been adopted with a view to exercising this control.[7]

Audit of taxpayers

Two kinds of basic procedures were developed for audit: (1) the general audit procedure laying down overall audit guidelines; and (2) specific procedures for each "audit plan," for instance, the VAT sales/purchases ratio and tax returns showing no transactions or an overall credit position.

The choice of cases to be audited was always made objectively, and rarely was there any discretionary selection. The new tax audit system began operating in December 1988. Unfortunately, as of June 1991, the expectations generated by its introduction have not been fulfilled, primarily because of problems related to personnel and to the heads of departments responsible for control. These problems remain unsolved.

Tax statistics

The system generates statistical files intended for the use of government agencies that request them.[8] In addition, a special module produces the relevant statistics for the tax administration itself.

Related Activities

The activities described below supplement the basic systems and procedures and are essential to ensure adequate operation.

---

[7]See Annex II.

[8]Annex IV shows in detail the format of some of the statistics produced.

Determining the size of the data processing department

When reform began, the DGRI did not have a computerized data processing department. The first task in this area was to make a comprehensive evaluation of needs projected over a period of five years, so as to define the requirement for computer equipment in light of available resources and investment possibilities. Also projected were the required staff resources.

Special records and invoicing rules

Regulations were issued on the formalities to be met by invoices before they can be considered valid tax notes that allow taxpayers to claim VAT credits. A prerequisite for the invoice to qualify as a tax note is that it must be validated with a seal by the DGRI before being used by the party making the sale. The manner in which purchases and sales were to be recorded, in cases where the taxpayer failed to keep adequate records, was also regulated.

Restructuring the tax administration

The organizational structure of the DGRI was inappropriate. A new organizational chart, a manual of duties and responsibilities, and operational profiles of positions in the first and second tiers of the organization were prepared. Key officials in the first and second tiers of the new organization were selected, and minimum staffing requirements were established. To select the new staff, public notices were published, directed in particular at persons under 35 years of age who had completed most program requirements or were graduates in the fields of accounting, economics, business administration, or law. The candidates hired were those who successfully completed a personal interview and passed a technical exam and a psycho-technical test.

Proposal to amend the tax code

The Bolivian tax code was enacted on July 2, 1970. The Tax Reform Law of May 20, 1986 introduced some changes in it, but further modifications are needed.

The most important changes expected to be introduced in the near future concern the following:

- The use of computers, by validating procedures related to this technology (the use of a facsimile signature, automatic computation of fines, and so on).
- The manner in which notices may be served, including the possibility of using private mail services.
- The system of fines, imposing more severe penalties than those now in effect.
- Ex officio assessments (refinement of the procedure).
- Enforced collection (refinement of the procedure).
- Assessments based on presumptions (procedures are being added with respect to estimated sales, differences in assets, and inventory differences).
- The system for temporary closure of businesses, which will spell out the procedures needed for its application (now governed by DGRI rulings).

Control of tax payments on the import of goods

Imports of goods are subject not only to customs duties but also to the VAT and the tax on specific consumption. Responsibility for assessment and payment rested primarily with the DGA, which did not always do an effective job. Of total VAT revenues about 50 percent pertain to imports of goods. In the case of the tax on specific consumption, the tax levied on imports accounts for about 25 percent of total revenues from this tax.

In view of these figures, a new system was established to process a redesigned import declaration form. The new form, along with payment, was processed through banks, similar to the DGRI system, and subject to a system of automatic verification. This procedure ensures control of tax receipts and the early availability of computerized data connected with imports. The system includes a control for the release of goods from customs warehouses, in which the form is checked to make sure it has been canceled.

Control of the tax on presumed income of property owners

The tax on presumed income of property owners is a tax on registered property.[9] From the standpoint of tax administration, its characteristics

[9]See Annex I.

prevent it from being grouped with other taxes because the persons who owe this tax are under no obligation to register with the single national register of taxpayers and because its enforcement is in the hands of other government agencies (municipal governments, for instance). Special systems were therefore designed for its control. A system was developed for monitoring the tax on motor vehicles, motor boats, aircraft, and urban real property, and another system was developed for controlling the tax on rural property. In both cases, the general system of collection through banks is used. For the taxes mentioned, tax return forms are sometimes distributed along with major newspapers in each city.

Special operations to increase tax collection

Throughout the period when tax reform was being implemented, a series of special programs, broadly known as "operations," were conducted for increasing tax collection. The main operations carried out were as follows:

- Control of taxpayers subject to the tax on specific consumption.
- Control of public companies, public agencies, and municipalities.
- Control of compliance with the VAT and the tax on specific consumption at customs (carried out before the new import permits were introduced).
- Control of tax compliance by banks (filing of tax returns and payment).
- Control of payments made by taxpayers under the simplified system.
- Making sure that public and private companies correctly withheld amounts due under the VAT supplementary system.
- Cross-checking of tax notes (checking invoices for significant amounts deducted under the VAT supplementary system).
- Control of tax return filing and payment by self-employed professionals.
- Control of relevant economic transactions (grouping of purchases made by major taxpayers, so as to verify whether they were reported by the sellers).
- Temporary closure of business establishments.

The temporary closure of business establishments was the most spectacular operation of all. It consisted of shutting down for a minimum of seven days establishments that did not issue a proper invoice to buyers. The operation was carried out by groups of two inspectors from the DGRI and two policemen, who asked persons coming out of stores to show them the invoice for their purchases. If an invoice had not been issued, the group entered the establishment and made a record of it. An order shutting down the establishment followed, and when the time ran out for the taxpayer to appeal this decision, the business was shut down. The front of the establishment was taped up with strips proclaiming in red letters that the business had been shut down on account of tax violations.

At first this operation ran into problems because politicians and high officials would intercede in favor of the violators. The firm attitude adopted by the Minister of Tax Collection and by the President of the Republic himself served to counter this pressure, and the operation was carried out with complete success. The first operation took place all over the country between October 8, 1987 and March 5, 1988. A total of 13,605 inspections were carried out and 1,374 establishments were ordered closed, of which 890 had been shut down by the relevant closing date and 484 remained pending, awaiting the expiration of the deadline for appeal to which every violator is entitled. By September 30, 1989, actual closings totaled 1,540, a very high number indeed in a country where this kind of action had never been taken.

Operational timetable and progress control

To control the progress of the work, an "operational timetable" was drawn up detailing all important activities to be carried out. Such a timetable makes it possible to monitor progress effectively. A system was also introduced to coordinate the work of area bureaus (units that provide advisory services to the General Bureau and develop and control systems) and regional administrations (operational units).

Assistance for advisory and operational areas

Once the main systems and the new structure of the DGRI had been put in place, an intensive program was carried out to assist the officials responsible for consolidating the installation of the new structure and operating the systems. This program was very useful because it helped to resolve specific operational problems. Furthermore, as a result of dealing with unforeseen situations, adjustments were made in the systems and officials were provided with the support they needed to improve the operation of those systems. In some cases this assistance lasted several months. That was the case in the regional administrations of La Paz, Santa Cruz, and Cochabamba and in the advisory areas for technical and legal affairs, collection, control regulations, and automatic data processing.

Training

Training courses were held for all systems and operations. In some cases, for various reasons, some of the training courses were repeated. The new structure of the DGRI includes a specialized training area.

Dissemination of information and advertising

Using the media deemed most suitable in each case (television, radio, newspapers, booklets, and so on), intensive publicity campaigns were conducted. The following areas were covered:

- Motivational area (explaining why taxes must be paid).
- Information area (telling how to do it), especially when taxes fell due.
- Enforcement area (describing what happens to those who fail to pay their taxes), especially in connection with closings of establishments and with control activities.

Spending on publicity between 1987 and 1990 was roughly US$2.1 million, which accounted for about 10 percent of all tax administration expenses.

Conclusions

There is no doubt that the approach used in Bolivia was successful. It brought together a comprehensive tax reform providing for very simple tax administration, a government that was firmly committed to attaining its goals, and a team of technicians with sound knowledge of tax administration and total dedication to the task. As mentioned earlier, the outcome was impressive: the tax burden increased from 1 percent of GDP in 1985 to 7.4 percent in 1990 and is likely to continue climbing, as indicated by figures for the early months of 1991.

Not all systems were equally successful, however. For instance, the audit system that was put in place has yet to be evaluated, and, if necessary, altered. As noted above, personnel and supervisory problems are the reason for this delay.

Some elements had a negative impact, such as low salaries and a high rate of personnel turnover, particularly among managers. The subject of salaries is now being worked on for finding a lasting solution. The idea is to supplement the budget through a fund that would be financed with revenues that exceed established goals. Thirty percent of this surplus would be earmarked for raising the compensation of employees, consistently with their performance. Ten percent of the surplus would go to improving office infrastructure and equipment.

Much has been accomplished, but much remains to be done. The next set of activities envisaged by the program are as follows:

- Continuing direct assistance to advisory areas and regional administrations in connection with systems already in place.
- Assisting the officials involved in the development of new systems, particularly in the audit area.
- Improving the quality of the staff.
- Improving lines of communication with the taxpayer and strengthening the image of the DGRI.
- Repeating training modules, particularly in light of the changes that have taken place at management levels.

In the reform of tax administration, each country needs to take stock of the existing situation and to plot the most desirable and practicable course. Bolivia set ambitious goals for itself. Even so, because of its political resolve and the proper use of technical tools, it has largely managed to attain those goals, perhaps to an even greater degree than was foreseeable when the work began.

III. Uruguay

Conditions Prevailing at the Outset

In 1985 the Dirección General Impositiva—DGI (Internal Revenue Service) of Uruguay was not effective in the task of ensuring tax compliance. Antiquated methods were being used and nearly all procedures were carried out manually.

Organizational Structure of the Tax Administration

The organization of the DGI reflected a functional approach. Collection, auditing, and technical-legal functions were well defined at the management level. In addition, there was an Administration Department and a Systems Support Department. The latter dealt, among other functions, with data processing, training, statistics, and the single register of taxpayers.

One unusual feature of the DGI was that, under the Collection Department, it had a special unit for the control of large taxpayers called Control Especial de Contribuyentes—CEDE (Special Control of Taxpayers). This unit was supposed to control filing and payment of the 2,700 largest taxpayers in the country, who accounted for nearly 70 percent of all DGI tax receipts. Control systems were manual, and this unit basically followed the same procedures employed for small and medium-sized taxpayers.

The main problems in the organizational structure of the DGI were (1) the structure of the DGI did not explicitly provide for planning and coordination functions, and responsibility for these was spread out among the various departments; and (2) regional offices in the interior of the country had very limited autonomy and reported directly to the Collection Department.

Staff Resources

One of the most important problems faced by the DGI was the lack of qualified staff. Having to compete with the private sector and even with other government agencies, the DGI found it hard to hire and retain personnel with the needed technical qualifications. The difficulty was compounded by a steady decline in the budget of the DGI. Furthermore, the whole organization operated with marked slowness, and there was great resistance to the introduction of changes in procedures. Sixty percent of the staff had served more than 20 years, and 25 percent of them had worked more than 30 years.

The Single Register of Taxpayers

The taxpayer register was made up of some 120,000 taxpayers, of whom approximately 40,000 were inactive (that is, they filed no tax returns and paid no taxes). In addition, some 20,000 taxpayers who regularly filed returns or paid taxes were not registered in the single register of taxpayers.

Forms

Taxpayer forms were excessively complex and asked for too much information. The DGI was incapable of processing the information it received. Tax return forms were neither suitable for automatic data processing nor had been designed to serve as payment forms at the same time. When taxes fell due, the taxpayers had to fill out two forms, a tax return and a payment receipt, both of which had to be received and processed.

Collection Lags

From the standpoint of revenues, one major problem was the lag in the established deadlines for payment of taxes. The VAT, for example, was payable as much as 85 days after the taxable transaction. Significant delays occurred as well in the area of the tax on income from industry and commerce, excises, and the taxes on assets. In light of the high rate of inflation, these collection lags significantly reduced real tax revenues.

Data Processing

The DGI received very limited support from its data processing center. Data processing was virtually confined to pre-printing (name and taxpayer identification number) payment receipts and processing them afterward. The data processing function was largely discredited. Indeed, in 1981 the authorities decided to disconnect the computer equipment because they did not find it very useful. Like other employees of the DGI, technicians working in the data processing center earned salaries that were far below market levels and even lower than the salaries paid by other government agencies.

Systems for Controlling Tax Compliance

Tax delinquency was controlled in two ways. First, the taxpayer was required to present his tax records every time he filed a tax return. These tax records had to include copies of payment receipts for any partial payments or payments on account made by the taxpayer, as well as copies of previous tax returns filed by him. The official responsible for taking delivery of these documents checked the information in the tax return against the copies of payment receipts and determined whether the taxpayer was delinquent.

The second means of control was the issuance of a certificate of tax clearance that was good for one year. Production of this certificate was a prerequisite for certain procedures. The certificate was issued only to taxpayers who were current with the DGI. To apply for the certificate the taxpayer had to show copies of tax returns and payment receipts.

Relations with Taxpayers

A major difficulty was the manner in which the tax administration related to taxpayers. All controls were based on the personal contact of a DGI employee with taxpayers or their agents. If a problem was not detected when the taxpayer was waited on at the counter, that is to say, in the presence of the taxpayer, it was never detected or resolved. There was no system for subsequent review. Incorrect information submitted by taxpayers was never corrected unless the mistakes happened to be detected at the counter. There was great resistance to contacting taxpayers by mail, and if the mail was used there was no follow-up to make sure that the mailing had been actually delivered. The postal service was considered inefficient. However, a study based on documents mailed to large taxpayers showed that a major portion of the returned mail was due to errors in taxpayer addresses that the DGI had in its records, rather than because of postal inefficiency.

Resistance to Change

The DGI staff strongly resisted any changes. They were ready to discuss proposals for change, but problems arose when time came to implement them. The organization was accustomed to using its traditional manual procedures, and the staff distrusted computer systems. The idea of giving the computer control over taxpayers was opposed, even though this meant that control would no longer need to be exercised on the basis of copies of payment receipts and tax returns provided by taxpayers. This distrust arose from earlier, unsuccessful efforts at maintaining computer records of taxpayer accounts. The DGI staff felt that these attempts had only resulted in an increase in their own work load and had never helped them in any way.

Tax Legislation

The main taxes administered by the DGI were as follows:

• *Taxes on assets*, including (1) a tax on personal assets; (2) a tax on corporate assets; and (3) a tax on bank assets.

• *Taxes on the transfer of goods and services*, including (1) the VAT, a broad-based monthly tax at the basic rate of 21 percent and a reduced (minimum) rate of 12 percent on unprocessed food products; and (2) excises, applying in particular to fuel, tobacco, beverages, and motor vehicles.

• *Income taxes*,[10] including (1) a tax on income from industry and commerce; (2) a farming tax on agricultural activities on the basis of estimated net income; (3) a tax on farm income, applicable to agricultural income based on real net income; and (4) a tax on the transfer of farming property.

• *Other*, including a tax on sales of foreign currency.

In terms of GDP, the contribution made by each of these taxes in 1989 is shown in Table 2.

Table 2. Uruguay: Revenues from the Main Taxes, 1989[1]

	Collection as a Percentage of GDP
Tax	
Value-added tax	6.6
Excises	3.5
Tax on income from industry and commerce	0.9
Farming tax, tax on the transfer of farming property, and tax on farm income	0.2
Tax on assets	0.7
Tax on bank assets	0.3
Tax on sales of foreign currency	0.4
Total	12.6

Source: Dirección General Impositiva.
[1]Changes over time in the composition of tax revenues are shown in Annex V.

Reform of the Tax Administration

General Strategy

The main idea was to separate the problems encountered in tax administration into parts and to try to make gradual progress. It was decided to design a program whose initial goal would be to monitor the filing and payment of the 2,700 largest taxpayers through a highly automated system.

[10]Uruguay has no income tax on individuals. Individuals, if employed, are subject to a social security contribution that equals nearly 26 percent of the salary received. Half of that contribution is paid by the employer.

The purpose of this program was to demonstrate that, despite adverse conditions (a staff that was advanced in age, the resistance to change, the low salaries, and so forth), it was still possible to bring about a major change. If the program proved successful, which was the expectation, the project provided for increasing to as many as 5,000 the number of taxpayers that would be monitored through the new system. This was estimated to be the maximum number that the operational unit known as Special Control of Taxpayers (CEDE 1) could handle. Later, another unit would be established, CEDE 2, with equipment and procedures identical to those of CEDE 1. CEDE 2 would monitor the 5,000 taxpayers domiciled in Montevideo who were next in order of importance after those controlled by CEDE 1.

After fully implementing CEDE 1 and CEDE 2, five other CEDE units would be set up in the interior of the country to monitor some 1,000 taxpayers each. Actual tax receipts from taxpayers in the interior of the country were far below potential, accounting for approximately 12 percent of total receipts, even though the interior of the country accounted for 50 percent of all business establishments, 50 percent of the employed population, and 50 percent of the electricity consumed in Uruguay.

The work would begin with the VAT both because it was relatively simple to control using the new system and because it was of major importance to tax revenues. The experience gained with the VAT would be useful in overhauling the systems to deal with all the situations that had not been originally foreseen. Later, the new system would be expanded to bring under control the tax on income from industry and commerce, excises, and all other taxes payable by large taxpayers.

The System for Monitoring Large Taxpayers

In line with the proposed strategy, a computerized system was developed and implemented to monitor large taxpayers. This system has made it possible for CEDE 1 to exercise effective control over stopfiling and delinquent taxpayers. The plan to control the 5,000 largest taxpayers has already been completed successfully. The system, which is managed directly by its user, covers the following areas:

- Registration of taxpayers.
- Control and receipt of tax returns and payments.
- Control of failure to file tax returns (stopfilers).
- Control of outstanding balances (delinquent taxpayers).

The main characteristics of the system are as follows:

Operational autonomy

CEDE 1, which monitors major taxpayers domiciled in Montevideo, has operational autonomy. It is responsible for entering the data, refining the information, and printing listings from printers installed within the unit itself. The operational dependency of CEDE 1 on the central data processing center is minimal. Although the terminals in CEDE 1 are connected to the central computer, the data processing center has no role in the operations of CEDE 1. All it has to do is to leave the central computer switched on. This is a fundamental change. Prior to the introduction of the new system, the printing of a simple listing by the central computer could take more than a month. The new system fully applies the concept of operational decentralization. The user is the actual owner of his information and has total control over its use.

DGI tellers

One important feature of the Uruguayan model is that the DGI, unlike tax administrations in other Latin American countries, uses its own tellers to collect tax payments from large taxpayers. Although this was already the practice when the new system was introduced, it was decided at that time that only the large taxpayers would be allowed to pay at the DGI. All other taxpayers were required to pay at branches of the BROU. This change enabled the DGI to expand its capacity to receive payments from large taxpayers.

By law, the DGI may delegate the task of tax collection only to the BROU. This restriction has slowed the development of the system of collection through the bank network and has hampered the system because the BROU is not as effective or as technologically developed as most private banks in the country.

Another feature of the Uruguayan system is that taxes may be paid using various means of payment such as checks, cash, or a number of credit certificates issued by the DGI or by other official agencies.

The single register of taxpayers (SRT)

Prior to the introduction of the new procedures for the control of large taxpayers, a new version of the single register of taxpayers' system was introduced. This system operates on-line. It checks by computer, in the presence of the taxpayer, the identification information supplied by the latter. Next the system issues, also on-line, the tax identification card (SRT card). The system operates out of the SRT unit, which, like CEDE 1, enjoys total autonomy in its operations. Entry and validation of data, as well as the printing of listings, are all carried out under the direct supervision of the SRT unit, with virtually no involvement from the data processing center. This system applies to all taxpayers domiciled in Montevideo. A similar system, based on microcomputers, is being installed in the interior of the country.

The first step in introducing the new system for controlling large taxpayers was to clean up within the SRT the identification data on these taxpayers. This was done by asking large taxpayers to review the data available at the DGI and to report any errors found. Each large taxpayer was issued a computer printout setting out the information on record at the SRT. These printouts were handed to taxpayers when they came in to file their tax returns. As a result, nearly 60 percent of all taxpayers reported changes in their identification data. Most changes had to do with telephone numbers and addresses, but there were also changes in names, the taxes payable by the taxpayer, business activities, balance sheet dates, and the legal nature of the taxpayer. Following this editing of the data in the SRT, new tax identification cards were issued to large taxpayers.

New forms

Introduction of the new control system made it necessary to redesign all existing tax return forms. The new forms have several characteristics in common: they may be used simultaneously for filing the return and for paying the taxes; they have a standard letterhead, a preprinted number, and a box to indicate whether the form is being used as an amended return, with a space to show the serial number of the amended tax return. All information lines are numbered in sequence.

Receiving the tax returns

Large taxpayers must file their tax returns in three copies directly with the CEDE unit. A supervisor receives the return, briefly checks over the formalities, and passes the form on to a data-entry operator to key in the information.

The data in the tax returns are entered into the computer, in front of the taxpayer or his agent. A rigid validation routine was developed in order to keep to a minimum the possibility of entering erroneous information into the system. Errors in tax identification numbers, arithmetic, and computation of rates or balance carryovers, among other mistakes, are shown on the screen operated by the person entering the data. If errors are detected, they are reported to the taxpayer and the tax return is rejected. When this happens, the taxpayer has the option of making a partial payment against the rejected tax return, thereby avoiding or reducing delinquency surcharges. At first, each return took two minutes to be entered into the computer; after three months of using the new system, this length of time was halved.

In order to distribute the work load more evenly, tax due dates have been spread out over five days. The due date for each taxpayer is determined by the last digit in the taxpayer's identification number. Taxpayers may go to the DGI with their tax return ahead of time in order to verify whether it contains any errors. If the taxpayer chooses to do this, the return is checked by the computer and, if found to be error-free, is accepted. Immediately thereafter the data in the tax return are filed within the system. Later, on the date when the tax is due, all that the taxpayer has to do is go directly to one of the DGI tellers and make the payment.

The reception area is equipped with ten terminals for entering data and one printer. Terminals are grouped in pairs. Each pair of terminals is assigned two keyboard operators and one supervisor.

The entry and validation of the data on-line before the return is accepted is one of the cornerstones of the Uruguayan system. It accounts in large measure for the high quality of the data available from the system, which has enabled the DGI to act in an effective and timely manner. After the data are entered, the CEDE unit keeps a copy of the tax return, stamps the other two copies and returns them to the taxpayer, who must then go to the collection unit to pay.

Receiving payment

The taxpayer goes to any teller station and shows the copy of the tax return filed.[11] The teller enters into the terminal the serial number on the form, to gain access to the data previously recorded in the system. The system displays on the teller's screen information on the amount to be paid and the means of payment that the taxpayer reported he would use. The information on the screen is checked against the means of payment now being tendered by the taxpayer. If there are no

[11]The procedure is exactly the same whether the tax return is filed on the day payment is made or has been filed earlier.

discrepancies, payment is accepted. The teller then asks the system to print the amount on the tax return form. As the amount received is printed, the system automatically credits the payment to the account of the taxpayer. Finally, the teller gives back one copy of the return to the taxpayer and keeps one copy as a cashier's receipt.

The collection unit employs seven tellers to handle large taxpayers. Each station is equipped with a microcomputer connected, in a network, to the central data processing system. Each microcomputer has a special printer to print receipts for tax returns and payments.

Detecting stopfilers

The new system introduced an effective routine for detecting stopfilers (registered taxpayers who have not filed tax returns). Nearly 300 stopfiling taxpayers (about 11 percent of all large taxpayers monitored) were detected with this routine the first time it was used. Many of these 300 stopfilers were taxpayers who were not being adequately monitored under the old manual system.

Physical storage of tax returns

Tax return forms are stored in batches of 100 forms. These batches are numbered in the sequence in which they are received. In addition, inside each batch, the forms are numbered in sequence from 00 to 99. Each document that comes into the computer system is given a batch number and a sequence number. This number is connected with the other data in the form (the SRT number, the serial number, the tax number, the tax period number, and so on). In this way it becomes possible to learn the exact place where a particular form has been filed. All that is required is to enter into the system the SRT number, the tax year, or the serial number of a form, and in a few seconds the system reports the sequence number and the batch number in which the form is physically stored.

Modules that make up the system

The computer system used to keep track of large taxpayers was designed in modules so as to allow the inclusion of new taxes and new routines as they became necessary. As previously mentioned, the new system was first used with the VAT. Other taxes were subsequently added. The average time required to include a tax in the system, including programming work, testing, and training, is less than one calendar month. The main modules are as follows:

- *Data entry.* This module deals with the on-line entry and validation of data set out in tax returns. Using the correct data the module updates the data base of reported information. The validation routine checks all fields in tax returns. The module uses validation tables (subroutines) that contain individualized validations for each item in each form checked by the system. This makes it easier to introduce changes when the validation rules for a particular item are altered or when tax return forms are amended. This module also processes amendments of previously filed returns. The criterion used in processing amendments is to logically (not physically) eliminate the entry being amended. That entry is replaced by a new entry, as long as the data common to the two returns are consistent.
- *Cashier.* This module controls the work of DGI tellers receiving payments from taxpayers. It provides access to the data in tax returns that have already been placed on record when received, and it records the payments received.
- *Closing balance.* This module helps the supervisor of tellers in the work connected with closing balances. It allows for partial closing of balances and provides totals for each of the various means of payment received.
- *Control of stopfilers.* This module produces notices to and listings of stopfilers. To generate these, all that the supervisor of the CEDE unit needs to do is to give the computer the appropriate command through his terminal. The resulting listings are printed directly at the CEDE unit. This module also produces statistics on the status of stopfiling taxpayers.
- *Control of balances.* This module processes partial payments, payments on account and payments made through tax returns, and reports any outstanding balances. It constitutes the current tax account of large taxpayers of the DGI and is also used to identify delinquent taxpayers.

Related Work

In addition to the development of the new system for controlling large taxpayers, a number of steps were taken to correct distortions:

Reducing the lag time in tax collection

Collection lags for the VAT and for partial payment of the tax on income from industry and commerce and the taxes on assets were reduced by approximately 60 days. These taxes are now paid in the final business day of the month following that in which the sales take place. Collection lags for excises were shortened by anywhere from 10 days to 30 days. The number of partial payments against the tax on income from industry and commerce was increased from 11 to 12 a year. Tax returns for the VAT payable by large taxpayers, which were quarterly, became monthly. The returns of small taxpayers, which had been yearly now became half yearly, with monthly partial payments.

Improvements in organizational structure

The DGI introduced some organizational changes to improve its operations. For instance, a coordination unit for the interior was set up to supervise regional units in the interior of the country. Further, within the Systems Support Bureau, a unit was established and made formally responsible for planning and controlling the work of the DGI.

Key Factors in the Success of the Project

Success in attaining the goals set for the project was due primarily to the following:

- The project received strong support from several international organizations: the IMF, which laid down the general guidelines for the project and exercised technical supervision; the IDB, which provided the necessary financing; and CIAT, which served as the executing agency for the project.
- The support provided by the Ministry of Economy and Finance in bringing about the necessary legal changes.
- The on-time delivery by the Government of the resources needed to carry out the project in accordance with the established timetable.
- The approach used by CIAT in managing the project, similar to that used by the international supporting agencies in Bolivia, which gave the consultants overall responsibility for implementing the new systems, not just for developing them.
- The strategy followed to overcome resistance to change. The approach used was to begin by developing simple systems that resolved minor problems, successful implementation of which earned the confidence of the staff. This made it possible to involve the employees and gain their support when the time came to implement more complex systems.

Conclusions

The most important gain for the DGI is that it now has available timely information of excellent quality about its largest taxpayers. The system for control of stopfilers, for instance, will indicate with full precision one day after taxes are due which taxpayers have not filed their tax return or paid the tax. Another example is the support provided by this system to the audit area. Analyses of sales-to-purchases ratios, by economic sector, led to a selection for auditing purposes of taxpayers whose behavior was presumably evasive. In some of those cases it was found that phony purchase invoices had been deducted as credits.

Furthermore, several proposals for changing the tax system have been developed from econometric simulations based on data stored in the system. The information now available makes it possible to take more informed decisions. The effects of changes in tax policy and tax administration can be better forecast.

A key question facing the authorities when the project was first set in motion was whether change was possible at all. The DGI needed to learn how to work using information systems supported by computers. It had to be shown to the organization that it was possible to identify and monitor stopfiling and delinquent taxpayers without having to ask them to produce copies of the tax returns they had filed or the payments they had made. With the control system designed and put in place for large taxpayers, change was shown to be possible even without changing the staff which for decades had been using obsolete manual procedures.

Still to come is the opening of CEDE 2 that will control 5,000 taxpayers in Montevideo, as well as of the five CEDE units in the interior of the country, each of which will control about 1,000 taxpayers. If everything goes according to plan, this work will be completed within two years and the new system will cover some 15,000 taxpayers who together account for more than 95 percent of total tax revenues collected by the DGI.

ANNEX I
Bolivia: Summary Descriptions of Taxes

Taxes Introduced Under the Tax Reform Law (Law No. 843 of May 20, 1986)

Presumed Corporate Income

The presumed corporate income tax is levied on the net worth of companies. It is assessed annually. The initial rate was 1 percent and the current rate is 3 percent. The tax exempts assets devoted to activities that are not commercial or industrial. It also exempts assets of the Government, savings and loan housing cooperatives, and public service cooperatives.

Presumed Income of Property Owners

The presumed income of property owners tax is a levy on the ownership of registered property (real estate, motor vehicles, motor boats, and aircraft). Its rates are moderately progressive. Payments of this tax made by companies are credited as partial payment of the presumed corporate income tax. It exempts property of the Central Government, the states (called "departments" in Bolivia) and municipal governments, public institutions, and diplomatic missions. This tax is subdivided into three chapters: chapter I, tax on rural property; chapter II, tax on urban real estate; and chapter III, tax on motor vehicles, motor boats, and aircraft. It is assessed and paid annually and may be paid in two installments.

VAT

The VAT taxes value added in primary production (cattle raising and farming), nearly all services, sales of personal property on a regular basis, the leasing of personal and real property, and imports. All stages of production and marketing are taxed. The nominal rate is 10 percent[12] and the actual rate is 11.11 percent, because the taxable net price includes the VAT itself. The VAT cannot be indicated separately on invoices. There are virtually no exemptions. The tax is assessed and paid on a monthly basis.

Tax on Transactions

The tax on transactions is a typical cascading tax. It taxes gross income from commerce, industry, liberal professions, trades, services, interest, and gifts. The tax is assessed and paid monthly. The initial rate was 1 percent and the current rate is 2 percent. It exempts the personal labor of employees as well as exports, services provided by the Government (except those supplied by private companies performing a public service), private education, diplomatic services, and interest from savings accounts, bank accounts, and fixed-term deposits.

[12]In March 1992, this rate was increased to 13 percent.

Tax on Specific Consumption

The tax on specific consumption is levied on the first sale or import of the following goods:

	Initial Rate (1986)	Current Rate (1991)
	(In percent)	
Product		
Beer	30	60
Cordials and liqueurs	10	15
Wines	7.5	10
Alcohol	30	30
Cigarettes	50	50
Perfumes and cosmetics	30	30
Jewelry and precious stones	50	50
Consumption of electric energy[1]	—	20
Bottled soft drinks[1]	—	20

[1]Included subsequent to the tax reform.

The basis for computing this tax is the net sales price. Neither the VAT nor the tax on specific consumption is included in the base of the tax on specific consumption. The tax is assessed and paid monthly.

Value-Added Tax Supplementary System

The value-added tax supplementary system taxes the income of individuals and undistributed estates, such as the leasing of personal and real property; the yield of invested capital (interest, dividends, and profits distributed by partnerships and amounts withdrawn from solely owned companies); wages and salaries; fees earned by self-employed professionals; and royalties, patents, and trademarks.

Only Bolivian-source income is taxed. There is a withholding system with monthly assessments and payments. For taxpayers not subject to withholding, the assessment and payment period is quarterly. Employees benefit from a nontaxable allowance equal to two national minimum wages. The rate is 10 percent. A unique characteristic of this tax is that taxpayers can credit against it 10 percent of the sales amounts shown in VAT invoices received on purchases of consumer goods. When this tax was established there was little hope of being able to collect any significant amount. However, in 1990 the amount collected was equal to 0.46 percent of GDP. The purpose of this tax is to encourage taxpayers to ask for an invoice when they make a purchase, thereby stimulating payment of the VAT by sellers.

Tax Amnesty—Special Tax

A tax amnesty was granted from December 31, 1985, calling for a one-time filing of a tax return and payment of tax. The special tax was levied on the registered property (real estate, motor vehicles, and so on) of individuals and the assets of legal entities. Payment of the tax ruled out tax audits or tax bills for periods preceding December 31, 1985, unless final rulings had been issued by the date of publication of the law.

Taxes Introduced After the Tax Reform

Gift Tax

The gift tax applies to inheritances and to legal acts by which property is transferred free of charge. It is levied on personal property, real property, shares of stock, shares of capital, and rights subject to registration. Government agencies and nonprofit associations, foundations, and institutions are exempted from this tax. There are three rates: 1 percent, 10 percent, and 20 percent. The tax is assessed and paid within 90 days of the death of the decedent or within 5 business days following the event that gives rise to the tax. This tax was enacted on March 18, 1987.

Tax on Travel Abroad

The tax on travel abroad is levied on all air travel to foreign countries by persons residing in Bolivia. Diplomats and persons entitled to that status are exempted. The tax is Bs 100 (approximately US$30) for travel to neighboring countries and Bs 150 (approximately US$45) for all other countries. This tax was established in February 1990.

ANNEX II
Bolivia: Summary Description of the Basic Tax Systems and Procedures

Single Register of Taxpayers

The current registration system handles the following functions: registration number allotments; new registrations, cancellations, and amendments; control of duplicate registrations; and data inquiries according to different headings and statistics.

Because of the high degree of decentralization of the registration process, and in order to avoid transcription errors, a form was designed with three sections: (1) registration application (to enter the information); (2) registration certificate (to be displayed on the premises where the taxpayer carries on his business); and (3) taxpayer card (for bank operations, processing of paperwork involving government agencies, and so forth).

When the form is filed, an adhesive label is placed on each section showing the registration number pre-stamped by the computer. Though simple, such labels were not produced in the country at the time the system was introduced and had to be bought abroad. This made their procurement more difficult, because of the processing involved in making an international purchase.

The registration code assigned to each taxpayer is fully numerical. It is made up of eight digits of which the last is a check digit. It includes no subcodes identifying special features such as type of taxpayer (individual or juridical), region, and so on. It is unique for each taxpayer, irrespective of the activities engaged in or the number of establishments or branches operated.

Registration was mandatory for all existing taxpayers liable for the taxes included in the tax reform and was carried out in February–April 1987. Following the closing of registration for existing taxpayers, inspections to verify registration were carried out in virtually all industrial, commercial, and services areas of the largest cities. To do this, university students were hired to work part-time. They were first assigned to verification teams (44,931 inspections were carried out) responsible for checking particular areas and were subsequently reassigned to teams that conducted a second verification, making sure that no person was assigned the same area as in the first operation (21,920 second verifications were conducted). A final control was done through sampling, without entering into direct contact with the taxpayers, to make sure that the single register of taxpayers certificate was being displayed.

Taxpayers could register under the following categories: (1) general system (of the VAT); (2) simplified tax system (special system); (3) comprehensive tax system (special system); and (4) unified rural tax system (special system).

New taxpayers are required to follow similar procedures. Changes in the number of taxpayers registered over time are set out in detail in Table 5 in Annex III.

Collection Through Banks

The system of collection through banks began operating on May 11, 1987, coinciding with the first due date for filing tax returns and paying taxes under the new tax reform provisions. Opposition to the introduction of the system came chiefly from the Bank Association (ASOBAN), which raised three basic concerns: (1) Banks might be held responsible for incorrect information provided by taxpayers in their tax returns. This was not true and the matter was duly cleared up. (2) Banks might experience delays in turning over tax receipts to the Government and might be liable to the penalties provided for in the proposed agreement. (3) Banks might make errors in the course of entering the data and might be fined on that account.

Opposition from ASOBAN reached such a pitch that only days before the first due date of May 11, 1987 the Government had to reaffirm its strong backing for the system as then developed and let ASOBAN know that a decision had been made to begin operations as planned, authorizing only the Banco del Estado (the State Bank), which had accepted the new system, to collect taxes.

The firmness demonstrated by the Government made the private banks reconsider their position and on May 7, 1987 they accepted the new procedures. The Government agreed to enforce the penalties stipulated in the accord only after it had been in force for six months, so that banks would have time to gain experience and to streamline their own internal procedures. The system began operating with ten banks that had a total of 250 branches throughout the country. A few banks, such as the Bank of Cochabamba, which had not signed the agreement initially, decided to join the system after it had been in operation for one year.

The basic structure of the collection system is as follows:

(1) Bank branches accept tax returns and payment of taxes directly from the taxpayers.

(2) At the end of each day, on the basis of a collection summary form, each bank branch transfers the proper amounts to the beneficiaries under the revenue sharing system: the Regional Development Corporation, the university, and the municipality (25 percent of tax receipts).

(3) The original summary is sent, along with the tax returns, to the head or central office of each bank in La Paz.

(4) This office then transcribes the documents onto magnetic media and validates by computer all the data recorded on the tax returns, issuing an order for a transfer from the account kept by each bank in the Central Bank to the account of the National Treasury. This order

is issued in the amount of the sum total of summaries prepared by bank branches (75 percent of tax receipts). In addition, each head or central office sends to the automatic data processing area of the DGRI a supporting disk containing (a) complete information on the transfer order; (b) complete information on each of the collection summaries that add up to the transfer order; and (c) complete information on each tax return included in each collection summary, as well as on those tax returns that show no tax payable or a balance in favor of the taxpayer.

(5) The DGRI, using computer controls, draws up and supplies to each head or central office a listing of all transfer orders not credited to the account of the National Treasury because they were never sent out. Likewise, it reports those transfers which have been credited by the Central Bank but for which the relevant documentation and supporting disks have not been received.

(6) The automatic data processing area of the DGRI checks the data processed by the banks and the documentation that the Central Bank has sent with its statements, including the validation process and supporting detailed data (tax returns and adjustments) sent by banks, and the reconcilement of the data sent by banks with the data in the statements received from the Central Bank.

(7) With the validated data, information on tax receipts is generated for various users. For example: performance charts, for the DGRI National Office; tabulations for the regional administrations; tabulations for control of bank reports filed late; information for beneficiary entities under the revenue sharing system; information for the accounting unit of the DGRI; information concerning bad checks; information on adjustments made by banks and awaiting cancellation; and distribution of bank commissions.

To ensure proper operation of the system, the following procedures were established: (a) delivery to banks of the software needed to retrieve information from tax returns and prepare collection summaries, generate transfer orders, validate data, and submit reports to the DGRI on magnetic media; (b) delivery of batches to test the system; and (c) supporting banks in the tasks of setting the collection system in motion, generating orders for the transfer of funds, and retrieving and validating data from tax returns.

Thanks to the system of collecting taxes through banks the DGRI can count on having, by the twentieth day of the following month, all of the previous month's tax receipts processed by computer. At that point the DGRI has all the information on the tax returns filed, with the sole exception of the presumed income of property owners tax, which is due twice a year and which, owing to its large volume, has a processing deadline of three months.

The system of collection through banks processes a total of about 190,000 tax returns every month.

Control of Large Taxpayers

A few months after the bank collection system went into effect computerized information was available on the amount of taxes paid and the monthly sales figures of each taxpayer. With this information a ranking was made from which it was seen that about 1,300 taxpayers throughout the country contributed more than 66 percent of all tax receipts. The decision was consequently made to monitor the largest taxpayers separately from all other taxpayers. Accordingly, there are now three sectors for monitoring large taxpayers:

(1) Since March 2, 1988, there is a sector for large taxpayers of the La Paz regional administration, which began operating with 602 taxpayers and now monitors 711 taxpayers.

(2) Since April 3, 1989, there is a sector for large taxpayers of the Santa Cruz regional administration, which began with 319 taxpayers and now controls 372 taxpayers.

(3) Since May 2, 1989, there is a sector for large taxpayers of the Cochabamba regional administration, which began with 317 taxpayers and now monitors 366 taxpayers.

Each sector is housed in a separate building of the regional administration to which it belongs, which also houses collection outlets of the Banco del Estado, where large taxpayers must file their tax returns and pay their taxes. The personnel of each of these sectors numbers between 30 and 40 persons, who are university graduates or students previously unassociated with the DGRI. Each sector performs, for the taxpayers under its jurisdiction, all the tasks assigned to the regional administration, with the sole exception of tax audits. Each sector has a computer to carry out all system operations.

When a large taxpayer wants to file a tax return and pay he goes to an office within the sector where the documents go through a first check (to make sure that all boxes have been filled in, especially the single register of taxpayers number and the tax period, and that the return is from a large taxpayer). If the return shows no errors detectable at first sight, it is passed on to the Banco del Estado cashiers for payment and acceptance. The Bank processes the documents and delivers a disk to the sector on the following day. Orders to file missing tax returns are drawn up within a maximum of three days and are then delivered to taxpayers in person by officials of the sector. Orders to pay taxes are delivered within a week, having been prepared by the tax return reassessment system.

The sector also makes preliminary checks to detect inconsistencies arising from a review of tax returns and special information requested from taxpayers. Such checks may raise suspicions of tax evasion, which in turn may prompt more formal and deeper tax audits.

The treatment accorded to large taxpayers is personalized and professional. The idea of creating a new DGRI, sponsored by some government officials, may be said to have become a reality in the large taxpayers sectors. Their staff have been especially selected and trained and are imbued with the esprit de corps they need to perform the task set before them. The first national meeting of large taxpayers sectors was held in February 1991 to discuss and seek solutions to their common problems.

ANNEX III

Table 3. Bolivia: Tax Receipts as a Percentage of GDP

1978	3.83
1979	3.59
1980	3.06
1981	3.09
1982	1.81
1983	1.39
1984	0.88
1985	1.12
1986	1.88
1987	4.91
1988	6.15
1989	6.59
1990	7.40

Source: Statistics Section of the DGRI.

Table 4. Bolivia: Tax Collections in Constant Values

(In bolivares of December 1990)

	Tax Collections *(In millions of bolivares)*	Increase over Preceding Year *(In percent)*
1986	346.4	—
1987	731.8	111.23
1988	939.8	28.13
1989	1,026.6	9.23
1990	1,190.9	16.00

Source: Statistics Section of the DGRI.

Table 5. Bolivia: Development of the Single National Register of Taxpayers

As in December	General System	Simplified Tax System	Comprehensive Tax System	Unified Rural Tax System	Total
1987	79,414	163,731	—	—	243,145
1988	105,403	188,237	10,455	—	304,095
1989	120,925	198,106	15,843	—	334,874
1990	138,759	203,748	15,987	7,065	365,559

Source: Statistics Section of the DGRI.

ANNEX IV
Bolivia: Statistics for the Use of Government Agencies

Following is an outline of the statistical data included in the magnetic files produced for the use of government agencies (summary of the fields that make up the record):

(1) Monthly statistics (large taxpayers)

DGRI unit code
Processing month
Tax
Economic sector
Number of taxpayers per sector in the month
Amount collected
- In the month
- In the previous month
  - At historical values
  - At constant values
- In the same month last year
  - At historical values
  - At constant values

Change in constant values
- Collection this month versus last month
  - Relative
  - Absolute
- Collection this month versus same month last year
  - Relative
  - Absolute

Total this heading
Country total by economic sector and heading
Total per agency and heading

(2) Annual statistics (all taxpayers)

Collections through bank network, broken down by tax and economic sector.

Collection through bank network, broken down by department and tax.

Data on particular tax reported, broken down by type of taxpayer and economic sector.

Data on balances in favor of the treasury and the taxpayer, broken down by economic sector (VAT).

Data on collection of presumed corporate income, broken down by agency and means of payment.

Collection through the bank network, broken down by tax, department, and economic sector.

ANNEX V

Table 6. Uruguay: Internal Taxes—Gross Receipts and Refunds

(In percent of total gross receipts)

Description	1985	1986	1987	1988	1989
Total gross receipts	100.0	100.0	100.0	100.0	100.0
Value-added tax	47.3	46.7	45.9	50.8	51.4
Excises	31.3	29.5	29.6	26.1	27.3
Tax on income from industry and commerce	6.5	6.2	7.1	8.1	7.1
IMPROME,[1] farming tax, tax on the transfer of farming property, and tax on farm income	2.9	3.3	3.6	3.3	1.7
Tax on assets	6.9	7.2	6.9	6.2	5.8
Tax on bank assets	—	0.9	1.2	1.3	2.5
Tax on sales of foreign currency	4.4	5.1	4.4	2.9	2.7
Other taxes[2]	0.4	0.4	0.3	0.3	0.6
Interest, surcharges, and fines	0.4	0.7	0.8	0.8	0.8
Tax refunds	−8.8	8.6	−8.5	−9.5	−8.9

Source: Dirección General Impositiva.

[1]IMPROME is an earlier form of agricultural taxation.

[2]Includes the additional real property tax.

Comments

Ramiro Cabezas M.

Background—The Situation in Bolivia in August 1985

To operate with reasonable efficiency, all administrations require constant adjustment and updating. When this is not done and the corrections are carried out all at once, the process is generally known as "reform."

In instances where the situation is chaotic and desperate, the required change is more drastic and sweeping. This is what happened in Bolivia, not only in the areas of tax legislation and tax administration but also in the administration of government finances in general.

In Bolivia, structural change in tax legislation and administration was part of a much wider overall strategy. To understand this, it is necessary to be aware of the background against which it was introduced and the forces that drove it.

Until August 1985, when the Government changed, the Bolivian economy was subjected to stringent government regulations. For instance, prices of a large number of essential consumer goods were controlled and only belatedly adjusted, as the Government was reluctant to appear responsible for unpopular measures; a number of basic consumer goods were subsidized; wages in both the public and private sectors were fixed by the Government; no private sector employee could be dismissed; bank interest rates were fixed by the Government; and the Government held a monopoly over foreign exchange transactions, and private foreign exchange transactions were illegal. Further, the exchange rate was fixed by the Government, and the domestic currency was kept artificially overvalued in the hope of avoiding price increases. This policy had a serious effect on exports, as foreign exchange had to be surrendered at an artificial exchange rate. Domestic industry was overprotected through quantitative restrictions on imports, foreign exchange rationing, and high import tariffs.

With respect to public sector finances, the situation was as follows: Under pressure from the trade unions, there were constant wage increases, which overshot the budget; the heavy burden of subsidies was inadequately financed; the tax base suffered from dramatic erosion, aggravated by inflation; and there was disarray in public expenditure, coupled with low investment. As a consequence, the public sector produced enormous fiscal deficits which were financed by credit from the Central Bank.

As was to be expected, such economic policies and the manner in which the public sector was administered led to a generally chaotic situation. Bolivia recorded the greatest hyperinflation ever known that did not arise from domestic conflict or foreign war. In August 1985, hyperinflation reached an annualized rate of approximately 23,500 percent; essential consumer goods could only be purchased on the black market; and international reserves were exhausted and Bolivia ceased to meet its external obligations.

Structural Changes in Economic Policy and in the Administration of Government Finances

In brief, Bolivia was in an intolerable situation. The Government was obliged to hold elections ahead of schedule. The new Government that took office in August 1985 was faced with the urgent need to take prompt, radical measures. These consisted of the following:

- All subsidies were eliminated.
- The economy was opened up by removing all restrictions on international trade and by drastically reducing customs tariffs.
- Prices were freed and made subject to market forces; domestic products were forced to compete with imports.
- Unrestricted employment and dismissal of workers was introduced; the obligation to pay social benefits for retirees was retained; and private sector salaries were to be negotiated between the parties, without government intervention, excepting in cases requiring arbitration. The Government, as employer, negotiated public sector salaries.
- Following a large initial devaluation, a floating official exchange rate was established, and private foreign exchange transactions became legal.
- Interest rates were made subject to market forces.

With regard to the administration of government finances, the Treasury's resources were rapidly increased through a tax on fuels; public spending was reduced to essential levels and public employee salaries were frozen for a six-month period; and, despite public spending cuts, the proportion of investment was increased. In addition, two laws were enacted for regulating the system of government finances: the Law on the Integrated System of Financial Administration and Control (SAFCO Law) and the Tax Reform Law.

Law on the Integrated System of Financial Administration and Control

The SAFCO Law was approved only in July 1990, under the Government that took office in August 1989. However, the previous Government began, to the extent possible within the framework of the laws then existing, to put into practice a large part of the law's content and philosophy. The SAFCO Law defines the characteristics of the following administrative systems: programming of operations, administrative organization, budget, personnel administration, administration of goods and services, treasury and public credit, government accounting, internal audits, and ex post external audits. The law establishes the relationship between the above-mentioned systems and those of planning and public investment. It also defines the institutional responsibilities of the Ministry of Finance, the Office of the Comptroller-General of the Republic, and the Central Bank, and sets out the responsibilities of individuals holding civil service positions.

Tax Reform Law and Its Application

The paper by Carlos Silvani and Alberto Radano on the Tax Reform Law enacted in May 1986 and on its implementation clearly describes essential aspects of the new law and the adjustments made in tax administration to provide for its implementation.

As I played a role in designing and drafting the new tax law and was responsible for implementing the reform during the first three years, I will take the liberty of expanding upon certain aspects of the reform.

To fully understand the reform, it is necessary to understand the main objectives that guided and characterized it.

The first objective was to increase tax collection, minimizing the distorting effects of taxes by applying low rates and broadening their base. We did not wish taxes to be a determining factor in the decision-making process of economic agents, and tried to keep taxes from becoming incentives or disincentives for any activity. On the other hand, by increasing the scope of their application, we hoped to increase tax collections and reduce the resistance that results from discriminatory treatment.

The second objective was to simplify the tax system so that taxes could be known and understood by taxpayers. Bolivia's level of development makes a broad common understanding of complex systems impossible. It was deemed preferable to disregard certain subtleties usually advocated in the name of tax "justice" or "equity" and instead to develop simple systems, especially taking into account that the rates are low.

The third aim was to design the system in such a way that tax evasion and fraud were more difficult than under the previous system. This objective led, for example, to the elimination of the income tax on businesses and to its replacement by a tax on net wealth, which is harder to hide than income. In this way the work of tax administration was simplified as well.

The fourth objective was to avoid contact wherever possible between the taxpayer and the administrator; thus, the taxpayer's direct responsibility was clearer.

With regard to the general strategy for implementing the reform, the temporary creation of the Ministry of Tax Collection was intended to demonstrate the political support the Government accorded the reform and the significance it attached to the reform, as well as to enable a Minister of State to propose to the Cabinet, directly and swiftly, the series of regulations that were essential to get the reform under way. The creation of the ministry also made it possible to reap prompt benefits from external advice and permitted political decisions to be taken quickly.

Part of the strategy consisted of contracting the services of a core group of Bolivian professionals, some with experience in taxation, to work closely with foreign advisors and thus develop into a cohesive unit and afterward go on to occupy key positions in tax administration. The selection process was not easy, and retaining these professionals was particularly hard in view of the low level of salaries in public administration. In order to retain them, financial support from international organizations was obtained. This support was very important, but it also had its drawbacks. For example, the Minister was questioned in Parliament as to why he was paying a small number of civil servants more than the rest and was using resources that could have a damaging effect on national sovereignty or dignity.

I was convinced that, at least during the initial phase of a far-reaching reform, the utmost priority should be given to the development of tax awareness among the population. I clearly recall that the first impressive leap in tax collection occurred before audit systems and techniques were in operation.

To everyone's amazement, after having stood in long lines outside banks to pay their taxes and having been unable to do so within the timetable set, tens of thousands of taxpayers marched in public demonstrations urging the banks to remain open so that they could pay their taxes. Such demonstrations occurred on several occasions. There were also, of course, public demonstrations against taxes, but these were to be expected.

A group of journalists, intrigued by the radical change in the attitude of the taxpayers, conducted a survey to find out the reason behind this remarkable change. The main questions were: You are now paying more taxes than before. Is this because you feel like a responsible citizen? Because you are confident that the Government administers your money well? Or because paying taxes helps control inflation?

Close to 70 percent of the taxpayers interviewed, even low-income taxpayers, responded that the payment of taxes helped to control inflation. This, among many others, was the message that had most captured the imagination of the people during the motivating and consciousness-raising campaign that was carried out.

Unfortunately, a taxpayer's spirit of responsibility does not continue unaided; it needs to be renewed through regular campaigns, and the taxpayer needs to be informed that the administration is able to keep an eye on him.

Immediate Results of the Structural Changes, the Administration of Public Spending, and the Tax Reform

To conclude, some of the immediate and most important results of the structural reforms, the administration of public spending, and the tax reform are summarized below:

- Prompt control of hyperinflation. In 1991, Bolivia had the lowest inflation rate in Latin America.
- The negative economic growth trend was reversed. Bolivia has now been growing for five years, though not yet satisfactorily.
- In general there is an abundance of consumer goods.
- The public sector deficit has been greatly reduced and is financed to a large extent with external resources. Central Bank financing of the public sector is now of little significance.
- The tax ratio has increased from 1.2 percent of GDP to approximately 7.5 percent of GDP.
- International reserves have reached reasonable levels and, because of skillful negotiations with its creditors, Bolivia is current in its external obligations.

The evolution of some of the key indicators of the Bolivian economy is shown in Table 1.

Table 1. Key Indicators of the Changes in the Bolivian Economy
(In percent)

	1984	1985	1986	1987	1988	1989
Growth of GDP	−0.3	−0.15	−2.9	2.12	2.81	2.41
Ratio of nonfinancial public sector deficit to GDP	25.5	10.8	3.3	8.3	5.7	4.9
Percentage of deficit financed with money creation	89.5	79.5	—[1]	55.0	38.8	40.9
Ratio of investment expenditure to total expenditure	9.7	11.5	16.4	18.4	23.0	21.9
Ratio of internal taxes to GDP	1.4	1.3	2.7	5.1	6.3	7.5[2]
		Aug. 1985	Dec. 1986	Dec. 1987	Dec. 1988	Dec. 1989
Inflation		23,500	66.0	10.7	21.5	16.5

[1]The availability of external resources to cover the deficit was greater in 1986 than the deficit itself.

[2]The tax ratio, including customs duties and taxes on hydrocarbons, reached 13 percent.

3

The Nexus of Tax Administration and Tax Policy in Jamaica and Guatemala

Roy Bahl and Jorge Martinez-Vazquez

It is almost inevitable that a report on taxation in a developing country, especially if prepared by an outside advisor or a donor, will end by pointing out that the primary problem is one of poor administration. Because low-income countries do not efficiently administer the systems they have in place, they fail to collect the true amount of revenue due, the efficiency objectives of the tax structure are not realized, and both the horizontal and vertical equity intent of the nominal tax structure are compromised.

There seems to be a consensus on why tax administration is so poor in developing countries and on what might be done about it. Most analyses center on three areas:

- The procedures used are antiquated, and staff are poorly paid and badly trained. This view of the problem has led bilateral donors and international agencies to provide massive amounts of technical assistance in tax administration. There are success stories, but in most countries the scorecard probably still shows a poor administrative effort.[1]
- The tax systems in developing countries are too complicated for efficient administration with the modest resources typically available to central government tax departments. Frequently, developing countries have imitated the complex tax structures of developed countries, but have found it much harder to replicate tax administration capabilities. Thus, the proposed solution for developing countries has been policy reform in the direction of simplifying the tax structure.
- The government is unwilling to enforce the existing system. The approach here is to wait for a crisis to move the government to improve its system, or for outside donors to use coercion (close

[1]We say "probably" because we can point to no analysis that compares and tracks indicators of tax administration efficiency across developing countries.

the loan window) or incentives (open the loan window) to "assist" the process.

If the problem is this well understood, the solutions are viable, and the needed technology is available, then one might ask why tax administration in developing countries has been so slow to improve. We would argue that there are three reasons.

- The modernization of tax structures, which usually involves following the golden tax rule of broadening the base and lowering the rate, does not always lead to a simplification of the tax structure. In general, the complexities of modern tax structures, which are partly due to the complexities of modern economies, require a higher level of administrative effort. A corollary to this rule is that as developing countries industrialize, and as the level of taxation rises, the incentives for evasion and avoidance go up, and tax administration becomes more difficult.
- Tax policy is used as an instrument of economic policy, and discretionary tax actions are inevitably "special case" tax preferences or penalties that complicate tax administration. Too often such policies are enacted under the assumption that there is no tax administration constraint.
- All governments, but particularly governments in developing countries, do not want high levels of enforcement, for economic as well as for political reasons. They are willing to accept a certain amount of evasion and leave open loopholes that permit avoidance. Outside advisors often confuse these deliberate policies with poor administration.

This paper is about the nexus between tax administration and tax policy in developing countries, and draws on the experience with tax reform in Jamaica and Guatemala in evaluating these three propositions. These propositions suggest a need to rethink the traditional remedies for poor tax administration in developing countries. To be sure, more training, better staff conditions, improved procedures, and a less complicated tax code remain sound advice. But, as we enter the 1990s, there are other aspects that need to be considered, including perhaps a need to begin breaking with the conventional wisdom of "go slow and keep it simple." Modern tax structures are complex, and the complexity grows with economic development. One need not survey too many tax systems to realize this. It may be time to move away from advising governments to shun complexities in their tax structures because of the administrative constraint toward relaxing the constraint so that the administration is better able to absorb the inevitable complexity.

The paper is organized as follows. A brief description of the two tax reform projects is given in Section I; Section II considers the influence of the economic and political setting on the probability of successful policy and administrative reform; and Section III describes the reforms that took place in both countries in the 1980s. These themes are analyzed further in Sections IV, V, and VI. A final section speculates on general lessons for tax policy and administration reform in developing countries.

I. The Jamaican and Guatemalan Tax Projects[2]

In 1986–87, the Government of Jamaica implemented a major reform of its income and property tax structure. The reform package was a success in that it was popularly accepted, the revenue targets were met, and the package was implemented without any major incident in tax administration. However, it was incomplete in that it did not include a restructuring of the indirect tax system or the payroll taxes. The impetus for policy and administrative reform disappeared after the 1987 reform, but in 1990 the Government moved to reconsider the introduction of measures complementary to those approved in 1986. The groundwork for a major administrative reform was also laid in 1986, and though much progress has been made, that effort is not yet complete.

The tax reform was preceded by a careful evaluation of the existing problems, quantification of the tax system, and simulation of the impact of possible changes. The proposals were subjected to public debate, deliberated upon by a blue-ribbon commission, and reported in the media. The second-round reform, presently under way, is taking this same quantitative approach and is modeling the revenue and tax burden impact of alternative reforms.[3]

---

[2]The 1983–87 Jamaican tax project is summarized in Bahl (1990a) and reported in detail in Bahl (1990b). The 1990–91 Jamaican tax project is under way, but no reports are yet available. The 1989–92 Guatemalan project is also under way, and at this time is reported only in a series of technical working papers produced under the direction of KPMG Peat Marwick and the Policy Research Center at Georgia State University.

[3]The initial tax reform project was carried out by the Revenue Board of the Government of Jamaica and the Metropolitan Studies Program of the Maxwell School of Syracuse University. The project began in mid-1983 and the collaboration ended in September 1987. A second round of the tax reform project is now under way, with the Revenue Board taking the lead and the Policy Research Center at Georgia State University doing the technical and advisory work. This project is scheduled for completion in 1991.

In 1987, the newly elected Government of Guatemala introduced a comprehensive tax reform. In the view of many observers this reform package was riddled with problems. It was unpopular with taxpayers, and it ultimately led to a dramatic decrease in compliance. In contrast to the Jamaican project, the 1987 Guatemalan tax reform was done almost in an ad hoc fashion. In part, this was because the Government could not afford the time to "do it right." Only a few Guatemalan experts were involved, little international expertise was used in assessing and formulating policy, and there was practically no quantification of revenue and burden effects. Consequently, the Government did not have in hand the necessary background information. The Government made no effort to improve tax administration, and the reforms were designed to accommodate the weaknesses of the existing administration. Rather than public debate, there were a number of presentations to the public through the media and public meetings. The presentation put little emphasis on the characteristics of the tax reform itself and much more on the political and social benefits to be derived from the increased tax collections the reform would provide. In retrospect, 1987 was a missed opportunity for successful tax reform, although it should also be noted that changes to the laws introduced by the Guatemalan Congress at the last minute contributed to diluting the quality of the 1987 reform package.

A new government took office in January 1991, and is considering the need for a more comprehensive reform of the tax system. The present reform project in Guatemala is being carried out jointly by the Ministry of Finance, the Policy Economics Group of KPMG Peat Marwick, and the Policy Research Center of Georgia State University. This effort started in 1989 and it is scheduled to end in early 1992. It is a comprehensive reform program in the same vein as the Jamaican effort.[4]

II. The Economic and Political Settings

Finding the right relationship between tax policy and tax administration in developing countries begins with choosing the right moment to carry out a reform. The Jamaican and Guatemalan cases show that comprehensive tax reform can take place in a weak economic setting.

[4]Funding for both the Jamaican and the present Guatemalan projects was provided by the U.S. Agency for International Development, but in neither case was the U.S. Government involved in the actual work.

Reform certainly took place in Jamaica in an economic crisis, and is under consideration in Guatemala in a similar crisis situation.

Jamaica

Jamaica was besieged by severe economic problems over most of the tax reform period. This made it difficult for the Government to keep its attention focused solely on improving the tax structure and its administration. The collapse of the bauxite industry in the early 1980s deprived the country of its major foreign exchange earner. The performance of the tourism industry, the second most important source of foreign exchange, was often weak, and recovery proceeded slowly. Continuous disequilibrium in the balance of payments put pressure on the exchange rate and led to a major devaluation of the Jamaica dollar in November 1983. During this period the debt-service burden was very heavy, averaging over 45 percent of export earnings in the mid-1980s. On the domestic side there was a substantial fiscal imbalance, with the budget deficit reaching about 8 percent of GDP in 1985. With not only high inflation but also high unemployment during the period, and the public sector being the most important employer of unskilled workers, it was difficult for the Government to adopt a policy of expenditure retrenchment.

All of this meant that at the time the reform project began, there was a great deal of pressure to take care of the short-run problem of the fiscal deficit mainly by finding ways to raise more revenue. This environment would not have seemed the most opportune time to focus on structural reform—in particular a revenue-neutral structural reform with an emphasis on reducing allocational inefficiencies induced by the existing tax system.

In other ways, however, the time was exactly right for comprehensive tax reform in Jamaica. Prime Minister Seaga had been elected in 1980 with a mandate to make the economy more responsive to market incentives and to get rid of a complex system of controls and regulations. The task was overwhelming but opportunities for improvement abounded. The foreign trade sector was rife with quotas and licensing, to restrict imports and to compensate for an overvalued Jamaica dollar. An inherited import-substitution growth strategy and a complicated tariff structure were in place, and there were substantial price controls, government ownership of some traditionally private sector activities, and very high marginal income tax rates. The Prime Minister's economic strategy of replacing government controls with market forces fit well with a structural tax reform program designed to "get the prices right." Moreover, the Seaga Administration won an overwhelming majority in Parliament in a 1984 election, which enhanced the possibility of eventually passing a tax reform bill. Another stimulus to action came from the external donors—the U.S. Government, the World Bank, and the IMF—all of whom were enthusiastic about Jamaica's plans for tax reform. Finally, the Jamaican income tax had become so onerous, so obviously unfair, and so out of control that there was substantial public sentiment for a major overhaul.

Guatemala

Guatemala's economy had performed satisfactorily, and by some accounts rather well, prior to 1980. Traditional exports of coffee, cotton, bananas, and sugar, and industrial production fueled by a policy of import substitution within the Central American Common Market (CACM), were the main engines of growth. During 1960–79, GDP grew at an average rate of 5.5 percent. Prior to the first oil shock in 1973, Guatemala enjoyed a particularly stable price level, with an average inflation rate between 1946 and 1972 of 1.5 percent. Between 1973 and 1979 the average inflation rate rose to 12 percent, but never reached the extremely high levels of other Latin American countries. However, observers also see the 1970s as the period when Guatemala developed most of the problems it faced in the next decade. High rates of effective protection with respect to trade outside the CACM, an overvalued exchange rate after 1972, and preferential credit policies for domestic business (which typically were able to borrow at negative real interest rates) resulted in an industrial sector that despite very low labor costs was not internationally competitive and absorbed little labor input.

In 1980 Guatemala entered a deep recession that lasted over five years. By the end of 1985 GDP per capita had fallen to levels of the late 1960s. The depth of the recession was due to a combination of domestic and international factors. Political instability in the region kept away foreign investors. Internal unrest led to capital flight. The international recession of the early 1980s meant higher interest rates for international loans and a deterioration in the terms of trade caused by large reductions in the prices of traditional exports. But perhaps the most important factor was the collapse of the CACM. Domestic economic policy was characterized during this period by a growing fiscal deficit frequently financed by increases in the money supply, and toward the end by multiple exchange rates. Changes in the tax structure in 1983 and 1985 were largely ineffective in eliminating the deficit.

The Guatemalan setting is similar to that in Jamaica in that the policies of the 1970s were a major contributor to the problems of the 1980s, and because the proposed tax reform would be considered by a new administration with a mandate to develop a new economic policy. In many other ways, however, the setting is quite different in the two countries—the most notable difference being that Guatemala has a small, and Jamaica a large, public sector.

The inauguration of the democratically elected Cerezo Government in January 1986 marked a big turn of events not only in Guatemala's politics but also in its economic performance. The Cerezo Administration started its mandate with a good economic performance. The average growth rate of real GDP was 3.6 percent. But the economy deteriorated in the last two years of the administration. By the end of 1990 it was obvious that the administration would leave the economy in no better shape than when it was inaugurated in 1986.

What happened between 1986 and 1990 to lead to the fundamental imbalances that occurred in the central government budget and the international accounts? In the external sector, imports grew at a brisk pace after 1986, fueled by continuous growth of private and public spending. However, exports grew at a more moderate pace over this period, because of the sluggish performance of nontraditional exports and deterioration in the terms of trade for traditional exports. Net capital inflows declined from a high in 1986, led by a marked drop in private capital net inflows. Despite repeated devaluations of the quetzal, and a floating exchange rate after 1989, Guatemala's net reserve position deteriorated. By the end of 1990 the Government had defaulted on most of its international loans, including those from the World Bank and the IMF.

By most accounts, fiscal policy was an even greater problem of the Cerezo Government. To be fair, the Administration inherited the disarray in public finances. It took two policy steps to resolve the problem. It first introduced a short-run program intended to close the fiscal gap. This program included a temporary tax on exports (to be phased out gradually), a temporary tax on international phone calls, and a selective consumption tax. The second, and most important, fiscal move of the Cerezo Administration was the tax reform program of 1987. In the same year, however, the Administration began to emphasize the need to undertake an ambitious domestic investment program in social services, mainly education and health. Because many in the private sector saw this program as creating more bureaucracy and exacerbating the government deficit, support for the Government's fiscal program was weakened.

Politics aside, the fiscal problem in Guatemala has been that the tax structure is not in step with such government objectives as export-led development. More important, the level of taxes is not high enough to cover the direct expenditures and subsidies desired by the Government. Interest and exchange rate subsidies by the central bank have been an important source of the overall government deficit in recent years. The projected overall government deficit for 1991 is Q 2 billion, or close to 6 percent of GDP.

The financing requirements of the public sector were partially offset in the first years of the Cerezo Administration by foreign aid, mainly budgetary support from the U.S. Government. As the government deficit grew, foreign aid was significantly reduced and the Government resorted to monetization of the deficit. This led to an acceleration of the inflation rate, which by the end of 1990 had reached 40 percent. There was an attempt to introduce new tax legislation in the summer of 1990 in the hope of arresting the decline in tax revenues. The measures included the elimination of a number of incentive laws, new taxes on foreign exchange operations, increases in a number of fees, and the introduction of a tax amnesty. Only a few of these measures were finally approved in Congress, and they were of little consequence.

The new government of Jorge Serrano, which took office in January 1991, faced the need to implement a short-run stabilization plan immediately and to offer a plan to control the fiscal deficit. Without a stabilization plan, approved by the World Bank and the IMF, the options for the new government are few: foreign loans are not available, foreign government donations have dried up, and the ability to borrow from the public and the private banking system is very limited. Increased foreign government grants and loans will depend largely on whether an agreement is reached with the international institutions. As of August 1991, a range of possibilities to reduce the current year's deficit was under consideration, and proposals for a longer-term tax reform were under preparation.

Comparative Economic and Fiscal Positions

Guatemala is the larger of the two countries, with a greater proportion of its population living in the capital city. Its economy is less open to foreign trade, and its income generation is more heavily concentrated in the primary (agriculture and mining) sector. Jamaica has a significantly higher per capita income. Both countries showed negative economic growth through most of the 1980s.

One of the most noticeable differences between the two countries is the level of taxation: Jamaica raises taxes equivalent to nearly one fourth of GDP, and Guatemala raises an amount equivalent to 5 percent of GDP. Of course, there is no definitive way to establish the appropriate level of taxation for a country, so we cannot jump quickly to the conclusion that Guatemala's taxes are too low. This is a normative issue to be resolved politically. However, one can ask how the levels of tax effort in Jamaica and Guatemala compare with each other and with those in other countries with similar economic structures and at similar levels of development.[5] We applied three different models to estimate tax effort for 66 countries for the mid-1980s (Bahl (1971); Chelliah (1971); and Lotz and Morss (1967)). Based on these indices, Jamaica was a high-tax country, ranking ninth or tenth, while Guatemala was a very low-taxing country, ranking fifty-ninth or sixty-first. For example, if Guatemala had taxed at the average level of the 66 countries in the sample in the mid-1980s, it would have roughly doubled the taxes it actually collected. These results also suggest why Jamaica may have been such a good candidate for a revenue-neutral reform.

The fact that Jamaica exploits its tax base more fully does not lead to the conclusion that Jamaica has a "better" tax administration. Some of the difference is due to a greater willingness of the population to pay taxes, and some is due to the broader scope of services financed by general taxation. Still, there is no escaping the fact that the Jamaican system does collect a great deal more in taxes. Jamaica has invested heavily in its tax administration: an extensive training program, significant progress on computerization of its system, and the establishment of a Revenue Board. The results of stable and good leadership in the Ministry of Finance are not easily separated from other influences, but the Revenue Board has protected the basics of the 1986–87 reform and extended it to indirect taxes. The training program has been steadily improved—a training plan has been adhered to since the mid-1980s—and there has been a continuous improvement in income tax administration. In Guatemala, where there is no such body as the Revenue Board, there have been five different ministers since 1988. There is no training

[5]There is some discussion among the IMF economists who developed these indicators, and others who critique them, about whether the term "tax effort" should be used in describing the indices derived. Some have suggested the less pejorative term "tax performance." Either way, the index has a numerator, which is the actual level of taxes collected, and a denominator, which is an estimate of the taxable capacity of the country. A country with an index greater than unity is one that taxes at a greater rate than we would expect, given its economic structure and the average practice among developing countries. Higher tax effort is not an unreasonable way to describe this situation, though a problem with the specification of the model is another explanation. In any case, these regression models were never meant to give more than a general idea of the difference in the rate of taxation. In this analysis, the results are robust in showing that Jamaica is a high-taxing country and Guatemala is a low-taxing country.

plan, and no consistent, long-term program for improving tax administration.

III. The Tax Reforms

Jamaica[6]

The 1986–87 Jamaican tax reform was meant to be comprehensive, that is, to include a restructuring of all taxes and to improve tax administration. In fact, the structural reform only reached the individual income tax, the company income tax, and the property tax.[7] It was also proposed to replace the present indirect tax structure with a value-added tax (VAT). Payroll tax reforms were proposed but not enacted. Both are under consideration in the current reform project.[8]

Individual Income Tax

Prior to reform, the statutory individual income tax base included all sources of income except bank deposit interest.[9] In practice, there was no tax on capital gains, and most self-employed income was outside the tax net. There were two rate structures—depending on whether income was above or below J$7,000. The top marginal rate was 57.5 percent. When payroll taxes were taken into account, the marginal tax rate on an income of J$14,000 was well in excess of 60 percent. There was no standard deduction, but taxpayers could qualify for 16 tax credits. These credits were for different purposes, including personal allowances, stimulation of savings, and even employment of domestics. Because credits were not indexed for inflation, their value had been substantially eroded during the early 1980s. The income tax administration did relatively little monitoring of the credit system.

The base of the tax was further eroded by the practice of permitting employers to grant nontaxable perquisites ("allowances") to employees. These perquisites were a matter of negotiation between employee and employer (including government ministries) and did not have to

[6]Monetary amounts are presented here in local currency units (Jamaica dollars). Exchange rates are reported in Annex I.

[7]The property tax reform is not discussed here, but it is considered in detail in Holland and Follain (1990).

[8]The VAT was implemented in October 1991.

[9]The system is described in detail in Alm, Bahl, and Murray (1990) and the reform measures in Alm, Bahl, Murray, and Riddle (1990).

be reported to the Income Tax Commissioner. The value of these allowances was estimated at 15 percent of total taxable compensation, but for higher-income workers it was much greater.

Simulation of alternative rate and base structures, with a revenue-neutral target in mind and with simplification and neutrality as primary objectives, led to the following reform program:

- Replacing the present graduated rate structure with a flat rate of 33⅓ percent.
- Replacing the 16 tax credits with a standard deduction of J$8,580 a year.
- With few exceptions, bringing all nontaxable allowances into the base.
- Including bank deposit interest (above a low ceiling) in the income tax base.

The Government enacted this program after a Tax Reform Committee representing private business, unions, and other nongovernmental groups spent several months scrutinizing and amending the proposals. The income tax reform became effective at the beginning of 1986 and was almost totally operative by the end of the first quarter.

The Company Income Tax

Prior to reform, companies paid a basic rate of 35 percent plus an "additional tax" of 10 percent, but the additional rate could be offset against a withholding tax on dividends (Wozny (1990)). To complicate matters further, there was separate treatment for agricultural companies, incentive firms, and financial institutions.

This system led to three basic problems. First, the tax was complicated, not easily administered, and was unfair to certain types of firms. Second, it discriminated in favor of debt and against equity finance; in favor of retaining rather than distributing earnings; and against risk taking. The "optimal" dividend distribution rate for a firm was about 27 percent of profits—above this amount "additional" profit tax liability would be due. Moreover, in the eyes of investors, dividends were taxed twice whereas interest received from savings accounts was not taxed at all. Third, the reduction in the top individual income tax rate to 33⅓ percent and the reduction in the U.S. corporate rate brought new pressures to lower the company tax rate.

The Government enacted a comprehensive reform of the company tax in 1987. The tax rate was reduced to 33⅓ percent and the "additional tax'' was eliminated. This removed the disincentive to larger dividend distributions, and though the Government did not eliminate the preferential treatment of retained earnings, it did bring interest income into the tax base, thereby removing another disincentive to equity finance. Full loss carryforward was introduced, removing some of the bias against risk-taking, and branch and subsidiary companies were given equal tax treatment. The proposal to exempt dividends from personal tax liability was rejected. The Government instead decided on a separate entity approach whereby company profits and dividends each would be taxed at 33⅓ percent.

Was Jamaica's Income Tax Reform Successful?

The impact of the flat rate tax reform is now being monitored. The major problem, of course, is to separate the effects of tax changes from everything else that is affecting the Jamaican economy. Even so, there are some indications of success. Perhaps the best indicator is the absence of major public discontent with the income tax reform. The press was not critical, the political opposition did not raise substantial objections (even during the recent national elections), labor seems to be pleased with the relatively high standard deduction and with the fairness of a flat rate, and the business community clearly has benefited from the lower company tax rate. To be sure, there was initial resentment over the taxation of interest income—this led to exemption for small deposits—and there was the expected grousing from special interest groups about the loss of tax preferences. The important point, however, is that the public adjusted to the initial shock of the change; and though taxes are never as low or even as fair as citizens would like, the new system would appear to be much more palatable than the previous one.

Since no monitoring program was put in place for the reform, it is not possible to estimate the effect of the structural changes. The evidence, however, suggests the following:

- The Jamaican economy grew rapidly in the immediate postreform period. Few would suggest that this growth was principally due to the tax reform, but it could be argued that so favorable a performance of the Jamaican economy could not have taken place under the old tax regime.
- The results of the 1990–91 project show that the combination of the lower, flat rate, the standard deduction (increased in 1990), and the broadened base did not worsen the regressivity of the system,

and that these measures together with the taxation of interest have improved horizontal equity.[10]

- The revenue neutrality target was not met: the reformed system produced faster revenue growth than the prereform system would have. This led the Government to increase the standard deduction in 1990.

Administration Reform

As regards the relationship between policy and administration in the Jamaica project, much of the administration work had a life of its own and was unrelated to the policy design. On the other hand, some of the administrative improvements were directly led by the policy design.

The prereform administration was characterized by an acute shortage of skilled staff. DeGraw (1984) reported that in 1983, a time when increased revenue mobilization was at a premium, there were 150 vacancies among the 449 positions authorized for the Income Tax Department. A disproportionately large number of these were technical positions. Throughout the tax administration service, there were too few skilled staff.

The reasons for the staffing problems were the same in Jamaica as in other developing countries. Salaries were too low, even given the job security and prestige that a government post might offer. In 1983, a trained accountant earning J$9,000 in the Income Tax Department could have earned J$14,000 with a private sector accounting firm. There was no formal career development program and little opportunity for promotion. In the case of the Customs and Excise Department, personnel were recruited primarily out of secondary school; entrants had little background in accounting. To compound the problem, no adequate training program was in place in 1983.

The methods used to assess and collect taxes in Jamaica were inadequate. There was no unique numbering system for either businesses or individuals; hence there was no up-to-date master file of taxpayers under the sales or the income tax. The system was completely manual, that is, there was little if any use of the computer other than to print bills. This effectively ruled out the use of third-party information, the cross-checking of sales and income tax returns, and so on. The income tax was essentially a pay-as-you-earn (PAYE) levy, and there was little if any use of presumptive assessments on hard-to-tax groups, such as self-employed professionals. The major problem was record keeping.

---

[10]This analysis is reported in "Jamaica Tax Review: Report No. 1" (1991).

The income tax file room was inadequate in size and all records were kept manually. Files were regularly misplaced or lost, and records were frequently out of date or incomplete. There was no monitoring of the performance of the tax system. No annual statistical volume reporting the distribution of taxpayers by taxable income brackets was produced, and there was no revenue forecasting model.

The reform project addressed several of these issues. The revenue services have been reorganized to better integrate assessment and collections; an extensive training program for revenue agents has been completed; a number of courses for income tax assessments and collections have been completed; and computerization of the revenue services is well under way.

The reform itself also had an impact on the administrative upgrading. The proposal to replace the existing system of extended excises with a VAT defined a training program for both the revenue agents and the sales tax inspectors. Moreover, the simpler income tax system seems to have made it possible for the Income Tax Department to concentrate more on enforcement of the system. There was a marked increase in the number of employer and individual returns filed, and an increase in the number of new enrollees.[11] Audit and special investigation activities in the postreform period, however, do not differ much from the prereform period.

It is difficult to infer much from available data on income tax collection activities, in part because of changes in reporting, in part because income tax administrative activities might be lumpy, as, for example, when campaigns[12] are undertaken; and in part because even these statistics may be too aggregated to describe any changes in administrative activities that may have taken place.

Guatemala[13]

As noted above, tax reform in Guatemala has a checkered history. The military regime attempted a stabilization plan in 1983 with the help

[11]Detailed statistics for the prereform and postreform periods are presented in Alm, Bahl, Murray, and Riddle (1990).

[12]Periodically, the income tax administration will mount a "campaign" against a particular sector of the economy where delinquency or nonfiling has got out of line. For example, during the course of this project there were special efforts with respect to informal importers, mini-van operators, and companies in arrears by more than a set amount.

[13]Monetary amounts are presented in quetzales. Exchange rates are reported in Annex I.

of the IMF. The plan called for a reduction in public expenditures and a tax reform. The latter was ambitious in scope: a new VAT was introduced, the income tax was modified, the stamp tax was eliminated, and export taxes were reduced. But the 1983 tax reform was preceded by little preparation, especially for such a radically new tax as the VAT. Predictably, the reform was accompanied by considerable confusion among taxpayers, as well as considerable resistance. The VAT rate was reduced from 10 percent to 7 percent only a few months after the introduction of the tax, and stamp taxes were reintroduced in 1984. The attempt by the military regime to introduce new fiscal measures in April 1985 met with strong opposition from the private sector.[14]

The program that is of most interest to us is the 1987 tax reform. The changes in the tax code affected not only individual and corporate income taxes but also the VAT, the property tax, and other taxes.

Individual Income Tax

The 1987 reform touched all aspects of the tax. Most of the changes, however, had the effect of *narrowing* the tax base. The increases in exemptions and deductions, particularly personal and dependent deductions, contributed significantly to the erosion of the base. The law also increased deductions for payments of professional fees and education and other family costs and provided an unlimited deduction for paid insurance premiums. The average household filing taxes can deduct nearly Q 20,000, which is over 150 percent of the country's average household income. The other main factor contributing to the narrowness of the tax base is a long list of exemptions, most prominently the exemption of interest income from financial deposits and most bonds. Repealing this measure alone would almost double personal income tax collections. The law also exempts holiday bonuses (*aguinaldos*) in amounts up to two months' salary, pension and retirement income, dividends and, de facto, most capital gains.

The reform also introduced a presumptive income tax for professionals who fail to file a tax return, a potential base-broadening measure. The presumptive (absolute) levels of income, however, were specified in the law, and with inflation, they have already become obsolete. By 1990, most professionals would find it advantageous to pay taxes according to the fixed presumptive income assigned to their profession in the tax law.

---

[14]A good discussion of the Guatemalan tax reforms of the early 1980s is contained in Bird (1985).

The tax rate schedule for individuals was simplified in the 1987 reform by reducing the number of brackets from 68 to 16, and the maximum rate cut from 65 percent to 34 percent. On the other hand, the reform made each rate effective for the entire level of taxable income, thereby creating "notches" at the bottom end of each bracket.

The Company Income Tax

The 1987 reform introduced several important changes in the tax treatment of company income. It reduced the number of tax rates from 5 to 3, and set the maximum rate at 34 percent—equal to the maximum personal rate. But, as in the case of the personal income tax, one rate is applied to all income, creating an incentive to fragment enterprises into smaller units. The reform eliminated the carryforward of losses and required the apportionment of costs between taxable and nontaxable (for example, tax holiday) activities. The reform also introduced a number of enforcement provisions, including limits on deductions (for example, royalties and payments to directors); presumptive measures of income based on revenues for several groups of companies (for example, film distribution and airlines); and minimum taxes for financial institutions (banks and insurance companies), which have to include interest income in their tax bases but are taxed at a lower rate of 18 percent. As a result of these reforms, companies in all sectors of the economy faced an increased liability, but the commercial sector experienced the largest increase.

The reform of 1987 has left a number of business tax issues that will require further attention, such as the tax treatment of foreign source income, the tax treatment of interest income and capital gains and consequently of financial institutions, the integration of personal and company taxes, the distortions in capital investment and finance induced by the absence of an inflation adjustment, and the widespread existence of costly fiscal incentives. The present tax reform project is addressing these issues.

VAT

The reform of 1987 maintained the 7 percent rate, but it introduced three major changes to the administration of the VAT. First, current period credits for the tax paid on a firm's purchases were limited to inputs of goods and services directly used in the process of generating the taxable sales. This measure had the goal of reducing the level of fraudulent credits, but it went too far; for example, under the present law the VAT paid on a typewriter and other office equipment needed for administrative purposes is not deductible from the VAT collected by the firm on its sales. Although the level of fraudulent credits may have been reduced, this has been accomplished at the price of increasing compliance costs for honest taxpayers and probably also administration costs, as well as tax cascading. Second, VAT paid on equipment and other capital inputs could be credited over a five-year period rather than being entirely refunded in the current year. Third, traditional exports and construction were stripped of their zero-rated status and are now treated as final consumers. These two latter reforms were revenue-raising measures, and the last one probably also helped reduce administration costs, though at the expense of introducing economic distortions. With the exception of these three measures, the basic structure of the VAT is sound. The rate of 7 percent, however, is quite low by world standards.

The most vexing problems with the VAT concern administration. Among the administrative problems, perhaps the worst is the slowness of the government refunding of excess credits; frequently, the policy has been one of auditing all (and only) those taxpayers who ask for a refund, no matter how small the refund is. Paying a small amount of tax saves most would-be evaders from government scrutiny.

Property Tax

The property tax underwent major changes in the 1987 reform. The previous two taxes—the national territorial tax and the municipal tax—were unified in a new single tax. Under this tax, the entirety of the taxpayer's property holdings are added up to a single base and then a progressive rate schedule is applied—although again, as in the case of the income tax, a proportional rather than a marginal rate structure. These reform features have contributed significantly to the unpopularity of the tax, and the implementation of the new tax system has exacerbated this unpopularity. Because tax records were incomplete and assessments outdated, the Government undertook a massive reappraisal of properties based on self-assessments by property owners. Many taxpayers, especially industrial and commercial landowners, boycotted the self-assessment process. The recording and processing of the new information has been very slow, because of the lack of proper planning and because of problems with software and hardware. These administrative problems and the low revenue yield of the property tax (less than 2 percent of total tax collections) have made it, at times, a candidate for elimination from the tax system.

Was Guatemala's Tax Reform Successful?

This program initially increased the central government share of GDP from 8.9 percent in 1986 to 10.1 percent in 1988, which was the revenue target for the reform. However, the share of government revenues fell back to 9.1 percent in 1989 and plunged to 6.5 percent of GDP in 1990. It is still not clearly understood what has been behind this dismal performance, but a dramatic decrease in compliance seems likely. Simulations with the VAT and personal and company income taxes show a decrease in compliance in 1990 alone of over 25 percent. In 1989, while GDP increased by 15.5 percent in nominal terms, central government revenues rose by only 4 percent.

To what extent has the decline in revenues in recent years been a product of the *structural changes* of the 1987 tax reform? Has the reformed tax structure yielded a greater or lesser flow of revenue than the pre-1987 tax structure would have yielded? Using simulation models, we found that for the personal income tax, the net effect of the 1987 reform was to reduce projected revenues in 1991 by 37 percent (Q 125 million), compared with what the prereform system would have produced. The main source of this reduction was the increase in personal exemptions granted in 1987. Very few taxpayers—fewer than 1 percent of all potential taxpayers—had an increase in tax liability as a consequence of the 1987 reform. In contrast, the business income tax reform increased projected 1991 revenues by 28 percent (Q 67 million). Most of the increase was due to the higher rates and to disallowing the carryforward of losses. On balance, it appears, however, that the 1987 structural reform may have reduced the built-in revenue elasticity of the tax system.

IV. Proposition No. 1: The Tax Administration Bottleneck Is Not Always Eased by Simplifying the Tax Structure

A view held by tax policy analysts in developing countries (see, for example, Gillis (1989)) is that simplification of the tax structure will lead to a lighter administrative burden. In its most general terms, the argument goes that a simplified tax structure will let administrators shift their attention from the difficult problems of assessment of firms and individuals that have been given special treatment, monitoring of eligibility for exemptions, and classification of income or commodities to more productive activities such as development of a master file of taxpayers, collections, and audit. In this view, complex provisions in tax structures that demand considerable monitoring and sophistication, generally yield poorer outcomes than rougher, less-refined provisions (see McLure and Pardo, Chapter 4 in this volume). The following are suggestive of the kinds of simplification that may lead to such improvement:

- Replacing Jamaica's system of over 60 indirect tax rates with a single-rate VAT would allow sales tax collectors to spend less time classifying goods and more time enforcing the system.
- Broadening the base of Guatemala's VAT by making exports the only zero-rated transaction in the system would greatly simplify administration.
- The substitution of a VAT for export rebates would simplify the approach to adjusting for an overvalued exchange rate and would eliminate the administrative task of monitoring the rebate applications.
- The removal of special tax treatments, such as industrial tax incentives, would reduce the amount of work required of ministry officials to evaluate applications and to participate in an approval process and monitoring.

Such considerations point toward the desirability of a broader-based tax and a less complicated rate structure, if not a single rate. This has long been the advice of most students of tax design, and this seems to be the trend in many developing countries that have recently enacted tax reforms. Clearly there is merit to the broad-base route to simplification of the tax system. For one thing, it may be easier for the administration to handle because of its uniformity, although special rules are often introduced to facilitate administration. It may also be easier for taxpayers to understand, and therefore comply with uniform rules, although here again special rules (for small taxpayers, financial institutions, and so forth) may facilitate compliance. And, finally, with a broader-based system, there are by definition fewer opportunities for tax avoidance. There is also less opportunity to evade by misclassifying income or commodities, or overstating deductions, exemptions, or credits. Another advantage is noted by Gillis (1989, p. 93) in discussing the Indonesian reform of the mid-1980s. "It was expected that simplification would reduce the scope for corruption, since complexities and ambiguities in tax law were used by tax collectors and taxpayers alike to cloak their transgressions."

The case for simplification of the tax structure through base broadening—as appealing and essentially correct as the argument may be—can be overstated. More precisely, in some instances it has been overtaken by modernization of developing economies. In fact, modernization of tax systems may in many cases increase the complexity of tax rate and base structures, and the cost of efficient administration. This could happen for a number of reasons:

- Economies become more complicated in the process of development. The financial structure of domestic companies becomes more complex with more suppliers, middlemen, and financial intermediaries; foreign tax considerations arise in more complicated forms; and the share of income earned from capital increases as local capital markets develop. A true broad-based tax in a more complicated economy poses a formidable administrative task for a low-income country with a tradition of taxing only wages in the formal sector, commodity consumption, imports, and large manufacturers.
- The change from specific to ad valorem bases in developing country sales taxes implies a switch to book audit from physical inspection. This can be a major shock to the tax administration system, and one that is costly, depending upon whether the country has an existing sales tax structure and on the complexity of the VAT structure chosen. With respect to the latter, the number of rates and the extent to which zero rating is used are particularly important (Casanegra (1990); Due (1990a)).
- A benchmark of economic development is an increased share of consumption in services. Services are difficult to tax, in part because of assessment problems, even in the industrial countries. Services are often provided by smaller firms or self-employed professionals who are typically "hard to tax." Tax systems with uniform rules extended to the service sector will require a higher administrative effort.
- As real property wealth grows, it becomes too important a component of income and wealth to be left out of a truly comprehensive tax base. But good property tax assessment, especially when there is a heavy component of business property and owner-occupied residential property, poses difficult assessment problems.
- Simplification of the tax laws and the introduction of uniform rules in the computation of taxes frequently means the elimination of special provisions that had been introduced in recognition of limitations of the tax administration.

A broad-based tax may well be the right way to go for a developing economy, and simplification is a goal that is to be strived for, but economic development brings with it the need for more complexity in taxation. This, in turn, places more burden on the administrative infrastructure of the country. Some specific examples of this phenomenon, drawn from the experience in Guatemala and Jamaica, illustrate the range of relationships between tax structure simplification and administrative cost.

Jamaica: Individual Income Tax

Perhaps the best case for simplification of the tax structure as a route to improving administrative efficiency is the individual income tax. Jamaica's reform is a case in point. There were three parts to the simplification of the tax. The first was the replacing of a system of 16 tax credits, and employer discretion to award nontaxable perquisites, with a single standard deduction. This structural change had the (potential) advantage of allowing the Income Tax Department to shift its administrative efforts away from monitoring allowances and credits (to the extent such monitoring was going on) to audit activities. Another advantage was that the number of taxpayers in the system was reduced by 100,000—nearly one third of the total. Finally, the use of a single standard deduction made withholding an easier process for employers, who now were relieved (theoretically) of determining the eligibility of workers for various types of credits.

Second, the adoption of a single rate in place of a progressive rate structure held advantages for the income tax administration. Reduction of the top rate from 57½ percent to 33⅓ percent could reduce the incentive for evasion and avoidance at the top income levels and presumably the efforts required of the Income Tax Department. However, it still leaves a "notch" problem, when a taxpayer moves from a zero to a 33⅓ percent liability position.

Third, interest income was brought into the system, broadening the tax base significantly. The interest tax is very revenue productive and now accounts for over one third of total individual income tax revenues.[15] The collections are made via bank withholding, at the full 33⅓ percent rate. Hence, relatively little administrative burden is placed on the Income Tax Department. It is a tax on the banks rather than on individuals. A privacy law prohibits the Government from inspecting the books of the banks, so there was no possibility for an effective tax at the individual level.

---

[15]It is difficult to estimate the revenue income elasticity of the interest tax because it is a new tax and the coverage has been broadened in each of the three years since its inception. Clearly, however, the elasticity is well above unity. The income elasticity of the remainder of the individual income tax is also above unity since the reform, but not so markedly as interest income.

The Jamaican individual income tax is a good illustration of the possibilities for administrative improvements through a simplification of the tax structure. But there also is a dark side to this story. The Jamaicans did not take on the difficult administrative problem of taxing the self-employed, who accounted for only 6 percent of total collections in 1986. Nothing in the reform program addressed this problem. By 1990, the percent of total individual income tax collections from the self-employed had not increased. Moreover, all of the nontaxable perquisites could not be eliminated—especially in the areas of housing and automobiles. Some fringe benefits are increasingly difficult to handle because the economy is more complicated (for example, business expenses), and it is necessary to make exceptions to the rule that all compensation shall be taxed at a uniform rate.

Jamaica: Company Tax

A textbook example of how complications in the tax structure impose administrative costs is the Jamaican company tax. Because of the many special features in its rate and base structure, the prereform company tax was not easily administered. The problems were magnified by a shortage of skilled staff and outmoded—and in some cases flawed—operating procedures. Such difficulties of administration not only raise administrative costs but lead to arbitrariness in assessing the tax base and inevitably to some unfairness in the way different firms are treated.

Examples of how a complicated structure can compromise administration relate to capital consumption allowances and inventory valuation. The system of capital allowances is quite complex (and was not changed by the 1987 reform). There are numerous schedules for asset types, special types of allowances for different industries, and incentive laws that provide special treatment to both favored industries and favored types of assets. Income tax officers spend too much time on classification issues at the cost of spending too little time on audit, with the consequence that monitoring is lax and abuses are invited. Compliance costs, in one form or another, are also raised by such a complicated system. Large enterprises make use of accounting firms to assist them in compliance, but smaller enterprises can less easily take advantage of the available options. This introduces an unintended but potentially important nonneutrality into the system.

The other example has to do with valuing inventories. The law requires that inventory be valued at the lower of cost or market value, and most firms use the FIFO (first in, first out) method for determining the cost of their sales. However, some firms have shifted to the LIFO (last in, first out) method, which has neither been sanctioned in the courts nor approved by the Commissioner. Others avail themselves of even more advantageous approaches, such as writing off stocks that are over a certain age and excluding the proceeds of their sales from chargeable income, and are successful because the Income Tax Department lacks an effective audit branch.

The complexity was exacerbated by inflation, which in concert with the present tax structure, drove up real company tax rates, influenced investment choices, and provided additional incentives for avoidance and evasion. The law contained no provisions for inflation adjustments, except for the crude 20 percent to 90 percent approximation on an initial first year allowance. Under inflationary conditions this approach will lead to understated capital consumption (to a differential degree for assets of different lives), and FIFO accounting will understate the cost of goods sold. Both practices cause profits to be overstated and, other things being equal, dampen the rate of investment (Wozny (1990)).

Finally, the availability of three important avenues of tax avoidance—the preferential tax treatment of incentive activities, interest income, and capital gains—encouraged enterprises to undertake tax arbitrage: to engage in transactions whose sole purpose is reduction in tax liability. Among the many avoidance techniques observed in Jamaica are revaluation and sale of assets with lease-back arrangements; revaluation and sale of assets with a distribution of the (nontaxable) proceeds to shareholders; and the leasing of capital equipment by firms receiving preferential tax treatment to affiliated firms that do not receive such treatment.

The point that structural complication burdens administrative cost would seem well made here. But, while removing some of the ambiguities in the company tax law and restructuring it to fit modern norms would help, it would also introduce new challenges to the tax administration such as the need to develop expertise to deal with inflation adjustments, transfer pricing, inventory valuation, and capital consumption schedules.

Jamaica: VAT

The adoption of a VAT has been offered as a solution to many of the problems of the present indirect tax system in Jamaica, and in many ways it is a simplification by comparison with the present system.[16]

[16]Parts of this section draw heavily, with relatively little modification, on Bird (1990a, 1990b); Due (1990b, 1990c); and Cnossen (1990).

However, it does not follow that administration of indirect taxes in Jamaica will be made easier or less costly.

A VAT was proposed for Jamaica as part of the 1986 reform. At the time of this writing, it is planned to implement it in October 1991.[17] It is to be a single rate tax, with a relatively short list of exemptions and zero-rated goods, and will extend through the level of large retailers.

It is proposed to replace the present indirect tax system, which has five components.[18]

- Excise duties levied at widely differing specific and ad valorem rates on domestically produced items, but not on beer, spirits, and cigarettes, which are subject to consumption duty.
- Separate or additional taxes, called consumption duties, levied at various ad valorem and some specific rates on nearly all domestic manufactures and similar imported goods. There are two principal rates, a basic rate of 15 percent and a "luxury" rate of 27.5 percent, plus two reduced rates (2 percent and 5 percent), one high rate (50 percent), and several specific rates.
- Taxes on luxury products, called retail sales tax, levied at ad valorem rates on the sale at retail or the importation of a limited number of consumer durables, such as automobiles and household appliances. The rates on automobiles range from 13 percent to 57 percent and household appliances are taxed at 10 percent. The value for tax includes customs, stamp, excise, and consumption duties.
- Selective taxes on services, such as travel (departures), hotel accommodation, entertainment (admissions), and betting, gambling, and lotteries.
- An import surcharge levied as a stamp duty. Broad classes of goods are excluded, including petroleum, drugs, fertilizer, and school and hospital equipment. The basic Jamaican customs duty includes a Caribbean Community tariff and an external tariff. Most rates are between 5 percent and 60 percent, but many manufacturing firms and government or quasi-government agencies enjoy low rates or exemption on imports of machinery, materials, and other goods used in production.

From the point of view of administration, there are objectionable features in the present indirect tax structure. First, it is complex. The

[17]See "Jamaica Tax Review: Report No. 1" (1991).

[18]Cnossen (1990) has characterized the Jamaican domestic indirect tax system as "an extended excise system."

levying of four different internal consumption taxes—with different rates, licensing and return requirements, and considerable overlap of the taxes on various firms and commodities—is a source of substantial confusion. Second, there is an excessive number of rates, especially of the excises. Some of these are so low that they are not worthwhile. Third, there is a continued use of some specific rates, without indexing for value changes, particularly on the high-yield traditional "excise" commodities now subject to consumption duties.

There are two reasons why introduction of the VAT may complicate administration. One is the expansion of the number of firms covered under the tax, and the other is the skills required to effectively assess and collect the tax.

The decision to extend the tax through the level of large retailers involves the registration and control of firms that are not now in the tax net. Moreover, the registration and control process will require more work for all registered firms than is the case for the present consumption duty, excises, or retail sales taxes. Due (1988, p. 212) has noted these difficulties with the implementation of a VAT, and underlined the need for a more modern tax administration system, stating that the VAT is more suitable in countries that have achieved higher levels of development.

The other complication is that a higher level of expertise will be required to operate the VAT, hence a more sophisticated and costly administration will be required. This is the main issue (Cnossen (1990)). Though the Jamaican indirect tax rates are generally stated as ad valorem, much of the assessment is done on a physical basis and makes use of notional estimates of selling price. The "excise man" who does this work is different from the sales tax officer who may be an accountant or an auditor. To ascertain taxable turnover and verify compliance with the law, sales tax staff rely on examinations of books of accounts payable and receivable, with cash and bank statements, but not with physical properties and quantities. A sales tax auditor is an expert in analyzing the flow of funds and in detecting the underreporting of sales, but he is not acquainted with the technicalities of production processes and warehouses.

An important conclusion here is that Jamaica's indirect tax system cannot be transformed into a more modern VAT system without substantial organizational and administrative changes. Excise staff cannot be molded into sales tax staff without considerable changes in personnel, additional training, and perhaps an upgrading of salary and substantially improved career opportunities.

Casanegra (1990) suggests that the transition to the VAT is markedly easier if a functioning sales tax is already in place. Jamaica may be in a situation where the transition to a VAT will be especially difficult. A major problem with the present system has been shortage of qualified staff. Prior to completion of the revenue agent program, most of the inspectors lacked the type of training necessary for effective auditing. The present inspection program is also burdened by operating procedures that are antiquated in some cases and weak in others. The ratio of the number of inspectors to the number of accounts is in an acceptable range, but the frequent visits to enterprises are not true audits. Due (1990b) reports that there is no system of priorities for inspection or guidelines for the inspectors, no system for them to report their findings, and little supervision. Even in the case of the traditional excises, where administration is relatively more manageable and physical methods of control are used, there is evidence that procedures are inadequate and qualified staff are in short supply. For example, Cnossen (1990) reports that consumption duty supervision of the largest beer factory in Jamaica is exercised by only one junior officer, largely on the basis of the brewing book.

Guatemala: Company Income Tax

Reform of the company tax, even if in the direction of broadening the base, will not necessarily simplify the tax or reduce the required enforcement effort in Guatemala. The present system was formulated with administrative ease in mind. The tax law tends to incorporate in the base activities that offer relatively easy tax handles; and the difficult things to tax, logically, are left out.

At a certain point in the development process, these "difficult things" must be dealt with. The following list is probably not atypical for a country at Guatemala's stage of development.

The Guatemalan income tax is based on the "territoriality" method of taxation. Foreign source income, both passive and active, earned by resident companies—and individuals—is exempt from income tax, and income accruing to foreigners in Guatemala is taxable. The issue is whether Guatemala should adopt a residence-based method of taxation and impose a tax on the worldwide income (domestic and foreign) earned by Guatemalan residents. Adopting a territorial system of taxation and ignoring foreign source income simplifies tax administration, but it also would narrow the tax base and consequently reduce revenues, if in fact foreign source income can be effectively taxed. A territorial system gives incentives to companies operating in Guatemala to undertake fraudulent operations to convert income earned in Guatemala into exempt foreign income. The territorial system also allows for highly inequitable situations to arise legally. Wealthy Guatemalans residing in Guatemala may pay no income taxes if all their income is, for example, interest income earned from foreign deposits.

Switching to a residence-based system of taxation would in principle eliminate many of these problems, but it also would clearly increase the complexity of tax administration. The worst (and not so unlikely) scenario, given the international experience, is that despite the administrative effort the residence-based system would not produce significantly larger revenues.

At present in Guatemala, most interest income—that from financial deposits and bonds—is tax-exempt, and de facto interest and other costs incurred to earn tax-exempt income are deductible from taxable income. This policy, together with a partial integration of the corporate and personal income taxes (dividends are exempt at the individual level), means that a considerable portion of capital income escapes taxation. Broadening the tax base by making all interest income taxable and adopting a more complete integration system will be very attractive from the policy side, but, again, there is no question that the changes would impose new demands on the tax administration. Identifying and tracking interest income will increase the complexity of audits. Taxing interest income effectively will also require the introduction of a withholding system for this type of income. A withholding scheme for interest income, of course, can become very complicated if the exemption of low incomes is attempted. Administrative considerations typically advise against attempting a more orthodox method of integration.[19]

Regulated financial institutions, mainly banks and insurance companies, are subject to a separate tax regime in Guatemala.[20] Generally, the income tax base includes interest income, but tax rates are lower. An interesting twist is that the administration of taxes on financial institutions is largely implemented by the regulatory agency, the Superintendent of Banks. In a way, one could interpret this arrangement as if the Ministry of Finance had contracted out the tax administration function for this sector.[21] The problem is that the regulatory agency and the Ministry of Finance have quite different objectives. For example, from the regulatory agency point of view, soundness may dictate

[19]The Jamaican scheme of taxing banks, and allowing banks to exclude the income earned on accounts below a certain level, has not imposed great administrative costs. However, because of secrecy laws, the Government has not done a thorough audit of the effectiveness of the program. Such audits seem less urgent when the revenue yield of a tax policy intervention exceeds rather than falls short of expectations.

[20]This is also the case in Jamaica. See Martinez-Vazquez (1990).

[21]In Jamaica, the banks are largely responsible for assessing and collecting the tax on interest income received by individuals.

conservative reserve policies, but for the Ministry of Finance this will mean lower tax collections. The issue here is whether the administration of the tax should be transferred back to the Ministry of Finance if a unified income tax were to be introduced. Many would argue that it should. But transferring the administration back to the Ministry of Finance will entail substantial specialized training of auditors in financial accounting and actuarial science. Keeping auditors with these high skills in the public sector would also prove difficult, given the salary limits in the public sector.

The lack of an inflation adjustment, coupled with the deductibility of interest payments and nondeductibility of dividends, imparts a significant bias in the Guatemalan tax system toward debt financing. With high inflation rates, the tax system de facto heavily subsidizes debt-financed investment. These distortions could be eliminated by introducing full inflation indexing.[22] Indexing the tax system for inflation may or may not broaden the tax base, but it certainly increases the complexity of the tax laws, the general difficulty of administering the tax system, and compliance costs. Full indexing would require extensive training of both tax administrators and accountants and others in the private sector who work as tax preparers.

The elimination of fiscal incentives is a notable exception to the proposition that base-broadening implies more complex administration. In Guatemala, as in many other countries, fiscal incentives are given to firms for all sorts of reasons (regional development and export promotion are common justifications). These actions narrow the tax base and indirectly decrease tax collections by providing opportunities for tax evasion. The proper administration and control of tax incentives is a very demanding task in terms of resources. Broadening the tax base by eliminating most of the fiscal incentives would not require additional administrative resources and could free up administrative resources.

In Guatemala, it appears that the Government does not at present put much effort into monitoring the fiscal incentives program. Does this imply there is no administrative cost? On the surface the answer would appear to be no. However, the lax administration of the present system probably encourages evasion and narrows the tax base. This, and the tax expenditure associated with the incentives, necessarily causes the Government to raise some other tax to make up the shortfall. The result is that there is increased administrative effort implied somewhere in the system. Elimination of the incentive program would thus free some administrative resources.

---

[22]Guatemala shares this problem with many other countries. For a comprehensive discussion of inflation adjustment issues, see McLure and others (1988).

V. Proposition No. 2: Administration Is Complicated Because Taxes Are Used to Achieve Multiple Objectives

Economic planners in developing countries regularly violate the neutrality maxim in taxation. Tax policy is used as an instrument of economic policy, even though it may not be the appropriate instrument and even though it may not have a significant effect. The reasons why tax policy is used to shape economic choices and macroeconomic conditions vary from country to country, but the major factors are that monetary policy and direct income policies are weak or ineffective, taxation is a tool that is available to the central government, and discretionary tax changes give the appearance that something is being done.

Not often considered is the fact that the use of taxation as an economic policy instrument has important implications for tax administration, usually in the direction of complicating the tax structure and therefore the administrative task. One possible outcome is that the administration is not up to the job, and the economic objectives are not attained. The other is that the tax administration is revamped to implement the program, but this imposes costs both on the government in terms of the other tax administration tasks that now may go undone, and on the private sector in terms of resources spent for compliance. In both cases, the new provisions may open loopholes or create ambiguities that present opportunities for evasion, avoidance, or corruption.

One reason why this problem occurs is because the designers of the tax policy measures in question are usually not "tax men," and are hence impatient with objections that the tax administration system cannot carry the changes proposed. Too often, they see this as an administrative detail that can be worked out in the short run, or simply want to ignore the administrative constraint because it causes them to back away from the policy program they most want. The international agencies are sometimes guilty here because they usually are in a hurry to get their programs in place, and there is rarely time to get the tax administration system geared up to do the job. Legislators may be even worse once they fix their sights on a politically popular reform program.

Tax policy is used as part of stabilization programs, to change the allocation of resources to better fit government development objectives, and to achieve social goals. The list of tax policy and quasi-tax policy measures used in Guatemala and Jamaica in the 1980s gives some idea of the variety of these discretionary measures. One could speculate about the extent to which these measures compromise the overall tax administration (see Annex II).

Tax Policy and Stabilization

Stabilization programs became more a regular than an extraordinary occurrence in developing countries in the 1980s, and taxation was usually a centerpiece in these programs. Developing economies are by their very nature exposed to external events because they are often dependent on a very few products to earn their foreign exchange, they trade in commodities that are subject to prices set on world markets, most are energy-poor, and many owe substantial sums to foreign governments and banks. There are numerous ways in which worldwide economic changes can be transferred to the local economy, as both of the countries under study here illustrate. U.S. recessions have affected Jamaica's tourism, changing world demand for aluminum has affected Jamaica's bauxite industry, the world price for coffee and bananas has affected Guatemala's financial position, and an increase in the price of oil brings inflationary pressures on both economies. In the case of small countries such as these even natural disasters (for example, Jamaica's hurricanes and Guatemala's earthquakes) can have major consequences for the economy and the budget. The imbalances to be addressed usually include a government budget deficit in addition to or in connection with a foreign exchange problem and inflationary pressures. An increase in taxation is, therefore, a reasonable part of the remedial program.

The conflict between policy and administration arises because stabilization programs are by their very nature emergency programs, and administrative preparation may be given little attention. Consider the situation where the government is under immediate pressure to address a revenue shortfall and introduces a new tax or a major new enhancement to the tax system. If the tax administration is not prepared to absorb the change, the results may be less than expected. In any case, the day-to-day job of the tax administration may be compromised, and effort may be diverted from other activities that are more in the long-term interest of the country.

Almost every tax advisor can cite an example. Guatemala's 1983 tax reform, which was part of a stabilization package, is a case in point (see Bird (1985)). The main objective of the package was to reduce the fiscal deficit with tax increases and expenditure cuts. In the tax area the most important changes were the introduction of a VAT to replace a turnover sales tax with a 3 percent rate and the elimination of the stamp tax. The VAT was hastily introduced without time to either educate taxpayers or plan its administration. It was placed into operation roughly a month after it had been announced. The new VAT had a rate of 10 percent and used the tax credit or invoice method. At the time, it was believed that the tax credit feature would make the tax largely self-enforcing.

The great expectations for the tax quickly turned into disappointment. Because of strong public protests, the VAT rate was reduced from 10 percent to 7 percent only months after its introduction. Because the revenue yield of the new VAT proved to be substantially less than anticipated, the stamp tax had to be reinstated only months after it had been removed from the tax code. The effectiveness of the new Guatemalan VAT was hurt most by the lack of planning and preparation in tax administration. Requests for refunds from taxpayers for whom credit for tax paid on purchases exceeded tax due on sales were much larger than anticipated. The avalanche of refund requests, many of which were thought to be fraudulent but could not be audited, led to the on-and-off suspension of crediting, and consequently reintroduced cascading effects in indirect taxation and damaged the confidence of the public in the tax system.

Tax Policy and Resource Allocation

In most developing countries, the allocation of resources is not in line with the government's development plan, and tax policy is frequently used to try and induce a change. There are many examples from the Jamaican and Guatemalan cases:

- to force additional savings;
- to increase employment of unskilled workers;
- to conserve foreign exchange;
- to discourage luxury consumption;
- to encourage equity investment in companies; and
- to encourage risk-taking.

Examples of how these special tax provisions complicate administration may be drawn from the experience in both countries.

Jamaica: Individual Income Tax

Economic planners adjusted Jamaica's individual income tax in an attempt to stimulate both savings and worker productivity. They did this by providing tax credits for savings and for the employment of household helpers and by providing a preferential tax rate for income earned from overtime employment. Each worker made an original declaration of credit entitlements to the employer; this became a basis for calculating his tax. There was little or no monitoring by the Central Government, and little incentive for the employer to verify the truthfulness of the declaration. The employee was more or less free to claim all credits, or to inflate the number of children for his personal allowance, and so forth. On the other hand, since the amounts of the credit were not indexed, their real value had eroded substantially by the time of the tax reform.

Two questions may be asked. First, did these credits have any significant impact on the level of savings and employment in Jamaica? Second, did the monitoring of these credits impose a significant burden on the tax administration in Jamaica? The estimates of the Jamaican project were that the credits were not used by a broad spectrum of the taxpaying population, and that their elimination would not significantly reduce either savings or the employment of household helpers.

- Only 4 percent of all filers and only 0.2 percent of all PAYE taxpayers claimed the household helper credit in 1983.
- The "savings credits" were more widely claimed, particularly that for life insurance. But the amounts allowed were small, equivalent to only about 10 percent of total individual income tax collections in 1983. When the amount of displacement induced from private sector savings is considered, it seems doubtful that elimination of these credits would have much effect on the aggregate amount of savings.

The second program was a preferential tax rate applied to income earned from overtime work. The split between overtime and regular earnings was reported by the employer, but there was again little or no monitoring. The amount of income reported from overtime activities was estimated to be between 5 percent and 7 percent of collections in 1983, but this ratio varied substantially across income classes (Alm, Bahl, and Murray (1990)). For the over J$50,000 income group, overtime income was estimated at between 20 percent and 45 percent of regular income, suggesting that "overtime" was simply a tax loophole.

The evidence seems to indicate that neither subvention—credits or overtime—has a significant impact on savings or work effort or on worker productivity and neither imposed new administration burdens. What would have happened if the Government had attempted to enforce these programs? Each taxpayer's status in terms of how much he invested in each of the savings programs would have had to be determined. Since the savings programs and the Income Tax Department do not use the same taxpayer numbering system, and since the Income Tax Department does not have a complete master file in any case, the problems would have been monumental. The monitoring of the household helper credit would have been even more difficult, even though only a small number of families claimed this credit. Monitoring the overtime provision would have required a combination of audits and spot visits to establishments. These programs were established without any provision for monitoring, and likely with the presumption that they never would be monitored.

Both the system of tax credits and the preferential tax treatment of overtime income were abolished with the 1986 tax reform.

Guatemalan Employment Credit

The present income tax law in Guatemala offers an employment credit equal to 100 percent (50 percent in Guatemala City) of the social security contributions paid by the employer for new workers earning less than Q 500 a month. This measure was introduced in 1987 to reduce the high unemployment rate in the country and to redress the openly pro-capital bias of the tax laws. From direct observation of tax returns, the number of businesses that have claimed this credit appears to have been very small. The Department of Internal Revenue does practically no monitoring of this or other credits and incentives. The income tax law also offers an education credit of 100 percent of teacher salaries paid by the company or employer under the supervision of the Ministry of Education. As in the case of the employment credit, only a negligible number of firms seem to have used the education credit.

VI. Proposition No. 3: Many Governments in Developing Countries May Not Want to Improve the Enforcement of the Tax System

Tax administration in developing countries may be weak because governments have deliberately chosen not to make it stronger. To be sure, no country has attempted, or even should attempt, *total* enforcement of its tax system. Ensuring compliance with the tax laws to obtain adequate tax revenues is only one objective of government. Other objectives, such as protecting citizens' right to privacy or their right to due legal representation and procedures, also have to be weighed indicating how far to go in tax enforcement. Full enforcement probably is not a sensible proposition, even from an exclusive revenue-raising perspective. After a certain level of enforcement is reached, the (administrative) costs of raising revenues any further are likely to exceed any additional taxes collected.

Governments in both developed and developing countries appear to apply a level of enforcement that is less than their capability (that is, they deliberately accept varying degrees of tax evasion and avoidance). A study of the Internal Revenue Service in the United States (Malanga (1986)) reports that for each extra dollar spent in administration, the U.S. Government could get seven additional dollars from audits and twenty-seven dollars from servicing delinquent accounts. If the return on stronger tax enforcement is potentially so high, why do governments refrain from exploiting it even in relatively "politically safe" areas such as delinquent accounts? The attitude of the Guatemalan authorities toward tax enforcement raises the same question. Even at times when there was a pressing need for additional revenues, and well-designed enforcement programs with a high expected payoff were available, the Government was reluctant to implement these programs. Frequently, programs for improving administration were ignored and attention was shifted to other "solutions."

In fact, this behavior is not necessarily irrational. There are a number of explanations.

Politics

Tax revenues raised to reduce the budget deficit or to increase expenditures produce short-run effects that are within the elected life of the politician. The politician must weigh the negative feelings of voters about higher taxes against the positive feelings about higher expenditures. The payoff from improvements in tax administration, on the other hand, is seen only after years of effort. To the extent they are successful, some future politician is likely to reap the benefits. To make matters worse, some of the costs of administrative upgrading are likely to be felt in the very short run. There are inevitably transition problems when a country moves to a new administrative setup, and the "shock" effect can create problems of discontinuities in collections, personnel disgruntlement, and taxpayer anxiety because of the uncertainty involved. This set of timing problems and the normally high discount rate of politicians is one reason why tax administration reform is so often on the back shelf.

A corollary is that since enforcement of the tax laws carries both economic and political costs as well as benefits, the preferred level of enforcement for the politician will involve a certain level of evasion or avoidance. Toma and Toma (1986) argue that tax administrators would be responsive to politicians' desires because they might be rewarded or punished though budget allocations. Hunter and Nelson (1991) find that the congressional power of a state congressional delegation in the United States (as measured by seniority and committee assignments) is a significant negative predictor of the enforcement activity of the Internal Revenue Service in that state. It should not be surprising to find that such political considerations play a similar and even stronger role in developing countries such as Jamaica and Guatemala. The number of taxpayers, especially large taxpayers, is fewer in developing countries, and they may find it easier to manipulate or control government policies because of less well-developed political institutions.

Evasion

A second reason for less than maximum enforcement has to do with the unwillingness of many governments to fully eliminate evasion. The level of evasion may be expected to vary with the level of economic development, the tax structure itself, and the idiosyncratic values and behavior of taxpayers. Every advisor working in a developing country has heard the same story: "You must understand that people in this country do not like to pay taxes." However, it is clear that for any level of economic development and so on, the government can choose widely different levels of enforcement. So, the question becomes, "Why is tax evasion allowed to continue?"[23]

The theoretical literature on tax evasion, and the practice in industrial countries, would lead one to believe that with the right combination of enforcement and penalties, and an administrable tax structure, evasion could be reduced to much smaller levels. But it is not, and the following are some hypotheses as to why not.

- As noted above, it is politically very difficult to impose widespread and harsh penalties if evasion is widespread, and if some of the major offenders are the wealthiest citizens and the biggest businesses. Such actions are inconsistent with the desire to stay in office for the longest possible time.
- Evasion could be eliminated or substantially reduced only if corruption in the tax administration were eliminated or substantially reduced, which would be expensive in monetary and perhaps political terms.
- Tax administration is costly, and the efficiency of assessment, collection, and audit depends on the amounts spent for this function.

[23]For a good, conceptual discussion of the issue, see Shoup (1969, Chapter 17).

It is difficult to convince the public to pay substantially higher taxes so they can be more effectively pursued by tax collectors.

- The economy may actually be served by evasion. Take the case of evasion under the income tax, which is most rampant for the self-employed. In neither Jamaica nor Guatemala is there any serious attempt to reach this sector of the economy by preparing a comprehensive master roll and introducing vigorous enforcement. While such action might increase revenues, it also might reduce the aggregate amount of savings and investment in the economy, since the self-employed are among the leading entrepreneurs in the economy.

Other Objectives of Tax Administration

A third justification that a government might use for choosing a less efficiently administered tax system is that revenue maximization may not be the only goal. There are a number of other objectives that authorities may be pursuing as part of the tax administration system, and some of these may be in conflict with revenue maximization.

One objective is to reduce compliance costs. A level of enforcement commensurate with reducing tax evasion could imply a substantial increase in compliance costs. Tax statutes (by design) and administrative practice can shift, or try to shift, administrative costs to taxpayers. Withholding systems do this with employers, printing costs may be reduced by distributing fewer instructional materials to taxpayers, and so forth. Also, as noted above, tax systems become more complicated as the economy evolves into a more complex set of market structures and the cost of complying with the tax law increases. Compliance costs may also be higher simply because the government has not taken them into account in its tax design. Moreover, compliance costs are often ignored at the time of writing the law. The law, of course, does not state that there is no need to pay taxes if it becomes very inconvenient or very costly to do so. But the government may be willing to ignore delinquency if compliance costs are high. For example, it was probably never imagined that employers in Jamaica would police carefully the eligibility of employees to claim each of the 16 individual income tax credits available.

Another objective that the government may have in designing its tax administration system is to protect the right to privacy. In Jamaica, for example, the tax on interest income is collected by the banks, but the Government does not have the right to make a blanket examination of individual accounts. Bank secrecy laws raise similar problems in El Salvador and Panama.

Casanegra (1990) has suggested that an important goal of good tax administration is to increase voluntary compliance. However, one does not often find actual tax administration behavior directly aimed at increasing voluntary tax compliance. For example, few tax administration policies are targeted at minimizing the amount of overpayments made by taxpayers. Goode (1981) states that some tax administrators have proposed this as an important goal of tax administration. The reality is that few tax administrations attempt to gain taxpayers' confidence by reducing overpayments. In Guatemala, for example, taxpayers believe that if they overpay they will never receive the refund. Indeed, the only firms audited under the Guatemalan VAT are those requesting refunds. Even in the United States it was recently disclosed that the Internal Revenue Service had not sent out notices to taxpayers for overpayment even though those overpayments had been identified by tax administrators.

The Attraction of Administrative Discretion

Another reason why governments may not want full enforcement is that some tax policies are popular and acceptable in their nominal form, but entirely unacceptable if fully enforced. In such cases, the government creates loopholes for avoidance or simply ignores evasion—so long as minimal revenue targets are reached. A more negative way to state this is to say that "bad" policy design, for instance, tax laws that are difficult to understand and interpret, may be intentional. Ambiguous norms provide more opportunity for interpretation by politicians and even corrupt administrators. Goode (1981) also makes the interesting point that since resources may be used less efficiently in the public sector, it may be that tax evasion is a safety valve in the economy against "excessive" or poorly designed taxes.

An example of deliberate policy by government to hold back on efficient tax administration in order to offset some of the undesirable effects of the legal tax structure is the following. Before the 1986 reform, the Jamaican individual income tax had a very progressive nominal rate structure, a separate rate for low-income taxpayers, and many tax credits that appeared to benefit the same group. This was politically acceptable rhetoric about how an income tax should look in the Jamaica of the late 1970s and early 1980s. This (nonindexed) structure yielded a built-in income elasticity estimated at 2.48. If the tax had been fully enforced the result would have been substantial automatic increases in the tax burden and in the progressivity of the system. Given Jamaica's economic and political setting, this clearly would not have been acceptable tax policy.

The solution to this quandary was to allow tax avoidance and to monitor compliance to assure an "acceptable" amount of revenue. The Jamaican system provided relief through permitting employer-determined amounts of nontaxable perquisites. These fringes, which were mostly cash payments not requiring proof of expenditure, were stated as allowances for all manner of expenses, including travel to work, housing, entertainment, and laundry. Allowances were widespread in the public and private sectors, with the result that the actual income elasticity of the individual income tax was less than unity in the period immediately prior to the reform.

The 1986 reform abolished most of these nontaxable perquisites and brought in a flat rate. This reversed the problem. The rate structure now had the look of a "big man's" tax package, and there was need to add some features that would give the lower-income workers some nominal benefits. The Government provided the loophole by giving the Income Tax Commissioner discretion to determine whether laundry and uniform allowances were "necessary." Within three years of the reform, about 20 percent of Jamaican income taxpayers were receiving one or both of these two allowances.

Some would argue against the thesis that governments want less than fully efficient tax administration systems, that it is in their interest to efficiently steer assessment and collection efficiency in the direction that best suits their objectives. But if the system is transparent, the government will find itself in a position of having to defend its actions to those who are the losers in the tax game. An opaque system makes government less accountable for the outcomes and permits tax administration discretion on a day-to-day and week-to-week basis.

VII. Summary and Conclusions: What Are the Lessons?

This work in Jamaica and Guatemala seems to offer two messages. The first is the traditional "poor country-weak tax administration" story. The theme is that tax structures are too complicated for the administrative resources available, the administrative staff is poorly trained and badly paid, and administrative procedures are inadequate. The second, perhaps conflicting, message is that governments in developing countries choose some degree of poor tax administration as part of their development strategy. They do this because enforcement complicates other goals they want to achieve (for example, protection of privacy), because administrative improvements do not have a strong political payoff, and because tax evasion may serve as a "safety valve" against "excessive" or poorly designed taxes. Taken together, these two points reinforce what all tax advisors should already know: There is no correct way to do tax reform.

The lessons learned from this work fall into two categories. The first concerns the place of tax administration in the reform process. The second is what we do next to improve the state of tax administration in low-income countries.

Tax Administration and Tax Reform

There is no general agreement about the best way to do tax reform. Should we shock the system with big changes, or proceed incrementally? Can administration reform be separated from policy reform, and what is the right order of the two? Is the technology now in place to permit governments to improve their administrative systems and live within their budget constraints? Under what conditions will governments agree to significant improvements in their tax administration? A way to answer these questions is to distinguish among three different views of the administrative constraints to tax structure reform.

The Incremental View

The first view is that going after a comprehensive tax reform is a mistake because it is always hard to find the right opportunity for it, and the interdependency between the different elements of the reform increases the risk of failure. Proponents of this view favor an incremental approach to tax reform.

The incrementalists consider tax administration as an institution that will change only very slowly. It follows that policy changes must be modest. In this view, tax administration is a reflection of the general level of development of the country and there is little that can be done in the short run. Complex or sophisticated tax schemes should be avoided in favor of simpler, more easily administered taxes. A possible corollary of this position is that efforts and resources used to accelerate the pace of change of tax administration institutions may be wasted. The main determinant of change—the general level of development in the country—is outside the control of the tax authorities. A second possible corollary of this view is that if it were possible to index the quality of tax administration, this measure would be highly correlated with the level of development and there would be relatively little variation in administration among countries with the same level of development.

The Insufficient Resources View

A second view is that it is indeed possible to produce significant improvements in tax administration in a relatively short period of time, say two years, if enough resources are invested and adequate expertise is put in place. This view would seem to hold that major administrative reforms can take place independently of policy changes. This would seem to be the view adopted in Guatemala, at least at times, by international donors, who have supported tax administration reform.

One test of the success of this approach is provided by Ecuador's tax administration project from 1985 to 1989 (financed by U.S. Agency for International Development). This project had some evaluation of policy, but no explicit reform component (Martinez-Vazquez (1986)). The main objective was to increase tax revenues by improving registration, collection, and audit procedures. No effort was made to change the tax laws, which were cumbersome and antiquated. The Ecuador project could not be described as a success. It started with several successful pilot projects, especially in collections, but fell short of its long-term revenue collection objectives. The problem was partly that the income tax structure was deficient, and many other things went wrong operationally, such as procurement by the donor agency and widespread corruption of public officials. But perhaps the heavy emphasis and dependence on computerization was the single most important factor in the failure of the entire project. The attraction of computers was understandable, given the backwardness of the tax administration system and the high level of corruption. However, making the administrative process dependent on computers (and their maintenance and replacement) in a setting where there frequently were no funds even for photocopying seems in retrospect to have been ill-advised.

A second phase of the Ecuador project was started in 1990, in conjunction with policy reforms and administered by CIAT. At that time, the Government gave serious consideration to the creation of a new "elite" team of tax administrators, mainly auditors, directly under the Minister of Finance and entirely disconnected from the regular tax office. These officers were to be put in charge of the largest taxpayers.

The "Policy-First" View

A third view about successful reform is that tax administration projects without policy reform are almost always doomed to failure. The policy-first view best describes Jamaica's successful tax reform, and it is the paradigm adopted for the design of the Guatemalan project. An Ecuador-type tax administration project would have failed in Jamaica. No matter how streamlined the Jamaican administration might have become, it still would have faced the task of monitoring the 16 income tax credits, a special tax regime for wages earned from overtime, and the ad hoc granting of nontaxable perquisites by private employers. To have left the job at administrative reform—as advisors from the U.S. Internal Revenue Service had proposed for Jamaica in the early 1980s—would have been folly.

Training

An illustration of the three different views is provided by the issue of personnel and training. One of the most difficult questions of tax policy and administration reform projects is what to do about poorly trained and ill-paid tax auditors, programmers, and other key personnel in tax administration. One strategy is to simply accept the fact; the problem of poorly paid public sector employees goes beyond the scope of any tax reform project, and it is better to adapt policy design to this constraint.

The opposite strategy may be to try to create an elite corps of tax administrators who are very well trained and are paid at least competitively with the private sector, and to go on to design tax policy that is clearly beyond the capabilities of the present administration but with hopes it can be handled by the "new" administration. Jamaica has taken this approach in preparing to implement its VAT. The most recent tax reform in Ecuador considered the introduction of full indexation for inflation in the income tax, requiring considerable new skills in both the tax administration and the private sector. A third strategy could be to target specific jobs for training and try to find ways to retain those individuals by upgrading positions.

Lessons for a Better Nexus Between Policy and Administration

This paper is about why tax administration in developing countries is not better. If the bottlenecks to improvements in tax administration can be identified then a strategy to improve matters can be derived. Based on experience in Jamaica and Guatemala, we offer the following guidelines for an improved nexus between tax policy and tax administration:

(1) If the objective is a "big" tax reform, the proper order of business is first policy and then administration. It makes little sense to invest in procedures to better enforce a tax that is unfair and has undesirable economic effects. The success in Jamaica and Indonesia and the lack of success in Ecuador are cases in point. We can also say that policy without administration is likely to be no more successful.

(2) Broader-based taxes are fairer and introduce fewer distortions to economic choices, and in some cases they simplify administration. In other cases—for instance, the extension of the VAT to lower levels in the chain of distribution—they do not. In fact, as economies modernize it is reasonable to expect that the job of tax administration will become more and more complex, even if a "good" tax structure is in place. To prepare for this complexity, countries should invest heavily in training in tax administration, updating procedures, and finding ways to improve the competitive position of government employees in the tax service.

(3) Single rate taxes offer significant administrative and policy advantages.

(4) Government planners often overuse tax policy to deal with economic problems. There is too little consideration of the ability of the government to administer these programs. Tax administration experts should have at least a "seat at the table" in the formulation of new tax policies. The expected benefits of such programs should be weighed against their administrative costs.

(5) Governments should have long-term plans for the improvement of tax administration systems, just as they have long-term plans in virtually all policy areas. A "capital budget" for this particular form of infrastructure could protect improvements in tax administration against short-sighted politicians who are afraid they cannot claim the benefits of the eventual improvements and who shy away from significant expenditures on enforcement.

(6) Monitoring systems for tax administration should be set up to track changes in the efficiency of taxpayer identification, assessment, collection, and audit. This is especially important in the postreform period, when new policies need protection from those with a vested interest in finding ways not to comply.

(7) Government planners (the leadership in the ministry of finance and the planning ministry) should cease using poor tax administration as a shield for poor design of tax policy.

(8) Invest the necessary resources to keep up-to-date statistics on tax performance. This will both provide information necessary to improve tax administration and will also help in the formulation of tax policy.

ANNEX I

Exchange Rates of the Jamaica Dollar and the Guatemalan Quetzal Vis-à-Vis the U.S. Dollar

(Annual averages)

	Jamaica Dollar–U.S. Dollar	Guatemalan Quetzal–U.S. Dollar
1980	1.78	1.00
1981	1.78	1.00
1982	1.78	1.00
1983	2.31	1.00
1984	4.41	1.00
1985	5.62	1.00
1986	5.05*	1.88
1987	5.55*	2.50
1988	5.49*	2.62
1989	6.49*	2.82

Sources: International Monetary Fund, *Government Finance Statistics Yearbook*, Vol. 24 (Washington, 1990), and for those with *, Planning Institute of Jamaica.

ANNEX II

Selected Tax Policy Instruments in Jamaica and Guatemala

Following are some of the tax "interventions" used by the Governments of Guatemala and Jamaica during the 1980s. These were introduced primarily for nonrevenue purposes. A reasonable proposition is that such interventions significantly complicate tax administration.

Individual Income Tax

Credits for savings
Credits for employment of domestics
Deductions for professional services and insurance premiums
Nontaxable fringe benefits
Preferential rate for overtime earnings
Nontaxable Christmas bonus
Separate rate schedule for low incomes
Tax-free interest income

Company Income Tax

Accelerated depreciation
Tax-free interest income and full interest deductibility
Tax rebates for dividend distributions
Limited or no carryforward of losses
Tax credit for issuance of bonus shares
Fiscal incentives

Taxes on the Foreign Trade Sector

Import surcharge
Export rebates
Export taxes
Fiscal incentives for partial exporters
Free-trade zones
Import licenses
Import quotas
Exemption of imports
Protective tariffs

Domestic Indirect Taxes

Exemptions
Zero rating

REFERENCES

Alm, James, Roy W. Bahl, and Matthew Murray, "An Evaluation of the Structure of the Jamaican Individual Income Tax," Chapter 3 in *The Jamaican Tax Reform*, ed. by Roy W. Bahl (Cambridge, Massachusetts: Lincoln Institute of Land Policy, 1990).

Alm, James, Roy W. Bahl, Matthew Murray, and Bruce Riddle, "A Program for Reform," Chapter 4 in *The Jamaican Tax Reform*, ed. by Roy W. Bahl (Cambridge, Massachusetts: Lincoln Institute of Land Policy, 1990).

Bahl, Roy W., "A Regression Approach to Tax Effort and Tax Ratio Analysis," *Staff Papers*, International Monetary Fund (Washington), Vol. 18 (November 1971), pp. 570–612.

_____ (1990a), "Jamaica: Tax Reform: Evaluation and Lessons," *Bulletin for International Fiscal Documentation*, Vol. 44, No. 1 (1990), pp. 37–44.

_____ (1990b), ed., *The Jamaican Tax Reform* (Cambridge, Massachusetts: Lincoln Institute of Land Policy, 1990).

Bird, Richard M., "A Preliminary Report on the Guatemalan Tax System" (Syracuse, New York: Metropolitan Studies Program of the Maxwell School, University of Syracuse, October 1985).

_____ (1990a), "An Introductory Overview," Chapter 14 in *The Jamaican Tax Reform*, ed. by Roy W. Bahl (Cambridge, Massachusetts: Lincoln Institute of Land Policy, 1990).

_____ (1990b), "The Taxation of Services," Chapter 22 in *The Jamaican Tax Reform*, ed. by Roy W. Bahl (Cambridge, Massachusetts: Lincoln Institute of Land Policy, 1990).

Casanegra de Jantscher, Milka, "Administering the VAT," in *Value Added Taxation in Developing Countries*, ed. by Malcolm Gillis, Carl S. Shoup, and Gerardo P. Sicat (Washington: World Bank, 1990).

Chelliah, Raja J., "Trends in Taxation in Developing Countries," *Staff Papers*, International Monetary Fund (Washington), Vol. 18 (July 1971), pp. 254–327.

Cnossen, Sijbren, "The Extended Excise Tax System," Chapter 20 in *The Jamaican Tax Reform*, ed. by Roy W. Bahl (Cambridge, Massachusetts: Lincoln Institute of Land Policy, 1990).

DeGraw, Sandra L., "Current Administrative Procedures of the Income Tax Department of Jamaica and Some Recommended Changes," Jamaica Tax Structure Examination Project, Staff Paper No. 4 (Syracuse, New York: Metropolitan Studies Program of the Maxwell School, University of Syracuse, February 1984).

Due, John F., *Indirect Taxation in Developing Economies* (Baltimore: Johns Hopkins University Press, rev. ed., 1988).

_____ (1990a), "Some Unresolved Issues in Design and Implementation of Value-Added Taxes," *National Tax Journal*, Vol. 63, No. 4 (December 1990), pp. 383–94.

_____ (1990b), "Jamaica's Indirect Tax Structure," Chapter 15 in *The Jamaican Tax Reform*, ed. by Roy W. Bahl (Cambridge, Massachusetts: Lincoln Institute of Land Policy, 1990).

______ (1990c), "A General Consumption Tax," Chapter 17 in *The Jamaican Tax Reform*, ed. by Roy W. Bahl (Cambridge, Massachusetts: Lincoln Institute of Land Policy, 1990).

Gillis, Malcolm, "Comprehensive Tax Reform: The Indonesian Experience, 1981–1988," in *Tax Reform in Developing Countries*, ed. by Malcolm Gillis (Durham, North Carolina: Duke University Press, 1989).

Goode, Richard, "Some Economic Aspects of Tax Administration," *Staff Papers*, International Monetary Fund (Washington), Vol. 28 (June 1981), pp. 249–74.

Holland, Daniel, and James R. Follain, "The Property Tax in Jamaica," Chapter 23 in *The Jamaican Tax Reform*, ed. by Roy W. Bahl (Cambridge, Massachusetts: Lincoln Institute of Land Policy, 1990).

Hunter, William J., and Michael A. Nelson, "The Political Economy of Federal Tax Evasion," paper delivered at the Public Choice Society meeting in New Orleans, March 1991.

International Monetary Fund (1990a), *Government Finance Statistics Yearbook, 1990* (Washington, 1990).

______ (1990b), *International Financial Statistics Yearbook, 1990* (Washington, 1990).

"Jamaica Tax Review: Report No. 1" (unpublished; Atlanta: Policy Research Center, Georgia State University, 1991).

Lotz, Jørgen R., and Elliot R. Morss, "Measuring 'Tax Effort' in Developing Countries," *Staff Papers*, International Monetary Fund (Washington), Vol. 14 (November 1967), pp. 478–97.

Malanga, Frank, "The Relationship Between IRS Enforcement and Tax Yield," *National Tax Journal*, Vol. 39, No. 3 (1986), pp. 333–37.

Martinez-Vazquez, Jorge, "An Evaluation of Personal Income Tax in Ecuador," Staff Paper No. 1, Studies of Fiscal Administration in Ecuador (Syracuse, New York: Metropolitan Studies Program of the Maxwell School, University of Syracuse, 1986).

______, "The Taxation of Financial Institutions in Jamaica," Chapter 10 in *The Jamaican Tax Reform*, ed. by Roy W. Bahl (Cambridge, Massachusetts: Lincoln Institute of Land Policy, 1990).

McLure, Charles E., Jr., John Mutti, Victor Thurony, and George R. Zodrow, *The Taxation of Income from Business and Capital in Colombia* (Bogotá: Ministerio de Hacienda y Crédito Público, 1988).

Shoup, Carl S., *Public Finance* (Chicago: Aldine Publishing, 1969).

Toma E.F., and M. Toma, "A Congressional Control Model of Treasury Revenue Collection," *Southern Economic Journal*, Vol. 53, No. 1 (1986), pp. 141–54.

United Nations (1990a), *Demographic Yearbook, 1990* (New York, 1990).

______ (1990b), *National Accounts Statistics: Main Aggregates and Detailed Tables* (New York, 1990).

World Bank, *World Debt Tables*, Vol. III (Washington, 1989).

______, *World Tables*, 1989–90 Edition (Washington, 1990).

Wozny, James, "The Taxation of Corporate Source Income in Jamaica," Chapter 8 in *The Jamaican Tax Reform*, ed. by Roy W. Bahl (Cambridge, Massachusetts: Lincoln Institute of Land Policy, 1990).

Comments

Edwin Tulloch-Reid

In the light of our recent experience in Jamaica, it may be useful to make three general observations before commenting on the specific propositions put forward in the paper.

First, our experience has not only confirmed the nexus between tax administration and tax policy but has demonstrated that a well-conceived tax policy developed from a thorough analysis of the tax system and with clearly defined economic and social objectives is the foundation for implementing sound tax administration measures.

Second, our experience has also taught us that tax administrators need to be constantly reminded that—and here I quote Vito Tanzi in his address at the 1991 CIAT Assembly in Washington, "Tax systems do not just raise revenue but are policy instruments that governments use to pursue their own goals."

Finally, our experience has again taught us that strategic planning, which has been strongly advocated by CIAT in recent years, is the single most important weapon in the armory of the tax administrator. Here we refer specifically to the methodical identification and consideration of the environmental factors that affect the planning and implementation processes.

It is within this context and in the light of the Jamaican experience that we offer comments on the three propositions put forward in the paper.

Proposition No. 1

The tax administration bottleneck is not always eased by a simplification of the tax structure.

In the case of the income tax, administrative bottlenecks were significantly reduced in Jamaica as a result of the simplification of the tax structure under the tax reform of 1987. For example:

- The cumbersome system of multiple tax credits (16) was eliminated and replaced by a single standard deduction.
- A single flat rate of 33⅓ percent for individuals as well as companies was introduced. This rate replaced, for individuals, a graduated rate with a marginal top rate of 57½ percent, and, for companies,

the basic company rate of 35 percent and the additional company tax of 10 percent.
- Bank deposit interest income was brought into the income tax base with collections withheld by the banks.
- Nontaxable allowances were also brought into the tax base, thereby limiting the practice of employers and employees "negotiating" the ratio of taxable and nontaxable income.

These changes drastically reduced the volume of tax computations for both taxpayers and officials and released staff to concentrate on the major problem of widespread tax evasion, particularly among the self-employed.

The proposed general consumption tax, a VAT-type tax, is specifically designed to simplify the system of indirect taxation by introducing a single rate of tax to replace the existing complex tax structure consisting of eight different forms of taxes and a multiplicity of rates. However, introduction of the general consumption tax may not remove administrative bottlenecks because it requires not only a background in more sophisticated accounting and computing skills but the administration of a far more complex tax base that includes zero rating, exemptions, and services.

In order to minimize administrative bottlenecks in the implementation of the general consumption tax scheduled to come into effect in October 1991, the following steps were taken:

- Revenue agents were specifically recruited and trained to ensure that the required managerial and technical skills would be in place.
- Computer systems for the general consumption tax were enhanced to accommodate the multiple tax type regime; and
- A modern office was built for the purpose and appropriately equipped for the convenience of staff and taxpayers.

In the case of the property tax, we have continued under the tax reform with the unimproved value (land value) tax base as the simplest and most cost-effective system of property taxation for a developing country. However, the property tax being a wealth tax, the overriding principle of equity will in time dictate that the land value system be modified to include improvements, particularly where the ratio of "improvements" to "land value" is far greater than the norm.

The land value system, modified to include improvements, is not expected to produce any unusual administrative bottlenecks in light of the experience gained over the years by the valuation authority in determining improved values for purposes other than taxation.

Proposition No. 2

Administration is complicated because taxes are used to achieve multiple objectives.

Ideally, the tax administrator would prefer the political directorate simply to indicate the revenue target and to be left free to identify what he considers to be the appropriate sources of revenue, taking into account not only the prevailing economic and social conditions but available resources in terms of manpower, equipment, and technology. However, as the authors have pointed out, if there is a tendency for monetary and direct income policies to be weak, the political directorate must give constituents the appearance that actions are being taken.

The case of taxes being used to achieve multiple objectives and at the same time giving the appearance that something was being done may be illustrated by the announcement made by the Minister of Finance of Jamaica in his 1991/92 budget presentation that it was necessary to provide tax incentives to encourage productivity by workers in the export and tourist industries. Tips received by hotel workers would therefore be free of tax, as well as payments received by workers under approved productivity schemes.

Some tax officials were of the view that these new measures would complicate administration, be difficult to monitor, and would create loopholes in determining taxable and nontaxable income. But the special tax preferences illustrate the use of taxation as an economic policy instrument.

The authors also contend that "things get out of hand" because the designers of the tax policy measures are not "tax men." Our experience points to the need for the tax administrator or "tax man," as a part of his strategic planning, to be more closely involved with the design and development of tax policy with a view to "influencing," as well as providing viable options for the political directorate. This approach would ensure that in any policy change important implications for tax administration would be fully taken into account.

Proposition No. 3

Many governments in developing countries may not want to improve enforcement of the tax system.

Since the 1987 tax reform, Jamaica has been fortunate to have ministers of finance who were fully committed to enforcement measures. However, it is understandable that the level of commitment of individual members of Parliament to the enforcement process often reflects the views of their constituents or special interest groups.

In practice, the effectiveness of the enforcement program is largely determined by the resources committed to it. Quite often, in Jamaica as well as most developing countries, the revenue agencies are not exempt from the overall budgetary constraints to which the entire public service is subjected. Consequently, enforcement measures are usually given priority by international funding agencies.

Notwithstanding these budgetary constraints, Jamaica has performed well in the area of compliance. Our economic and social survey for 1990 shows that revenue yield was maintained at 32 percent of GDP for that year. As the paper shows, Jamaica ranked high in terms of tax effort.

The extent of support received from the Government for compliance and enforcement activities is demonstrated by the initiatives currently being implemented to improve tax administration in Jamaica.

Recent Initiatives Taken to Improve Tax Administration

Arising from the policy decisions taken by the Government in the tax reform of 1987, the following initiatives have been taken to improve tax administration.

Development of Staff Resources

A specially designed revenue agents scholarship program was introduced under which 115 revenue agents were recruited and trained from 1987 to 1990 to strengthen the assessment and compliance capabilities of the six revenue departments. The program consisted of a one-year full-time course for university and college graduates and included classroom and on-the-job training, continuous assessment, and written examinations.

A special professional category of revenue agents with competitive salaries and a defined career path was established within the public service to accommodate this new cadre of tax officials.

An evening program for training serving officers as junior tax auditors was also started. Financial assistance is provided to cover tuition, books, examination fees, and travel expenses. Forty auditors have participated in this program since its inception in 1989.

The U.S. Agency for International Development, in collaboration with Georgia State University, is sponsoring a public finance program in tax policy development and tax analysis to develop the capability of the Revenue Board to monitor the tax system on a continuous basis by undertaking tax policy analysis and tax burden studies.

Tax Compliance Measures

A comprehensive audit program has been implemented to improve compliance through in-depth audits. Experienced tax accountants from the Revenue Board coordinate audit teams drawn from all revenue agencies in auditing groups of companies and large enterprises in all aspects of taxation including income tax, excise taxes, property tax, and statutory contributions. This approach supersedes the practice by which companies were subjected to a number of unscheduled and uncoordinated audits.

Tax compliance certification is required by all importers, building contractors tendering for government contracts over a specified sum, and businessmen who require foreign exchange to travel abroad. A tax compliance certificate is issued on production of satisfactory evidence that all tax obligations have been discharged or suitable arrangements for payment have been made. Since the introduction of this measure, revenues have improved significantly.

A business enterprise numbering system (BENO) has been implemented as a first step in the development of a unique taxpayer identification system for all businesses and individuals. This is an integral part of the registration of businesses for the new general consumption tax.

New Technology

A computer center for revenue services has been established to develop an integrated tax information system for the entire revenue services and to improve the assessment and collection facilities.

Micro-filming and laboratory processing facilities have also been introduced in the Income Tax and Land Valuation Departments to store and retrieve vital assessment and land ownership records in the respective departments. Preliminary steps have been taken to develop a land sales data bank in the Land Valuation Department. The data bank will facilitate more frequent revision of land values for property tax purposes, thereby improving elasticity in the tax yield. In practice, the values are only revised every ten years, which results in loss of potential revenue and gross anomalies in the tax base.

Voluntary Compliance

A modern Revenue Services Center was established in 1991 as part of a network of centers to be built throughout Jamaica over the next five years. These centers will be linked by a computer system to improve services in the areas of tax collection and taxpayer assistance, information, and education.

Taxpayer participation as part of the education process is encouraged through seminars and forums in which tax officials speak directly with the public and invite questions. This approach has been widely adopted in the general consumption tax program.

The foregoing initiatives are being pursued in accordance with our strategic plan, and the program is adjusted from time to time as economic circumstances dictate.

Jaime F. Pineda S.

We agree with the authors of this paper that inadequate tax administration is a major problem faced by developing countries. This problem is characterized by the use of antiquated administrative procedures, poor training of staff and contractual personnel, and insufficient compensation for public officials and employees, at levels clearly lower than the remuneration for equivalent positions in the private sector.

In Guatemala one must add to these problems a generalized skepticism about public management ("the government is a bad administrator"), which has led to a very low level of tax awareness and compliance. The tax ratio has not increased in the past twenty-five years. In 1965–67, on average, the tax ratio (tax revenue as a percentage of GDP) was 8.2 percent, with a direct tax burden (the ratio of direct taxes to domestic income) of 4.7 percent and an indirect burden (the ratio of indirect taxes to domestic private consumption) of 7.5 percent.[1] As shown in the paper, in 1990 the tax ratio dropped to 6.5 percent, despite the tax reform of 1987.

To a large extent, inefficient tax administration is reflected in an inability to monitor taxpayers. With a total of about 30,000 registered businesses, only 200 audits a year have been performed on the average, accounting for less than 1 percent of all taxpayers. Moreover, there is real leniency in administrative and criminal prosecution for tax noncompliance, owing to the imperfections of legal procedures, the inadequacy

[1]Congreso Nacional de Economistas, Contadores Públicos, Auditores y Administradores de Empresas, *Una política para el desarrollo económico de Guatemala* (Administración de la Revista Economía, Instituto de Investigaciones Económicas y Sociales, Universidad de San Carlos, Guatemala, 1969).

of executory instruments, and the leniency of clerks in charge of procedures. In recent years, the constitutional elimination of the advance deposit on appeals (*solve et repete*) has led to a large increase in the number of appeals against additional assessments.

The following figures illustrate the level of tax evasion. In the 1966–67 income tax period, of 24,300 registered taxpayers, 49 percent paid no taxes because they reported a fiscal loss, and the amount of deductible costs and expenses of those who did pay taxes averaged 82 percent of gross income. For the period prior to the 1987 tax reform (fiscal years 1985–86), taxpayers reporting a fiscal loss still accounted for 33 percent, but for sole proprietorships and business corporations that reported taxable income, the average relative weight of deductible costs and expenses represented 95 percent of the reported gross income.

The Tax Plan of Guatemala

Guatemala's 1987 tax reform was implemented under extremely pressing conditions, with the participation of a limited group of Guatemalan advisors and staff and the help of only one international expert. A political struggle developed in Congress between the representatives of the Ministry of Finance and the deputies of the various political blocs, particularly with the involvement of representatives of the business sector and their attorneys (CACIF). The deputies of the ruling party (DCG) wavered on fundamental decisions, especially with regard to income tax. Improvised modifications were made, with textual errors and the elimination of some paragraphs that made the text of several articles unintelligible. As a result of these and other political and business pressures, Congressional Decrees 90-87 and 95-87 were issued, largely distorting the plan originally sent to Congress. Eliminated from the scope of income tax at that time were interest accrued on savings and time deposits, and on bonds and credit instruments issued or guaranteed by the Government, public entities, financial institutions, banks, and private enterprises, whose issues are classified by the Bank of Guatemala's Securities Commission as first-class; interest on treasury bonds, notes, or bills issued by the Government, its autonomous institutions, and municipalities; and profits on the sale, transfer, or trading of shares, securities, or credit instruments listed on the stock exchange.

When the tax laws that formed the 1987 tax reform took effect, political campaigning and passive resistance by entrepreneurs began, culminating in a three-day business strike. Then, private sector attorneys began to file appeals for unconstitutionality, eventually totaling 28 appeals (mainly against the income tax, the value-added tax (VAT), the stamp tax, and the single tax on property), of which 6 appeals were successful. These actions partially crippled the tax laws, since unconstitutionality only suspends application of the rule in question and the other provisions of the legal text remain in effect.

At the same time as the tax laws that formed part of the 1987 tax reform were being drafted, a seminar was held on restructuring the organization of the Internal Revenue Office. Participants included all heads of departments, sections, divisions, and administrative units, under the coordination of the General Director and Deputy Directors, with advisory assistance from an expert in procedural simplification and administration (Ing. Luis Melgar) and the logistic support of the Research Department. The seminar concluded by recommending a functional organization. There was, subsequently, great resistance to the changes proposed, due especially to fear of elimination of the "proceedings," an anachronistic mechanism for issuing routine orders from office to office and even from desk to desk within the same unit, without resolving the matter at hand. The modernization of the administrative infrastructure was delayed.

The unit that monitors large taxpayers' compliance with filing and payment requirements was not institutionalized nor was its effectiveness increased, although a study showed that 8 percent of taxpayers (approximately 2,400 taxpayers) accounted for 95 percent of the income tax and VAT collections.

The auditing methods were, however, changed. The auditors of the VAT Department were combined with those of the Audit Department. A model report for field audit adjustments was designed, and a new concept of verification was formulated, called selective "integrated auditing." Under this procedure, no longer would all substantiating documentation be verified; the only items analyzed would be for income, costs, and expenses, which determine the amount of taxable income.

Smaller taxpayers (92 percent of the registered taxpayers), whose income tax and VAT payments represent only 5 percent of collections, would be audited selectively through grouping by economic activity and within the same activity, by comparability factors such as levels of purchases and sales, operating capital, paid-in capital, stock turnover in relation to purchases and sales, and average profitability indices. In these cases, instead of sending the tax auditor to the company, the Office of Desk Auditing would require taxpayers to justify certain revenue and expenses and to explain their irregular behavior with respect to a norm estimated from analysis and behavior of the other taxpayers in the same economic activity.

Unfortunately, there was no support for recruiting 300 additional auditors, though these were requested repeatedly for more than four years. Guatemala continues to be a tax haven, where taxpayers know that they will probably not be audited and, if audited, it is now less burdensome for them to pay attorneys to defend them since the advance deposit on appeals (*solve et repete*) no longer exists. If any additional assessment results, it is possible that government action will become unenforceable because of the statute of limitations or because a tax amnesty will be enacted.

The Political and Economic Framework

Guatemala is at a crossroads because, in agreement with international funding agencies and donor countries, it has pledged to adopt structural adjustment policies so as to achieve monetary, fiscal, and financial stability with modest economic growth in real terms and an increase in per capita income.

Faced with the political impossibility of undertaking a deeper tax reform that would increase the tax burden on those sectors with the highest income and greatest wealth concentration, the Ministry of Finance has had to resort to offering treasury bonds on the open market in order to attract money in circulation, especially quasi-money (savings and time deposits) institutionalized in the banking system, which early in 1991 surpassed Q 5 billion. The financial cost of this undertaking is very high and means greater pressure on the public finances in the next few years, because the bonds were offered at an interest rate of 33 percent on 360-day investments.

If the current government does not undertake an immediate tax reform that substantially raises revenues, it is likely that the fiscal deficit will reach the unprecedented figure of Q 2 billion, equivalent to 6 percent of GDP.

At the time of these comments (June 1991), the Ministry of Finance has sent one bill to issue economic emergency bonds for Q 700 million (forced saving), which has not been very well received in Congress. If approved, it will most likely be enacted together with a one-time special tax on net wealth, which may not yield the expected revenue. As these comments are being written, the Minister of Finance has announced that Congress has been sent a draft Fiscal Adjustment Law, which is equivalent to a new amnesty on taxes, penalties, and interest.

Economic and Fiscal Positions Compared

The comparison with Jamaica is stimulating, since the most conservative segments of the Guatemalan business sector have used as their argument against tax reform the large *nominal* increases (from 1985 to 1991) in government revenues and expenditures. However, the deficit in 1985 was 5.9 percent of GDP, while the expected deficit for 1991 will equal about 6 percent of GDP, a difference which in relative terms is insignificant.

In 1988, during President Cerezo's administration, the tax burden reached its highest level equaling 10.1 percent of GDP, while expenditures remained at about 14 percent of GDP during the five years of that government (1986–90). While Jamaica currently collects over 26 percent of GDP in taxes, Guatemala barely exceeds 7 percent.

Another eloquent comparison relates to tax effort, where the authors' calculations show that Jamaica ranks as a high-tax country—between ninth and tenth, whereas Guatemala ranks as a low-tax country, between fifty-ninth and sixty-first (out of 66 countries). For Guatemala, the decision to modify the current tax structure cannot be postponed. It has had no fundamental changes in the past 30 years and is characterized by one of the lowest tax burdens in the world and a highly regressive distribution. In fact, indirect taxes on consumption have a weight that fluctuates around 85 percent of tax revenue, while direct taxes on income, real property, and equity transfers represent only 15 percent.

Fiscal Reforms

The authors point out that the 1987 reform of the personal income tax reduced the tax base by increasing the basic exempt allowance, the number of dependents, medical expenses, life insurance premiums, and other deductions for education and transportation. These expanded allowances were granted mainly to favor wage earners, whose only income is from providing their personal services. The Social Security Institute's statistics showed that, of 835,000 workers and employees registered in 1987, only 1 percent earned salaries over Q 1,000 a month, and a typical family of five (parents and three children) had to earn over Q 1,650 a month in order to have taxable income, since their personal deductions amounted to over Q 21,300 a year. Thus, the plan was to tax only approximately 8,300 employees who earned incomes above Q 1,500 a month, generally business executives and senior public officials. In addition, the tax administration was freed from receiving over 50,000 returns with refund claims.

In regard to the authors' observations on the provision establishing a system of presumptive income for professionals, we accept that the absolute figures established "have become obsolete" due to the effect of inflation and that professionals may find it advantageous to pay the tax according to that presumptive income. Such income was fixed in absolute figures, with no possibility of indexing or periodic adjustment, in keeping with the constitutional limitation found in Article 239 of the Constitution (legality principle) that gives Congress the exclusive power to establish the tax base, which cannot be delegated according to the private sector lawyers who raised objections to the 1987 tax reform.

VAT

With regard to the three major changes analyzed by the authors, we shall explain the reasons for the following VAT reforms:

(1) To grant tax credit exclusively for purchases of manufacturing inputs and merchandise for resale, eliminating the tax credit for indirect administrative and sales expenses, including purchases of furniture and office equipment. This reform was based on the fact that auditing of tax credits showed that taxpayers channeled through their businesses the purchase of luxury goods such as televisions, satellite dishes, and all types of electrical goods and home appliances. They also included expenses such as bills from restaurants and supermarkets, air fares for pleasure trips, and business expenses for executives using credit cards (which are also used as a way of augmenting the salaries of officials and employees).

(2) Tax credits for the VAT paid on local purchases and imports of capital goods (investments in manufacturing equipment and machinery) were deferred. Taxpayers were allowed to deduct them in five yearly installments, on each anniversary of the acquisition, to lower the monetization of the economy derived from cash refunds of excess tax credits. At the time of the 1987 reform, because of the freezing of tax credits decreed by the previous government, which also reduced the VAT rate from 10 percent to 7 percent, net VAT credits of over Q 120 million had accumulated. As a result, before the reform, Congress had authorized the issue of VAT bonds at 9 percent for up to a total of Q 80 million.

(3) Traditional exports and construction were excluded from the zero rate.This was justified because traditional agricultural exports would no longer be subject to the special tax after March 1990 and because the effective income tax paid by producers of such goods did not exceed 5 percent of reported taxable income, which was lower than the effective rate of close to 7 percent on the income of professionals and on wages. In the case of construction, despite the fact that large amounts of VAT were refunded to this activity, it was found that the VAT paid on purchases of construction materials had been charged to the cost of

construction. The VAT is currently Guatemala's main tax, despite the fact that evasion is estimated at 20–30 percent, between noninvoicing and the informal economy.

It is hoped that the financial problems stemming from the Government's obligation to refund excess tax credits will be solved with the establishment of a system for computerized record keeping of taxpayers' current accounts, which is expected to be fully operational in the first half of 1992. This will allow the Internal Revenue Office to issue, via the computerized system, a tax credit certificate whose value can be applied to payment of any other tax except import duties; or, if the taxpayer so requests, it will be refunded in cash or with bonds, depending on the prevailing monetary circumstances.

Tax on Property

As the authors state, the single tax on property combined the existing municipal tax in the municipal jurisdiction of Guatemala City and three other municipalities of the Department of Guatemala (Mixco, Villa Nueva, and Chinautla). About 2 million self-assessments were expected; only about 1.2 million were actually received. Recording of the self-assessment data for updating the pre-existing tax registers was flawed. The new collection bills were issued consolidating all the properties of each taxpayer, and collections were frequently duplicated. To date, the deficiencies in controlling and billing this tax have not yet been overcome and, despite the fact that the payment was authorized via the banking system, the taxpayers had to go to the tax offices to clear up billing errors.

Currently, Congress has been presented with a draft Law on Municipal Property Tax that seeks to transfer to the municipalities the administration, control, and collection of this tax at a single proportional rate of 6 percent of the value of each property, revoking the single tax on property of the 1987 reform.

The single tax on property did not yield the expected collection results. In fact, from the Q 18.9 million collected in 1986, collections during 1989–91 have remained at about Q 50 million, except for 1990 when collections fell to Q 39.4 million, achieved with high administrative costs and extreme unpopularity among the taxpayers.

According to the authors, "Not often considered is the fact that the use of taxation as an economic policy instrument has important implications for tax administration." However, there is no getting around the fact that fiscal and tax policy form part of the national economic policy and must be embodied in specific actions. The Ministries of Finance and Economy, along with the central bank (Monetary Board), make up the financial public sector, which must systematically evaluate the behavior of the principal macroeconomic variables while correcting imbalances or deviations from the policies adapted.

It is undeniable that this complicates fiscal and tax administration and eventually violates tax neutrality, but what is needed is to set verifiable goals and objectives, especially in public finance administration. At the Seminar on Data Processing held in Costa Rica in March 1990 under the auspices of the Central American Institute of Public Administration (ICAP), it was recommended that an office of data processing be established under the presidency of each country, to incorporate into the data base the principal macroeconomic variables, development programs and monetary, banking, credit, fiscal and tax policies, with ongoing monitoring of quantitative goals and objectives as well as achievements in economic stability.

4

Improving the Administration of the Colombian Income Tax, 1986–88

Charles E. McLure, Jr., and Santiago Pardo R.

Over the past thirty years, the Colombian income tax has undergone more or less constant change as the result of efforts by some to reform it and efforts of others to reverse that process. On balance, the system has been improved greatly, and Colombia now has one of the best income taxes of any developing country.[1] Progress, however, has often lagged in one important area, that of the administration of the tax.[2] This is especially troubling since, in the words of Milka Casanegra, an expert from the Fiscal Affairs Department of the IMF, in developing countries "tax administration *is* tax policy."[3]

From late 1986 to the end of 1988 Colombia was again engaged in a fundamental reform of its income tax system. While the sweeping changes in tax structure—especially the elimination of the taxation of dividends and the movement to a comprehensive system of inflation adjustment—have drawn the most attention, there have also been important administrative changes that should greatly improve the implementation of the tax; furthermore, some of the structural changes will simplify tax administration.[4]

This paper describes the administrative improvements that were made during 1986–88. Section I describes the structural changes that were introduced to simplify compliance and administration. Section II describes the administrative changes per se that were made during the period. And Section III comments on the general applicability of lessons from the Colombian experience for other developing countries.

---

[1]For detailed discussion and evaluation of the recent history of tax policy in Colombia, as well as references to literature on that topic, see McLure (1989) and McLure and Zodrow (1991). On the landmark 1974 reforms, see Perry and Cárdenas (1986) and Urrutia (1989).

[2]McLure (1982) called for a high-level commission of experts—analogous to the 1968–69 Musgrave Commission on tax policy—to examine tax administration.

[3]Casanegra de Jantscher (1990, p. 179). McLure (1982) noted that "the finest tax structure can be subverted by tax avoidance made possible by carelessly drafted statutes and regulations and especially by tax evasion facilitated by poor tax administration."

[4]The structural changes are described and analyzed in McLure and others (1990).

I. Improving Administration Through Structural Reform

As in most developing countries, Colombia has traditionally collected most of its individual income tax through withholding on wages and salaries. In 1970, for example, such withholding represented 70 percent of all individual income tax revenue. Colombia does, however, include income from virtually all sources in the tax base of its income tax, which is a global tax, not a schedular one. Like most countries, Colombia has traditionally employed deductions and/or credits to adjust tax liability to the economic circumstances of taxpayers—notably marital status, number of dependents, and expenditures thought either to reflect diminished taxpaying ability or to deserve public support through the tax system. Credits have been allowed for residential rent, health care, educational expenses, and mortgage interest. These deductions and credits, as well as multiple employment, the earning of nonlabor income, and the ceding of income to spouses, have made it impossible for amounts withheld on wages and salaries to reflect closely the ultimate liability of individual taxpayers, except in relatively simple cases (one job; no nonlabor income; no itemized deductions). As a result, many taxpayers have been obligated to file returns, either to report liabilities not covered by withholding or to claim refunds for excess amounts withheld.

In common with most developing countries, Colombia lacked the administrative capability to monitor compliance by the vast majority of individual taxpayers; this was clearly true for itemized deductions, and even for marital status and personal exemptions.[5] All that was really possible was a check of forms for mathematical errors, a process for which the term "desk audit" would be too ambitious. As a result, many taxpayers failed to file returns as required by law; for them withholding was a final tax. Many who did file claimed exemptions and deductions for which they were not eligible. On the other hand, claiming refunds was a laborious and uncertain process.

In 1986 the Government decided to adapt the individual tax system to administrative reality. It eliminated the personal exemptions for the taxpayer, spouse, and dependents; it repealed a form of income splitting that allowed the taxpayer (commonly the husband) to "cede" a limited amount of income to the spouse (commonly the wife) for income tax

[5]In the pre-1986 system, most taxpayers subject only to withholding claimed the largest number of personal exemptions possible—"three or more." Those filing returns could claim even larger numbers of dependents. Though the extent of cheating has not been documented, that it was widespread is part of the conventional wisdom in Colombia.

purposes; and it eliminated many of the itemized deductions.[6] (The only itemized deduction remaining is that for mortgage interest on the principal residence of the taxpayer. The Government wanted to repeal the mortgage deduction, but the Congress exerted political pressure to keep it.)

Repealing the personal exemption for dependents might appear to make the income tax unfair. But this exemption was virtually impossible to control, since taxpayers could claim nonexistent dependents to gain the maximum benefits from this deduction, with little risk of detection. The Government believed that eliminating the deduction would create less inequity than retaining it. Evidence from polls taken since the 1986 reforms suggests that the general public accepts this view.

With these changes, withholding would be much more accurate for most taxpayers with incomes largely from wages and salaries; the primary exceptions would involve multiple employment and income not subject to withholding on wages and salaries.[7] Withholding was made

[6]The net wealth tax was also eliminated under the 1988 reforms, to come into effect in 1992. This was not done for administrative reasons, but to lower the tax-induced incentives to invest abroad. This change reduced the progressivity of the system. The net wealth tax is applied to the wealth of individuals, on a base consisting of assets minus liabilities. In 1989 nearly 700,000 individuals were subject to this tax; these constitute the universe of income tax filers. The rate is progressive, ranging from zero to 1.8 percent. The 1987 revenues from this tax were C$34,000 million, or 8 percent of total collections from the income and complementary taxes (C$427,000 million). In 1989, C$48,000 million was collected, compared with total income tax revenue of C$590,000 million. As the tabulation below shows, net wealth tax collection is concentrated in the 20 percent of taxpayers with net worth in excess of C$10 million, who pay 80 percent of the tax.

Ranges of Net Wealth *(In Colombian pesos)*	Number of Taxpayers	Accumulated Percentage	Net Wealth Tax *(In Colombian pesos)*	Accumulated Percentage
0–5,000,000	330,593	48.7	1,374	2.8
5,000,000–10,000,000	221,341	81.2	7,706	18.9
10,000,000–50,000,000	114,642	98.3	18,973	58.3
50,000,000 or above	11,338	100.0	20,067	100.0
Total	677,914		48,120	

Eliminating the filing requirement for those who have net wealth of less than C$15,000 million and meet the above-mentioned conditions should cause a maximum loss of revenues estimated at 1.6 percent of all income and complementary tax collections. The loss is presumably even less, since many taxpayers with net wealth of less than C$15,000 million receive income from nonlabor sources and thus are required to file an income tax return and pay income and net wealth taxes.

[7]The taxation of dividends was also eliminated. This is unimportant for most Colombian taxpayers. Interest income is subject to withholding at a rate of 7 percent; amounts withheld can be credited against tax liability on global income.

a final tax for those meeting the following criteria: at least 80 percent of total income is from wages and salaries subject to withholding; other income has been subject to withholding; net wealth is not more than C$15 million (US$25,000); there is no obligation to collect sales tax; and total income is less than C$8 million (US$13,000).[8]

It is estimated that this change eliminated the need for 1.5 million individual taxpayers (out of 2.2 million) to file tax returns, thereby greatly simplifying compliance and administration. Moreover, it removed a factor that erodes the social fabric of a country: Income tax laws that are known to be impossible to administer invite the taxpayer to cheat in self-defense, knowing that everyone else is cheating. Perhaps equally important, elimination of the need to file tax returns, where filing is largely pointless, improves taxpayer morale.

Beginning in 1979 Colombia has steadily extended the scope of withholding beyond wages and salaries. In that year, withholding was applied to interest payments. Two years later it was extended to honorariums and commissions, and in 1983 to services. In an important move made in 1985, the Government began to apply withholding to all payments for purchases made by corporations, limited liability companies, and the Government. Initially set at ½ of 1 percent, the rate applied to purchases was raised to 1 percent in the 1986 reforms. The current withholding rates are as follows:

Wages and salaries	0 to 30 percent
Honorariums and commissions	7 percent
Interest	7 percent
Services	4 percent
Rents	2 percent
Purchases	1 percent

The differences in these rates are intended to reflect differences in ratios of net income to receipts. Thus, for example, it is assumed that the costs of generating a peso of honorariums and commissions are less than the costs of generating a peso of sales of merchandise, and that the ratio of income to receipts is correspondingly greater.

All amounts withheld are credited against ultimate tax liability on global income for those filing tax returns. Only for those filing no returns (primarily low-income recipients of wages and salaries) is withholding a final tax.

---

[8]These limits are for the 1990 tax year; at the time of enactment in 1986, the two limits were C$6 million and C$4 million, respectively. In December 1990, the exchange rate was roughly C$600 per US$1.

Table 1. Colombia: Withheld Taxes as a Percent of All Income Tax Collections

Year	Percent Withheld
1975	14.5
1976	15.8
1977	18.2
1978	18.3
1979	22.6
1980	27.3
1981	29.4
1982	31.3
1983	27.7
1984	32.3
1985	38.0
1986	41.9
1987	49.2
1988	51.8
1989	49.7

Source: Directorate of National Taxes.

In 1989 withholding accounted for 70 percent of all revenue from the individual income tax. Of this, withholding on wages and salaries accounted for 21 percent, and withholding on other payments 49 percent. Overall, in 1989, withholding generated 50 percent of all income tax revenues (Table 1).

The 1986 reforms included many other changes that simplified compliance and administration. Though these are far too numerous to discuss in detail, or even to list, the following are worthy of mention.

First, many forms of labor income that were formerly exempt were made taxable.[9] This eliminated the need for rules drawing lines between exempt and taxable income.

Second, Colombia repealed a provision under which imputed income from owner-occupied housing was taxed. Though attractive in theory, this rule was not administrable.

Third, in order to "integrate" the corporate and personal income taxes and reverse the perceived "decapitalization" of the economy, Colombia eliminated the taxation of dividends. For administrative reasons, this route was chosen over conceptually preferable techniques

[9]The 1974 reform had eliminated most exemptions for nonlabor income. For constitutional reasons, exemptions for labor income could not be eliminated under the emergency procedures used at that time. Thus, payments such as vacation pay, "*primas*" (the thirteenth month salary), severance pay, pensions, and per diem payments had remained exempt.

such as a deduction for dividends paid, different rates on corporate income that is distributed and retained, and shareholder credits for dividends received.

Fourth, the rates applied to the income of corporations (formerly 40 percent) and limited liability companies (formerly 20 percent) were unified at 30 percent, and the top individual rate was reduced from 49 percent to 30 percent.

Finally, it should be noted that not all the 1986–88 reforms simplified the tax system. For example, the adoption of a comprehensive system of inflation adjustment for the measurement of income from business and capital adds to the burden of compliance and administration. This makes it doubly important that simplification and administrative improvements be adopted where possible.

II. Administrative Reforms

The 1986 reform legislation gave the Government legal authority (via the grant of "extraordinary powers" allowed under the Constitution) to restructure the tax administration and to change the procedural law governing relations between taxpayers and the fiscal authorities. This section describes the changes made under that authority.

The starting point for the exercise of the extraordinary powers was an analysis of the primary objectives of the Directorate of National Taxes. The objectives identified were the auditing of taxpayers on a current basis and the collection of amounts due. Further analysis showed that the first of these goals was being sacrificed to the second and that the second was not being discharged satisfactorily. This realization provided the foundation for the reforms described below.

Elimination of Certificates of Tax Payment

Traditionally, Colombia has placed great emphasis on *paz y salvos* (tax clearance certificates) stating that the taxpayer has no outstanding tax liabilities. These certificates have been required to leave the country, to transfer real estate, to register an automobile, to export or import, to enter into contracts with the Government, and so on. The idea is that the use of this technique will guarantee that those who have tax liabilities will meet them.

There are several problems with this approach. At best it helps to identify taxpayers and to collect taxes once liability has been established. It does nothing to ensure that correct liabilities are established—

which can be accomplished (in the case of taxpayers for whom withholding is not a final tax) only if adequate trained personnel are devoted to auditing.

Even worse, the tax clearance certificate system did not even achieve the purpose of ensuring payment of known liabilities. There was an active market in these certificates, some of them initially obtained legitimately by taxpayers who had no use for them (as they did not contemplate foreign travel, the transfer of real estate, contracts with the Government, and so on) and some of them counterfeit.[10] Only honest taxpayers needed to go to the trouble and expense of obtaining the certificate by legal means; for them the time and expense required to comply with the law could be considerable indeed.

Besides being ineffective and unfair, the tax clearance certificate system absorbed an enormous amount of administrative resources; some 60 percent of the 6,000 employees of the tax administration were involved in collecting taxes and issuing certificates. Moreover, the system created a false sense of security that the income tax was being administered effectively.

Again, the Government decided to face reality. It simply made no sense to devote so much effort to certifying that established liabilities were being met, and so little to establishing the liabilities. In February 1988 the Government eliminated the tax clearance certificate system for all taxes collected by the Directorate of National Taxes, thereby freeing up 3,600 employees for more productive activities, notably auditing with greater care the reduced number of taxpayers still required to file tax returns.

Collection of Revenue and Data Processing

As is the case in many developing countries, Colombia has long had problems in processing both tax payments and the data needed for tax administration and policy analysis. Part of the data processing problem has been the lack of legal authority to require that large corporate taxpayers (including limited liability companies, an important form of business organization in Colombia) provide data in machine-readable forms.

In addition, the 1974 reforms required that taxpayers file copies of many documents supporting claims for deductions and credits. In theory this information assists in the audit of those supplying the goods

[10]False tax clearance certificates were said to sell for C$10,000, the equivalent of about US$16.

and services for which deductions and credits are claimed, as well as the taxpayer in question. In practice, the result has been quite different. The Directorate of National Taxes has been physically overwhelmed by the avalanche of paper produced by this system. In some cases large taxpayers have used trucks to deliver their tax returns, together with boxes of the supporting documents required by law, implicitly challenging the directorate to try to find the discrepancies between the amounts reported and their legitimate deductions and credits. Rather than assisting in the audit and cross-checking of the tax returns of buyers and sellers, the filing requirement actually impeded these tasks; at best the documents filed could be used only for auditing the taxpayer, not for cross-checking the returns of others. Moreover, the quantity of documentation required slowed down the processing of information from returns.

Auditing has been hampered by the practices of some unscrupulous taxpayers who have exploited an overly generous interpretation of a provision of the law intended to protect taxpayers' rights. The law provides that a taxpayer whose return has been audited and corrected cannot be subject to audit again on the same return. Some taxpayers have deliberately included glaring errors on the first page of their returns (for example, omission of the taxpayer identification number of suppliers, without which no deductions are allowed), hoping that the errors will be found and corrected, making them immune from auditing that might lead to the detection of evasion based on far more serious errors buried deeper in the tax return.

Collection of taxes also involved serious problems. Collection officials in the Tax Directorate could conveniently "lose" returns accompanied by cash, or they could alter amounts of payments reported on returns; in either case they could pocket the money with relatively little fear that such pilferage would be detected by the lax internal controls. Yet another possibility was that the collecting officer, in collusion with taxpayers, would issue receipts for payment not actually made; this would allow the taxpayer to support false assertions that tax liabilities had been met.

In yet a third compromise with reality, the Government greatly simplified the tax return and eliminated the requirement that supporting documents be filed with tax returns. Now such documents must be retained and made available to the tax authorities on demand, but the information they contain need only be reported in summary form on actual tax returns. Moreover, large taxpayers (chosen by the tax administration on the basis of the size of their liabilities) must now provide information on magnetic media that can be processed by computer. As noted above, the 1986 reforms reduced drastically the number of individual taxpayers who file under the new system. Auditing the relatively few who do file will be easier.

Collection techniques have also been changed fundamentally. Since February 1988 the tax administration no longer handles either the initial receipt of tax returns or tax collections. Rather, all returns and tax payments (for all taxes under the jurisdiction of the Directorate of National Taxes—that is, income tax, value-added tax, stamp taxes, and so on) are now made entirely and solely to banks, which act as collection agents for the Government. This allows reliance on the well-developed internal controls of the banks. Moreover, banks are required to process and transcribe onto magnetic media all the data on tax returns and revenue receipts and forward them to the Tax Directorate in machine-readable form. To compensate the banks for their expense, the Government allows the interest-free use of the funds collected for 18 to 25 days before they must be credited to government accounts. As part of the arrangement, banks must process returns with no tax liability, as well as those with liabilities.[11]

This change has improved service to taxpayers, as well as tax administration. Whereas declarations and payments had previously been accepted by 900 government tax offices, they are now accepted by the 3,000 offices of banks located throughout the country.

Within 15 days after tax returns are presented, the Government has data in machine-readable form. Thus, cases can be selected for audit and collection follow-up on a current basis. This contrasts sharply with experience under the old system when data processing could take as much as two years from the time of filing of returns. Such delays create a number of serious problems. Tax collections decline in real value, especially when inflation is rapid. Even worse, chances of collection are reduced for a number of reasons: taxpayers may go bankrupt; there is a greater likelihood of collection being foreclosed by the statute of limitations (two years from the date of filing); and the "scent" of evasion is much colder when auditors attempt to do their work.

As a result of this step, an additional 400 government employees formerly engaged in receiving tax returns and tax payments have been made superfluous. Elimination of these jobs saves an estimated C$1 billion a year over and above amounts saved through avoidance of pilferage.

[11]In Chile, by comparison, banks accept returns only from those with tax liability. Moreover, Chilean banks do not process data on tax returns.

Use of Supplementary Information

The fiscal authorities now have access to information that is invaluable in identifying taxpayers and assessing liabilities. First, banks must file information returns identifying individuals or companies having accounts with more than C$120 million in transactions (the sum of debits and credits) annually.[12] This has proved to be an effective means of identifying wealthy "taxpayers" who have never filed returns.

Credit cards issued by banks and others provide another important source of information. Issuers of credit cards must identify (1) all businesses that have charges to credit cards in excess of C$10 million a year and (2) all holders of cards who charge more than C$1 million to their card in one year. Thus far there does not appear to be much problem with a switch to cash payments, perhaps because of security problems associated with cash payment.[13] On the other hand, a taxpayer can circumvent these rules by having several credit cards, perhaps at different banks.

Finally, notaries public are obligated to inform the fiscal authorities of all real estate transactions in excess of C$10 million.

These measures have been exceptionally effective. For the first time the tax administration has begun to audit those who have never filed. (Experience suggests that the worst mistake a taxpayer can make is to file a first return and thus become known to the fiscal authorities.) In 1990 the tax administration identified 26,560 taxpayers who had never filed a return; 15,815 of those were summoned and 4,607 filed a return before the end of the year with a tax of C$600 million (US$1 million).

Also, in that year, the tax administration visited 24,650 taxpayers who did not issue invoices as required; afterward 17,948 of those corrected their behavior. After a second visit, 125 taxpayers did not cooperate. As a penalty, their businesses were temporarily closed for one or two days. (See also below.)

The auditing capacity of the tax administration has been increased by the decisions to eliminate tax clearance certificates and use banks to collect both revenues and information. As shown in Table 2, in the last three years the results of auditing have increased dramatically. In 1987 the fraction of the income tax collected due to auditing represented

[12]This figure was initially set at C$6 million, which was so low that for five months—until it was revised to C$120 million—the reform threatened to induce a financial panic as depositors withdrew funds to avoid detection by the fiscal authorities.

[13]It appears, however, that the use of credit cards is decreasing for other reasons, notably a government requirement that 30 percent of the initial balance must be paid in the first month after debt is incurred.

Table 2. Colombia: Effectiveness of Audit
(In millions of U.S. dollars)

	1987	1988	1989
Income tax collections			
Total collections	1,335.4	1,426.9	1,534.0
Result of audit	21.6	143.8	240.9
(In percent)	(1.6)	(10.1)	(15.7)
Sales tax collections			
Total collections	717.5	762.4	797.1
Result of audit	18.9	25.8	52.6
(In percent)	(2.7)	(3.5)	(7.1)

Source: Directorate of National Taxes.

only 1.6 percent of the total income tax revenue; in 1989 it represented 15.7 percent. While this experience could be given a variety of interpretations (for example, unchanged auditing effort and worse voluntary compliance), the proper interpretation is almost certainly improved audit performance.

Processing Refunds

Refunds pose problems for the tax administration of most developing countries. Colombia does attempt to meet its obligation to make refunds of overpayments where there is no evidence that the taxpayer has understated his liability. This is essential if there is to be an effective system of widespread withholding. Unfortunately the processing of tax refunds creates an opportunity for dishonest tax officials to extort money from taxpayers applying for refunds. The technique is simple: paperwork is "lost" or moved along slowly in the absence of bribery.

New administrative regulations designed to eliminate this abuse allow the dismissal of an employee who does not move paper through the system within a set period of time—ordinarily 30 days from the time the claim is presented; 5 days in the case of a claim for an "expedited" refund, supported by a warranty from a bank or an insurance company. (There are, of course, safeguards to protect employees who express to their superiors legitimate concerns about the propriety of claims for refunds.) The system of expedited refunds has largely solved the problem of getting refunds to those who have large excess amounts withheld (and of exporters under the value-added tax). The primary remaining problem involves the many small taxpayers who may lack the sophistication or resources to request an expedited refund. There is still some opportunity for extortion in these cases. A system of automatic refunds of small amounts (for example, less than C$50,000 or about US$83) with random spot checks would eliminate delays and opportunities for bribery—but not without some risk of lost revenues due to fraudulent claims for refunds. Such an approach would free further resources for auditing.

Morale of Taxpayers and the Tax Administration

Both the reforms just described—in processing collections and refunds—have led to an improvement of taxpayer morale—at least, the morale of honest taxpayers. Rather than facing the prospect of dealing with dishonest officials who will demand bribes or otherwise cause trouble for the taxpayer (such as by "losing" the record of his payment), the taxpayer can be relatively confident that payments will be handled properly by the receiving bank and that claims for refunds will be processed expeditiously by officials who lack the leverage to demand bribes.

The various reforms described above have also had a salutary effect on the honesty and morale of the tax administration. In the prereform system, corrupt officials had many opportunities to demand bribes, both in the collection process and in the processing of refunds. Because of laws regulating public employment, such officials could not be discharged without proof of illegal activity. Yet graft and corruption were difficult to detect and prove because controls were inadequate. Worse, the presence of corrupt colleagues undermined the morale of those inclined to be honest, causing the spread of discontent and dishonesty.

The reduction in opportunities to extract bribes from taxpayers has changed this environment. Without the possibility of supplementing their incomes through bribes, some tax officials—presumably those who were corrupt—have resigned. The officials who remain are inevitably more honest than those who have moved on to greener pastures.

Penalty Provisions

Before 1986 certain violations—notably "inexactitude," that is, omission of income and overstatement of costs—carried a penalty equal to twice the amount by which the tax had been understated. But the penalty did not become due until the final resolution of liability, after the taxpayer had exhausted all appeals. Moreover, penalties were not indexed for inflation. Even worse, penalties did not carry interest because of the interpretation of a constitutional provision that prohibited the tax authorities from collecting two penalties based on the same violation. With interest rates at 25–40 percent a year, there was a substantial incentive to contest assessments, since the real present value of a penalty postponed several years was reduced substantially.[14] Finally, the recent history of repeated amnesties made it virtually certain that liabilities would be forgiven even before they were established. Under the prior system, ten-year delays in settlement were not unusual.

Tax lawyers were the primary beneficiaries of this process. Thus, there was room for reform that would benefit both taxpayers and the government, at the expense of tax lawyers.

New rules have been adopted to encourage quicker settlements. The basic sanction has been reduced to 160 percent of the amount at issue, but it can be reduced still further by quick admission of liability by the taxpayer. A mistake not yet discovered by the tax administration can be corrected by paying only a 10 percent penalty (formerly the penalty was 100 percent). If the taxpayer agrees to settle at the time of the initial field audit by the tax authorities, the penalty is 20 percent (formerly 200 percent) of the underpayment. If a formal demand for supplementary payment made by the tax administration is accepted by the taxpayer before the case goes to court, the penalty is 40 percent. If the taxpayer agrees to the increased assessment after the case goes to court, but before the final judicial determination of liability, the sanction is 80 percent.

The result of this revision of the penalty system has been greater willingness to settle claims quickly. Disputes on some 80 percent to 90 percent of audited returns have been settled with sanctions of 20 percent to 40 percent. In 1990, of 3,248 audits, 2,640 taxpayers had corrected their returns within two to three months, resulting in increased tax collection of C$2.3 billion (US$3.9 million). Under the law prior to 1986, this process would have taken eight or nine years of controversy and might have yielded less additional revenue.

Under another form of sanction, the Directorate of National Taxes has been authorized to close a business that does not issue receipts to customers or that is found to have more than one set of accounts. (Procedural safeguards for taxpayers include the requirement that there be a formal written accusation, to which the taxpayer has a specified time within which to prove innocence of the charges.) There has been television coverage of the tax administration closing shops for one day and posting public notices reading "closed for tax evasion."

[14]At an after-tax interest rate of 20 percent a year, a three-year postponement reduces present value by 42 percent.

Organizational Changes

In addition to the types of reforms just described, important changes were made in the organization and conduct of the Directorate of National Taxes. There were too many administrative layers between the Director General of National Taxes and the taxpayer, which reduced the effectiveness of vertical control. Moreover, the responsibilities assigned to the various divisions in the directorate were so broad that expertise suffered in some cases. A streamlining of the organization reduced the number of administrative levels, increased control, and allowed more qualified personnel to deal with particular problems.

Since relatively few large taxpayers generate a widely disproportionate amount of revenue, special administrative offices were established to deal with such taxpayers in the three largest cities, Bogotá, Medellín, and Cali.[15] In other cities, special units within local tax offices were created to deal with large taxpayers. This change is intended to provide better service to taxpayers, as well as to improve tax compliance.

Tax administration has long been favored by politicians as a means of rewarding supporters with government positions. Such political appointees are generally poorly qualified, and some are dishonest. To combat this practice—which also exists in other agencies—a career civil service has been created for the public sector, including the tax administration. With hiring and promotion based explicitly on merit, it should be easier to resist unqualified political appointments, as well as to weed out unqualified employees by preventing their promotion. This new system also allows greater ease of dismissal of officials hired after 1988.

A National Tax School has been created to provide instruction in tax law for both the public and private sectors. Inexpensive day-long seminars have brought together tax administrators, practitioners, and business employees; 2,000–3,000 persons have attended such seminars at one time. Besides serving an important instructional function, such seminars provide valuable interaction that leads to a two-way process of learning—about taxpayer problems and about the goals of the tax administration. Such interaction can help dispel the feeling of mutual distrust that all too often characterizes relations between taxpayers and tax administrators.

[15]The largest 2,000 taxpayers in the country—all companies—account for 80 percent of all revenue. Some 800 of these (accounting for 50–55 percent of all revenue) are located in Bogotá. There are 40,000 other companies, as well as 2.5 million individual taxpayers.

III. Lessons for Other Countries

Colombia's experiences with problems of administering its income tax system have valuable lessons for other developing countries. As with the discussion of the previous two sections, these conveniently fall into two categories, implications of tax structure for tax administration and broad issues of tax administration.

Implications of Tax Structure

The tax systems of many developing countries closely resemble those of the advanced countries that colonized or otherwise exercised hegemony over them. (These sometimes seem to be "frozen in time," containing features since discarded by the developed countries.) Thus, former British colonies have tax systems that resemble that of the United Kingdom, francophone countries follow the French system, and the tax systems of Latin America have been strongly influenced by the U.S. tax system. Unfortunately, not enough attention has been paid to the fundamental question of whether the tax structure of a developed country is appropriate for a developing country, considering especially differences in administrative capabilities, as well as cultural attitudes toward taxation. For present purposes, we focus only on limited features of the personal income tax.

The standard paradigm for personal income taxation is similar to the following: Add together income from all sources. Subtract deductions for personal exemptions and itemized deductions. (Alternatively, allow analogous tax credits once tax has been calculated; this distinction is not important for present purposes.) Then apply the rate structure to calculate tax liability. Employ withholding on wages and salaries in order to ensure collection on a "pay-as-you-earn" basis. In some countries, the individual is the taxpaying unit, in others the married couple or the family unit. In some instances, the rate structure depends on marital status, by means of income splitting. With this paradigm in mind we can see where problems arise.

The theoretical justification for deductions for personal exemptions is a venerable and attractive one. There is no taxpaying ability until income exceeds a certain minimum level; deductions for personal exemptions prevent the taxation of income below the level of the exemption. Since the minimum level below which there is no taxpaying ability is clearly related to family size, personal exemptions are commonly allowed for the taxpayer's spouse, children, and perhaps other dependents.

In developed countries that have good records on vital statistics, there is relatively little difficulty monitoring claims for personal exemptions. In principle, in some developing countries the relevant information on vital statistics could also be made known to the tax authorities; in Trinidad and Tobago, for example, the Department of Inland Revenue is responsible for vital statistics. But in many developing countries, the communication and use of these statistics is quite inadequate. In such cases, the provision of deductions or credits for all dependents is an open invitation to cheating; in essence, it creates a tax on honesty. Under these conditions, it is far from clear that personal exemptions make the tax system more equitable, rather than less.

Many countries allow itemized deductions. Although such deductions often show an amazing variety of response to local customs and political forces, there is a rather standard "core" group that is found in many countries. The deductions include interest on mortgages on owner-occupied housing, certain taxes (especially those on real estate), medical expenses, charitable contributions, and various forms of saving (life insurance, purchase of mutual funds, and so on). Many of these deductions can be questioned on grounds of public policy, but that is not our objective in this paper.[16] Our concern is whether they can be administered satisfactorily.

As with personal exemptions, many of these expenditures could, in principle, be subject to audit; most mortgage interest is paid to financial institutions, as are commonly deductible payments to institutions holding the savings of taxpayers; taxes are paid to governments; and medical payments are made to hospitals and to doctors, who can be required to register and issue receipts. In fact, it is difficult to cross-check such information unless evidence of payment—commonly copies of receipts—is attached to the taxpayer's return; after all, it is only in the last few years that the United States has begun to require that financial institutions and state and local governments file information returns covering interest and taxes received. Falsification of receipts is a potential problem unless either (1) the amounts involved are so small that the deductions could just as well be repealed or (2) safeguards are taken to prevent falsification, in which case administrative costs skyrocket. Given the dubious policy grounds for many itemized deductions, repeal seems an attractive option.

The case for the elimination of both personal exemptions and itemized deductions is strengthened once we consider their implications for with-

[16]For an analysis of the deductions allowed in Colombia in the late 1960s, see Musgrave and Gillis (1971); on the credits allowed under the 1974 reforms, see Gillis and McLure (1977).

holding. Given the levels of literacy and of legal and economic sophistication found in most developing countries, it is desirable that withholding be a final tax for those with little nonlabor income. Yet this is possible only if withholding takes account of the taxpayers' personal exemptions and itemized deductions. In principle, the employer's information on personal exemptions could be communicated by the government, as it is in Jamaica, and therefore be accurate—or at least as accurate as the government's information. But we have seen above that the government does not necessarily possess these data.

The problem is far worse for itemized deductions. At least the vital statistics do not change during the year for most taxpayers, and the changes that do occur are objectively clear and easy to verify, at least in principle. By comparison, itemized deductions generally are not known even by the taxpayer at the beginning of the year, and they can be known accurately and certainly by the fiscal authorities, only with great difficulty, after the year has passed. This information, which is needed for withholding, is not likely to be known accurately by the employer during the year, even if the employee has a good estimate of the relevant expenditures. Moreover, unlike the government, the employer has little direct incentive to attempt to verify that the itemized deductions of its employees are legitimate. In short, if taxpayers are actually to claim itemized deductions, there is little chance that withholding can be a final tax. Of course, what commonly happens in practice is that many taxpayers forgo filing returns and claiming itemized deductions, so withholding is de facto a final tax.

The approach used in Venezuela illustrates the problem. At the beginning of the year taxpayers indicate to their employers the number of personal exemptions and estimate their itemized deductions. Employers then base withholding on this information. If personal exemptions or estimated deductions change during the year, the employee is to inform the employer, who calculates the implied change in tax liability and alters the amount withheld to spread the resulting change in liability over the remaining wage and salary payments for the year. Finally, the taxpayer is obligated to file a return at the end of the year, reporting actual figures. This system is clearly quite cumbersome for both taxpayers and employers; moreover, it is easily abused. It appears that far fewer taxpayers file returns than are legally required to do so.

The upshot of this discussion is fairly obvious. In many developing countries, neither personal exemptions nor itemized deductions can be monitored with enough precision that we can be sure that they contribute to equity among taxpayers. Moreover, many itemized deductions lack justification on policy grounds. Finally, personal exemptions and itemized deductions make it very difficult to design a satisfactory system of withholding. As a result, either scarce resources are squandered on complicated withholding systems and the filing and auditing of returns, or else the equity objectives underlying these provisions are not realized. All things considered, it does not seem that these provisions involve enough net benefit to justify their continued use by many developing countries. Their elimination—and the possibility that withholding could be a final tax for many taxpayers—would raise taxpayer morale and would free scarce administrative resources for more productive uses.

The choice between individual filing and filing by married couples or family units generally reflects deeply held social views; we do not comment on these. But the choice also has important economic and administrative implications. First, making the couple or the family the taxpaying unit has adverse incentive effects, since any income earned by secondary workers is taxed at marginal rates determined by the income of the primary earner. Second, and more relevant for present purposes, this choice complicates withholding, since ultimate tax liability depends on the aggregate income of all members of the taxpaying unit. Accurate withholding is simpler under individual filing, since ultimate liability depends only on the income of the individual.[17]

Administrative Reforms

The type of administrative reforms implemented in Colombia seems to be widely applicable to other developing countries. One important lesson of the Colombian experience is that tax clearance certificates are valuable to taxpayers if they can be counterfeited or obtained illegally—perhaps even more valuable than money. Yet they are often printed with no safeguards against counterfeiting and theft. The point is not simply to print these certificates under the same control as bank notes. Rather, the lesson is that if the tax administration can certify the discharge of tax liability, it can also upgrade collection for everyone to the point that such certificates are unnecessary.

In all developing countries, owners of small businesses and noncommercial professionals are notoriously difficult to tax; indeed, experience from many countries indicates that the tax administration may not even know the identity of some such potential taxpayers. Cross-checking the membership lists of professional societies against tax returns can help identify professionals; this technique was used effectively in

[17]On the other hand, the need to allocate capital income among members of a family complicates matters.

Jamaica.[18] Tax administrators can also ascertain that owners of relatively large businesses have filed tax returns. But there may remain a residual of relatively well-to-do persons who do not file. Use of information on bank accounts, credit cards, and transactions in real estate can help to locate such potential taxpayers.

The tax administrations of most such countries probably suffer from the same types of corruption that has plagued the Colombian system. Thus it is important to eliminate opportunities for corrupt officials to practice extortion and theft. Using the banking system to collect taxes is one such approach; imposing sanctions against undue delays of refunds is another.

While many tax administrations are understaffed and underpaid, many—including some where understaffing and low pay are problems—are saddled with employees known to be dishonest, who cannot be dismissed for lack of evidence. Eliminating opportunities for extortion can help to force them out of positions they would not otherwise voluntarily leave.

Under the laws of some countries, only written documents can be used as evidence. This is sometimes interpreted as implying that copies of such documents must be filed with tax returns. The resulting flow of paper to the fiscal authorities is acute if there are no legal requirements that data be provided in machine-readable form, even by large taxpayers. Colombia's experience illustrates both this problem and its possible solution.

Data processing can also be improved by using the banking system to process the data from tax returns, as well as to collect money. In most countries, the banking system is among the most highly computerized sectors of the economy; it is thus generally likely to be far more capable of processing tax return data than are the fiscal authorities, which are commonly understaffed, underpaid, and not computerized.

The structure and application of penalties are also a common source of problems in developing countries. In some cases, the statute of limitations is written in such a way that a taxpayer can escape liability entirely by employing delaying tactics. This was true in Colombia during the 1960s. More commonly, the provisions for penalties and interest are so generous to the taxpayer that delay is attractive, even if it is certain that penalty and interest will eventually be assessed. Again, the Colombian experience in reducing the incentives for delay may have instructive lessons for other countries. Finally, even if, in principle, penalties and interest are adequate, they will have little effect unless

[18]See Alm, Bahl, and Murray (1990); this experience is summarized in Bahl (1989).

they are applied consistently and fairly. This has also been a problem in Colombia.

Many of the reforms discussed here can improve the image of the tax system and the tax administration. These include requiring fewer ordinary citizens to file tax returns, elimination of tax clearance certificates (especially where the system is abused), fewer requirements to provide copies of documents with the tax return, dealing with efficient banks instead of inefficient public tax offices, more accurate public record keeping and more timely refunds, fewer dishonest tax officials, and quicker settlement of disputes. Such improvements may be among the most important benefits of tax reform. Taxpayers are not likely to meet their obligations fully when the tax system is seen to be unfair and the tax administration is thought to be corrupt or inept or both. This is especially true where there is a strong distrust of government. An improved image will not induce taxpayers to trust the government or to pay taxes with glee. But it will almost certainly help to reduce distrust and improve compliance.

REFERENCES

Alm, James, Roy Bahl, and Matthew Murray, "Income Tax Evasion," in *The Jamaican Tax Reform,* ed. by Roy Bahl (Cambridge, Massachusetts: Lincoln Institute of Land Policy, 1990).

Bahl, Roy, "The Political Economy of the Jamaican Tax Reform," in *Tax Reform in Developing Countries,* ed. by Malcolm Gillis (Durham, North Carolina: Duke University Press, 1989).

Bird, Richard M., "The Administrative Dimension of Tax Reform in Developing Countries," in *Tax Reform in Developing Countries,* ed. by Malcolm Gillis (Durham, North Carolina: Duke University Press, 1989).

Casanegra de Jantscher, Milka, "Administering the VAT," in *Value-Added Tax in Developing Countries,* ed. by Malcolm Gillis, Carl S. Shoup, and Gerardo P. Sicat (Washington: World Bank, 1990).

Gillis, Malcolm, and Charles E. McLure, Jr., *La Reforma Tributaria Colombiana de 1974* (Bogotá: Biblioteca Banco Popular, 1977).

McLure, Charles E., Jr., "Income and Complementary Taxes" (unpublished, 1982).

______, "Analysis and Reform of the Colombian Tax System," in *Tax Reform in Developing Countries,* ed. by Malcolm Gillis (Durham, North Carolina: Duke University Press, 1989).

______, John Mutti, Victor Thuronyi, and George R. Zodrow, *The Taxation of Income from Business and Capital in Colombia* (Bogotá: Ministerio de Hacienda y Crédito Público, 1988; Durham, North Carolina: Duke University Press, 1990).

McLure, Charles E., Jr., and George R. Zodrow, "Tax Reform in Colombia: Process and Results," in *Tax Policy in Developing Countries*, ed. by Javad Khalilzadeh-Shirazi and Anwar Shah (Washington: World Bank, 1991).

Musgrave, Richard A., and Malcolm Gillis, *Fiscal Reform for Colombia: The Final Report and Staff Papers of the Colombian Commission on Tax Reform* (Cambridge, Massachusetts: Harvard University International Tax Program, 1971).

Perry R., Guillermo, and Mauricio Cárdenas S., *Diez Años de Reformas Tributarias en Colombia* (Bogotá: Empresa Editorial, Universidad Nacional de Colombia, 1986).

Urrutia, Miguel, "The Politics of Fiscal Policy in Colombia," in *The Political Economy of Fiscal Policy*, ed. by Miguel Urrutia, Shinichi Ichimura, and Setsuko Yukawa (Tokyo: United Nations University, 1989).

Comments

Jaime Vázquez-Caro

The purpose of these comments is threefold: (1) to describe the political, economic, and fiscal environment that led to the Colombian tax reforms in the 1980s; (2) to challenge the underlying approach used by the authors to define and organize the various administrative categories; and (3) to examine certain substantive aspects of tax policy and to propose possible explanations for developments to date.

The authors discuss what has been accomplished on the basis of what could be called the income tax's "manageability" in terms of its substantive and procedural features. In addition, they examine the organizational strategy, which was based on a greater recourse to the private sector—as a withholding instrument for the bulk of taxes—and the banking system as the principal teller which, in addition, performed the initial processing of tax returns. This strategy was intended to simplify anything that could pose administrative difficulties and to privatize activities that had previously failed. After explaining the characteristics of the reforms, the authors draw conclusions in the form of lessons that might apply to other countries.

The Climate for Tax Reform in Colombia

Colombia's macroeconomic policy has changed gradually. By Latin American standards, it has opened up its economy to the rest of the world cautiously and has undertaken conservative external credit and monetary policies. Much the same has occurred with regard to its tax system, which was reformed after many background studies.

After the 1974–76 tax reforms, Charles McLure and Malcolm Gillis, who were members of the Musgrave mission of 1968, returned to Colombia as World Bank consultants to make their assessment. They were surprised at the manner in which the Colombian working group had adapted the recommendations they made in the late 1960s. In 1974, the administrative aspects (of which I was in charge at the time) were not regarded with the same interest as the economic and the design aspects of the tax reforms. As a result, the Gillis and McLure study (1977) described the Colombian tax system as among the most advanced in Latin America. Economic reasoning at the time accepted the duality of solid tax theory and ineffective tax administrative practices.

Between 1977 and 1981, very little happened in the country with respect to taxes. During that period favorable external circumstances generated nontax revenue (from foreign exchange operations of the Central Bank) on a scale matching total value-added tax (VAT) receipts. Instead of adopting offsetting fiscal measures when this revenue dried up in 1980, the country resorted, between late 1980 and 1982, to foreign credit, which doubled the external debt but allowed the ailing tax system to breathe easier. Once the supply of external credit was exhausted, Colombia financed its deficit by issuing new money, thereby prolonging the fiscal lethargy still more.

Tax policy began to be redefined only when the scale and monetary implications of the fiscal deficit had demonstrated the urgency to consider the issue of taxes seriously. The earlier magical period of public finance gave way to a period of fiscal crisis. During the 1980s the signal given to the Colombian tax authorities—both from within and from the outside—was to increase tax collections. There was no alternative. The directive was clear.[1] Like the rest of Latin America, during the debt crisis of the 1980s, Colombia was forced to generate fiscal surpluses to meet its external debt repayment obligations. The only long-term solution was for the tax system to meet these imbalances and maintain current public spending levels.

These macroeconomic imperatives became clear and the microeconomic framework used to set policy was simplified during the 1970s. The consensus among economists was to lower tax rates and to simplify tax laws. More and more people were convinced that a plethora of tax incentives had made it impossible to control the tax evasion masked within tax avoidance. Moreover, even the very existence of the income tax was questioned because of its effects on economic efficiency. The VAT was assigned a prominent role in many countries because of its neutrality and for its potential for generating revenue. Furthermore, an awareness that procedural legislation had to be streamlined to increase effectiveness had already taken hold in the country. Colombia has been a pioneer in developing procedural frameworks based on legal efficiency. The procedural reforms enacted in 1967 (Decree-Law No. 1366), 1974 (Decree-Law No. 2348), and 1977 (Law No. 52) provided an important framework for the conceptual development of a national tax structure for the economic development of the 1980s.

[1]Although these fiscal problems created the conditions that brought about reform, it should be noted that the best condition for changing taxes is certainly not during periods with the largest fiscal deficits. Perhaps the lost period (1977–82) would have been much more appropriate for modifying the tax system, given the extrabudgetary considerations.

The Colombian income tax endured despite the growing popularity and importance of VAT. The modifications made were primarily aimed at achieving compatibility with the new economic doctrines and the new emphasis on administrative viability. These doctrines improved the conditions for tax administration implicitly, because they were based on notions of simplification and lowering of tax rates.

The informal sector continues to account for a large share of the Colombian economy. The fact that widespread smuggling is tolerated leads not only to tax evasion on imports but also on VAT as many taxpayers' transactions occur under the table. The counterweight to this structural trend is that during the last decade Colombia's economy has been characterized by an affluence of dollars as a result of the drug trade. Tax amnesties (in 1982, 1984, 1986, and 1990) have played a central role in promoting the legalization of this new money. In all likelihood, these amnesties have had an impact on income tax elasticity, but there has been no research on this subject.

The Importance of Tax Administration

In the medium and long terms, the success of a tax system depends less on the soundness of the laws governing taxation and procedures than on the administrative practices that emerge during the course of its development. The administrative implementation of any tax system is critical to its long-term survival. Casanegra's (1990) fitting remark, "in developing countries, tax administration *is* tax policy," applies not only to developing countries. I believe that the secret to success in the developed countries has been this emphasis on implementing tax laws. Enacting legislation in the absence of administrative planning is useless, and also frustrating for those in charge because their systems are actually better "designed" for failure than for success. An indicator of the implicit effectiveness of tax legislation might perhaps be constructed by identifying the specific provisions in the laws that are inconsistent with the implementation of the system, the "monkey wrench" indicator. For instance, studies of Argentine tax laws show that in some of these laws one out of every five provisions contradicts the rest of the text. In the case of the Colombian reform process, one of the major accomplishments of tax policymakers and administrators during the 1980s was the deliberate removal of the monkey wrenches that had been thrown into the tax system.

Administrative analysis of each separate tax is not easily performed, because in many cases the administrative units are concerned with such overall aspects as identifying taxpayers, systems for recording and monitoring a taxpayer's total obligation, control of tax evasion in general, custody of the supporting documentation pertaining to tax arrears, and tasks related to improving tax compliance.

Obviously each tax will require a specific administrative approach that will depend on the degree of procedural and administrative integration of the overall system. One approach has a separate tax identification number for each tax combined with a single current account for each taxpayer, specific collection system for each tax, and an integrated audit system, as was the case in the Argentine system until recently. Another system, used in Colombia until a few years ago, uses a unique tax identification number for all taxes and separate accounts and auditing schemes for *each* tax. The possible combinations of administrative strategies are countless.

Examining the administration of a tax requires separating the integrated administrative aspects from those aspects that are specific to that tax. In Colombia, for example, for many years the trend has been toward integrating collection systems for the VAT and the income tax. Tax audit is performed separately for each tax, however, and a taxpayer can be visited by more than one tax inspector, each of whom is looking for evasion of different taxes. In Argentina, on the other hand, until quite recently each tax had a separate account but auditing tended to be integrated.

The study fails to consider these distinctions. After explaining the specific aspects of the income tax, the authors discuss the modifications made to all taxes as if they were dealing only with the income tax. To keep matters straight, I suggest the classification used in Table 1, which lists the various ways of organizing procedures according to the sequence in which they occur and the functions observed in the Colombian system. The table indicates that procedures can be grouped as

Table 1. Colombia: Administrative Procedures

Procedure	By Type of Tax	Common to All Taxes
Identification		x
Withholding	x	
Tax filing	x	
Payment	x	
Amended return	x	
Investigation	x	
Discussion	x	
Accounting		x
Collections		x
Tax amnesty	x	x

"atoms," that is, individually by tax, or as "molecules," that is, encompassing several taxes. In practice, because laws on procedures are not defined systemically, procedural design is often incoherent in many countries.

Critique of the Study's Conclusions

What are the main points made in the McLure and Pardo study?

First, the role of the income tax. The income tax continues to play a decisive role in the structure of Colombian tax revenue. As noted above, the reforms preserved the major revenue-generating taxes. The income tax and the VAT underwent a parallel evolution. Following developments that seemed to indicate that the VAT would overshadow the income tax, the latter recovered its leading role. This occurred despite government policies favoring the VAT. Much the same occurred in Mexico. More recently, Ecuador has also undertaken to strengthen both taxes. Curiously, Colombia did away with the wealth tax which had supplemented the income tax.[2]

The generalization of the VAT in 1983 and the sales tax, its predecessor, in 1965, had always been intended to supplement income tax revenue. The trend followed by some Latin American countries in the 1980s was to rely mainly on the VAT and to reduce the role of the income tax. In Argentina, for example, the tax structure continues to include a complex income tax that collects little. Chile kept the income tax but with less revenue-generating importance. Uruguay virtually abolished the income tax in the early 1980s, although schedular tax schemes have recently been reintroduced. In Colombia, the relative importance of both taxes has been kept in balance. Experiences in Argentina and Uruguay suggest that neither tax should be used exclusively. As the income tax has been practically eliminated, governments have been forced to raise VAT rates on a regular basis to levels that may be undesirable from both economic and administrative viewpoints.

Second, the timely consideration of administrative aspects. The Colombian tax system has been greatly improved by an approach to reform that sought to integrate in a coherent fashion the substantive aspects of the reform process—taxes themselves—with the administrative process and organization. It was decided to do whatever was needed to make the system work. Rather than seek new solutions, implementation was the main preoccupation. For the first time in the

[2]The stamp tax, an administrative nightmare which generates very little revenue, was inexplicably maintained.

country's history, the decision to enforce the tax system was accompanied by changes to the laws aimed at facilitating and simplifying administrative procedures. Establishing a sound tax administration was set as a parallel objective to tax structure reform. In brief, the administrative aspects of the tax system were taken seriously. For years, Colombia had suffered setbacks that prevented an operational tax system from being developed. At the political level, taxes were continually redefined, while the tax administration maintained rigid management systems. The measures described in the study attest to the progress made in the case of the income tax. The demands imposed by "what should have been done" were eased, and the focus was put on doing what could be done.

In particular, progress was made in extending the inflation adjustments introduced to a certain extent in the 1974 reform, the tax treatments of business partners and businesses were integrated in a simple manner, and tax rates were lowered to levels in line with U.S. rates. These modifications to the system brought it closer to the realities of the economy and overall enforcement became somewhat easier. The standardization of tax paid by most individuals was unquestionably a reform in which administrative considerations were taken into account to the greatest degree. In a sense, the Colombian strategy consisted in striving for what is possible while accepting that perfection cannot be attained. This acceptance resulted from the recognition by those who analyzed the system of the need for simplifying tax legislation.

Clearly, the Colombian system was improved with the easing of demands on the administration and the elimination of procedures previously considered to be necessary safeguards. Operations became smoother, and previously unchallenged procedures were changed. An assessment of what occurred is incomplete without an analysis of the total cost of operating the system. This cost should include the cost to the private sector. The arrangements with the banks imply an opportunity cost to the budget, which should be measured in terms of its public debt cost. The widespread levying of taxes at source has a financial impact on liquidity and implies administrative processing of tax withholding forms by those that prepare them. Despite noticeable improvements and taxpayer satisfaction with the new system, it should be noted that higher administrative costs are being incurred because of the need to remunerate banks for processing tax information and cash handling and because more work is required from withholders.

What are the flaws in the analysis?

The authors fail to emphasize sufficiently what I consider to be of paramount importance for tax reform: the legal design of a penalties system based on rewarding compliance. The penalties set up in Colombia over the years were so inconsistent that in many cases they actually encouraged noncompliance. Even worse, they became a weapon in the hands of officials intent on corrupting the system. The fact that tax inspectors can come to an agreement with taxpayers on assessment and impose penalties whose severity increases according to delays caused by taxpayers' opposition, has restored leverage to the tax administration.

The problem posed by *paz y salvos* (tax clearance certificates) was part of a broader diagnosis performed in the 1970s that failed to result in action, because of political factors and not because of a lack of understanding of the issue among those who participated in the reforms of the 1970s. Moreover, the study may leave the mistaken impression that tax clearance certificates were an invention of the 1974 reforms and that the 1980s were spent trying to solve the problems of the 1970s. Tax clearance certificates were a product of the 1960s that remained in force as testimony to administrative inability to set up and manage an accurate taxpayer current account that could have been the basis for an effective collection system. The problems of tax procedures encompassed much more than just the tax clearance certificates.

The study also criticizes the tax administration for requesting huge amounts of information that were never actually used. With the implementation of the 1974 tax reform, magnetic media could be legally used for submitting information. At the time, it would have been out of the question to make such a requirement mandatory. Therefore, submitting tons of information on paper was the taxpayer's privilege. The fact that much of this information was unused is more a reflection of carelessness and lack of purpose than of any redundancy. Moreover, the Directorate of National Taxes has always reserved the right to require additional information. Tax reform was not needed to modify this aspect of compliance. Simply eliminating the annexes would have sufficed.

The decisions made were based more on conjecture than on a comprehensive evaluation of the various options. Income tax withholding on wages and salaries could have been monitored together with payroll taxes. Checks on withholding at source appear to have structural weaknesses because employers are not required to report amounts withheld for each employee, which thereby precludes cross-checking between withholders and taxpayers. This situation allows for fraudulent behavior from both sides. Withholders may pocket the withheld amounts and taxpayers can file claiming a tax refund.

What are the points on which I disagree with the study by McLure and Pardo?

A simpler tax cannot be justified on grounds that Colombia is a developing country, if the technology for supporting the administration of more equitable tax systems is available. To a certain extent the pragmatic approach used in making the decisions was based on the constraints of computerization during the 1970s and ignores the fact that the hardware of the 1980s has tremendous potential and that Colombia has adequate human resources for designing an appropriate system. Paradoxically, in the 1970s we may have made the opposite mistake: we had great faith in the computers that were being developed and tended to overestimate their potential.

I do not share the view that administrative problems justified the elimination of deductions for children and other dependents and for health expenses. It is true that nonexistent spouses and children were made up for "tax purposes." This occurred because the administration never tried to keep the situation under control. No one seems to have remembered that the Cajas de Compensación Familiar (Family Allowance Funds) maintain an updated roster of all dependent children of employees and that the Directorate of National Taxes could have obtained this information on magnetic media. Moreover, keeping the deduction for housing expenses is unfair and undermines the streamlining effort.

I do not share the view that the cause of the computer systems problems lies in the organizational structure of the Ministry of Finance, in which a separate Systems and Information Center operates as a Directorate-General having the same level as the Directorate of National Taxes. The problems encountered with the computer systems were not organizational but rather technological: mainframes used obsolete languages, and procedures were based on standards used in the late 1960s. Incidentally, I have found this to be true also in Argentina, Brazil, Chile, Ecuador, Mexico, and Venezuela.[3] In Colombia, redefining the current account and achieving viable alternatives in data processing were more important than organizational changes.

I have serious reservations regarding the consolidation of the tax return and the payment slip in one document. This was not necessary to solve the current account problem. Because of the consolidation, some information useful for audit had to be sacrificed, including information that previously had been processed on applications such as "SACUATO," which was the first real attempt by the Tax Directorate to come up with a clear and systematic picture of taxpayers. As opposed to tax collection, audit requires more data, which are used in more varied ways. This approach essentially creates a hybrid for managing the continuous tax collecting process, and audits, which are a discontin-

[3]In Mexico, data processing systems began to be changed in 1988 and the process has now been completed.

uous or discrete process. Revenue collection is hampered because of data checks performed for the auditing process, that is, information other than payment of the tax requires substantially greater validation and processing than is required by the mere entering of the payment amount. Before the current account is fully updated in Colombia, a new payment cycle is already beginning, which, by definition, once again renders the account obsolete.

For two reasons, it is unlikely the new tax system will be successful in the long run. First, the system is based on a few taxpayers who, in addition to being responsible for the collection, payment, and paperwork of the taxes of third parties, are required to file and make payment on their own taxes. The administration is no longer administering. Most taxpayers are excluded from the system. The system relies on huge penalties on withholders-at-source who fail to comply. In other words, the system relies on the administration's capacity for monitoring compliance of these withholders in the medium term. The problem is that although the elimination of tax returns has reduced the number of persons the administration must deal with, the transactions that must be closely watched and that are taxable are still the same. The periodic filing of tax returns marks the close of the accounting period, the double entry of the system. I disagree with the view that the capacity of the present computerized system is insufficient to process the tax returns of all taxpayers.

I disagree also with the way the banks are remunerated for processing tax return data. The system is a poor one for the following reasons:

- It results in a "Tanzi effect," which benefits banks; the greater the increase in inflation, the greater the loss to the Government.
- To encourage tax payments from major taxpayers, banks give them loans with low interest rates, thus effectively reducing the taxes paid by major taxpayers.
- Finally, at the time the banks must hand over the taxes to the Government, the fierce battle for liquidity that ensues distorts interest rates.

In broad terms, it can be said that Colombia took a major step forward when it decided to give a leading role to administrative considerations when formulating tax policy. Unfortunately I believe too much importance has been given to the public side of administration; the result is that the private sector now carries a heavier load—including banks, withholders, large-scale informants—and there are shortcomings in the fairness of the system.

On the whole, the study provides an excessively optimistic picture of the Colombian reform process of the 1980s. It also presents it as the only available alternative. I do not share these views. The merits of the process were, as the authors note, its ability to implement new efforts. The pragmatism shown by the reformers in objectively assessing the situation permitted progress to be made. This was possible because the reformers also took it upon themselves to create the conditions necessary for progress.

Richard Gordon

Charles McLure and Santiago Pardo R. have written an excellent paper. They describe a number of important techniques used by one Latin American country to improve administration of the income tax, most particularly as it affects individuals.

The following comments expand on a few of the points raised by the authors that relate primarily to substantive tax law. More specifically, these comments will address (1) administrative aspects of the design of substantive tax law and (2) some techniques for enforcing that substantive law. The comments are designed to add to McLure and Pardo's suggestions for improving income tax administration in developing countries that are engaged in substantial income tax reform, particularly in the area of personal tax reform.

Design of the Substantive Income Tax Law

The first key to effective income tax administration lies in the design of the substantive income tax law itself. McLure and Pardo describe how certain changes in the Colombian income tax law greatly eased the job of administration. The most successful of these changes resulted in three important benefits: (1) they reduced the complexity of the system; (2) they reduced the dependence of administrators on those facts that were difficult to verify; and (3) they reduced the number of individuals who were required to file returns.

In effect, perhaps the most important role of the first two benefits, that is, simplicity and reliability, is to permit the last, that is, reducing the number of filers. The fewer the people who must themselves file returns (including those whose final income tax is remitted by their employer and who do not have to file returns themselves), the fewer the returns that must be processed, the fewer the refunds that must be made, and often the fewer the audits that will be required.

Complexity

As McLure and Pardo correctly point out, reducing the theoretical "complexity" of a system may not always make it easier to administer. The theoretically least "complex" system would tax a flat percentage of every person's "global income," that is, the actual net accretion to wealth of an individual over a specific period of time. Many tax policy experts would contend that such a system would be optimal from an economic perspective. Of course, determining actual global income would be virtually impossible.

Nevertheless, at the outset, complexities should generally be avoided when designing an income tax. "Complexities" should only be added when there are compelling policy reasons to do so, or when tax administration would be greatly simplified.

When looking at the initial design of a tax system, one of the most important aspects of tax simplicity is treating all taxpayers and all income as similarly as possible. By so doing, incentives for shifting income from taxpayer to taxpayer, or from type to type, are reduced. This also reduces problems regarding defining different types of taxpayers or income.

In most cases, treating different taxpayers as similarly as possible requires keeping the number of marginal tax brackets relatively small. Also, in most cases, treating most different forms of income alike requires eliminating deductions and credits that are not a legitimate part of determining real income.

For policy reasons, however, different taxpayers cannot always be treated alike. Most tax jurisdictions conclude that a zero bracket, and at least a small number of graduated rates, are desirable. Although graduated rates complicate administration, they nearly always constitute a compelling policy reason for violating simplicity.

Treating all forms of income alike can also result in substantial administrative problems. For example, capital gains can usually be taxed effectively only on realization. Because the timing of realization is often under the control of the taxpayer, deductibility of capital losses must normally be limited in some way to net capital gains. If not, taxpayers would tend to realize losses and not gains.

There are also substantial administrative problems, in addition to policy ones, in treating all taxpayers alike. Individual taxpayers at the higher end of the income spectrum normally owe more in tax than do individual taxpayers at the bottom. It is therefore usually preferable for tax administrations to expend more resources in evaluating and confirming the income of an upper-income individual than that of a lower-income person.

In sum, the simplification of income tax administration often requires making exceptions to the rules of taxing all taxpayers and incomes alike.

McLure and Pardo suggest that reducing the tax administrator's dependence on facts that are difficult to verify, and reducing the number of individuals who are required to file returns, are important factors in improving the ease of administration. Accomplishing these two objectives sometimes requires making exceptions to the "treat alike" rule (although in some of the examples cited by the authors, it also means sticking to the "treat alike" rule).

Approximation

One of the most important methods of accomplishing McLure and Pardo's goal is to substitute approximations of certain types of income for actual income, and to restrict the applicability of those approximations (or restrict their effect) to certain taxpayers. As discussed above, while tax policy theory suggests that an income tax should be based upon the taxpayer's global income, the accurate measurement of global income can often be difficult. In general, the greater the accuracy of measurement, the more emphasis will be placed on facts that will be difficult to verify and that will vary from individual to individual. Other things being equal, the rougher the approximation of income, the easier the system will be to administer.

Individuals will normally have income from various sources. The process of approximating income and collecting tax will involve two steps. The first will be to make relatively accurate assessments of some types of income. The second will be to approximate other types of income. In many instances, "approximation" will involve exempting certain amounts of certain types of income (see Bird (1983, p. 4)).

In order to make accurate assessments of income with ease, that income must be relatively easy to identify and verify. Tax on that income must also be relatively easy to collect. As will be discussed below regarding employment income, for most taxpayers, virtually all of their income will fulfil these criteria.

It should be noted, however, that it will not always be easy to identify and verify all substantial sources of income. In some cases, large amounts of income will not be easy to identify. In those instances either approximation (and simplified collection techniques) or relatively difficult, expensive, and time-consuming evaluation and collection techniques will be required.

Of particular importance is the fact that there are fewer taxpayers at the top of the income pyramid than at the bottom. Relatively speaking, by limiting income approximations to taxpayers from the relatively lower-income groups, and by making more accurate income evaluations of taxpayers from the relatively higher-income groups, the number of taxpayers whom the tax administration would need to examine carefully would be limited. Therefore, in the trade-off between accuracy and ease of administration, income approximations should be limited to (1) smaller amounts of income; (2) a smaller part of a taxpayer's total income; and (3) to the lower-income earners. On the other hand, more accurate measurement should be made of income that is (1) relatively easier to assess and verify; (2) relatively large; (3) constitutes the bulk of a taxpayer's income; and (4) is earned by wealthier taxpayers.

When referring to "income," it should be understood that income is equal to gross income minus deductions. Those issues regarding verification and approximation of gross income also apply to deductions. Deductions are discussed in greater detail below.

Wage Income

Certain types of income are relatively easy to identify and verify, and so can be taxed easily. Such income does not need to be approximated. The most important is wage income. Depending upon how much of an economy is organized into entities, and the extent to which the organized sector is concentrated in relatively larger firms, wages can constitute a substantial portion of an economy's personal income. At the lower end of the economic spectrum, they often constitute virtually all of a taxpayer's income.

Salary income is usually easier to verify than other types of income. Companies can be required not only to report gross wages to the tax authorities but also to calculate the amount of tax actually due. If the taxpayer has no other income or deductions (a big *if*, which is addressed below), the company's calculation will equal the employee's final tax due. The company can then remit the taxpayer's final income tax due as part of a wage withholding system, making the filing of a return by the employee unnecessary. In effect, the taxpayer need have no contact with the tax authorities at all. The employer acts as a "mini-assessing authority" for the government (see Bird (1983, p. 6)).

Audits at the company level are easier and more efficient to perform than audits at the level of the individual taxpayer. Deductions at the company level for wages paid are linked to the amount of wages declared as income to the employee, and the relative ease of audit means that substantial tax penalties for misreporting employee wage income have a deterrent effect.

Therefore, companies should be required to compute, withhold, and remit income taxes due on the wage income of employees. Which entities should count as "companies" for withholding purposes is an empirical question. Often, the answer is any entity registered or incorporated, or any entity with more than a small number of employees, or any entity with a capital value or turnover in excess of a small amount.

The obvious problem with treating withholding tax on wages as a final tax lies in the phrase, "if the taxpayer has no other income or deductions." However, in most cases the lion's share of most taxpayers' income will be employment income, and deductions will be few. The treatment of nonwage income, and of deductions, is addressed further below.

Another problem arises when an employee has more than one salaried employment. In a system without graduated rates (including a zero rate) of income tax, this would not be a problem. However, the existence of graduated rates means that a single taxpayer would often owe more tax on the same income than if it were earned by two different taxpayers.

In systems that maintain substantially graduated rates, and where multiple wage employment is common, this problem can be alleviated by requiring the taxpayer to provide information to his employers about his other employment. Although this complicates the system somewhat, the use of a unique taxpayer identification numbering system and simple cross-checking may make the administrative burden less onerous. How effective this technique would be will depend on the particular features of the economy, including the degree of concentration of the wage economy into a limited number of firms, the extent to which salaried individuals work at different jobs, the completeness of taxpayer identification records, and the degree of computerization of the tax administration.

McLure and Pardo discuss certain taxpayer-specific criteria that some jurisdictions use for specific tax policy reasons to reduce tax, such as the number of dependent children. If supplied by the taxpayer, these criteria could be used by the employer to compute total tax owed. As discussed earlier in this paper, distinctions among different taxpayers should be avoided wherever possible. This is particularly true when, as McLure and Pardo point out, the information is hard for the employer, and the tax authorities, to verify.

In certain circumstances, however, policy planners will insist on deductions being based on such information. One way of reducing problems is to disallow cumulative deductions beyond some amount. Limiting deductions in this way, which is really a variation of income approximation, is discussed below. When a deduction is based on information that is difficult to verify, a specific limit on the amount of deduction can also be helpful. For example, a deduction could be allowed for each child, up to a limit of two. It might then simply be assumed that everyone will declare two deductions.

Business Income

It is much more difficult to estimate the income of farmers, sole proprietors, and small partnerships. When a taxpayer's total income consists of only a small amount of business income, it might make sense to exempt such income from tax. Excluding income from the tax base is merely another method of approximating income. The issues involved in excluding minimum types of income is discussed below.

Taxing business income in excess of the exempt amount is more problematic than taxing employment income. It requires some contact between tax administrators and taxpayers, since there is no easily identifiable third party to assess the amount of tax due and to collect it.

A possible alternative is to enact withholding on certain types of payments *to* the taxpayer. Such withholding would not only serve as a mechanism for ensuring that tax payments are remitted but would also serve as an approximation of tax due by the taxpayer. Estimates can be made as to the average profit made on a particular input (for example, purchases) or output (for example, sales of services). Tax can then be withheld on a gross basis, with a rate that yields an amount approximately equal to the tax on the estimated profit. The sum of gross withholding taxes could be treated as a final tax. Which inputs and/or outputs should be subject to such withholding depends on the particular facts and circumstances unique to the economy. However, inputs and/or outputs of businesses that normally have income that is relatively greater than those at the bottom of the income spectrum, but that are particularly hard to tax, might be good subjects for such withholding taxes. Such businesses might include the major professions, as well as contractors (see Gison (1984)).

Estimates of business income should be relied upon less when such income is relatively large or constitutes a large percentage of the taxpayer's income, or constitutes income of taxpayers at the upper level of the income spectrum. Of course, the exemption discussed earlier accomplishes some of this. Gross withholding taxes should not serve as final tax on large amounts of business income, although they may serve as a minimum tax in some cases.

Taxpayers with sufficiently large amounts of business income should be required to keep detailed books of account. The income of such taxpayers would, if large enough, justify the difficult and time-consuming audits necessary to verify the taxable income computed by the taxpayer.

For taxpayers whose business income lies between the exempt amount and the amount for which books of account would be required, it will often make sense to make approximations of income more accurate than withholding but less complicated than keeping books of account. Such approximations would be based upon simple and relatively easily verified facts, such as a forfait-style system. These approximations could also serve as a minimum tax for the books of account cases. In some instances, one might want to give taxpayers the opportunity to challenge the forfait-type approximations.

The cut-off amounts for exemption, approximation, and books of account systems, as well as the methods of implementation to be used, need to be determined by an empirical analysis of the facts in the particular economy.

Exclusions

The first and most obvious type of exclusion is the zero tax bracket. Excluding the lowest-income earners from the income tax system entirely can eliminate a large number of filers. However, in excluding these taxpayers, attention must be paid to the operation of any withholding system. As noted above, withholding can serve as a method of approximating income tax due as well as a method of ensuring collections. Withholding on payments made to tax-exempt taxpayers would still act as final gross taxes, an issue discussed in greater detail below. The refunding of such withholding would necessarily complicate tax administration and require the exempt taxpayers to file.

One of the advantages of salary income is that the company can determine the amount of gross wages to be paid to an employee over the course of the year. However, income received from outside sources cannot easily be taken into account by the employer.

This problem can be dealt with by having the taxpayer report all income to the employer. The employer could then adjust the withholding, using a pay-as-you-earn (PAYE) system. In such systems, the employer, in effect, becomes the tax administrator.

But such a system creates a number of problems. Verifying that the employee has in fact reported all income to the employer can be difficult indeed. Moreover, a substantial amount of additional paperwork would be involved between employee, employer, and tax administration.

Excluding some such income from the income tax base would be an administratively easier method of solving the problem, as suggested above with regard to business income. Employees at the lower end of the income scale are unlikely to have much income outside of their salary or part-time business income. By excluding such income from tax, only the employees' salary income would be subject to tax. This would greatly increase ease of administration.

Probably the most common form of such income is bank interest. As noted above, part-time business income may also be important. In some economies, although in few, if any, developing countries, income from dividends and capital gains may also be important, particularly where mutual funds are a common form of investment for taxpayers at the relatively lower end of the income scale.

Other forms of nonlabor income, such as rent or royalties, are likely to be earned only by a relatively small number of people, or are likely to be earned only by upper-income wage earners. In the case of such income, the administrative benefits of exclusion are unlikely to outweigh other considerations; they therefore need not normally be subject to an exclusion. The one exception to this rule might be imputed rent on owner-occupied housing.

Relying again on the principles of income approximation outlined above, nonlabor income should be excluded (1) only if it is small; (2) only to the extent to which it constitutes a relatively small portion of the taxpayer's income; and (3) so that, where possible, it primarily affects taxpayers at the lower end of the income spectrum. The amount of exclusion should be set low enough to satisfy the above criteria, but high enough to ensure that most taxpayers do not need to file returns. Lower-income taxpayers for whom nonlabor income constitutes a substantial percentage of total income would still be taxed on a substantial portion of that nonlabor income. Upper-income taxpayers, whose income normally includes a substantial amount of nonlabor income, would be taxed on most (relatively speaking) of that nonlabor income. Estimation would be largely confined to lower-income taxpayers and would apply only to a relatively small proportion of the lower-income taxpayer's income. Administrative resources would be concentrated on more accurate evaluation of the real income of the few upper-income taxpayers.

In most instances, a single fixed amount of exclusion should be set for the sum of interest, dividends, and capital gains. In other instances, separate amounts might be set for each category. The optimal nature and size of fixed amounts can be determined only by empirical analysis.

Deductions

As with gross income, deductions of expenses related to the earning of income, as well as deductions for special incentives, create two problems, Deductions may be difficult to verify, and, by allowing deductions, income computation is made more complex. Also, as with gross income, deductions can be estimated and limited, particularly with regard to the smaller portion of a taxpayer's income and to relatively lower-income earners.

First, as discussed above regarding PAYE systems, deductions that have little or no economic basis (meaning that they are not legitimate expenses in the earning of income) should be disallowed, particularly deductions that are difficult to verify. In some instances, "tax expenditures" that have valid social goals could be replaced with spending targeted to the intended groups of beneficiaries. They can also be limited in other ways, as suggested earlier.

Some other deductions might also be denied, even though they may have some economic validity. These might include deductions that are likely to have a personal component, or a component that is hard to value and therefore prone to abuse. Expenses relating to passive or investment income, commuting expenses, and entertainment expenses usually fall into this category.

As with the exclusion of nonlabor income, only deductions in excess of a certain amount should be taken into account by the tax system. The rationale of such a system is virtually identical to the rationale for excluding minimum amounts of nonlabor income.

In most instances, a single fixed amount can be set for the sum of all allowable deductions. In other instances, some of which are discussed below, separate limitations might be set for different categories of deductions.

While the exclusion of income from tax is generally likely to be popular with taxpayers, excluding deductions is likely not to be. Therefore, it may make political sense to provide a general deduction for taxpayers, up to the excluded amount. Rate brackets can be adjusted accordingly.

Withholding

The objectives of withholding have already been discussed. In principle, withholding rates must be set based upon factual information as to (1) what a particular taxpayer's liability should be and (2) what rate of withholding is likely most closely to approximate that liability.

First, it is necessary to determine what income should be subject to withholding. As noted above, employment income in firms with over a certain number of employees, as well as certain other payments, should be subject to withholding.

In a system with graduated rates, taxpayers' liabilities should differ based upon their total income (see Dixon (1985, pp. 39–40)). Withholding rates should, therefore, vary on the basis of the personal circumstances of any particular taxpayer. The lowest-income taxpayer should suffer no withholding, while the highest-income taxpayers should suffer relatively higher withholding.

With regard to wage income, the personal circumstances of a taxpayer can be taken into account. Withholding at the company level can be based upon the total amount of wages that the taxpayer will earn. But with regard to other types of withholding, it would be administratively difficult to vary withholding based upon the personal circumstances of the individual taxpayer.

Determining the rate of withholding likely to approximate a taxpayer's final liability is also difficult. An income tax is, by its very nature, based on net income, not upon gross amounts. One cannot tell with any degree of certainty what a taxpayer's final income will be by looking at any gross amount that contributes to the computation of that income, whether the gross amount be interest, dividends, or gross input purchases.

Some factual analysis can help set withholding amounts. In general, for most individual taxpayers, interest and dividend income is net income; in a pure global income tax system, interest and dividends would properly be taxed at the taxpayer's marginal rate. The fact that withheld amounts will be final taxes primarily for taxpayers at the lower end of the income scale suggests, however, that these amounts should be less than at the top taxpayer's marginal rate.

The rate of the most typical taxpayer would probably be appropriate for most interest income. The rate for dividend withholding might possibly be set higher, if it is likelier that dividend recipients would be higher-income taxpayers than interest recipients (see Jenkins and others (1991, p. 10)). However, such differentiation might set up a disincentive for equity investment or create an incentive to disguise dividends as interest.

Withholding on other forms of periodic income would also vary depending on circumstances. Withholding on inputs or outputs in a business enterprise can be even more problematic. Empirical analysis is of even greater importance here.

Loss Limitations

Several other approximations can help make an income tax system more easily administrable. One, discussed earlier, relates to the usual "realization" requirement before capital gains or losses are taken into income. Because taxpayers may control realization, limits on the deductibility of capital losses—allowing them only to be deducted up to the amount of capital gains—restricts the ability of the taxpayer to realize only losses.

Other limitations include restricting the deductibility of business costs and expenses only against business income, passive losses against passive income, or foreign losses against foreign income. In these instances, limitations on losses make it easier for a tax administration to avoid repeated detailed investigations as to the economic validity of the losses.

Some Techniques for Enforcing the Substantive Law

Many of the substantive tax law changes outlined above involve the use of income approximation, particularly for those at the lower end of the income scale. Different types of approximations, based on exclusions, withholding, and certain types of loss limitations, are based both on the form and the amount of income. In general, the goal is to reduce the information needed to assess tax due, and, in turn, to make it unnecessary for large numbers of taxpayers to file returns.

Verification

Verification of the relevant information will always be necessary. For lower incomes, this will often mean verification of employment income, which was discussed above. But it is also necessary to verify who actually is at the lower end of income distribution.

Withholding allows tax authorities to collect at least some of the tax that is likely to be owed to the government. In some cases, it also allows for a final approximation of income tax due. Of equal importance is the reporting of various income-producing transactions, particularly wages and passive income. Such reporting can help tax administrations to verify how much income should be subject to exclusion and whether any additional tax is due. In most instances, transactions subject to reporting requirements will also be transactions subject to withholding. This may not always be the case, however.

The use of taxpayer identification numbers, and the reporting of income by identification number to the tax authority, can play an important role in this process, even in developing countries. A taxpayer identification system can allow the matching of income, particularly employment, interest, and dividend income. This matching can determine whether or not a taxpayer has exceeded various exclusion amounts and whether he should have filed a tax return. As McLure and Pardo point out, the services of banks can often be used in assisting the tax administration in this task.

Reporting of types of transactions involved in business income, along with any withholding, can also help identify taxpayers who should be filing returns. The reporting of transactions by identification number can be useful when verifying the returns of taxpayers who exceed the amounts for exclusions and who should be filing.

As McLure and Pardo note, there is always the danger that tax administrations might be flooded with information that they cannot efficiently use. They discuss the benefits of the requirement that, whenever possible, information be supplied in machine-readable form. What information should be reported, as suggested above in the various discussions regarding withholding, would depend on the facts and circumstances of the particular economy.

As McLure and Pardo also discuss, there are other sources of information, from bank and credit card accounts to notices of real estate transactions. These may reveal whether taxpayers have been concealing income that is statutorily subject to tax and whether they (and perhaps withholding agents) should have filed returns.

Penalties

I have written elsewhere in detail about the design of taxpayer penalties (Gordon (1990)). Only a few points are emphasized here.

Penalties for failure to carry out a legally required act should be designed to encourage the taxpayer to carry out that act. Optimal penalties are often expressed in terms of probability of detection and potential tax savings (Mansfield (1987, pp. 18–19)). But, as with any aspect of tax administration, the most effective penalties are those that relate to activities most easily discovered and verified. Therefore, they should be used sparingly to increase the likelihood that transactions that are difficult to discover or verify are brought into the tax net.

Some of the most effective penalties are those that apply to withholding agents: employers, companies, and banks. Because the transactions are relatively easy to define, because the amount of tax owed is relatively easy to evaluate, and because the taxpayers are therefore relatively easy to audit, stiff penalties can act as a substantial deterrent. With regard to most withholding agents, investigation for failure to carry out withholding and reporting requirements is often quick and easily resolved.

Interest charged on late payments is not a "penalty" at all, but an adjustment designed to ensure that neither taxpayer nor tax authority gains the time value of money from a delayed payment or refund. However, an interest-like penalty can be used to encourage taxpayers to settle disputes. McLure and Pardo discuss a sliding scale of penalties depending on when taxpayers settle claims. Another possibility is to base the applicable penalty on a multiple of the applicable interest rate. This would ensure that for each day a taxpayer failed to settle, his penalty would increase at a rate greater than the cost of money.

Conclusions

The design of the substantive income tax law can play a crucial role in determining the ease of tax administration. To ensure a well-designed tax law, it is necessary to identify effective ways of easing implementation and to scrutinize carefully the facts unique to the particular economy. Careful legislative and administrative drafting are also required. As the process of tax reform continues, the process of identification of methods, examination of facts, and drafting of provisions will continue to improve. The work of McLure and Pardo contributes substantially to this process.

REFERENCES

Bird, Richard M., "Income Tax Reform in Developing Countries: The Administrative Dimension," *Bulletin for International Fiscal Documentation*, Vol. 37, No. 1 (1983), pp. 3–14.

Dixon, Daryl, "Tax Avoidance and Withholding Tax," *Australian Tax Forum*, Vol. 2, No. 1 (Autumn 1985), pp. 33–52.

Gison, Cornelio C., "The Philippine Expanded Withholding Tax System," *Asian-Pacific Tax and Investment Bulletin*, Vol. 2, No. 3 (1984), pp. 95–100.

Gordon, Richard K., Jr., "Income Tax Compliance and Sanctions in Developing Countries," in *Taxation in Developing Countries*, ed. by Richard M. Bird and Oliver Oldman (Baltimore: Johns Hopkins University Press, 4th ed., 1990).

Jenkins, Glenn, James Owens, and Ian Roxan, "Income Tax Reform for Zambia: Administration and Policy" (unpublished; Cambridge, Massachusetts: International Tax Program, Harvard University, 1991).

Mansfield, Charles Y., "Tax Administration in Developing Countries: An Economic Perspective," IMF Working Paper No. 87/42 (Washington: International Monetary Fund, June 1987).

5

The Introduction of a Value-Added Tax in Trinidad and Tobago

John F. Due and Francis P. Greaney

Trinidad and Tobago is a member of the Caribbean Community (CARICOM), one of the Community's "big four" (together with Barbados, Guyana, and Jamaica). Following independence and the formation in 1973 of CARICOM, the four countries had many features in common: unusually high dependence on income taxation,[1] with steeply rising marginal rates, a uniform (with minor exceptions) external tariff that the countries could not unilaterally raise under terms of the CARICOM agreement, and the traditional excises applying only to domestic production.[2] However Trinidad and Tobago differs from the others in that it is an oil exporting country—petroleum exports accounted for 84 percent of its exports in 1965 and 72 percent in 1987.

Table 1 shows Trinidad and Tobago's major tax sources for selected years as a percentage of GDP. Oil revenues rose sharply through the 1970s as the dominating source of revenues; all other taxes declined as a percentage of tax revenue, especially levies on domestic goods and services. As a percentage of GDP, however, individual income taxes increased substantially, whereas customs duties fell.

Development of Interest in the Value-Added Tax

As long as Trinidad and Tobago had substantial oil revenue, it was less concerned than the other three major CARICOM countries about modifying the indirect tax structure to increase revenues. But with the decline in world oil prices, the Government turned increased attention to the question. In his budget speech of 1983, the Prime Minister and

---

[1]Twenty-one percent to 27 percent of total revenues from individual income taxes, and 37 percent to 75 percent from all income taxes.

[2]The experience is described by Roy T. Gobin, "An Analysis of the System of Sales Taxation in the Caribbean Common Market," *Public Finance*, Vol. 35, No. 2 (1980), pp. 269–88, and "The System of Indirect Taxation in the Caribbean Common Market," *Bulletin for International Fiscal Documentation*, Vol. 33, No. 6 (June 1979), pp. 252–57.

Table 1. Trinidad and Tobago: Major Tax Sources
(As percentages of GDP)

	1972	1980	1986	1987
Direct taxes				
Oil companies	2.5	23.5	6.8	9.2
Other corporate	2.3	2.7	2.6	2.4
Individual	3.6	4.8	7.6	7.1
Indirect taxes				
Domestic goods and services	4.5	1.7	3.8	4.4
Import duties	3.4	2.8	2.8	2.2
Property and other	0.2	0.3	0.4	0.4
Total	16.5	35.8	24.0	25.7

Source: Ministry of Finance.

Minister of Finance of Trinidad and Tobago stated, "We have been giving consideration for some time to the introduction of a general sales tax. I am advised that there are numerous problems in the administration of such a tax. I therefore propose to seek the assistance of the International Monetary Fund as to the form which would be most appropriate in our circumstances." This request resulted in a report by the IMF entitled *Trinidad and Tobago: Sales Tax and Other Options of Indirect Tax Reform* (May 18, 1983). No immediate action was taken on this report, however, because it recommended a sales tax to be imposed at the manufacturers level and the existing purchase tax was already being imposed on the wholesale value of goods.

In his 1986 budget speech, the Prime Minister indicated that changes in that year in the purchase tax represented movement toward a full implementation of a general sales tax. The Acting Permanent Secretary of Finance requested the Board of Inland Revenue to develop a proposal for a general retail sales tax, and to this end the Board appointed a committee headed by Michal Christian, Assistant Commissioner of Inland Revenue, to prepare such a plan. During 1986, the Committee held a number of meetings, gathered relevant information, and prepared a report. The Committee concluded that with a retail sales tax, a rate of 21 percent would be required to raise the same revenue as the purchase taxes, which had relatively high rates. A 40 percent rate would be required if food were exempted.[3] If various service sectors were included, the necessary rates would be 13 percent (food taxed) and 19

[3]*Report of the General Sales Tax Committee*, by its Chairman, Mrs. Michal Christian to Mr. Randolph Kong, Chairman, Board of Inland Revenue, September 17, 1986.

percent (food exempted). The Committee did not regard a tax with such rates as feasible, given rates in other countries, and sought to avoid multiple rates, which would allow a lower basic rate.

Preliminary Measures

In the 1988 budget speech, the Government announced that it had established in 1987 a Tax Performance Committee, with Steve Ferguson as Chairman, to further consider plans for a general sales tax, and indicated that a sales tax would be introduced in 1988. The establishment of a tax committee, comprised of representatives from labor, business, and the Government, to examine the tax system and recommend changes to the Government was not new. This approach had often been taken in the past, with formal committees established in 1967, 1981, and 1986 to review the tax system and recommend reforms in the system. The terms of reference of the Tax Performance Committee were not limited to the indirect tax system, but rather included an examination of the entire system of taxation.

In early 1988, the business community invited to Trinidad R. Watson of Price Waterhouse and Co. (U.K.), an expert on value-added tax (VAT) operations in the United Kingdom, for discussions about the feasibility of a VAT. Following a meeting on January 16, 1988, at which the participants were Mr. Watson and representatives of the private sector and the Government, a draft report on the introduction of a VAT was prepared by a committee headed by Mr. Ferguson.[4] This brief report considered the relative merits of a retail sales tax and a VAT and indicated that the business community favored the VAT. A schedule of work was set up, with the hope that the tax could be introduced January 1, 1989, and steps in the operation of the tax were outlined. The report noted the necessary educational program, favored administration by Inland Revenue rather than Customs and Excise, and stressed the need for simplicity and for care in designing the new tax.

In May 1988 the Policy Economics Group of KPMG Peat Marwick formally entered into an agreement with the Government of Trinidad and Tobago to assist the Tax Performance Committee and the Ministry of Finance in developing a comprehensive tax reform program. The scope of work of the Policy Economics Group was divided into three phases and included the issuance of various reports which are referred to below.

---

[4] *Draft Report on the Introduction of a Value Added Tax, 1988.*

Phase I of the study consisted of two principal components: (1) a review of the current tax system covering indirect taxes, individual income taxes, corporate income tax, petroleum taxes, and tax administration; and (2) the development of preliminary recommendations for directions for reform.

In phase I, particular emphasis was to be placed on (1) simplifying and expanding the system of indirect taxes; (2) improving the structure of the individual income tax with special attention paid to the equity of the system; and (3) reforming the corporate income tax to broaden the base and lower the tax rate to improve the environment for economic growth.

Phase II was focused on the development of models to analyze the entire tax system. Three microsimulation models were developed for the individual income tax, the corporate income tax, and the system of indirect taxation.[5] These models, based on detailed tax and economic data, were designed to estimate the revenue and distributional effects of proposed changes in the tax system. The models provided the Government and the Tax Performance Committee, for the first time, with a reliable means of quantifying the effects of proposed tax changes.

Phase III called for developing specific recommendations for a comprehensive tax reform program along with a detailed plan for implementing the reforms. The aim was to have a final report of the overall tax reform program completed by the end of 1988, together with a detailed implementation plan.

Peat Marwick assembled a team for the project, and team members visited Trinidad and Tobago on various occasions in 1988 and 1989. The team worked closely with the Tax Performance Committee, Inland Revenue, Customs and Excise, and other government agencies and private sector firms, and held a series of discussions concerning their findings and recommendations with the Tax Performance Committee and the Government. To assist in the work of the tax reform team, a specially appointed technical committee was formed. This committee included representatives from the Ministry of Finance, the Board of Inland Revenue, Customs and Excise, and the Central Statistical Office.

[5]The models are called "micro" because they use a stratified sample of income, expenditure, and demographic data for individuals or businesses as the foundation for the analysis. The effects of alternative tax policies are calculated for each individual or business in the data base and then aggregated to obtain the results for the entire country. This method of analysis provides aggregate results for the entire country as well as results by various categories of taxpayers (for example, by income class and economic activity). It also provides information on the number of tax units experiencing increases and decreases in tax liability because of changes in the tax law.

Of great benefit was the assignment of two government officials to assist the members of the team working on indirect taxes.[6]

Analysis of the Existing Indirect Tax System

A detailed review of the existing indirect tax structure and administration was the first step on the part of those members of the team who were involved with policy on indirect taxes. This work resulted in a report entitled *Indirect Taxation in Trinidad and Tobago: Initial Report*, May 12, 1988, which was combined with analysis of other aspects of the tax system and was formally presented to the Tax Performance Committee and the Ministry of Finance on June 1, 1988. A report entitled *Draft Phase I Report: Initial Overview of Trinidad and Tobago Tax System* was also prepared. The Ministry and the Committee provided considerable feedback on the direction of change, and the team developed more specific recommendations concerning the design of a tax reform program for Trinidad and Tobago.

Indirect taxes yielded about 32 percent of total tax revenue. Of this, import duties plus a stamp tax on imports, purchase taxes on various goods applying to both imports and domestic production, and excises (applying only to domestic production), each yielded about 8 percent, or 24 percent in total. As of 1988, there were four ad valorem rates of purchase tax (at 20, 40, 60, and 85 percent), plus specific rates on tobacco products. Tax applied to importation and to sale by manufacturers. The total purchase tax coverage was broad, only a few basic necessities being excluded plus various inputs of industry. Over one third of the revenue from purchase taxes was obtained from alcoholic beverages, tobacco products, food and soft drinks, and building materials. The purchase tax did not apply to services. There were about 600 active manufacturers paying tax. The tax was administered by Customs and Excise.

While the tax had some desirable characteristics, there were serious limitations. The designation of taxable items by tariff number resulted in unnecessary restriction of coverage. The relatively high rate—40 percent on many commodities—inevitably resulted in misclassification and adverse economic effects. While relatively few inputs in production were taxed, the lack of a general rule for excluding them resulted in some cascading and restricted the ability to extend the coverage of the

[6]The members of the team would like to express great appreciation to T. Boodoosingh of the Budget Office and Ken Superville, Superintendent of Enforcement for Customs and Excise, for their assistance.

tax to goods used both as production inputs and for consumption. The levies did not constitute a broad-based sales tax.

There were also serious inadequacies in administrative requirements, particularly the lack of penalties for failure to file and pay. There was no trained audit staff. Failure to cover any part of the distribution sector restricted potential revenue. Overall, the purchase tax was unnecessarily complex, restricted in scope, and applied unusually high rates on many transactions. Compliance requirements were inadequate.

In the excise field, petroleum products had become the major revenue source, yielding two thirds of the total excise revenue. Excises applied only to domestic production under the traditional British Commonwealth practice, and all had specific rates. There were in addition several special levies on sales of motor vehicles and on hotel, telephone, and electric services.

The overall evaluation was that the indirect tax system was in urgent need of reform, to lessen complexity, broaden the scope, reduce the number of separate taxes, introduce computerization, establish an audit program, improve equity and buoyancy of revenue, end adverse economic effects, and strengthen administration.

Development of Proposals for Change

The report prepared by the team initially proposed the establishment of a general sales tax, merging in the existing levies (except customs), with the suggested title of General Indirect Consumption Act.[7] The report also reviewed alternative forms of general indirect taxes. It recommended the value-added technique, but stressed the need for further review before making the key decision on the extent to which the tax should go forward beyond the manufacturing sector. It also noted other issues to be resolved, such as exemptions, taxation of services, choice of single versus multiple rates, the tax rate, exclusion of small firms and location of administration, and presented a list of steps to be taken in developing the tax.

Following further work in May and June 1988, a supplement to the initial report was prepared. A substantial portion of the supplement discussed how far the tax should be extended forward to the retail sector. Consultations with various trade and industry groups, three

[7]The experience with developing the proposals for change is reviewed in the paper by Michal Y. Christian, *VAT: The Trinidad and Tobago Experience*. It was presented to the Caribbean Community Secretariat's Seminar on Value Added Tax held in Barbados on June 18–22, 1990.

major firms involved in importing, manufacturing, wholesale distribution, and retailing, the Chamber of Commerce, and other business groups, plus examinination of data from the Central Statistical Office, led to the recommendation that the scope of the VAT not be defined in terms of sector (manufacturing, wholesale, retail) but in terms of size of establishment. Given the complexities in the distribution system, many firms were carrying on business in several sectors, and the inevitable influence of the sector approach would encourage firms to shift functions forward beyond the point of impact of the tax. The decision was partly influenced by the high literacy rate of the country and the adequacy of record systems; the same reasoning does not necessarily apply to other developing countries. Trinidad, which ranks thirty-sixth from the highest level of human development among the 130 countries listed in *Human Development Report, 1990* is vastly different from the typical developing country.[8]

The discussions showed substantial support in the business community for increased reliance on indirect taxation, as well as the value-added approach, primarily for enforcement reasons. There was no sharp division in the business community on the preferable form of the sales tax, as there was in New Zealand and Australia.

Several major issues remained, however, including the treatment of agriculture, the selection of the threshold figure above which registration, collection, and payment of tax would be required, and exemptions and zero rating. Further investigation by the team and discussions with various persons involved in the private sector, ministries, the Agricultural Development Bank, and faculty at the University of the West Indies, St. Augustine, facilitated making recommendations on these issues.

Indirect Taxation in Trinidad and Tobago: Second Report was completed in July 1988. This report incorporated the various recommendations, noted the issues that remained, and made a number of more specific recommendations, based on equity, administration, and economic efficiency considerations:

- The threshold figure should be TT$50,000 (about US$12,500).
- Tax credit should be allowed to registered firms for tax paid on all business inputs.
- Exclusion from tax should be limited to a very small number of unprocessed foodstuffs and a few other commodities. This recom-

[8]United Nations Development Program, *Human Development Report, 1990* (New York: Oxford University Press, 1990).

mendation was based in part on analysis of data from household budget studies.

- Taxation of all services was not recommended, for equity and operational reasons; a limited number of services considered suitable for taxation were listed.
- A single rate for the VAT was strongly recommended. Only the excises (except a few minor ones) and one special levy would be retained—a simplified ad valorem rate on sales of motor vehicles.
- Administration should be placed with Inland Revenue, because of the importance of audit and the fact that the staff of Customs and Excise did not have the appropriate training and skills for this function. It was also thought to facilitate the integration, to some degree, of VAT and income tax audit.
- Farmers, comprising a small portion of Trinidad's economy, in general should not be registered for the tax, but major farm inputs would be zero rated to relieve their produce of tax.

This report was supplemented with additional analysis of the revenue and distributional effects of the current tax system and of alternative tax policies. This analysis was undertaken with the help of a computer-based indirect tax model designed specifically for that purpose.

The indirect tax model was constructed around a detailed data base of tax and economic data that captured all the important flows of goods and services in the economy. This approach provided a single tool with which to analyze a wide variety of indirect tax policy alternatives and allowed for the explicit modeling of the operation of the VAT.

The data base was constructed from detailed data compiled from trade statistics, national accounts, surveys of business establishments, household budgetary surveys, and actual tax collections, all of which were generally available for 1987 from the Central Statistical Office and the Ministry of Finance. After the data was integrated into a comprehensive and consistent form for the base year 1987, it was extrapolated to future years using the Government's forecast of future economic activity.

The model used this data to replicate or simulate the operation of the entire indirect tax system. Taxes on international trade (that is, import duties, stamp tax, and purchase taxes on imports) were calculated based on the detailed data on the value and type of imports, categorized by tariff heading. Domestic indirect taxes (that is, purchase taxes, excise taxes, and other special indirect taxes on domestic production) were calculated based on domestic production data and the tax base implied by current tax collections. The modeling of the VAT was more involved. Not only were import and domestic production data used to determine the tax base, but data on import destinations and interindustry flows were used to model explicitly the crediting mechanism of the VAT. This approach enabled the model to account explicitly for the differential effects of exemption and zero rating at various stages of the production and distribution process. It also captured the revenue effect of zero rating exports. The model took into account not only VAT paid directly by consumers but also the indirect effects of VAT paid by exempt firms, such as small businesses, that was assumed to be passed along to consumers in the form of higher prices.

The distribution of the tax burden by household income class was estimated, based on detailed expenditure data from the household budgetary survey that was included in the model's data base. An overview of the indirect tax model is presented in Annex I.

The report's recommendations on both indirect and direct taxes were formally presented to the Cabinet and the Tax Performance Committee in separate meetings held on September 7 and 8, 1988. While the recommendations were well received, both the Government and the Tax Performance Committee offered numerous comments and alternative proposals that required further analysis. Throughout the entire process, a heavy emphasis was placed on the quantitative analysis of the tax reform proposals. This emphasis served to focus on developing a sound tax reform program that met not only the structural objectives of good tax policy but also satisfied the revenue and distributional goals of the Government. On October 17, 1988, the proposed tax reform program, with appropriate modifications, was submitted to the Government and the Tax Performance Committee.

Finalizing the Tax Reform Package

The revised tax reform program was presented to the Government in a formal report entitled *Tax Reform Program for Trinidad and Tobago, Final Report* (December 1988), which covered all the taxes. While primarily presenting the recommendations of the previous reports, this report contained a major addition, proposing a rate of 18 percent for the VAT. This figure was based upon estimates of revenue necessary to make up for that lost from the repeal of the purchase taxes, repeal of a number of miscellaneous special levies (but not the excises), and a reduction in the individual and corporate income taxes.

The tax reform program was formally announced in the budget speech of the Minister of Finance in December 1988 and a Provisional Collection of Taxes Order was issued to effect the changes. The first phase of the reform took effect in January 1989 with the introduction of extensive income tax reforms.

The overall income tax reform called for:

- Substantial reductions in marginal income tax rates for both individuals and corporations. The number of rates was reduced from 11 to 4 and overall tax rates were reduced. The top individual income tax rate was reduced from 55 percent to 35 percent, with the proposed rate schedule being 5, 15, 25, and 35 percent.
- Raising the threshold for imposition of the tax significantly, the allowance being replaced by credit against tax—TT$600 for the taxpayer and spouse and TT$100 for dependent children. The base was broadened by eliminating various special allowances.
- Cutting the corporate income tax rate from 49.5 percent to 35 percent. A wide range of allowances (investment, initial, and so on) were repealed.

The VAT Implementation Plan

Continued work resulted in a report entitled *Proposed Program for Implementation of a Value Added Tax in Trinidad and Tobago* (January 10, 1989), which defined in detail the responsibilities of the consultants and the Government and outlined the steps to be taken in 1989 so that the tax could become operational on January 1, 1990, the date indicated in the 1989 budget speech. The program provided a detailed month-by-month statement of the objectives to be attained in four areas: policy and planning; organizational analysis, staffing and training; public education and publicity; and computerization.

To facilitate the implementation of the VAT program, experienced tax administrators from Customs and Excise in the United Kingdom and Inland Revenue in New Zealand were recruited to assist in policy decisions, framing of legislation, and training. Additional personnel were also recruited to work with the Port of Spain office of Peat Marwick to complete the computerization program. A detailed checklist of issues on which decisions had to be made was developed, and discussed at length among persons on the consulting team, government officials, and the Tax Performance Committee.

A VAT Implementation Team was appointed by the Ministry of Finance to carry out the implementation program for the VAT. This team was drawn from the Board of Inland Revenue and Customs and Excise and included the following: an assistant commissioner of Inland Revenue, who was designated head of the VAT office, a tax lawyer, a tax officer, a tax training specialist, a computer systems analyst, and a customs and excise tax officer. Members were assigned specific responsibilities in their area of expertise. The group met frequently to formulate key policy and administrative recommendations for the Government.

The consultants held weekly meetings with the VAT Implementation Team to review the accomplishments of the previous week, to plan activities for the following week, and to address any problems that arose. They also met periodically with the Tax Performance Committee and the Minister of Finance to review and discuss detailed policy and administrative recommendations. In the course of these meetings, unresolved issues were reviewed and decisions were made—in the end by Inland Revenue and the Ministry of Finance—on almost all issues, although some new ones appeared later. The Government decided to call the tax the value-added tax, rather than general consumption tax (as in Jamaica) or goods and services tax (as in New Zealand and Canada). It is not feasible to list all of the issues that were considered, but their general nature can be summarized briefly:

(1) Final decision on services: specified, or all services except those specifically excluded.

(2) Restrictions on credits for tax on business inputs.

(3) Exclusions: zero rating versus exemptions for food, medicine, clothing, and so on.

(4) Actual coverage of the services category.

(5) Special rules on imports; zero rating of exports.

(6) Sales to and by the Government and various organizations.

(7) Sales of used goods.

(8) Tax treatment of farming and fishing.

(9) Exact rules for small firms.

(10) Rate structure: single versus multiple.

(11) Rate level.

(12) Quotation of tax; tax invoices.

(13) Elements in taxable price.

(14) Time of tax liability.

(15) Building construction, rentals, and sale of buildings.

(16) Allowance of refund of excess input tax credits.

There were likewise a number of issues relating to operation of the tax, legal aspects, and operating procedures, on which decisions were made as noted below.

Final Decision on the Structure and Operation of the VAT

During March–July 1989 work intensified on all aspects of the tax, preparatory to the introduction of legislation in the summer period. Major activities included the following:

(1) Final decision on policy issues, which resulted in the legislation subsequently drafted, as noted below. This involved cooperative effort between the consulting team and the VAT Implementation Team. In addition, the Tax Performance Committee and the Minister of Finance were involved in discussions concerning the major VAT policy issues.

(2) The selection of a director of the VAT office and the recruiting of personnel. Michal Christian, Assistant Commissioner of Inland Revenue, was named VAT Commissioner and was also appointed to the Board of Inland Revenue. For several years, she had been involved in consideration of a general sales tax. The VAT Administration Center, as it came to be called, proceeded to recruit personnel, largely from Inland Revenue, but some from the outside.

(3) An extensive program of training persons in VAT operations.

(4) Development of the computer system, assisted by personnel of the Port of Spain office of Peat Marwick, technical consultants from outside the country, and personnel within government.

(5) Establishment of an informational and educational program, with guidance from an official of the New Zealand Government and the contracting of a local advertising firm.

At this time, a number of key decisions were made about the operation of the tax:

(1) The tax would be administered by a separate unit in Inland Revenue, with its own enforcement and audit staff, rather than under a functional system, in which audit, enforcement, and other activities would be administered by units involved with all taxes. It was agreed by all that the tax should be handled by Inland Revenue, and not by Customs and Excise.

(2) Three local offices, in Port of Spain, San Fernando, and Tobago, would be established.

(3) A bimonthly system of returns would be adopted, with half of the firms filing in each two-month period.

The organizational structure would consist of five units: (1) operations, to deal with registration and returns processing, records and office management, and accounts; (2) the compliance unit, including two sections: enforcement, which would have jurisdiction over the regional offices and which would ensure that returns are filed and taxes are paid, and audit, which would be concerned with the payment of correct amounts; (3) the information systems, with control over the computer system (which would be wholly under the jurisdiction of the VAT administration); (4) the policy unit, which would be responsible for audit selection, policy, and research, as well as liaison with Customs and Excise; and (5) the legal unit, which would be involved with interpretation and changes in the act.

The Tax Reform Program: The Second Phase

The policy discussions and decisions resulted in the preparation of two policy documents. The first, *A White Paper on Tax Reform for Trinidad and Tobago: The Second Phase,* placed the introduction of the VAT in the context of the overall tax reform effort. The first phase of the tax reform, put into effect in January 1989, focused on reforms of the income tax system, broadening the base through eliminating a wide variety of special exemptions and allowances, reducing taxes, and generally simplifying the system. The second phase focused on implementing the indirect tax reforms, principally the elimination of the purchase tax and numerous other indirect taxes and the introduction of the VAT. Also, because the tax mix changed, the second phase led to a further reduction in income tax rates.

The second paper, *The Design of a Value-Added Tax for Trinidad and Tobago,* presented in some detail the structure and operation of the proposed VAT, including the following:

- A rate between 15 percent and 20 percent would be used, with a single rate to avoid operational complications.
- The threshold for small business would be raised to TT$75,000.
- Specified services would be included in the tax; financial, insurance, and professional services would not be taxed.
- Zero rating would be limited to exports and a few basic foods and medicines requiring a prescription.

Late in March 1989 the consulting team presented the recommendations to the Minister, the Permanent Secretary, and the Tax Performance Committee, and with minor exceptions the recommendations were accepted, approved by Cabinet, and served as the basis for ultimate drafting of the legislation. The check list for policy issues was replaced by a statement of proposed decisions on the tax, and this aided the preparation by the Legal Counsel, in cooperation with consultants, of the statement on which the draft of legislation would be prepared.

Drafting the VAT Legislation

The Chief Parliamentary Counsel drafted the VAT legislation. It was completed in July 1989, and a number of meetings were held between members of the consulting team and the Minister of Finance and the Permanent Secretary. Several major decisions were made by the Government:

- The VAT rate was set at 15 percent, instead of 18 percent as proposed originally; the lowering was made possible by an expansion of the base and the maintenance of the same level of taxation on traditional excise tax goods.

- The threshold annual sales figure for registration of firms was raised to TT$120,000 (about US$30,000).
- Crude oil and natural gas were zero rated, to avoid liquidity problems in the petroleum industry. (Since natural gas is used solely by a few particular industries, there would be basically no revenue effect from the change.)
- A decision was made to tax construction services, but not the sale of newly constructed buildings. Since this change reduced the tax on new housing (many small contractors would be below the threshold), an initial provision for a refund of tax on new housing was eliminated.

Subsequently, as a result of debate in Parliament, the structure of the VAT was changed to tax all services except those explicitly exempted.

The legislation, the passage of which required a three-fifths majority of all members, was passed by the House on August 18, 1989, and by the Senate on September 8, 1989. By no means were all the issues resolved, however. In subsequent meetings between the VAT officials and the consultants, various decisions were made, though issues continued to arise through 1990.

Following the enactment of the legislation, booklets and other instructions for the business community and the public were prepared and the services of an advertising firm were used to provide substantial newspaper and television publicity. The Minister of Finance traveled throughout the country giving presentations to various community and business groups explaining the objectives of the overall tax reform program, its anticipated revenue and distributional effects, and many of the specifics on the structure and operation of the VAT. Again, the overriding theme was that the VAT must be viewed as part of the overall tax reform program, which was designed to provide a stable basis for economic growth.

At all three local offices, staff members were available to provide information. Forms for registration were prepared and distributed, and tax return forms were developed. Recruitment and training continued. Registration was required by October 31, 1989.

Response to the Tax and Criticism

No new tax is ever popular—but on the whole the tax was received relatively well. The business community favored it—unlike the reaction in many countries—partly because the tax allowed income taxes to be reduced and partly because of the unsatisfactory nature of existing indirect taxes. Cooperation between the Government and the business community obviously facilitated a favorable reaction. The downturn in the economy and the sincere desire of both business and the Government to take possibly difficult actions for the good of the country as a whole played an important role in reaching consensus on the appropriate tax reform program.

Inevitably, the opposition in Parliament criticized the new tax, arguing that the shift to VAT reduced income tax and luxury tax burdens on higher-income groups and increased the burden on lower-income and middle-income groups. The Government did make a strong effort to minimize the burden on the poor, but some shifting between upper- and middle-income groups was inevitable, given the general objectives of the overall tax reform. Furthermore, there had undoubtedly been considerable evasion or avoidance of income taxes at the higher-income levels. Those objecting to shifting burden to the poor argued for excluding all medicines, not merely prescription ones, from the tax, and for excluding books, or at least textbooks. But driven by important revenue goals and with special attention paid to the distributional effects of the tax system, the Government kept to several politically difficult decisions concerning the appropriate coverage of the VAT. The Government also committed itself to increasing the funding of certain transfer programs, such as old-age pensions, food subsidies, and public assistance, aimed at assisting low-income and elderly persons.

In everyday discussions, much of the criticism was against the 15 percent rate; 10 percent was often mentioned as a reasonable figure. But the purchase taxes being removed had rates of at least 20 percent. Revenue needs and the desire to increase reliance on indirect taxes largely dictated the rate level.

Concern was expressed about inflationary effects of the tax and fear that the tax would be added to prices without downward adjustments reflecting the elimination of the purchase taxes. There was also concern that small firms would adjust prices upward by the amount of the tax rate applied to sales even though they were only taxed on inputs. Some of the criticisms included outright misinformation—the argument, for example, that registered firms would shift forward the taxes on their inputs even though these amounts were deductible against tax due on sales.

People involved with various activities were fearful of adverse effects. For instance, promoters of various Carnival activities were afraid that they would have to pay tax on goods purchased in 1989 for delivery in 1990 at Carnival time; this potential problem was alleviated by the introduction of transitional provisions. The hotel industry was concerned that the 15 percent tax on hotel charges was out of line with taxes in neighboring countries—and thus would hamper the tourist trade that the country was trying to develop. However, the evidence showed that the major impediments to the development of the tourist industry related more to infrastructure and marketing decisions, including the quality, availability, and accessibility of resort hotels, than to the rates of existing hotels. Farm groups sought zero rating of additional farm inputs.

There was concern over the lack of clarity in defining zero-rated commodities and various taxable services—a problem that was gradually lessened by interpretations of the provisions. But questions continue to arise about the meaning of "unprocessed" food. Further, the issue of taxing second-hand goods has not been resolved.

Finally, there were concerns about firms advertising to buy early to avoid the tax (ignoring the fact that the purchase taxes would come off), and after the tax became effective, advertising claims by firms that they were not shifting the tax to the consumer.

Experience with VAT Operation, 1990–91

As scheduled, the tax went into effect on January 1, 1990. By June 1990, the revenue yield from the VAT was in line with the original estimates; the estimates proved to be reasonably accurate. As of June 1991, there were 10,145 registered firms, somewhat lower than the original estimate of 12,000. Of these, 66 percent were in Port of Spain district, 31 percent in San Fernando, and 3 percent in Tobago. During the initial registration period, 52,144 registration packets had been mailed out, the list based on a number of sources of potential taxpaying firms. Many of these names were duplicates, and a significant number of firms had gone out of business but had never been removed from the various registers. By October 10, 1989, 15,929 of the applications were completed and returned to the VAT Center. Of these, 6,343 were found to have sufficient sales to be subject to VAT. Of the remainder, 17,104 were returned as duplicate, unclaimed, out of business, and so on; 18,478 never responded; and 633 applications were returned incomplete.

By December 12, 1989, 8,215 registrations were completed; by August 8, 1990 the number of registrants was 9,729, by December 1990, 9,688, by June 1991, 10,145. The figure for population divided by the number of registered firms, 118, compares favorably with countries in a similar situation; it is unlikely that the number is substantially less than should be expected.

The nonfiling or delinquency rate—that is, the number of registered firms not filing—was initially very high; it had fallen to 25 percent by the bimonthly period ended May 25, 1990, but was still 24 percent in November 1990. Roughly half of these delinquencies were cleared a month later.

By January 1991, the chief deficiency was the failure of the computer system to perform all desired functions. There were delays in developing the computer system along the way, and for reasons by no means obvious the completed system was inadequate. The most serious failure was the initial inability of the system to identify nonfilers and prepare a list and notices for mailing. The department responded quickly to develop a substitute approach manually. Ultimately, the system was brought into full operation. Meanwhile the delinquency rate remains relatively high.

The audit program was under way by mid-1990, but it is not adequately staffed because of training requirements and illnesses. As of July 1991 there were 16 active auditors. During March 1990–June 1991, there were 330 audits of refund cases and 222 audits of payable cases. Of the total, 140 cases involved no change. Additional tax assessed was TT$5 million.

The budget estimate of revenue from the tax for the calendar year 1990 was TT$863 million. The actual yield after refunds was TT$899.7 million, approximately 4 percent higher than anticipated. The gross yield was TT$1,213.1 million, of which TT$581.7 million (48 percent) was collected at customs, TT$630 million on domestic sales (52 percent), and a negligible TT$1.4 million from government departments. The total figure of refunds for input tax credit was TT$313.4 million, or 26 percent of the gross yield.

For the 1991 budget year, the tax is expected to yield 25 percent of total tax revenue; in 1987, the replaced purchase taxes yielded only 8.8 percent of total revenue.

The general situation after more than a year of operation was reasonably satisfactory. The VAT office has effective leadership and competent staff, a potentially good computer system, excellent physical quarters, and the support of the top level of the Government. The overall program of design and introduction of the tax proved to be satisfactory. Some difficulties arose, as is almost inevitable.

There were considerable delays in staffing and obtaining physical resources. The rigidity of public service administration and procedures caused much of the staffing delays. As in many countries, both developed and developing, more importance was placed on seniority than capability. On the whole, however, the VAT office was successful in obtaining exceptionally capable personnel.

Implementation efforts fell several months behind the original schedule because of a late start and the other unavoidable delays. Delays in staffing, training, development of legislation, and decisions on many basic policy issues adversely affected both information for the public and staff training. The difficulties with the computer system should have been avoidable. Striking a balance between authoritative leadership and committee decision making is always difficult, and it may be argued that too much emphasis was placed on the committee approach, in terms of utilization of time. But these problems should not be exaggerated: the tax became operational on schedule without serious difficulties; it has proved to yield the desired level of revenues; and it is now an important feature of the Trinidad and Tobago tax system. The main problems that remain are a delinquency rate that is still excessive and an inadequate audit program.

The act, as enacted in September 1989, proved for the most part to be satisfactory, but some changes became necessary. Several were made in December 1989, mostly minor, but some of substance: baby formulas and baby milk substitutes were zero rated, for example, and travel between Trinidad and Tobago zero rated instead of being exempted. In early 1990, tax invoices were simplified for specified types of business, requiring much less information. During the spring, a number of rather detailed changes were developed, primarily to schedules in the act, to explain the meaning of various categories of goods and services. Clarifying zero-rated goods such as unprocessed food and exempt services in a workable manner is a serious problem in any VAT. Other provisions of the act could be questioned—for example, the various alternative "schemes" for simplified accounting for tax, which had their genesis in the U.K. VAT and are themselves complicated and may be regarded as unnecessary. The most significant one allows a firm to calculate taxable sales on the basis of the ratio of taxable inputs to total inputs. The explanation of this rule in the act is unnecessarily complex.

Because firms selling to unregistered persons had the choice of quoting the tax separately or quoting tax-inclusive prices, some confusion arose. This, again, was the result of the compromise between the U.K. and New Zealand approaches to VAT. Typically, prices were readjusted to a tax-included basis, and some stores closed down for one or two days to make the changes. These firms were fearful of confusion at the tax register if the tax were added separately.

Data on price increases showed that prices of goods subject to tax rose between 5 percent and 11 percent between December 1989 and January 1990, while nontaxed goods rose by only 2 percent. Even by April 1990, none of the commodity groups had risen in price by as much as 15 percent, an indication that some downward adjustments were made for the repeal of purchase taxes. Prices were relatively stable in 1989; the tax was not introduced in a strongly inflationary period.

While refunds are being paid, there have been some delays. However, the Government is required to pay interest on refunds delayed for more than six months.

Summary of the Tax as of 1991

The major features of the VAT as introduced and modified slightly in 1990 are as follows:

Nature. The tax is a value-added levy of the usual tax credit or invoice type. It applies to imports, as well as to domestic sales. Credit is allowed for tax paid on inputs for business use by registered firms, without exception. The tax extends through the retail level, although small firms in all sectors are free of the requirement to register and collect and remit tax; they pay tax on their purchases and are not eligible for input tax credit.

Coverage. The tax applies to all sales of goods and to all services, except as otherwise specified. The sale of land and buildings is not included in the scope of the tax, although the rental of business property is taxable. Commodities specifically excluded from application of the tax are zero rated; thus, the tax does not apply to sales of these goods, and sellers receive input tax credit for tax paid on inputs to produce them.

Zero rating is limited to (1) unprocessed food and a few basic processed foods, such as flour, bread, milk, and margarine; (2) medicines sold by prescription; (3) live animals, livestock feed, seed, fertilizer, and farm machinery; (4) water sold through pipes; (5) exports and certain export-related activities; (6) natural gas and crude oil; and (7) veterinary and pest control services.

Specified services are exempted, and thus while not subject to tax, suppliers do not receive input tax credits. The principal exempt services are (1) medical, dental, hospital, and other health-related services; (2) most education; (3) rental of residential property; (4) bus and taxi service and postal service; and (5) real estate brokerage, insurance, banking, and stock brokerage.

Small firms. The threshold for registration of firms is set at TT$120,000 (about US$30,000) in annual sales. This figure appears to be satisfactory. Voluntary registration is permitted for firms under the threshold in certain important industries such as farming and manufacturing.

Operations. Returns and payment are required on a bimonthly basis, due by the twenty-fifth of the following month.

Tax invoices are required, with a simplified form for use by gas stations, car parks, and supermarkets. Firms selling to unregistered buyers have the choice of quoting the tax separately from the price or quoting tax-inclusive prices, although the latter is increasingly common.

The tax is administered by the Value-Added Tax Administration Center of Inland Revenue, under the VAT Commissioner, who is a member of the Board of Inland Revenue.

Reasons for the Successful Introduction of the Tax

Despite delays in the full operation of the computer system and problems in acquiring adequate staffing for the audit function, the overall introduction of the tax has been quite successful. There are several reasons for this:

(1) The careful planning that went into the development of the tax structure and administration. Heavy emphasis was placed on the quantitative analysis of the proposed changes.

(2) The close cooperation between business and the Government from the beginning of consideration of the tax. This cooperation was facilitated by the formation and participation of the Tax Performance Committee in the development and review of the VAT proposals.

(3) The extensive publicity program to acquaint the public and taxpaying firms with the operation of the tax.

(4) The introduction of the tax in conjunction with repeal of the purchase taxes and significant reduction in income tax rates.

(5) The selection of competent persons in key positions. The VAT Implementation Team appointed by the Minister of Finance included some of the most capable members of the Board of Inland Revenue.

Lessons for Other Countries

The introduction of the VAT in Trinidad and Tobago in the context of an overall tax reform program enabled the Government to formulate a consistent set of policies with an appropriate mix of winners and losers. The reduction in income tax rates greatly facilitated the introduction of the VAT by providing the benefit of lowering or eliminating income taxes for the lower- to middle-income groups, and increasing benefits to the poor lessened complaints of burden on these persons.

Based on the experience in Trinidad and Tobago, the following suggestions are offered for countries considering a VAT:

(1) If at all possible, the rate should be kept down to 10 percent when the tax is introduced. Much of the complaint in Trinidad was against the 15 percent rate.

(2) If the tax is to yield substantial revenue at a tolerable rate, it is imperative that most food be taxable.

(3) Delineation of exempt from taxable food is difficult in a workable and acceptable fashion; the exemption of unprocessed food, plus a few other items such as milk and bread, was the approach used in Trinidad, and this seems to have been accepted although there are definitional problems, especially about what constitutes "processing." This approach provides adequate protection to the lowest-income group while maintaining a broad base and lower rate by taxing processed foods, much of which is consumed by middle- and high-income families.

(4) If services are to be taxed, it appears desirable to tax all services other than those exempted or zero rated, in the interest of simplicity. It is desirable to include types of services provided mainly to businesses (which is highly undesirable in the usual sales tax) given the political repercussions of not doing so, and because most businesses will be able to obtain input tax credit for the tax on these services.

(5) Studies in many countries have demonstrated the difficulties of applying a VAT to financial and insurance services, and it is better not to attempt it; the concept of value added is not clearly definable in these fields. Taxation of rentals of nontransient housing is not feasible because of the consequent discrimination against the tenant compared to the homeowner.

(6) It is important to accept zero rating rather than exemption for categories designed to be free of tax; otherwise, the major inputs used to produce the exempt goods must be exempted also, and firms producing both exempt and taxable goods must segregate inputs between the two. Exemption is desirable when there is justification for not taxing the item, but it is considered appropriate for some tax burden to rest on the purchasers of it. Zero rating has to be controlled carefully to prevent fraudulent requests for refunds.

(7) Registration of all farmers is clearly not feasible, in terms of compliance and enforcement. Accordingly, major farm inputs—fertilizer, feed, seed, livestock, and farm machinery—should be zero rated, but not hand tools and items widely used also for nonfarm use, such as batteries for farm and other tractors.

(8) One of the most confusing issues in Trinidad was the question of how firms should indicate tax to unregistered buyers. Clear instructions are necessary for the firms about their policies. There is merit in a

requirement for separate quotation, in the belief that this facilitates exact and uniform shifting, as is intended, but the tax-included approach appears simpler.

(9) A major issue is the criterion for excluding small firms from the registration requirement. The aim is to draw the line at the level above which most firms have records sufficient to ensure control of the tax. This figure cannot be determined scientifically, but must be based on the views of persons familiar with the business community, particularly retailing and crafts.

(10) Another important issue relates to allowing credit for previous consumption or purchase taxes on stocks of goods on hand when the tax is introduced. No allowance was given in Trinidad, primarily because that would have had major negative effects on revenue in the first year of operation, as the experience of other countries shows.

(11) Use of consultants from countries that have a VAT obviously has merit. They bring a significant amount of experience to the task at hand. However, one must take care to understand the background, experiences, and points of view of the consultants. Advisors with experience in a number of countries are usually preferable to those whose experience is limited to one country. VAT advisors whose background is in Customs and Excise, such as in the United Kingdom, will have a different approach from those whose background is in Inland Revenue, such as in New Zealand.

(12) There are a number of issues that must be resolved, many of which often escape attention when the tax is first considered. For example:

- Are hotel service charges to be included in the taxable charge for hotels?
- How are transient rentals, usually taxed, to be delineated from permanent housing, which is usually not taxed?
- What sort of invoices must retailers give to registered customers, showing tax paid? These must not be too complex, as many taxable purchases by registered firms will be small in amount.
- If fertilizer and seed are to be exempt for farm use, how about small packages sold primarily at retail for nonfarm use? Attempts to make the latter taxable in Trinidad were not successful for operational reasons.
- Are trade-in allowances to be deductible from the taxable price? If not, are the subsequent sales of goods taken in as trade-ins to be taxable?
- Are sales of second-hand goods to be taxable?

- What is the appropriate treatment of construction of real property for business purposes? How should residential construction be treated?

(13) *Implementation schedule.* An initial study of the tax structure and operation, computer facilities, and so on, will require about 6 months. Then, a further 6 months are needed from the completion of this study until basic decisions on tax reform are made, and at least another 6 months until implementation. Thus, 18 months from the start is a minimum time; two years is more realistic. Once these decisions are made, several aspects require careful planning and scheduling:

Legislation. Early enactment of the new act is necessary. Plans should be made early for regulations and for instructional booklets. Use can be made of other acts but adapted to circumstances in the country.

Staffing. If a new tax such as a VAT is to be introduced, it is important to acquire staff immediately, particularly a suitable director of the new tax, which typically should be located in Inland Revenue.

Training. One possibility is to send for two months two key officials to a country using a VAT to become well acquainted with the tax and its operation. New Zealand is one of the best, from this aspect; Ireland is another, and Canada once its goods and services tax is in operation for a time. These officials will then direct the training of others when they return. The alternative is to bring a person familiar with the VAT from another country to direct the training. Obviously, this person must be selected with great care.

Public information. Publicity for the new tax must be developed early in the process and made widely available. In this field, both New Zealand and Trinidad have done very well. Both the public and the taxpaying firms need to be instructed about the new tax.

Computer systems. The development of a new computer system is a major effort and can be a lengthy process in itself. It includes analysis of requirements, system design, hardware and software procurement (often done through competitive bidding), software development testing, installation, documentation, and training, and each step can give rise to substantial delays. In Trinidad, the use of advanced software and the temptation to be too ambitious in the initial design resulted in a delay in delivering a fully operational computer system prior to the effective date of the VAT. However, the use of modern data base management software allowed the flexibility to develop isolated applications to address the major needs of the VAT administration, particularly in carrying out the important function of taxpayer registration on a timely basis.

ANNEX I
Overview of the Trinidad and Tobago Indirect Tax Model

Trinidad and Tobago's indirect tax model was designed to estimate the revenue yield and distributional impact of alternative structures of indirect taxation. The model treats the indirect taxes as a complete system and explicitly takes into account the interaction between each of the taxes. Import duties, for example, are included in the base of the purchase tax; therefore, if import duties are increased, the base on which the purchase tax is levied is also increased.

Data Base Construction

A primary focus of the model was to calculate the potential yield from a broad-based VAT. Therefore, substantial effort was devoted to developing a data base detailed enough to estimate the potential revenue yield from alternative rate and exemption policies under the proposed VAT.

The data base was constructed from a variety of sources that included national income and product accounts; surveys of business establishments; import and export data, by tariff heading; household expenditure data; interindustry flow data; tax collection data; and an economic forecast.

These data were used to construct an integrated data base that captured all the important flows of goods and services throughout the economy. An overview of the data base construction is presented in Figure 1.

Structure of the Model

The model was designed to estimate the effects of alternative policies. These included changes in tax rates; changes in tax base (including the effects of cascading in the system); changes in exemption criteria; and changes in the overall structure of the indirect tax system (for example, single-stage taxes versus VAT).

An overview of the operation of the model is presented in Figure 2. The model uses the detailed economic data to simulate the operation of the entire indirect tax system. Taxes on international trade (that is, import duties, stamp tax, and purchase taxes on imports) are calculated based on the detailed data on the value of imports by tariff heading. The value of dutiable imports is then determined (by accounting for the share of exempt imports) and the statutory tax rates are applied to

Figure 1. Overview of Indirect Tax Data Base Development

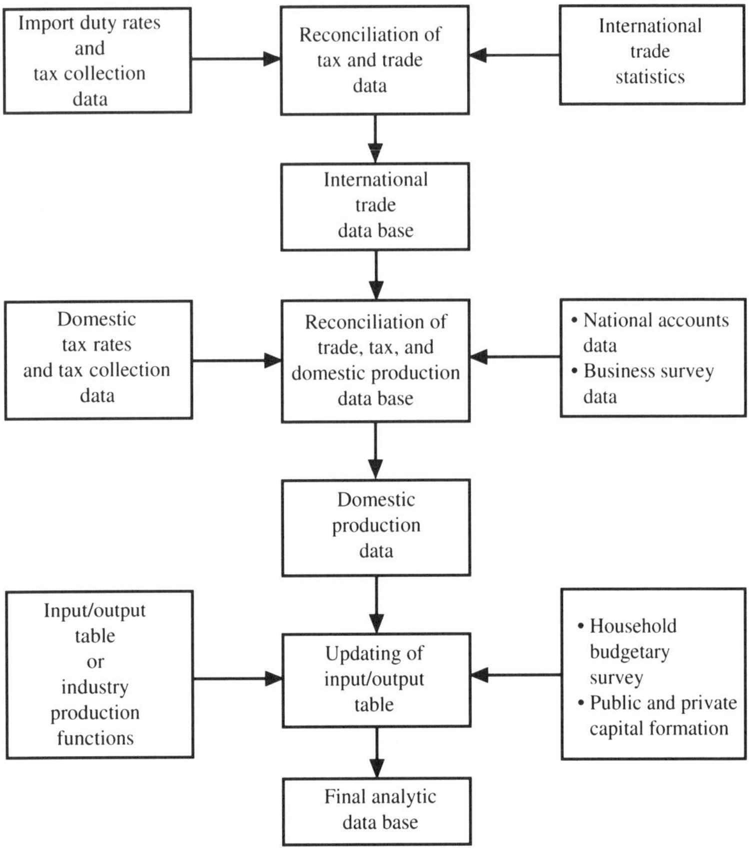

calculate the duty paid. The duty-paid value of imports then forms the base of the other indirect taxes levied on imports, including the VAT.

Domestic indirect taxes (that is, purchase taxes, excise taxes, and other special indirect taxes on domestic production) are calculated based on domestic production data and the implicit tax base of the current system. Essentially the same procedure is used as with imports—the tax base is determined and then the statutory tax rates are applied to calculate taxes paid on domestic production. The tax-inclusive value of domestic production then forms the basis of the taxable value for the VAT.

The modeling of the VAT not only uses import and domestic production data to determine the tax base but also incorporates data on import destinations and interindustry flows to model explicitly the crediting

Figure 2. Overview of the Indirect Tax Model

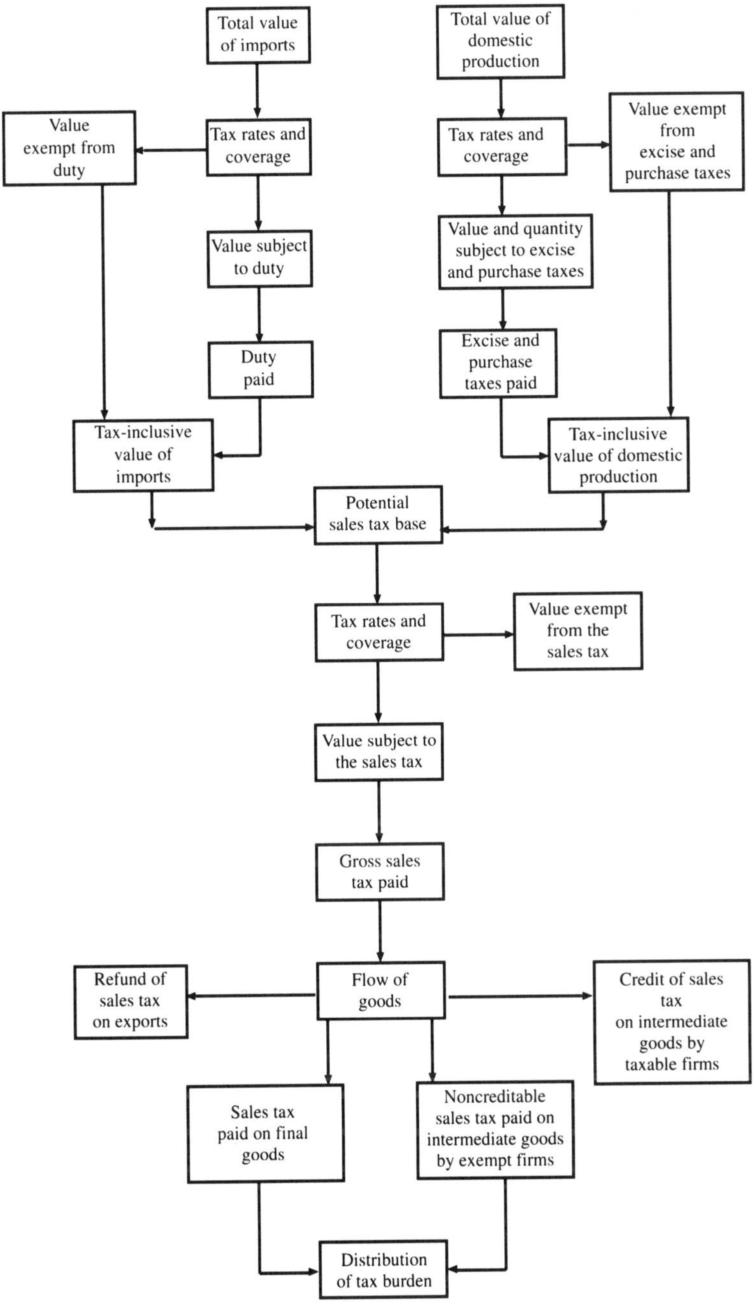

mechanism of the VAT. Parameters specifying the coverage of the VAT are used to determine the base of the VAT. Taxable imports are specified by type of good, and taxable domestic production is specified by subsector. The model applies the statutory VAT rate or rates to the tax bases to calculate the gross VAT paid. It then uses information on the destination of the goods and services to determine how much tax will be credited by taxable firms later in the production and distribution process. The remainder of the tax is either paid directly by consumers or by exempt firms, which will in turn pass the tax along in the form of higher prices.

After calculating the indirect taxes paid on each type of good and service, the model uses information from the household budgetary survey to allocate indirect taxes across income classes according to their patterns of consumption.

Model Results

Each execution of the model calculates the revenue and distributional effects under two alternative scenarios, generally referred to as Plan X and Plan Y. The results of each simulation are presented in a series of output tables. Tables 2 and 3 present two types of output from a simulation of the indirect tax reform program in Trinidad and Tobago. In this simulation, Plan X is current law (pretax reform) and Plan Y is the revised tax reform proposal.

The top part of Table 2 presents the revenue yield of each of the indirect taxes under the two alternative plans, and the dollar and percentage change in revenues between the two. The taxes are grouped into three categories: taxes on international trade, taxes on goods and services, and VAT. The simulation shows the revenue effects of eliminating a number of indirect taxes and introducing a new VAT.

The bottom part of Table 2 shows the distribution of indirect taxes by income classes for the two plans, again including the change in dollars and percent between the two plans.

Table 3 presents a summary of the operation of the proposed VAT by Trinidad and Tobago system of national account (TTSNA) category. Plan X, the prereform law, is presented at the top of the table, and Plan Y, the revised tax reform proposal, at the bottom of the table. The major steps in calculating VAT revenues is summarized in the table:

(1) The first two columns deal with VAT paid on imports. The first column, "VAT on imports" presents the VAT collected on imports originating from the corresponding TTSNA sectors abroad. The second

column, "Credit VAT on imports," presents the amount of VAT collected on imports that is credited when purchased by taxable domestic firms. The credit appears as a negative value in the table and is a loss in revenue remitted to the Government.

(2) The next two columns deal with VAT on domestic sales. The third column, "Calculated domestic VAT," presents the VAT collected on taxable sales by taxable domestic firms. The fourth column, "Credit VAT domestic production," presents the amount of VAT paid on domestic purchases that will be credited by taxable domestic firms. Again, the credit appears as a negative value in the table.

(3) The fifth column, "Refund VAT exports," presents the amount of VAT that will be refunded on exports.

(4) The final column, "Total," contains the total net VAT revenues to the Government.

Table 2. Trinidad and Tobago: Indirect Tax Model

	Revenue Yield of Indirect Taxes			
Type of Indirect Tax	Plan X[1] *(Million TT$)*	Plan Y[2] *(Million TT$)*	Change *(Million TT$)*	Change *(In percent)*
Taxes on international trade				
Import duty	203	203	0	00.0
Stamp duty	173	173	0	00.0
Special consolidated levy	53	0	–53	–100.0
Subtotal	429	376	–53	–12.3
Taxes on goods and services				
Purchase tax (imports)	108	12	–96	–88.7
Purchase tax (local)	338	93	–246	–72.6
Excise taxes (spirits)	42	42	0	0.0
Excise taxes (beer)	37	37	0	0.0
Excise taxes (petroleum)	313	313	0	0.0
Excise taxes (tobacco)	89	61	–28	–31.7
Excise taxes (edible oil and matches)	0	0	0	–100.0
Motor vehicles tax	52	52	0	0.0
Wireless licenses	4	0	–4	–100.0
Electricity tax	12	0	–12	–100.0
Telephone tax	25	0	–25	–100.0
Hotel room tax	1	0	–1	–100.0
Airline ticket tax	14	0	–14	–100.0
Domestic stamp duty	28	28	0	0.0
Miscellaneous taxes	0	0	0	0.0
Subtotal	1,065	638	–426	–40.0

VAT				
Imports	0	425	425	0.0
Domestic	0	441	441	0.0
Subtotal	0	866	866	0.0
Total indirect taxes	1,493	1,880	387	25.9

Distribution of Indirect Taxes

Income Class	Plan X[1] *(Million TT$)*	Plan X[1] *(In percent)*	Plan Y[2] *(Million TT$)*	Plan Y[2] *(In percent)*	Change *(Million TT$)*	Change *(In percent)*
0 < 10,000	107	7.2	136	7.2	28	26.4
10,000 < 20,000	115	7.7	142	7.6	27	23.7
20,000 < 30,000	191	12.8	230	12.2	39	20.4
30,000 < 40,000	184	12.3	231	12.3	46	25.2
40,000 < 50,000	182	12.2	232	12.3	49	27.0
50,000 < 75,000	327	21.9	412	21.9	85	26.1
75,000 < 100,000	179	12.0	227	12.1	48	26.9
100,000 < 200,000	190	12.7	247	13.2	58	30.9
200,000 and above	18	1.2	23	1.2	5	28.2
Total	1,493	100.0	1,880	100.0	387	25.9

Source: Policy Economics Group of KPMG Peat Marwick.
[1]Plan X: Current law; all indirect taxes.
[2]Plan Y: Revised proposal 15 percent VAT; reduced purchase tax on alcohol and tobacco.

Table 3. Trinidad and Tobago: Indirect Tax Model—VAT

(In millions of Trinidad and Tobago dollars)

I. CURRENT LAW; ALL INDIRECT TAXES

TTSNA Category	VAT on Imports	Credit VAT on Imports	Calculated Domestic VAT	Credit VAT Domestic Production	Refund VAT Exports	Total
0 Export agriculture	0	0	0	0	0	0
1 Domestic agriculture	0	0	0	0	0	0
2 Sugar	0	0	0	0	0	0
3 Petroleum	0	0	0	0	0	0
4 Food, drinks, and tobacco	0	0	0	0	0	0
5 Textiles	0	0	0	0	0	0
6 Printing paper	0	0	0	0	0	0
7 Furniture	0	0	0	0	0	0
8 Chemicals	0	0	0	0	0	0
9 Assembly	0	0	0	0	0	0
10 Miscellaneous manufacturing	0	0	0	0	0	0
11 Electricity and water	0	0	0	0	0	0
12 Construction	0	0	0	0	0	0
13 Distribution	0	0	0	0	0	0
14 Hotels	0	0	0	0	0	0
15 Transportation	0	0	0	0	0	0
16 Business and financial services	0	0	0	0	0	0
17 Government	0	0	0	0	0	0
18 Education	0	0	0	0	0	0
19 Personal services	0	0	0	0	0	0
Total	0	0	0	0	0	0

II. REVISED PROPOSAL 15 PERCENT VAT; REDUCED PURCHASE TAX ON ALCOHOL AND TOBACCO

TTSNA Category	VAT on Imports	Credit VAT on Imports	Calculated Domestic VAT	Credit VAT Domestic Production	Refund VAT Exports	Total
0 Export agriculture	0	0	0	0	0	0
1 Domestic agriculture	3	−1	0	0	0	1
2 Sugar	5	−2	98	−30	−16	55
3 Petroleum	67	−41	947	−230	−607	135
4 Food, drinks, and tobacco	27	−2	179	−48	−11	144
5 Textiles	30	−11	30	−4	−3	43
6 Printing paper	29	−11	35	−13	−6	33
7 Furniture	17	−3	6	0	−1	18
8 Chemicals	51	−30	74	−34	−13	48
9 Assembly	143	−93	81	−37	−24	69
10 Miscellaneous	20	−8	16	−9	−3	17
11 Electricity and water	0	0	57	−28	0	29
12 Construction	14	−7	17	−5	0	18
13 Distribution	0	0	81	−38	0	43
14 Hotels	0	0	11	−5	0	6
15 Transportation	0	0	153	−47	0	106
16 Business and financial services	0	0	110	−28	0	82
17 Government	19	0	0	0	0	19
18 Education	0	0	0	0	0	0
19 Personal services	0	0	0	0	0	0
Total	425	−221	1,894	−557	−685	866

Source: Policy Economics Group of KPMG Peat Marwick.

Comments

Michal Y. Christian

The paper presented by John Due and Francis Greaney gives a very accurate account of the introduction of the value-added tax (VAT) regime in Trinidad and Tobago, albeit as seen through the eyes of consultants who were contracted by the Government of Trinidad and Tobago to provide it with the specialized technical expertise and support necessary to implement such a VAT system. Each party to this contract had clearly defined responsibilities—the consultants were required to take the lead in the technical and administrative aspects of the implementation effort and the Government had the responsibility for final approval of all decisions relating to matters of policy, administration, and work output. The Government also had the critical responsibility for supplying the necessary resources, including manpower, materials, and facilities, to enable the timely implementation of the VAT.

I would like to highlight some of the significant practical issues that we, as administrators, had to address during the implementation stages of the VAT, and share with you some of my observations on the paper.

Requirements for a Successful VAT Implementation

During the initial stages of our implementation effort, concerns were expressed as to whether a small country like Trinidad and Tobago could really introduce a VAT system, since this system is viewed as the most sophisticated type of sales tax so far designed. As the paper points out, one of the earlier studies done by the IMF recommended that Trinidad and Tobago adopt a sales tax at the manufacturing level rather than a VAT system. These fears were based mainly on the fact that Trinidad and Tobago had no experience in operating a sales tax, whereas most countries that had successfully implemented a VAT system had previously operated some type of simple sales tax and thus both traders and administrators in these countries were able to assimilate a VAT system more easily. In spite of this lack of experience, Trinidad and Tobago was able to implement, in the view of the experts, a very successful VAT and is able to dispel the perception that without such prior experience, countries ought not to attempt a VAT system.

I am firmly of the view, however, that one of the key factors to the successful implementation of the VAT system in Trinidad and Tobago, and one that is not included in the paper's list of "reasons for the successful introduction of the tax," is that of the strong commitment to the implementation displayed by our Government. This commitment was a genuine one and was not just articulated to satisfy the requirements of an international organization. The Minister of Finance in particular was very dedicated to the project and was also knowledgeable about the system, and this allowed him to resist effectively a great deal of lobbying that took place to extend the range of zero-rated and exempt goods and services. Most countries embarking on a VAT system initially conceive of a well-designed system. However, in my view, it is the ability to withstand the inevitable lobbying that determines the extent to which the system that is finally implemented represents a good VAT system. From an administrator's point of view, the Government's commitment is also of vital importance, since it is needed to ensure that all government agencies that have a role to play in the implementation of the system are made aware of the importance of the tax and the need for their cooperation if the established goals are to be achieved.

In my opinion, one of the more difficult areas in the implementation process was staffing for the VAT Administration Center. Because the Inland Revenue Division of the Ministry of Finance was selected to administer the VAT, the first decision that had to be made was whether a separate category of officers should be created for the VAT administration. Two things militated against this. First, there was the problem of time. Traditionally, it takes a very long time to create a new category of officers in the public service since a number of agencies are associated with this process. For example, it involves the Director of Public Administration, who is responsible for determining job specifications, and the Chief Personnel Officer, who is responsible for determining the pay classification, as well as the terms and conditions of employment. Second, it was felt that a special category of officers would make the VAT Center a closed division and would limit promotional opportunities for staff. Since only 76 technical officers were to be assigned to VAT, this number was considered to be too small to have a closed office. After much deliberation, it was decided to use the same classes of technical officers as were used by Inland Revenue, thereby allowing promotional opportunities for existing officers. However, since technical officers for the Inland Revenue are recruited only at the lower levels, a number of experienced officers from the Inland Revenue Division had to be transferred to the VAT Center to fill middle- and higher-level staff positions. This resulted in severe hardship to the other Inland Revenue sections, given the length of time it takes to train replacements.

Another area of concern for us was the time given to implement the system. It is very important to provide adequate time for implementation in order to ensure that the infrastructure is in place. The paper suggests that at least 18 months are needed for this process, and I certainly agree. As you may know, Trinidad and Tobago implemented its VAT system in only 10 months, and during this relatively short time a great deal of planning had to be done. It certainly was not an easy task, and I would not suggest that you attempt to do likewise since there were a number of areas which, in my view, could have been improved upon if more time was available.

I would like to add another note of caution with regard to the timetable. I would urge you to resist setting a time frame that is too far removed from the present. The adage "work expands to fill the time to do it" is found to be true in this situation, since if too long a time period is allowed, the earlier months are often not used productively and the administrators still end up having to rush to complete the implementation within the time allocated. It should also be noted that, regardless of what length of time is given to prepare for the implementation, when the appointed day approaches some traders will still not be ready. This, in my view, will occur especially where the government is not fully committed to the project and traders, recognizing this, adopt a wait-and-see attitude in the hope that the implementation would be postponed and they would be saved from having to learn the system. My advice therefore would be that, provided the administration is at least 90 percent ready, the implementation should be carried out as planned, because in practical terms it is virtually impossible by the due date to have all aspects of the system in place and to have all traders registered and adequately briefed.

The date chosen for the implementation should also be considered carefully. Like Trinidad and Tobago, many countries have implemented their VAT system from January 1. At first glance this date seems to be a good choice, because it is at the start of the calendar year and any laws that need to be abolished to coincide with the introduction of the VAT can be accommodated in a tidy fashion. However, my experience has been that this date is a bad choice from the trader's point of view. The period from September to December is one of the trader's busiest periods, when he is preparing for the Christmas season and end-of-year sales and during this time he is also required to do most of the preparatory work on VAT to be ready for the appointed day. Thus, he is often either unable or unwilling to devote as much time as is necessary to implement the system properly. I would therefore suggest that the period chosen for the implementation be one that is slow for businessmen since their cooperation is vital to the success of the venture.

Training of VAT Staff

I would now like to mention some specific aspects of the paper. The paper refers to the extensive program that was introduced during March–July 1989 to train personnel in VAT operations. During that time we trained a core team of eight officers in the VAT law on the understanding that they would act as trainers and instruct all the other technical officers who join the VAT administration. Initially, this proved to be a somewhat frustrating exercise, since at that time all that was available was an outline of the proposed VAT law. When the law was finally enacted, a lot of time had to be spent in retraining the officers in those areas of the law that had subsequently changed.

I would therefore advise that it is critical to enact the VAT legislation early in the schedule. So many things hinge on this that if the law is delayed it can seriously jeopardize the implementation date. Apart from the training aspect, unless the law is in place a full-fledged publicity campaign cannot be begun, nor can the prescribed forms required for the system be designed and published since, more often than not, relevant sections of the law will be quoted on the forms.

We received advice from our New Zealand counterparts on another aspect of training. They suggested that we learn from their mistakes and commence our VAT audits as early as possible. Their audit program was not begun until the year after the implementation date and in the interim they discovered that a number of fraudulent practices had occurred. Bearing this in mind, we hurried to start our audits three months after the implementation date, but because our auditors had initially been conducting advisory visits to registrants we did not have enough time available to train them properly in conducting VAT audits. This lack of adequate training manifested itself in the results of the early audits, which were conducted with minimal effectiveness. We are only now in the process of continuing this training, some 15 months later.

The paper further suggests that to obtain the expertise for a VAT system "one possibility is to send for two months two key officials to a country using a VAT system to become well acquainted with the tax and its operation." It further suggests that "the alternative is to bring a person familiar with the VAT from another country to direct the training." I would like to suggest, however, that as a prerequisite to either of these alternatives, key personnel should be exposed in a formal classroom setting not only to the theory and classical operations of a VAT system but also to the variations employed in different countries.

It should be noted that adjustments to a country's VAT law may be a direct result of influential lobbying, and the systems and operations of the VAT may be tailored to accommodate these representations. When examined closely, the particular operations employed in that country may thus in fact have little, if any, relevance to your own country.

The danger, in my view, of the paper's suggestion is that, without some general background, the persons selected for training may be inclined to adopt wholesale the systems to which they have been exposed. If, on the other hand, these persons had attained a wider knowledge of VAT systems they would be in a better position to understand fully the background, experiences, and points of view of any foreign consultants and thus be able to examine their proposals constructively and ensure that the consultants deliver what is appropriate for the country introducing the VAT system.

A point which I would like to share with you and which is not mentioned in the paper, but from which we benefited a great deal, is that it may be worthwhile to also visit a country whose VAT system, to all intents and purposes, was not successfully implemented. Such a country may have experiences to share and might give insights into what mistakes should be avoided.

Treatment of Stocks on Hand at VAT Introduction Date

I would now like to highlight some of the practical legal issues of the VAT system that administrators also have to deal with.

Most countries, prior to the introduction of a VAT system, have in place some type of indirect tax that will be eliminated with the introduction of VAT such as the purchase tax in Trinidad and the manufacturers tax in Canada. These taxes are usually imposed at a multiplicity of different rates on various commodities. One of the major decisions that will face policymakers and administrators during the design of the VAT system is whether to give some kind of relief to traders who, on the commencement of the VAT system, have stocks on hand that have borne the existing tax. Most countries agree with the very valid arguments cited by traders, that to give no relief for such stocks would mean that on the implementation of the VAT these stocks will bear tax twice and the prices of goods will have to increase. To address this issue some countries introduce complex mechanisms to allow traders to credit against VAT payments the amount of the previous tax that is contained in the stocks on hand. In my opinion, such a system has endless opportunities for abuse and, since purchase-tax-type taxes are cascading in nature, it is also very difficult to determine precisely what percentage of the final purchase price of the goods relates to these taxes.

Trinidad and Tobago did not succumb to this type of pressure, principally because we benefited from the experiences of one of our Caribbean neighbors which had gone that route and paid dearly for it, in that for the first six months of the implementation of their VAT, the country received very little revenue and, as a result, had to keep modifying its VAT system to the point where today it bears little resemblance to a classical VAT system. Another factor that diverted us from this route was that, because of some deficiencies in our purchase tax law, arrears had accumulated and thus it was not considered prudent to give credit for taxes which we were not sure we had collected.

The strategy used by Trinidad and Tobago to avoid having to give such credits was to establish very early that there would be no refunds for purchase taxes previously paid and to advise traders to run down their stocks at the end of the year so that they could take advantage of the lower VAT rate on implementation. Experience also shows that where a substantial change occurs in a tax system, such as the introduction of a VAT system, traders take the opportunity to raise their prices and, thus, in such a scenario credit may be given to the trader with no real benefit accruing to the consumer. It was also felt that, at worst, any increases would be short term and, at best, the market forces and aggressive competition would prevent excessive increases. As far as we are aware, this strategy worked, and, in a report published by the Central Bank of Trinidad and Tobago, it was reported that the increase in the consumer price index attributable to VAT was only 4 percent during January–March 1990. In light of our experiences, I would therefore strongly recommend that, especially in a small economy, one should avoid giving relief for stocks on hand which previously bore purchase-tax-type taxes.

How VAT Should Be Indicated

An issue on which I entirely agree with the paper is the question of how firms should indicate the tax to final consumers. I am of the view that the tax-inclusive approach is simpler and is the better system. Under our VAT law, a trader has a choice and may show either VAT-inclusive prices or VAT-exclusive prices. In such a scenario, the element of VAT is always an issue. Every time someone goes to buy an item where the VAT is not included in the price but is added at the cash register, it is a source of annoyance and the issue of the VAT is brought to the fore on each such occasion. Contrast this for example with the United Kingdom where all prices are quoted VAT-inclusive, so although one is aware that there is a VAT, which incidentally was recently raised to 17½ percent, it is not an issue in the final price.

Level of VAT Rate

Another important question is the choice of a rate for the VAT. The paper lists this as number one in the suggestions relating to the introduction of a VAT and states that, if at all possible, the rate should be kept down to 10 percent when the tax is introduced. This is a very valid recommendation. Trinidad was not able to do this because of revenue considerations since its whole reform package was designed to be tax-neutral and was predicated on a shift from direct taxation to indirect taxation. The first part of the tax reform exercise was implemented in 1989 and involved substantial reductions to the income and corporation tax rates. The second part dealt with the introduction of the VAT in 1990. When the VAT was in the design stage, the consultants had originally proposed an 18 percent VAT to compensate for the reduction in direct taxes and the elimination of certain indirect impositions, but word of this high rate caused such a hue and cry from the population that policymakers were forced to re-examine the rate. Taking into consideration that revenue had already been forgone with the reforms on the direct tax side, the lowest rate that could have been sustained was that of 15 percent. On hindsight, however, I would recommend that, where VAT is to be introduced as part of a package, the VAT rate should be decided on first and any other reforms adjusted to accommodate a relatively low rate of, say, 10 percent. Experience will show that taxpayers soon forget the benefits they received from a reduction in income and other taxes, but they constantly have to face the rate of VAT set, and when this is too high it becomes a source of contention and inhibits general acceptance of the VAT system.

Other Implementation Issues

Further to the paper's point on our bimonthly filing of VAT returns, our computer system was designed to allocate registrants randomly to alternate periods. If one is contemplating a similar system, care should be taken to ensure that registrants who make significant contributions to the VAT revenues are not all placed in the same reporting category as this could result in an imbalance of revenue flows.

There is also sound merit, as the paper suggests, in creating a different name for the tax. A new name affords you the opportunity not only to distance yourself from any adverse connotations that the name VAT may carry, but also to create the perception that this tax is unique to your country. Reference is made to the goods and services tax of Canada and New Zealand and the proposed general consumption tax of Jamaica. Since Trinidad and Tobago had already been using the term "VAT," it was decided that there would be no advantage in changing the name at the implementation stage.

Problems Outstanding

The paper points out that our nonfiling or delinquency rate remains relatively high. Several factors contributed to this situation initially and we are only now in a position to correct them effectively.

The noncompletion of the design of our computer system has not only seriously hampered most of our operations but also has had dire effects on our enforcement procedures. A number of manual checking systems had to be introduced to counteract these deficiencies, but, as expected, these were a lot slower and thus the monitoring function was not as efficient as it should have been.

Further, because most of the offenses under our law, such as failure to file a VAT return, had to be prosecuted through the Magistrates Court, this was a lengthy procedure and we have only recently been able to obtain some judgments against persons who failed to file their returns on time. As a result of the latest amendment to the VAT Act (Finance Act, 1991), however, the Board is now able to impose administrative penalties for some of these offenses. It is anticipated that this measure will go a long way in lowering the delinquency rate since monetary penalties can now be imposed automatically for these offenses.

Conclusion

Finally, I would like to give a word of encouragement to those countries who are at present in the throes of implementation and are getting the full brunt of bad press and public outcry. The experience has been, in a number of countries such as New Zealand and more recently in Canada, that once the system is implemented the majority of these criticisms quickly subside. We have a local saying in Trinidad which is applicable to this situation; we say, "it boils down like *badji*." (*Badji*, otherwise known as spinach, is a green leafy vegetable which, in its raw state, is very bulky but during the cooking process shrinks considerably.) This was also our experience, and, provided that certain key elements of your legislation are perceived to be acceptable, I am sure that this will be your experience as well, and after implementation you can quickly get down to the serious business of administering the system.

In this regard, I would like to extend our cooperation and goodwill to any country that may wish to avail itself of the knowledge and experience gained by Trinidad and Tobago in the implementation of its VAT system.

Alberto H. J. Radano

According to the paper by Due and Greaney:

- Total indirect taxes accounted for about 32 percent of tax revenues in Trinidad and Tobago.
- About 600 manufacturers paid purchase tax; the Customs and Special Taxes Department was responsible for administering and auditing it.
- Oil and its derivatives accounted for two thirds of total revenues from excises.
- While oil was a substantial source of revenue, scant interest was shown in reforming the indirect tax structure; as world oil prices declined, the Government turned its attention to introducing a general sales tax.

Background

Several studies were conducted for introducing a broad-based sales tax. In fact, the Prime Minister and Minister of Finance had already referred to that tax in his presentation of the 1983 budget and the IMF referred to the same tax in a report dated May 1983.

In 1986 a committee chaired by Mrs. Michal Christian was established to prepare a reform plan that would include a general retail sales tax. The committee concluded that the tax rates would have to be very high to generate revenues equal to that obtained from the purchase tax, a fact that made its introduction hardly feasible.

In 1988 members of the business community brought a representative of Price Waterhouse & Co. to Trinidad and Tobago. Following a meeting attended by him and representatives of the private and public sectors, a report was drafted on the adoption of a value-added tax, specifying that the business community was in favor of introducing such a tax.

Development

The groundwork for the tax reform was launched in 1988 and involved three stages: (1) Review of the current tax system and preliminary recommendations for reforming it; (2) the development of analytical models for assessing the changes to be introduced in the tax system; and (3) recommendations for a comprehensive reform program.

The basic proposal for change involved the introduction of a general sales tax, using the value-added method. The tax would apply to activities generating an annual turnover of over US$12,500 (the amount was ultimately set at US$30,000) and would have a single rate.

The name finally given to the tax was "value-added tax" (VAT). The responsibility for monitoring it was assigned to the VAT Administration Office within the Department of Inland Revenue, which has three local offices located in the country's major cities (Port of Spain, San Fernando, and Tobago).

A detailed work plan was prepared. This included an intensive information campaign. The law, which came into force on January 1, 1990, requires that returns be filed and payments made bimonthly.

Results

During the first year in which the new tax was levied, the results were generally positive. Revenues for the first six months were equal to the estimates made. As of December 1990, 9,688 enterprises had registered. On the other hand, 24 percent of registered taxpayers failed to file returns. Perhaps the main shortcoming was the failure of the computer system to carry out all the desired operations. The audit program was also inadequate.

Conclusions

While it is extremely difficult to analyze a country's tax reform experience without visiting the country and witnessing the prevailing situation, a few comments can nevertheless be made.

According to the paper, all measures usually suggested were taken to introduce the VAT. Thus, the experience of other countries was assessed. International consultants were recruited who have contributed experience gained in countries in which they had worked. Exhaustive studies were carried out regarding the methodology to be applied. Computerized microsimulation models were applied to study the impact of alternative tax policies on collection and income distribution. The situations of specific economic sectors and activities were studied. Finally, detailed programs were launched to publicize the new tax.

A single rate (15 percent) was adopted, which simplifies administration of the tax. Tax administration was entrusted to the VAT Administration Office which, although a separate unit, is part of the Department of Inland Revenue. This decision appears to be more reasonable than assigning such responsibility to the Customs and Excise Department.

The failure of the computer system to carry out all the desired operations is a source of concern. Efforts should be stepped up to identify the causes of this failure and to make the necessary corrections or to change the design of the system for monitoring filing and payment requirements. It would appear that the number of enterprises registered is sufficiently low to permit the use of methods similar to those applied in some other countries (for example, Argentina, Bolivia, and Uruguay) for monitoring compliance with filing and payment requirements by large taxpayers.

The establishment of inspection offices that could each handle 5,000 taxpayers, receiving and checking information from returns and payments in real time, would make it possible to know which taxpayers were delinquent the day after every deadline. This option should be studied by the tax authorities of Trinidad and Tobago.

The alternative "plans" for a simplified accounting method for the VAT stem from the British VAT. They are complicated and unnecessary, and illustrate how care must be taken when incorporating technical features from other countries in which they may operate smoothly, only to lose their effectiveness when transferred to countries where they are inappropriate.

The decision that returns should be submitted on a bimonthly basis may benefit the tax authorities because it halves the work load involved in receiving and processing returns and payments. It may, however, also result in financial problems, particularly in the event of high rates of inflation. The widespread trend in CIAT countries is to collect indirect taxes in the month following that in which the taxable transaction takes place.

The option given to enterprises selling to unregistered persons of itemizing the tax on sales slips or of including it in the price is not recommended. Ideally, there should be a single method so as to avoid confusion that might encourage tax evasion.

6

Information Technology: Strategy of the Spanish Tax Administration

Rafael Moya and José-Damián Santiago

This paper analyzes the role that information technologies play in the Spanish tax administration and the role that we expect them to play in the future.

In the paper we highlight the impact that electronic data processing (EDP) has had on the Spanish tax administration. Without this technology, it would not have been possible to manage efficiently a generalized tax system such as that of Spain, with 10 million income tax returns to process. It is also one of the pillars on which the Spanish tax administration has based its strategy to offer taxpayers the best possible service.

It cannot be claimed that the EDP system introduced by the Spanish tax administration is the best option available. Before the final selection, several systems were evaluated. But the Spanish authorities believe that the system chosen has yielded positive results. However, there will always be some doubt as to whether a different system might not have achieved better results.

Considerable caution must be exercised when evaluating the transferability of the Spanish system to other administrations. In particular, the existing telecommunications technology and the computer skills of employees have to be taken into account. It is all too easy to succumb to the temptation (and computer applications for tax administration are no exception) of thinking that what is appropriate for one country will apply equally to another. In fact, Spain's experience can only be valid for other countries to the extent that it can help better evaluate the various options available; the choice has to be the country's alone, and adapted to its particular circumstances.

I. Overview

The Scope of Tax Administration

Until the new Government Agency for Tax Administration, created under Article 103 of the 1991 Budget Act, becomes operational, the

Secretariat General of Finance, an agency of the Ministry of Economy and Finance will continue to be responsible for tax administration. The functions of the Secretariat General are the usual ones of a tax department, including, however, responsibility for both internal taxes and customs duties.

The Government Agency for Tax Administration will have considerable autonomy and a variety of responsibilities. Apart from the functions previously performed by the Secretariat General, the Agency's responsibilities will include preparation and management of its budget, management of its acquired property, staff recruitment, and centralized accounting for the government taxes administered by it.

Tax Data Processing

Single Unit Responsible

The Spanish tax administration has opted for a single data processing organization, in the form of a separate Directorate General within the Secretariat General of Finance, as opposed to other possibilities, such as each functional directorate having its own data processing. It is not clear which of these two options is preferable. The option Spain selected has led to a certain amount of competition between the user directorates and the EDP Directorate. This tends to keep the systems operating smoothly—since some officials develop them and others use them, there is no advantage to concealing errors. Experience has shown that errors are frequently concealed when it is the same unit that develops and uses a computer application. The option chosen, however, requires considerable cooperation between the users and the teams that develop the technology.

Before the selection was made in 1983, the Secretary of State for Finance was frequently called upon to arbitrate among the various alternatives. Under the option chosen, there is considerable transparency between the users and those in charge of EDP. The advantages of this transparency outweigh the higher cost of the coordination that is required. A good example of this transparency is the DEFENSOR application, which is available to all users from any part of the central and peripheral tax administrations. Through DEFENSOR, users can voice their complaints or offer suggestions on EDP applications. The Directorate General of Tax Data Processing has agreed to respond to queries within a maximum of seven days. The main advantage of DEFENSOR is that, since all issues raised get registered, the senior officials of the organization can find out at any time the degree of satisfaction of users with their EDP systems, as well as any deficiencies. This application is, in fact, an additional user safeguard, offered by those in charge of EDP. This type of transparency is possible only when there is clear separation between those who use the applications and those who develop them.

Processing and storage capacity is available at the central office and at the 56 provincial centers. The other offices have peripherals, terminals, and printers, which provide access to the central processing units. Development and maintenance of software is centralized at the main office of the Directorate General of Tax Data Processing, from where the software is distributed to the 56 provincial processing centers.

Resources

The emphasis that the Spanish tax administration has placed in recent years on information technologies is self-evident. Between 1983 and 1991, processing speed rose from 36 MIPS to 291 MIPS, central memory from 67 MB to 2,110 MB, and the number of terminals from 663 to 9,600.

All the hardware available is compatible, which means it is not dependent on any one manufacturer or supplier. The hardware is acquired from the supplier that makes the best offer, and no purchase from any single supplier is allowed to exceed 25 percent of the EDP Directorate's budget.

The basic software used is the most standardized one on the market and for which products and compatible packages are available from other manufacturers. This means that there are a broad range of options from which to choose. The data base software is of the "relational" type, as this is best suited to our needs. Increasingly, we are using more powerful languages and "CASE" tools. Even though these require more resources, it is justified because they enhance our productivity.

The Data Network

The EDP system is a single, integrated system linked by a private teleprocessing network. This makes all applications and all data bases accessible from any tax office. The data network is the most valuable part of the system. It helps us to overcome time and space constraints in our operations with regard to the data available.

Even though much remains to be done, the technological level of telecommunications in Spain has made the integrated system a viable solution. It is obvious that if this kind of integration had not been feasible, another solution would have had to be envisaged. Telecommunications has enabled us to make better and more intensive use of the hardware and software capabilities we have. As Table 1 shows, the data network has 370 point-to-point lines, radiating from the main office to the provincial centers and from these to the administrations and customs.

Applications Software

The software systems used and their main functions are as follows:

- New tax management procedure (NPGT), for management.
- National data base (BDN), for inspection.
- National collection system (SIRENA), for collections.
- Mechanized customs management (GEMA), for customs.
- Regional administrative economic tribunals (TEAR), for the appeals function.

NPGT

The NPGT is the basic component of Spanish tax data processing, which brought about a new era in tax administration. It is a decentralized

Table 1. Spain: Data Network

	1983	1988	1991
Number of teleprocessing lines			
Management centers	0	9	20
Provincial centers	11	56	56
Administrations	0	201	204
Customs	0	0	62
Other	0	9	28
Total	11	275	370
Network traffic			
(Millions of characters a day)			
Electronic mail		0	40
National data base		60	300
Files		0	100
Provincial data bases		1,380	2,800
Total		1,440	3,240

system, that is, it resides in the 56 provincial centers. The four most important parts of the NPGT are (1) the tax register; (2) self-assessments; (3) annual returns; and (4) notices.

The purpose of the *tax register* is to identify taxpayers by their fiscal identification number (NIF). The register also shows the tax due by each taxpayer, according to his self-assessed return. At present, there are 722,580 registered taxpayers with the obligation to withhold income taxes on wages and salaries, 2,418,811 enterprises required to make estimated (advance) income tax payments, and 1,831,515 VAT taxpayers.

The purpose of the *self-assessment* part is to register payments made by taxpayers, usually quarter by quarter. The aim is to control fully these operations, as well as to have participating financial entities collaborate in the process. Taxpayers must submit their returns to a participating financial entity and the entity, in turn, must record the following four data: (1) the NIF, verifiable with a check digit, through which the taxpayer is identified; (2) the number of the return form, verifiable through a control character, through which the item under which the payment is made is identified; (3) the date, which identifies the payment period; and (4) the amount being paid, checkable against the corresponding amount declared. The corresponding magnetic files are processed by the provincial centers. In 1990, 39,109,165 self-assessments were processed.

The main purpose of the *annual returns* is to process the summary returns submitted by taxpayers once a year, which include the data from self-assessments filed during the year, together with any withholding to which the taxpayer has been subjected. The envelope used to file the annual form should also contain a copy of all self-assessment returns submitted during the year, kept until that time by the taxpayer himself.

The number of annual returns submitted in 1990 was 10 million for individual income tax; 900,000 for net wealth tax; 350,000 for companies; 720,000 reports by income tax withholders; 950,000 for third party transactions; and almost 2 million for VAT.

The constitutional requirement that the individual income tax be progressive and that it also take due account of numerous personal circumstances means that all income earners, above a given amount, have to file a return, even though their income, whether from work or from capital, is subject to prior withholding. It cannot be claimed that the Spanish option is the best compared with other possible options, such as where wage or salary earners do not have to file a return. But the solution adopted in Spain arises out of this constitutional requirement.

The final part of the NPGT is *notices*, the purpose of which is to get in touch with any taxpayer failing to meet an obligation. The notices cover such items as incomplete returns, requests for further information, full notices (in which all self-assessments that have not been submitted for any tax and for any period are demanded), and notices for annual returns, sent out when the taxpayer declares self-assessments or has been submitted to withholding but fails to submit a return.

BDN

The BDN is used mainly, although not solely, for audit purposes. It is a centralized system accessible on-line from any point in the network. The three original parts of the BDN are (1) identification; (2) information; and (3) preselection of taxpayers.

The purpose of the *identification* part is to identify the taxpayer, so that he can be matched with information about his activities. The system is very powerful and can identify a taxpayer even from incomplete or erroneous data. So far, about 21 million individuals and 1.5 million legal entities have been identified.

The purpose of the *information* part is to consolidate all the data received by the tax administration, both from returns filed by taxpayers and from third parties. The total amount of data stored in the BDN is 1.25 billion. These data are used to support the auditing services in their dealings with taxpayers.

Taxpayer preselection assists auditors in selecting taxpayers to be audited. The best results have been achieved through information matching, which makes it possible to compare what taxpayers report with third party information. The most recent step taken in this area is to align the cross-references with the data bases and with the continuous updating of data in the CLASE system, which is discussed later.

SIRENA and GEMA

SIRENA and GEMA are the systems used for managing collections and customs, respectively. These are two decentralized systems located in the provincial centers. At present, their full integration into the NPGT data base is under way.

SIRENA has a very broad range, mainly covering assessments made by the tax authority, payments of settlements by taxpayers, compulsory payments, injunctions, compensations, and deferments. So far, 2,861,078 assessments have been incorporated into SIRENA, not all related to taxes administered by the Secretariat General of Finance, since this organization also collects arrears for some other agencies and certain nontax assessments.

GEMA annually handles more than 65 million import and export declarations. Foreign trade transactions are highly concentrated in a few enterprises and a few customs points. For large enterprises, factory customs clearances are permitted. These enterprises submit their returns once a month on magnetic tape.

TEAR

The TEAR system is independent of the rest because it deals with appeals. Of the four phases of administrative economic tribunals, TEAR deals with three: initiation; preparation of the proceedings file; and enforcement of the decision. It also helps in the decision phase. In this last phase, judgments are automatically generated for cases in which identical appeals are submitted, which has led to a considerable increase in the productivity of the tribunals. There are currently 177,684 outstanding appeals in the system.

Monitoring of Large Enterprises

The data processing system of the Spanish tax administration is common to all taxes and to all taxpayers. However, for the largest enterprises, there is an additional application, known as ONI. Because of their tax significance (in 1990, 4.28 percent of self-assessments generated 87.25 percent of tax collections), these enterprises are subject to more immediate and detailed monitoring, in addition to being subject to the same data processing procedures as other taxpayers.

The additional monitoring of large enterprises consists of having their monthly (for other taxpayers, quarterly) self-assessments processed with all the details of the assessment month to month. For other taxpayers, only the four items that the participating financial entities record for all self-assessments, as previously discussed, are processed.

It is not that there are two separate systems, one for large enterprises and the other for the rest, but that for the former the common system is used with the addition of continuous detailed verification. The two systems are complementary—the system for large enterprises acts as an effective barometer for the whole economy, thereby ensuring some guarantee of collections, whereas the general process applies to the entire system and prevents any given sector of taxpayers from transferring the tax burden to the rest.

II. Information Technologies and Management of Tax Administration

Position of Management

Over the past nine years, the Spanish tax administration's management has had a clear and unwavering position in favor of the use of information technologies, a position that has not only been reflected in the budgetary appropriations for investment in EDP and communications but also in the decision to use them intensively. Management has also consistently borne in mind the difference between building and maintaining a basic information structure, on the one hand, and ephemeral and sometimes showy computer applications, on the other.

If management had not adopted this position, the present configuration of hardware and software would not have been possible, because, when short-term considerations prevail over medium-term and long-term considerations, one has to start anew continually without producing any practical results.

The support of management in the use of information technologies in the Spanish tax administration has not been purely passive. Its active support was critical when the systems were being established, which is when users tend to be most negative, because the cost to them is greatest, often more than the cost of continuing to use the old ways. It is obvious that during this phase, which is when applications have the most teething problems, the support of management is crucial.

At present, management's support is still necessary because, while it is less difficult to break the inertia, expectations are also higher. This is what is called "the paradox of success," in that the more successful you are, the higher are the targets set for you.

The use of information technologies in management has varied in parallel with the development of new applications. Their use by various managers has also differed, since all managers are not uniformly enthusiastic about computerization. Appropriate action needs to be taken to promote the use of these technologies. This is one of the challenges currently facing tax data processing, and there is little sign of any major successes on the immediate horizon.

Among the various applications available to the tax administration management, we will mention here INFO, PANINFO, and the monitoring of collection targets. Later, we will comment on other data processing support that are also available.

INFO

INFO (information for management) was established in the NPGT environment as a basis for decision taking and has been extended to all other areas. At present all applications, from their first phase, are included in INFO.

INFO records and makes available to users on-line statistics on data processing applications and the results of such use. This statistical information is very valuable for management decisions and tax data processing itself, since it is, among other things, an authentic measure of the acceptance or rejection of the applications.

The data derived from INFO are tantamount to a constantly updated balance sheet of the tax administration. INFO provides detailed information of the type desired, such as functional (collection, audit, and so on), geographical (such as provincial and administration), or the kind of tax (income, VAT, companies, and so on).

When the INFO application was started within the NPGT, the statistics were updated monthly, and gradually replaced the manual reports that lower-level units send to management centers. At present, updating is daily, in many cases even instantaneous; when an operation takes place, it is "posted." The information from decentralized INFOs is incorporated into the national INFO both to facilitate comparison between the various territorial entities and to have aggregate magnitudes available.

INFO has been widely accepted, but there is still some reluctance. In some cases there is overlapping with the manual operations that still remain, mainly because of the considerable inertia that exists in such a vast organization as the Spanish tax administration.

Apart from original data, INFO also offers derived data, that is, information appropriately analyzed so as to make it more useful. One example of the type of statistics that INFO provides is the taxpayer census, which gives details at the national, regional, provincial, and administration levels on the taxpayers registered, their tax obligations, their description, their distribution by economic sector, and their VAT regimes.

PANINFO

The volume of data collected by INFO from the NPGT is such that even the smallest details of the activity of the tax administration can be analyzed. However, at times, this vast amount of data makes it difficult to see the overall picture. In other words, there is a surfeit of data in INFO, so that for analytical purposes it becomes necessary to complement it with PANINFO.

The PANINFO application provides for the present and past fiscal years (for the future, the time series will be expanded) aggregated and analyzed INFO data. This facilitates an overall picture of the action of the tax administration, as a prior step to detailed analysis via INFO. PANINFO groups this information in three major segments: (1) statistics on taxpayers, self-assessments, and annual returns; (2) statistics on the effects of tax notices, proceedings, and injunctions for returns; and (3) statistics on the use of information tools.

The PANINFO application has its decentralized as well as its centralized version, incorporating day-to-day data by teleprocessing from the provincial centers to the central office of the Directorate General of Tax Data Processing.

Collection Targets

The purpose of this application is to monitor compliance with collection targets throughout the budget year, according to the selected breakdown. That is, this application makes it possible to establish the targets, adjust them as and when needed, and supply detailed on-line information.

The decentralized application has four subsystems: the establishment of targets, adjustment, confirmation, and consultation.

Targets can be established for the current year and for the following year. Collections for any of the two preceding years can be used as the basis. To establish a target, the reference year first has to be selected and the total figure given for that year. The application allows one to carry out the distribution by budget item automatically, on the basis of the distribution for the reference year, or to do it separately. If the automatic option is chosen, the budget target is distributed according to the distribution of collections for the reference year by item, for the various models of returns, and by month. The data for the established target are presented together with the information on effective collections for the two preceding years, the index of change between them, and the index of change in the target from the reference year. If the nonautomatic option is chosen, the distribution of budget targets can be done in one of three ways: indicating the corresponding amounts item by item; indicating the percentage weight of each item within the total target; or indicating the coefficient of change under each item from the reference year.

Once the target has been set, it can be adjusted as desired. The application makes it possible to do this item by item or month by month.

The system enables the user to select any of three options: to change the total amount of the target in keeping with performance; to keep to the previous target, automatically redistributing the difference between the rest of the items in keeping with their weight within the total; or to keep to the target, redistributing the difference between selected items. The function for making the adjustment by months is similar to the one just described.

With the combination of options for setting targets and adjusting them, any simulations considered necessary can be performed, not just at the start of the fiscal year but throughout. The possibility of having up to three targets defined produces more detailed monitoring.

At headquarters, targets can also be set and adjusted using the same methodology as at the provincial centers. Distributions and adjustments can be performed by territorial level, an option that makes it possible not only to monitor collection targets as the sum of peripheral targets but also as a national target distributed among the territorial entities.

III. Information Technologies and the Administrative Strategy

Public Service and Effectiveness

The ultimate objective of the Spanish tax administration is to implement the tax system effectively, to fulfill the constitutional requirement that all citizens bear the burden of public expenditure according to their economic ability.

Within this general framework, the Spanish tax administration's strategy is based on the notions of public service and effective implementation of the tax system. This involves a series of actions aimed at reducing tax evasion to a minimum, taking into account the following considerations:

- Respect for the privacy of taxpayers, in terms of both confidentiality of the information the administration obtains from them and in the procedures employed.
- The point of reference in the daily work of the tax administration should be the taxpayer and not the organization itself, especially regarding the amount of time the taxpayer spends in his dealings with the Secretariat General of Finance, which should be kept to a minimum.
- Relations between taxpayers and the administration should be as incident-free as possible.

- The reliability of these relations should be increased by ensuring that the taxpayer gets the same answer from the tax administration, regardless of the place or the official dealing with his affairs.
- Reduction of the administrative burden, especially for those taxpayers who produce correct returns, by an efficient selection of taxpayers to be audited.
- Rigor and effectiveness vis-à-vis tax evaders.

Confidentiality of Information and Proceedings

To fulfill its mandate, the tax administration needs resources, of which information on taxpayers is one of the most important. The Spanish legal system regulates what information the tax administration can have and also stipulates that it can only be used in the administration of taxes.

Tax data processing guarantees what is stated in the law through its security systems for data storage and access thereto. Thus, for example, for on-line access, security is extensive. First, the system has to recognize the terminal from which access is being sought, that is, it has to be identified in advance. Second, the user has to be identified. And, third, the user has to use a code word, which only he knows and can change when he wishes. Only after these steps can the user gain access to the level of information he is authorized to access, which guarantees that the information will only be reached by the rightful user.

Apart from these ex ante controls, there are also ex post controls. The system records all accessing, who enters the system, where from, when, whom he consults, as well as the reason or justification for doing so. The system permits on-line checking of access to information, in terms of both a particular user, to check which taxpayers he is accessing, and a taxpayer, to check all the users who have accessed his data.

The ex post control system even records accesses to the controls, which guarantees that the control takes place, and that there is no exception or discrimination. All users are included in the system, from the highest officials of the tax administration to the lowest, as are all taxpayers.

The computerization of the tax administration's procedures also guarantees nondiscrimination among taxpayers, as the system makes it necessary to apply each procedure in the same way to all taxpayers, guaranteeing that any decision taken regarding them be taken exclusively by the officials responsible and authorized to do so. Identical treatment meted out only by authorized persons cannot be guaranteed under traditional procedures.

This security system is required for all procedures, from the simplest, such as sending a certificate that the taxpayer has sent in his returns, to the most important, such as the decision to attach the property of a delinquent taxpayer.

Taxpayers' Time as a Measure of Efficiency

In the private sector, strategic decisions on the use of information technologies, like many other decisions, are based on competition among enterprises to gain and maintain a share of the market. There are many examples in which it is precisely the timely and appropriate use of computers and communications that marks the difference between enterprises.

This competitive market does not exist for tax administration; there is no other administration to compete with it, so the motivation has to be other than competitiveness. Spain's experience shows that management and control of the tax administration through concrete targets, measurable in clear and precise terms, can substitute for the incentive that competition provides for private enterprise, and is, therefore, a way of introducing and of getting information technology accepted and used.

The choice of one way or another of measuring targets is in many cases not neutral. The world looks different, depending on which yardstick we use, and this is true for data processing in the tax administration. The manner of using it will not be the same when it is a question of minimizing the time officials spend on a task, as when the objective is to minimize the time that taxpayers spend on meeting their tax obligations.

The EXPRESS application makes it possible to set targets in terms of taxpayers' time, which is obviously a good criterion for evaluating a public service and can also promote competition among provincial centers and officials to achieve that target. There are three parts to the EXPRESS application: (1) defining the procedure; (2) monitoring files; and (3) statistics or control.

Defining Procedures

The EXPRESS application allows the user to determine his procedures; it is an open tool, which he can adapt according to his own requirements and not the other way around.

A procedure may contain one to four phases and in each phase up to three processes can be distinguished. A responsible user must be assigned to each phase and users can also be assigned to processes.

In each process, tasks that do not change can be standardized, for instance, certain written communications between the tax administration and the taxpayers or between different units of the administration.

The freedom of the provincial centers to establish their own procedures is criticized by those who feel that procedures should be identical for all provincial centers. This criticism is leveled when the focus is on procedures, whereas what is important is the result—the public service that is provided. The ability of the provincial centers to incorporate their own experience, knowledge, and skills is what makes it possible to improve performance by adapting procedures to their capabilities, which will obviously differ from provincial center to provincial center. This approach also makes it possible for the more successful experiments to be transferred from one provincial center to another.

Of course, if management believes and decides to ensure that some procedures will be identical for all provincial centers, that can be accommodated under the EXPRESS application.

The definition of procedures is also open over time; at any time new procedures can be defined or old ones redefined differently.

Processing Files

The EXPRESS application allows files to be processed according to the procedures previously defined. The data processing function is very simple and briefly consists of the following.

The initial point is always the registration of the file as it reaches the administration, which consists of recording the identification data of the taxpayer and allocating a number that is printed on a self-adhesive label and given to the taxpayer so he can identify the file in the future. Registration can be performed at any terminal in the network, which makes it possible to have what we call the "single window."

After the files have been registered, they must be assigned to the appropriate procedure. This is done by the person in charge. When he sees the unprocessed files appear on his screen, he examines them and assigns them to the appropriate procedure.

The data processing functions carried out by those in charge of each phase and of those who process the files are similar to what has already been described. Their terminals indicate the work remaining and as they do it they pass it on to the next phase or process until its conclusion, which is registered in the outgoing register.

The status of a file can be retrieved from any point in the network by anyone authorized to do so. To look at a case, it is not necessary to refer to the point at which the file originated or is being dealt with:

from any point and at any time, the location of the file, who is responsible for the task being performed, how long it has been in the system, what decisions have been taken, what remains to be done, and so on, can all be ascertained.

The EXPRESS application allows specialized units to be set up to deal with specific problem areas, with the consequent external savings. It also makes file processing more flexible, the benefit of which is felt by the taxpayer.

Control of Procedures and Files

The EXPRESS application supplies on-line statistics that are immediately updated as the procedures and files go through the system, which allows those in charge of the organization to monitor the situation.

These statistics supply information on the procedures defined, their phases and their processing, the incoming and outgoing registrations, and the number of files in the system. The incoming and outgoing registrations supply data for that day, the current month, and overall data measured by the month. For files in the system, there are data on those finalized and pending, by phase and by month, showing the average time for their resolution and the distribution of the overall time taken to deal with them by phase.

The EXPRESS statistics are a basis for taking decisions on a file or on a batch of files, on the way in which a procedure has been defined, as well as for evaluating staff assigned to a given task. Perhaps the most striking aspect of the EXPRESS application is that it can define targets in the work of the tax administration as a function of the time it takes to resolve taxpayers' questions. EXPRESS also makes it possible to make comparisons between the statistics of different provincial centers.

The INSPECTOR procedure application is derived from the EXPRESS application. Its purpose is to guarantee nondiscriminatory treatment of taxpayers during auditing and to ensure that audit is carried out only by those so authorized. This application is not as flexible nor is it used as broadly as EXPRESS, but it has the advantage of being fully integrated with the rest of the audit support systems, from the preselection of taxpayers for audit to bringing legal action at the conclusion of the audit procedure.

INSPECTOR works in the following manner. The Directorate General of Audit prepares an annual national audit plan, grouped in several concrete plans, and establishes the procedures to be followed and the phases and the tasks for each of them. Once the plans and the procedures are in place, the INSPECTOR application allows the audit units to include the selected taxpayers in the system and to follow up on them. The INSPECTOR application also makes audit work easier by making it possible to perform some tasks, such as summonses and reports, automatically.

Reducing Inconsistencies—The Prior Verification of Returns

The classical processing of returns starts with the recording of the data, after which the identity of the taxpayers and consistency of the data in the returns are checked. In case of discrepancies, the taxpayer has to be contacted to resolve them, with the resulting cost both to the taxpayer and to the tax administration.

To minimize these inconsistencies and to reduce the need to contact taxpayers repeatedly, a number of steps have been taken that have had very positive results.

The identification labels and the fiscal identification number (NIF) are used to facilitate the identification of taxpayers. To help taxpayers check both the arithmetical and the legal consistency of their returns, they are supplied with programs to help them prepare their returns or to check them, such as the PADRE program for income tax returns and other programs for returns on magnetic tape containing reports from payers of wages and salaries, dividends, interest on bank deposits, and other reports on third-party transactions.

Since the NPGT was introduced, the tax administration has been providing self-adhesive labels giving the taxpayer's identification, adding a check digit to the number on the national identity document. With these labels affixed to the tax forms, any possibility of misidentifying taxpayers is eliminated. This procedure has made it possible for participating financial entities to take part in the NPGT in the way that they do, by recording a figure to identify the taxpayers (9 digits maximum), rather than all the data with an average of 80 characters, which would have involved an unsustainable cost. Thus, by establishing the compulsory use of the NIF in tax-related operations, and by giving taxpayers a card with the number on it, the application and therefore the advantages of the check digit have been extended.

The PADRE program helps taxpayers to complete their income tax returns and, in the case of family units, it finds the most advantageous option for them. Taxpayers can go to their provincial center or administration to have them fill in their returns or they can obtain the PADRE program on a diskette so that they can do it themselves. The PADRE program includes an analysis of consistency, which means that returns completed in this way will not contain internal discrepancies.

In 1991, 1,313,004 taxpayers had their returns completed after directly asking for this service, which is the equivalent of 10 percent of all returns. Twenty thousand copies of the program diskette were also distributed, most often to tax consultants.

The programs used to check other annual tax returns work the same way. Taxpayers and consultants are given the same programs used by the administration in its processing. This simple action has saved a significant amount of effort on both sides.

A Single Response to Taxpayers—The INFORMA Application

The Spanish tax administration encourages queries from taxpayers, as tax regulations are not simple and they change frequently. In the 1991 income tax operation we have started using, through the INFORMA application, some basic software developed by the Directorate General of Tax Data Processing to standardize replies to questions raised by taxpayers and to facilitate training of staff responsible for answering them.

The basic software of the INFORMA application makes it possible to perform the following tasks:

- Create data bases of information incorporating the experience of the organization.
- Find the answers to taxpayers' questions. The function is very simple and it is not necessary for the official taking care of the information service to be a tax expert, which is unavoidable without the INFORMA system. The main advantage of the application is that all taxpayers get the same answer to the same question no matter where they are and no matter which official answers the question. Furthermore, by registering and sorting the questions, the system can determine which parts of the tax regulations the taxpayers find most troublesome.
- Ask those managing the system the questions for which no answer has been found in the system. The managers answer these questions on an individual basis and, if they think it worthwhile, incorporate them into the system.

At present, a software package is being developed that will enable answers to these new questions to be generated automatically, which would give us an expert system, not only because we would have learning bases but also because we would have the capacity to learn without the need to incorporate more inputs from administrators.

The basic software for the INFORMA application can also be used to simplify staff training and above all to ensure that the training is identical for all and is permanently being kept up to date. One application of this type is the so-called procedures manuals.

The documentary data bases held by the Directorate General of Tax Data Processing fit in with these systems. At present, apart from having JURI (from tax jurisprudence), which is run by the Central Administrative Economic Tribunal, we also have the Official Government Journal. These bases are accessible from any terminal on the network.

With the same intention of providing more exact information, in the latest campaign undertaken by the tax administration to send letters to taxpayers who do not submit returns, a new kind of relationship was initiated. It consists of introducing an on-line application by means of which the taxpayer can be told to ask for the reason or the reasons for the letter. This means switching from generic answers, which were provided before this application was introduced, to specific answers.

Minimization of the Compliance Burden—The CLASE System

One important objective of the tax administration is to have efficient systems for selecting taxpayers to be audited, so as to concentrate on suspected tax evaders and not on those who meet their obligations.

The Spanish tax administration has used information technologies intensively in this selection process, and the CLASE system is the most powerful and up to date. It was the first data base the Spanish tax administration acquired, and it was also the first step toward expert systems. Compared with the applications available until then, it represented a very significant increase in the efficiency of the administration in fighting tax evasion.

The basic software of the CLASE system categorizes various elements of a data base and combines them based on their characteristics.

The way in which the user selects taxpayers is very simple. From any terminal in the network and on-line, he can choose the geographical and time frame he wishes and the system offers him a decision matrix through which the user can "talk" interactively with the system until he finds the subset of taxpayers he is looking for. Once the system provides the results he needed to obtain the list of the taxpayers in the set thus formed, he merely presses a key and the screen shows the corresponding listing. From this listing, those making the selection can include taxpayers in the different audit plans.

One further step in the computer applications for selecting taxpayers is the class generator, which makes it possible to share information and experience among all those responsible for selecting taxpayers for audit. It allows the work of the members of the organization to be available for use by all the others.

Decentralized Operations, Centralized Management, and the Basic Framework of a Central Accounting Office

Senior central and local responsible officials of the tax administration determine the targets, and there is an interactive process among them until the targets are actually set. The targets must be uniform throughout the country, although they must be specified separately for each regional and local center. Actions to meet the targets are of an eminently territorial, decentralized character, and take place near where the taxpayers are located, which is a reversal of the centralized process of establishing the targets.

A case to illustrate this is the Central Accounting Office, which is currently being established in the Government Agency for Tax Administration, and which will perform the accounting for the agency and for the Government's tax revenue. The accounting system followed by the Central Accounting Office will be different from the current system: it will be a single accounting process for the entire country, although details will vary at the territorial level. Under the present system, there is a different accounting procedure for each provincial center, although they are subsequently grouped together.

The new centralized system will be possible because of the computer resources available today and because of the teleprocessing network already in place, which permits on-line updating of the single accounting system, with the elimination of a number of intermediate steps that information technologies make unnecessary.

The accounting plan has to be approved by the Office of the Auditor General of Government Administration. The Directorate General for Tax Data Processing will be responsible for the equipment for the central accounting system. The Economic Financial Department will be in charge of the Central Accounting Office.

The data processing management systems—NPGT, GEMA, and SIRENA—will generate necessary summary accounts data. These summary accounts will be transmitted by teleprocessing, and the accounting automatically will follow the plan approved by the Auditor General.

The Central Accounting Office will provide details on everything from each individual account to all the accounting statements required, updated daily, which will be the basic data source for management.

Maximizing the Efficiency of Administrative Work—Office Automation Applications

Two striking characteristics of the administration's work are the vast amount of information that has to be processed and the number of administrative tasks. To a large extent, the latter consists of dealing with case files.

These two characteristics make the use of EDP in tax administration so appropriate. A substantial portion of the tax data processing applications already described include what is called office automation. A number of additional office automation tools have also been introduced for the convenience of users.

In the data processing system of the Spanish tax administration, office automation tools were chosen over personal computers (PCs) for two main reasons. First, to avoid the duplication of information and tasks that occurs when PCs are used in a large organization as a basis for the system, with the high cost of maintaining consistency of data or of suffering from their inconsistency. Second, to avoid the creation of closed, self-justifying environments working out their own modest programs and using systems without the required transparency. Obviously, this does not mean that the tax EDP equipment does not include any PCs. They exist and will continue to do so as a part of the system, like any other network terminal with access to the whole system, but with an additional independent processing capacity (albeit with corporate software and tools). In an inspection of software loaded on the tax administration's PCs that are not part of the tax EDP system, a fairly large number of games and pirated programs were found, a circumstance not peculiar to our organization and indeed mentioned as typical in EDP manuals. The risk that this use involves is very large, and the work time lost very costly.

The office automation system in use provides access from any terminal on the network to a group of very powerful corporate applications. It also gives access to a second group of tools which, in practice, provides all the 9,600 terminals in the network with the capabilities of a PC.

In the first group we have electronic mail, the appointments calendar, and applications for the issuance of reports and certificates and for the design and capture of audit cards and the file (ARCHIVO) application. In the second group we have text processing, calculation sheet, calculator, and the tools for calculating interest on arrears, for calculating income taxes, and for calculating withholdings.

Electronic mail is the office automation application most widely accepted and used in the organization, although its full potential is a long way from being realized. The ARCHIVO application enables one to call up a taxpayer's file from any terminal on the network, record its formation and the withdrawal of the documentation from the file, its return, and recognize the documents in it. It also allows issuance of documents needed to manage the files, such as the receipts that have to be signed by those retrieving documentation, and reports and requests to those who are late in returning the files to do so.

Recruitment of Computer Staff

The most critical factor in information technologies is the human factor, the need for professionals to design, develop, and maintain applications. This is even more critical in the public sector than in the private sector because remuneration paid by the government is not competitive, which leads to a continual brain drain from the public sector to the private sector.

The annual turnover rate in the tax administration computer staff is 30 percent and the average time taken to fill a vacancy is 18 months. Much effort has gone into resolving this problem, especially in the area of recruitment.

The 1990 Budget Act created a computer corps with three levels of staff—higher, medium, and administrative—because there was no category of civil servants specifically composed of computer technicians. The 1991 Budget Act created the tax specialty for these three categories, together with the Government Agency for Tax Administration to which they were attached.

With the autonomy granted to the agency, many of the problems connected with the scarcity of computer staff can be resolved, by creating a more transparent, broader, and more dynamic labor market that is flexible enough to cover the vacancies that occur. It will also be necessary to structure an administrative career for computer staff so that they have medium- and long-term prospects within the administration and not, as today, the goal of leaving it.

IV. Information Technology Strategy

The Right Time and Place

The Spanish tax administration uses information technologies to achieve its targets. With the new hardware, software, and communications now available, the Directorate General for Tax Data Processing is exploring how it can help to provide taxpayers with the most effective public service.

From a functional viewpoint, the present strategy in information technologies can be summed up as an attempt to overcome time and space constraints, in the sense of having the necessary information and the processing capacity at any time and from any place.

To have information available means not just moving from numerical or graphical data to information, but using it for better decision making. It also implies moving from information to the image and the voice, so that understanding can be immediate without the need for prior training or explanation. From the technical point of view, this means using various resources jointly. The use of multiple media will be decisive in the overall consolidation of information technologies at managerial levels and, as in our case, for a closer relationship with taxpayers.

To have the software available at the right time and in the right place means for the users to have open systems that they can adapt to their problems, needs, and capacities. This "customization" means, on the one hand, enhancing the software by meeting the users' needs and, on the other hand, that users not only accept it sooner and more willingly but also adopt it as their own.

To have the processing capacity means that from any terminal in the network the user can set in motion processes for which he is authorized. To do this, it is not sufficient to have adequate hardware and software; adequate communications facilities are also needed, and this, together with the staff resources, is the most critical factor in quite a few data processing organizations. The Spanish tax data processing system has a substantial and powerful teleprocessing network, but there is an imbalance between hardware and software, on the one hand, and available communications, on the other. From 1993, we expect to be able to make full use of communications satellites, which will mean a major qualitative change and a better balance between communications and the hardware and software currently available.

An Administration Closer to Taxpayers

The data bases, the public information systems, and the technologies of security and protection of access to EDP systems have been used to advantage by the Spanish tax data processing system to help the taxpayer in his dealings with the administration, thereby saving him time and avoiding the need for visiting a tax office.

For example, this year, the PADRE program was introduced in the videotex network, which means that anyone who can access this program can use it to complete his income tax returns. In Spain, in recent years, the number of videotex users has risen considerably, not only in enterprises, but also among individuals, who are installing it at home.

The INFORMA application is currently being installed in the videotex system, so that both professionals and individuals can access it from home, and at any time of day through its 24-hour service. Consideration is currently being given to the possibility of opening a mailbox in this system through which taxpayers can contact the tax office easily.

The technologies for the protection and security of EDP systems are being used in a pilot experiment with tax consultants involving the retrieval of taxpayers' identification labels. By using this facility, an authorized consultant can access the data base of a provincial center from a PC via the public telephone system and ask for the identification labels. The system offers him the possibility of issuing them on-line from his office or via the provincial center, which will send them to him. This service may be expanded if the pilot experiment is successful. The service eliminates the need to visit a tax office and removes the limitations of opening hours.

In the future, consultants too will be able to access the INFORMA application, and we are sure that a new form of relationship with the tax administration will open up.

Optical Reading and Storage

The full integration of image technologies into the world of data processing and communications is one of the main strategies of information technology. The advantages this would bring to tax administration are considerable, as they open up many possibilities.

Work is currently developing in various directions: on the automation of the processes for classifying and counting envelopes containing annual returns, simplifying and, in some cases, substituting the classical ways of inputting documents and replacing traditional paper files by image files.

The classification and counting of annual returns envelopes is carried out manually, with a high cost in human and space resources and many repercussions arising from the frequent errors committed. The process consists of classifying the envelopes received through the mail from the participating financial entities according to different categories. Thus, in the case of income tax returns, it is according to whether they are the ordinary or simplified model, whether the taxpayer is claiming a refund or making a payment, and whether the refund is to be by transfer or by check. This prior classification is justified by the subsequent order of processing, which is designed so that refunds can be dealt with as quickly as possible. The returns are then grouped in batches of about 100, counted, and passed on to the next stage at which the envelopes are opened, their contents formally checked and, if they are complete, they are accepted and the copy separated for registering and then passed on to the appropriate service. The rest of the contents of the envelope is filed.

The alternative on which we are working in a joint project with a supplier of hardware, software, and robotization components is mainly based on the optical recognition of characters. An ad hoc prototype is being designed for the Spanish tax administration that consists of equipment with a feeder for the annual return envelopes, which optically reads the identity of the taxpayer from the identification label on the envelope. To do this, the labels are already being printed with characters that can be read by this technology. It will also read optically what kind of return it is by reading the bar coding of the envelope. By reading the check marks made by the taxpayer on the envelope, the system will indicate whether a refund or a payment is due, and if a refund, whether it is requested to be made by check or transfer. The system will prepare batches of envelopes automatically, having opened them by mechanical means.

This will not only make the classification more reliable, with a considerable saving in cost and time, but also the identity of all the taxpayers concerned will be immediately available. At the moment, it is necessary to wait for such information until the end of the data entry period, which in the case of the income tax is estimated to occur 100 days after the start of the process. It is expected that by 1992, this type of equipment will be installed in some of the provincial centers that have the greatest work load.

Regarding the replacement of classical entering of information by optical reading, there will shortly be a real-life experiment in the Barcelona Customs, based on the technology and design that are already being used in Germany in the Cobra Project, called the unified customs document (DUAS), which can be used for import and export declarations. The tests already conducted have proved satisfactory and confirm the possibilities of this technology for the tasks of converting information on paper to a digitalized format.

The equipment that is to be installed in Barcelona performs in one hour twice the work that a data entry operator can do in a whole day, as its productivity is 14 times greater and it can work around the clock because the down time required for maintenance is negligible. In economic terms, the equipment will be fully amortized four months after installation.

The optical filing of documents will start with the EXPRESS application in Madrid and Barcelona to evaluate its possibilities and yield. The need for the tax administration to find some alternative to the present filing system is urgent, as a lot of money is being spent on space and people while the users are not very happy with the service being provided. There are two main disadvantages to this technology. One is psychological—associated with the culture of the organization—how to get image-based information accepted, even if it may seem identical to the original document when printed out. This may seem like an insignificant problem but, in fact, is a major difficulty. The other problem is the limitation we currently have on remote image transmission, which requires lines with capacities that the Spanish tax administration currently does not possess. However, the advantages and the savings are so great that they far outweigh all of these difficulties.

Comments

Luis Fernando Ramírez Acuña

The paper presented by Rafael Moya and José-Damián Santiago provides an excellent description of the technology currently applied by the Spanish tax authority, its development over the past decades, and, in some ways, the sophistication of the data bases used in information processing.

Moreover, the paper vividly relates the authors' personal experiences regarding changes in the Spanish tax authority's computer system, not only through technological advances introduced into the system, but also through the "in-house plan" they designed to meet the administration's needs.

I have had the opportunity to assess at close range the dramatic changes in the Spanish tax administration during the past decade, and to exchange ideas with José-Damián regarding his project since 1983. I have also had the privilege of closely following the development of computerization in Spain up to the present time, when there is a special autonomous directorate for electronic data processing (EDP) with a separate budget, as reflected in a sophisticated computer system serving the Spanish tax administration.

In the past decade the Spanish tax administration has increased the speed of computer processing from 36 MIPS to 291 MIPS; the system's central memory has been expanded from 67 MB to 2,110 MB; its disk storage capacity has grown from 56 GB to 893 GB; the number of terminals has increased from 663 to 9,600; in 1983 there were only 83 printers, whereas now there are 4,493; and the number of teleprocessing lines has grown from 11 to 370, including those in the internal revenue and customs authorities.

Budgetary support for computerization has certainly been of great help to the computer specialists' work, and there seems to be a clear commitment to continue to allocate a substantial share of fiscal resources to the tax administration for information processing.

Moreover, since the EDP Directorate provides support in collection, audit, and recovery of delinquent taxes, new software packages have been designed to meet the basic needs of the tax administration, such as NPGT (new tax management procedure), BDN (data bases for audit), SIRENA (national collection system), GEMA (automated customs management), and TEAR (programs for regional administrative economic tribunals). In addition, such statistical applications as INFO and

PANINFO make it possible to follow up on the administration's actions, and ONI facilitates control of large enterprises.

All these resources, fourth-generation tools and relevant data bases, together with the expertise of highly specialized officials, have enabled the EDP Directorate to meet the challenge of administering the Spanish tax system effectively.

However, I should like to comment on three aspects of system efficiency.

Greater Effort to Streamline Procedures

Some legislative changes with a view to streamlining procedures could increase efficiency. For example, enactment of legislation establishing that salaried workers' income tax (up to a certain level of income) is equal to the amount withheld by their employers would make it unnecessary for taxpayers in that category to file returns. By doing so, the EDP Directorate could well spare itself the work of processing 30 percent or 40 percent of the 10 million returns it currently receives, without any loss in revenue.

Elimination of annual returns (returns summarizing assessments that are submitted during the year) would make it possible to release additional substantial resources. To this end, the assessments submitted by taxpayers during the year should be considered final returns. This would not only increase the administration's efficiency but would also reduce taxpayers' compliance costs.

Currently there is duplication of work, as stated by the authors: "The envelope used to file the annual form should also contain a copy of all self-assessment returns submitted during the year, kept until that time by the taxpayer himself."

Wouldn't it be possible to do away with all these attachments and mailings of information? Doesn't the administration already have a copy of the assessments made during the year for which the taxpayer must send another copy at the end of the year? Wouldn't the EDP Directorate reduce its work load in processing files if by law the assessments made during the year were deemed to be tax returns or if tax returns were filed bimonthly or quarterly?

Priorities and Amount of Computerized Information

My feeling is that the Spanish tax administration system contains too much computerized information, which makes sorting it out difficult. In fact, for tax inspectors, the difference between having all taxpayer information in the computer or in traditional files may be marginal if the information is not classified according to pre-established priorities and provided to them selectively.

The EDP Directorate is endeavoring to sort information, as the authors state when referring to PANINFO. The volume of data collected by INFO from the NPGT is such that it enables the smallest details of the tax administration's activity to be analyzed. However, at times, the amount of data makes it difficult to see the overall picture. In other words, there is a surfeit of data in INFO that does not invalidate it but makes if necessary to complement it with PANINFO.

Microcomputer or Minicomputer Systems Versus Mainframe Computer Equipment

The decision concerning computer equipment poses serious dilemmas for most tax authorities. They must first decide whether to rent or buy the equipment and then whether to purchase large, costly equipment (mainframe computers) with greater potential for processing information or to use average, less costly equipment, and divide the pool of taxpayers to be administered.

Specialists usually recommend renting if the equipment consists of mainframe computers and buying in the case of microcomputers, as mainframe computers are becoming obsolete because of ongoing technological innovations, and microcomputers or minicomputers can now perform nearly the same applications, with greater versatility in the case of obsolescence, notwithstanding the somewhat more limited capacity of the smaller computers.

In Spain, the tax authority has large, powerful mainframe computer equipment. In fact, the system is designed to centralize information, while providing for decentralized access to it. Teleprocessing lines make it possible to consult and update information on-line, that is, in a more timely manner than with batch processing. The information is processed with data base systems. BDN is loaded with approximately 1.25 billion data.

Contrary to the aforementioned example, many tax authorities have separated taxpayers into different groups and have even set up separate services, as in the case of the so-called large taxpayers, in order to facilitate management of a reduced group of taxpayers.

In the case of large taxpayers, transactions can be processed efficiently with microcomputers. This option is considerably more economical than the use of an on-line centralized system, and data can be consulted and updated almost as speedily.

In most countries, a small group of taxpayers contributes a substantial share of tax revenue, a fact that considerably facilitates separate processing of transactions. For example, in Spain itself 4 percent of the enterprises contributes 87 percent of tax revenue.

In Mexico, where the largest taxpayers also contribute a large share of total revenues, a new strategy of data processing is being developed, based on using microcomputers and minicomputers to process the files of different groups of taxpayers. Colombia, too, is developing a large proportion of its software applications for microcomputers. The advantage is that this software is transferable and can easily be tested in one regional tax office and applied in the others within a very short period of time. Moreover, it is easy to alter these software programs to reflect legislative changes.

The essential point in this case is to design a centralized information storage system and uniform software in all the regional tax offices so as to prevent information anarchy.

The alternative of dividing the pool of taxpayers into groups and using microcomputer and minicomputer networks is at the very least innovative. Thanks to technological progress, the tax authorities can easily implement it, within budgetary limits, to achieve very good results in the administration of the tax system.

Malcolm G. Lane

In countries around the world, computerization can be a stumbling block that deters the success of new tax administration or proposed policy reform. If not done correctly, computerization can become a negative rather than a positive element. Certainly, if a computerized system does not provide obvious benefits to tax administrators, it serves no purpose.

In one recent experience, a tax commissioner was asked, "Where would you go to get information about receipts or other information about return filings for a particular period?" He responded that he would go to a paper cash book and manual cards and that he could not trust the information in the computer system. In this case, the computer was viewed as a "big black hole" into which data were keyed and from which nothing of value was returned for use by the commissioner or department staff.

Often times, this situation arises because too much is attempted too soon. Computerization is not a trivial task. It cannot be viewed as an afterthought to tax policy or administration reform. Experience shows that even computer professionals find it difficult to estimate the amount of time it will take to implement a particular application. Some feel that even if one were to double the estimates, it often is only half the amount of time required to implement the computerized application fully. The reason for this in most cases is that requirements are ambiguous and incomplete.

Approaches to computerization used in Spain, the United Kingdom, the United States, and other developed countries cannot simply be "transported" to a country in which application of computer technology is in its infancy. In many cases, tax administrators barely know what a computer is, much less how to operate one. There are many instances in such countries where a computer system is installed in a tax administrator's office, but is never turned on, is covered with dust, and really is for show rather than actual use.

Experiences in Spain

There is much that can be learned from the experiences of computerization of tax administration in Spain, presented in the paper. The paper states that the Spanish system provides many capabilities. Among them are the following:

- the determination of who should file tax returns;
- the determination of who did not file;
- the identification of incorrect submissions;
- the identification of those who did not pay their full liability (no payment or short payment); and
- assistance in tracking and resolution of disputes.

The above are certainly capabilities of a computerized system that are desirable in all countries. And, of course, implied in all of the above is the capability of a taxpayer accounting system that tracks liability and payments by tax period. Just how they are delivered via a particular computerized system will differ. Other functions mentioned, such as budget preparation and internal auditing, are not likely to be priority computerization tasks until tax administration has been computerized.

Spain chose a single electronic data processing (EDP) organization in an independent directorate general to provide computerization for all tax administration. This is a common organization for developing countries where personnel resources are scarce. In many cases, computer personnel have been assigned to specific tax departments and are directed by the appropriate tax commissioner and senior staff, even though they are a part of the centralized computer organization. This provides the benefits of centralized coordination and standards, while delivering specific systems designed for and controlled by user departments.

Mainframe Technology

Mainframe computer technology has been successful in Spain and other large developed countries. The capacity and volume of equipment used in Spain is far greater than that required in most developing countries. The application of mainframe technologies has been attempted in many of these countries. It is very costly and the training and retention of technical support staff for such installations is extremely difficult, if not impossible, in most developing countries. In one instance, there was a mainframe computer stored in a "back room" near an open window. This computer had been in this room for over a year (estimated purchase cost for this computer was at the time about $2 million) and it had never been used!

Many mainframe computer installations indeed do not work or operate very poorly. Often they serve as large filing cabinets in which data are stored, but seldom, if ever, read or analyzed. Furthermore, with hardware and system software maintenance costs often in the hundreds of thousands of dollars, mainframes consume vast and scarce financial resources with unsatisfactory results. Mainframe technology is certainly not the future technology for tax administration in developing countries.

Compatibility and Data Base Environments

Spain has adopted vendor independence with compatible equipment. The EDP Directorate relies on relational data base software and powerful languages and CASE tools for software implementation. These are important in all countries and are highly recommended even in microcomputer environment that is extremely attractive in developing countries.

Distributed Environment

The "new tax handling procedure" in Spain is distributed, that is, decentralized to 56 provincial centers and includes four aspects:

- Census (the tax register).

- Self-assessments.
- Annual tax returns.
- Notices.

A decentralized environment places data entry and collection at the source of data, which is always desirable. However, early stages of computerization in developing countries must go through stages of using centralized, regional, and finally district computers. This is because it is impossible to provide the training and implement the procedural changes and site modifications in all district offices.

The large data network used in Spain is perhaps ideal for the timely movement of data in a distributed environment, but at present it is not realistic in most developing countries because of poor or nonexistent communications facilities. In planning computerized applications, network capabilities should be included to ensure that they can be used when available.

Taxpayer Identification

In Spain, a fiscal identification number (NIF) provides unique identification of all taxpayers. The NIF identifies literally millions of taxpayers. While developing countries have far fewer taxpayers, there is the same need for unique identification. In most countries, local file reference numbers identify taxpayers, but these are unique to a district office. If a taxpayer moves, the number changes.

One of the more difficult problems is to define and control a taxpayer numbering system that can be applied in these countries. It is not only an administrative problem but requires legislation to force the use of this number for all taxes in the country. Often the introduction of such a numbering system can take years in a given country. However, it is possible to rely on "local identifying numbers" along with computer-generated internal numbers so that computerization can begin in advance of the availability of a unique taxpayer identification number. The computer "master file" can later be used to assign the new number and prepare notifications that are mailed to the taxpayers to inform them of their number.

Personnel

Even in Spain recruitment and retention of data processing personnel is a problem. It was stated that Spain actually trains experts for the private market because loss of personnel is 30 percent per annum.

This is exacerbated even further in developing countries where salary differentials between the government and the private sector can be as high as a factor of ten. This problem will remain in developing countries for the foreseeable future.

Management Support

Support from the management of an organization in the use of information technology is essential. Even in Spain there is a need to train executives on these matters, and the paper states that there has really been no great success in this area and none is envisaged in the near future.

Many developing countries have a similar problem, but there have been some successes because of early training of management at senior and intermediate levels.

Other Issues in Developing Countries

Manual Procedures

There is a false assumption that many have made in the past—"computerizing any system will solve problems in that system." Often, problems in tax administration or other applications are caused by poor manual procedures. Unless the procedures are reviewed and corrected, computerization will likely make things worse.

In Spain, tax administration procedures are well organized. However, in developing countries, it is very important to review existing manual procedures, identify weaknesses in these procedures, and, for new taxes, define new procedures. Only after appropriate manual procedures are well defined can a tax administration be successfully computerized.

Requirements Definition[1]

Defining the requirements of a particular application is difficult enough in developed countries with experienced users. Doing this in

[1]Requirements definition is the process of studying an organization's activities (income tax return processing, collection activities, and so forth) and formally describing which activities are to be computerized and how these activities will be changed as a result of computerization.

a developing country that has little or no experience with computers is even more difficult. In many developing countries, computerized tax administration systems have been developed with absolutely no requirements. This is like building a house without any plans. Few would pay a builder for such a house because they would not know what the end result would be. And it is even possible that it could fall down because of poor architecture or engineering.

Developing a computerized application requires similar definition and design. In particular, there must be user involvement to define the requirements. Yet, how does one involve inexperienced users in the process?

Unless the users and the systems analysts actually begin to feel there is much repetition in the questions asked and the material reviewed, it is likely that the analysis has not been done with the right amount of detail. It is not sufficient to "almost" understand the requirements; the refinement of requirements must continue until there is an exact understanding and presentation of the requirement.

There are many instances where computerized systems were implemented that were simply not what the user required. On the other hand, it is extremely difficult to define accurately what the user requires. Experience has proved that the use of rapid prototyping[2] that allows users to "test drive" the proposed computerized system prior to full implementation is the best way to guarantee user involvement and to produce user-defined systems that truly meet the users' requirements.

"Rightsizing"

Advances in microcomputer technology have made computerization in all countries cost effective and far easier than the mainframes of the past. They can provide multi-user environments for tax administration. The new laptop and notebook computers can provide an easy means of demonstrating the potential computer applications via a prototype right in the offices of the tax administrators. They have been used quite effectively to collect data on-site in tax offices where the movement of ledger cards and "master file" data was impractical or impossible.

Companies and organizations around the world are using what has been called "downsizing" to move applications from expensive mainframe systems to microcomputer systems. A better term is "rightsizing." The success of rightsizing is being published regularly in computer

---

[2]Prototyping is a technique in which a scaled-down software "model" is implemented very quickly to illustrate how the computerized system will eventually operate.

publications around the world. It is most definitely an approach that is being and will continue to be successful in tax applications around the world.

Realistic Expectations and Scheduling

Computerization in any organization is not simply a matter of purchasing computers and some software, plugging in the system, and beginning operation. There are many stories of failures of computerized applications in developing countries. Many of these failures have resulted from unrealistic expectations and attempting far too much in too short a period of time.

Careful planning and coordination

There are many "players" in the computerization of any application (management, users, contractor(s), and computer staff). Each new application affects other applications within the organization. Total success in computerization requires planning and coordination to avoid incompatibility problems and to provide for realistic phasing of the implementation of application within the organization.

Realistic requirements and expectations

Too many computer projects have failed because of the "too much, too soon" syndrome, that is, there was an attempt to computerize "everything" in too short a period of time. The requirements for the initial computerized systems must be realistic so that the application can be successfully implemented by the delivery dates specified. International organizations must guide developing countries in their computerization efforts so that each step is successful. Everyone must understand what is possible and what is not.

When unrealistic schedules are requested, computer center management and computerization advisors must be willing to inform high-level government officials that what is being requested cannot be accomplished by the stated deadline. It is far better to modify the plans for what will be delivered than to have the delivery date arrive with the computerized system not being ready for use.

Patience

Production software cannot be developed overnight. It must be understood by all concerned that it is far better to wait for a correct, properly tested product than to attempt the use of a product that is not ready for use (for example, incomplete, untested, wrong features), for once a computerized application fails, it is extremely difficult to regain credibility and trust in the computerized system.

Transfer of Technology

Without excellent documentation and training, a computer system cannot be successful. A system exists in its documentation and training. Hence, these are essential components of all successful computerized projects. Education of users before computerization begins, during requirements definition and system installation, and immediately prior to the production use of a computer application is important to the success of computerized applications in developing countries.

The transfer of technology to personnel in the EDP department is mandatory if computerized systems are to continue to be successful and evolve with change within the tax department. Technical personnel should be part of the computerization efforts from the beginning and trained with formal courses and seminars as well.

Simplicity

Simplicity, above all else, is perhaps the best strategy for success. Computerized systems should be delivered as simple components in a phased manner so that when all components of a system are delivered, each has been successful on its own and the collection of components is successful when operating as an integrated system.

Every aspect of computerization must be defined and reviewed with the object of keeping the solutions as simple as possible. It is far better to deliver fewer capabilities in an initial computerized system that indeed work, than to attempt to deliver everything that was ever asked for. The general rule should be to simplify procedures, simplify requirements, and guarantee success. It must be remembered that with one initial failure, computerization could be doomed for years. One country tried computerization in 1968 and failed; it did not attempt it again until 1990.

One important point to remember is that what appears to be a trivial computerized system in a developed country can have high paybacks and be viewed as a great success in a developing country. One example is the creation and maintenance of a master file that can be used to generate labels for mailings to taxpayers. When preparation of labels takes four to six weeks of most personnel handwriting labels, the production of a complete set of mailing labels by the computer in one day can make quite an impression on tax officials!

Conclusion

There is obviously much that can be learned from the experiences of the computerization of tax administration in Spain. Many aspects of the approach in Spain are applicable in developing countries. However, rightsizing (to powerful and inexpensive microcomputers) and the definition of simple systems are two other important keys to successful computerization in these countries. When used along with realistic scheduling of computerization projects, computerization will certainly be successful and tax administration will be very much improved.

PART II

Reforming Tax Administration

7

Tax Administration and Inflation

Milka Casanegra de Jantscher, Isaias Coelho, and Arturo Fernandez

This paper discusses the impact of inflation on tax systems and analyzes the revenue and administrative effects of measures designed to adjust tax systems for inflation.

In a monetary economy most transactions, including the payment of taxes, are carried out by means of money. Because inflation erodes the purchasing power of money, it ends up affecting all aspects of economic activity. Money has several important functions in the economy: it serves as a means of exchange, an accounting unit, a wealth reserve, and as a standard for deferred payment. As a unit of exchange, money is involved in almost all transactions; as cash, it serves as a measure of the value of goods; as a wealth reserve, money grants a right to acquire goods that can be exercised at any time; and as a standard for deferred payment, money acts as a credit or liability account.

The effects of inflation on the functions of money apply directly to the tax system:

- The unit of measurement employed by tax statutes to determine tax bases is the same monetary unit which devalues with the passage of time.
- Taxes are paid with lags and they are measured in monetary units, the value of which decreases over time.

This paper assesses the impact of inflation on the tax system's ability to produce revenues, giving special emphasis to administrative aspects such as the frequency of payments, payment periods and advance payments, and calculation of the tax base, mainly with respect to income taxes paid by businesses (corporations, partnerships, and sole proprietorships). It also analyzes the problems created by inflation with respect to late payments, and, in general, those relating to penalties and surcharges.

I. Collection Lags

Collection lags reduce the tax system's ability to generate a certain level of real revenue during inflationary periods. These lags arise from the way the assessment and the payment periods are defined.

Income, profits, and other taxable items are generated over time, with a particular purchasing power. In order to impose taxes, tax statutes define assessment periods, that is, periods during which an obligation to pay a particular tax arises, that generally coincide with specific calendar periods. This is why income taxes are generally applied on income earned in the calendar year, whereas taxes on consumption are levied with respect to shorter periods (monthly, bimonthly, or quarterly).

Most tax statutes establish a time interval from the end of the assessment period (when taxes are generated) to the time when payment must be made, in order to allow taxpayers to calculate correctly their tax liability. Several countries' tax statutes also provide taxpayers the opportunity of requesting deferral of tax payments.

Inflation, combined with the above-mentioned collection lags, weakens the tax system's revenue-generating ability. The cost of collection lags is reflected in the ability of the tax system to produce a particular real amount of revenues.

The lower the inflation rate, the greater the frequency of provisional payments, and the shorter the assessment period, the lower will be the revenue loss resulting from collection lags. The relationship between collection levels, frequency of payment, and inflation rates can be illustrated with the following example. Assuming a country has an inflation rate of 20 percent and one yearly tax payment, if inflation increases to 200 percent, 20 tax payments will be required during the year to collect the same real amount. If inflation increased to 2,000 percent, there would have to be 200 payments a year (one every 1.82 days!).

There are several methods for reducing the impact of collection lags on revenue during periods of inflation. These include the following: shortening assessment and payment periods; establishing a system of payments on account (provisional payments) or increasing the frequency of such payments; and lastly, indexation of tax payments.

Provisional Payments

If a system of advance payments or provisional payments does not exist, it seems logical to introduce one. Payments on account are relatively common with respect to the business income tax. The choice of a suitable formula, however, is not an easy one. If the provisional payments are to be equal to a fraction of the previous year's final tax, it is important to establish a mechanism for adjusting this amount to the new price levels. Another way of calculating the provisional payment is to establish it as a percentage of gross income. This percentage is equal to the ratio of taxable profits to gross income for the previous year. However, this formula is inequitable for economic sectors in which gross income and expenditure do not take place in the same time period. It also creates complications when dealing with income from interest.

In periods of high inflation some countries have established biweekly provisional payments of monthly taxes. In Chile, for example, in the mid-1970s large enterprises had to make advance fortnightly value-added tax (VAT) payments. This measure was very effective from a revenue point of view, given that in Chile, as in other countries that apply a VAT, a small number of taxpayers account for a considerable percentage of the total VAT yield. From an administrative point of view, the system did not cause any great problems as it affected a relatively limited number of taxpayers.

Shortening Payment Periods

One option that is frequently exercised in highly inflationary circumstances is to shorten payment periods. In Uruguay, for example, between 1987 and 1988 the VAT payment period was reduced by approximately 60 days. In other countries the period for payment of monthly taxes has been reduced from 20 to 15 or even to only 7 days from the last day of the month in which the tax is generated.

In the case of annual taxes, such as income taxes, the period for filing annual tax returns and making final payments can be shortened from three months to one. It is not advisable to shorten it further since the data needed to calculate the tax due may not be available to the taxpayer (for example, profit statements, bank statements, or the settling of accounts with clients or suppliers).

Indexing of Payments

The third measure aimed at decreasing the negative revenue impact of collection lags is to index tax payments. This involves, in practice, abandoning the legal tender as a unit of account for tax liabilities and replacing it with a fiscal or tax unit adjustable according to a selected index (consumer price index (CPI) or other). This measure is indispensable when the inflation rate exceeds 100 percent per annum, in which case even with monthly payments the loss in tax revenues exceeds 4 percent. In order to implement this measure, it is essential to take into account the frequency with which the CPI is calculated and published. These elements are fundamental in establishing the payment periods and the time lag that necessarily has to exist between the period to be indexed and the index that is applied in practice (for example, payments to be indexed month 2 to month 5, index variation month 1 to month 4).

The Mexican Experience

Several Latin American countries, particularly those in the southern cone, have a great deal of experience in using different combinations of the methods described above to decrease the revenue impact of collection lags.

Mexico's experience is worth analyzing since it is the most recent and therefore is little known. At the beginning of the inflationary spiral of 1979, politicians refused to recognize explicitly the effects of inflation in the hope that anti-inflationary measures would eliminate or at least substantially reduce them. This position forced the administration to introduce isolated and not always consistent changes; first, the provisional payments of company taxes were changed from four-monthly to quarterly, later to bimonthly, and finally to monthly. At the same time, payment periods were reduced from three to two and finally to one month, and even to ten days. This process caused discontent among taxpayers, who saw their compliance costs increase, until some elements of indexation were finally introduced starting in 1987. The administrative changes prior to 1987 gave rise to constant modifications in the regulations and forms of payment, causing uncertainty and confusion not only among taxpayers but also within the tax administration.

Perhaps the most important lesson from this experience is that, in countries unaccustomed to high levels of inflation, the introduction of tax adjustments aimed at maintaining revenue levels can be quite traumatic, both for taxpayers and for the tax administration. Adjustments that in Argentina, Brazil, and Chile are part of the tax culture may cause political and administrative problems of great magnitude in countries where previous levels of inflation have not been so high as to justify the introduction of such adjustments.

Administrative Cost of Measures to Decrease the Revenue Impact of Collection Lags

Reducing the periods of assessment and payment of taxes or increasing the number of provisional payments may give rise to substantial costs for the tax administration as well as for taxpayers. These costs constitute a "deadweight loss" for the economy as a whole, since in order to make a payment it is necessary to employ resources that benefit nobody.

As far as the tax administration authorities are concerned, introducing or increasing the number of provisional payments requires a significant increase in the administration's ability to monitor liabilities, check tax returns, and account for revenues. If collection is done through the banking system, the cost of this service rises in proportion to the number of tax returns and payments made. A greater number of periodic payments implies higher compliance costs for taxpayers.

If taxes normally paid quarterly become due monthly, the tasks associated with controlling collection are multiplied by three. There might, however, be surplus processing capacity if the personnel and material resources of the administration are employed intensively for only four months a year. In Mexico, when inflation rose above 100 percent, provisional payments for business income taxes were required monthly instead of the previous arrangement of one payment every four months. This change disrupted tax administration, and the control of provisional payments totally broke down. Data entry personnel and existing computer facilities were insufficient to handle four times the previous workload.

Some of the costs associated with increasing the number of provisional payments can be reduced considerably by consolidating in one return form the main monthly taxes paid by enterprises: VAT, withholding taxes, provisional business income taxes, and excises. Further savings can be obtained by eliminating the payment form, and making the tax return function as a payment form. These measures are beneficial even without inflation. However, when inflation accelerates, these measures markedly reduce the administrative costs associated with increasing the number of provisional payments.

A consolidated tax form of this nature allowed Chile successfully to implement and control a system of monthly provisional payments for business income taxes. However, the option of a unified or consolidated form faces great difficulties in countries in which the VAT is administered by state authorities while income taxes are administered federally (as it is in Brazil and was in Mexico until 1990).

As mentioned earlier, an alternative to increasing the frequency of payments or shortening payment periods is to index such payments. Depending on the type of tax, one solution may be more appropriate than the other. For example, the annual income tax return and final payment of business taxpayers cannot be advanced like the monthly VAT, because, as previously explained, it requires time for the necessary data to be available. In this case, indexation of the final payment is appropriate. Usually, increasing the number of advance payments or shortening payment periods can be done directly by the tax administration while indexation requires the enactment of legislation.

II. Delinquent Taxes, Additional Assessments, and Penalties

The previous section discussed various methods of reducing the negative revenue impact of legal collection lags. This section analyzes payments made after the legal payment period, including delinquent taxes, additional assessments, and penalties.

Taxes Paid After the Legal Payment Period (Delinquent Taxes)

Whatever the mechanism chosen to adjust delinquent taxes, it must protect the real value of the tax due (principal obligation). In addition, it must ensure that delinquent taxpayers incur a real financial cost so that there is no incentive to default. In principle, there are two options for indexing delinquent taxes. The first is to adopt a variable interest rate based on a market rate, or to apply an interest rate that includes an estimate of inflation. The second option consists of indexing the value of the tax liability and fixing a real interest rate.

The use of a market interest rate as a reference (for example, the banking system's borrowing rate, the prime rate, or the rate of government bonds) poses certain difficulties that should be taken into account. In a high-inflation economy, financial markets tend to contract, reduce the time span of operations, and be extremely volatile. These features intensify when financial operations are not indexed. The resulting interest rates can be excessively low in some cases, thus encouraging delays in tax payments. Generally, after an abrupt devaluation, real interest rates become negative and if interest on delinquent taxes is fixed according to market rates, taxpayers will prefer to finance their operations by incurring late payment of taxes. On the other hand, an interest rate that includes an estimate of inflation must be reviewed periodically so that the real cost proves to be greater than that of the market.

The second option—to index taxes owed—protects the real value of the tax liability. In principle, a periodic review of the (real) interest rate applicable to the indexed tax liability is required to prevent such interest from being equal to or less than the real cost of credit in financial markets. However, periodic reviews of nominal or real interest rates are not always possible; in most countries these charges require legislative approval and it is not always feasible or advisable to initiate tax legislation on this matter.

Decisions concerning indexation of the tax liability and the interest rate to be applied will generally depend on the institutional structure of each country and the level of inflation. The mechanism that is adopted should, however, comply with three conditions:

(1) The real value of the tax liability must be preserved.

(2) The real cost to the taxpayer of incurring tax delinquency must always be higher than the real cost of bank finance.

(3) The elements for calculating the cost of tax delinquency must be known before the payment is calculated and their evolution must be foreseeable.

Penalties

The previous section discusses options for preserving the real value of delinquent taxes and fixing an appropriate real interest rate. Besides interest for the delay in tax payments, tax statutes generally establish penalties for noncompliance with tax obligations. In some countries, most penalties consist of a percentage of the tax due, whereas in others penalties are expressed in fixed amounts of local currency even in the case of unreported taxes.

Where high inflation prevails, fines expressed in fixed amounts lose their effectiveness if they are not indexed. This of course has a negative impact on tax compliance levels. Solutions generally adopted are the following: (1) expressing penalties as a percentage of the indexed unpaid tax; (2) if that is not possible because the penalty is for nonfulfillment of a formal requirement, expressing the penalty in an automatically adjustable unit (as is the case of the tax unit in Chile)[1]; and (3) periodically modifying the tax statutes to adjust (index) penalties expressed in local currency.

The most practical solutions are those indicated in (1) and (2), as they do not require continuous legal modifications. In some countries solution (3) is also automatic, in the sense that the tax statute authorizes the administration to undertake this adjustment periodically. In this case, the problem of having to depend upon periodic legislation in order to make adjustments is eliminated.

Finally, we should point out that in periods of high inflation there is a tendency to confuse the concepts discussed in this section: (1) the

[1]The tax unit is an amount determined by law which is continuously updated according to CPI variations. There are annual and monthly tax units.

indexation of delinquent tax payments in order to maintain their real value; (2) the interest rate charged by the government for the use of the money; and (3) the penalties for noncompliance. In countries that are familiar (unfortunately) with the problem of inflation, such as those in the southern cone of Latin America, these concepts are relatively clear. In others, where experience with this problem is limited, there is a tendency to believe that indexation of tax payments is a kind of penalty, thereby making it unnecessary to apply additional penalties. As previously indicated, the indexation of tax due and the charging of interest are not intended to penalize the taxpayer. In order to maintain an adequate level of tax compliance it is also necessary to apply effective penalties for noncompliance.

III. Credits Against the Treasury

The above sections referred to the indexation of claims that the treasury has against taxpayers. For reasons of equity, and in order to increase the level of voluntary compliance, equal treatment should be given to claims that taxpayers have against the treasury. In practice, countries that have indexed late tax payments also permit an adjustment of the refunds owed to taxpayers. A number of countries have recognized, however, that the problem of equal treatment is not limited to the question of refunds. This is why, for example, excess VAT credits can generally be indexed by the taxpayer when VAT statutes require them to be carried forward. In Brazil and Chile, taxpayers are allowed adjustments for inflation in a variety of situations, including refunds, carryforward of losses, payments on account, and so forth.

These measures, similar to those used to index late tax payments, give rise to administrative costs because they complicate the calculation of claims against the treasury. But their cost is low compared with the equity that they introduce in the system.

IV. Calculation of Business Income

Generally accepted accounting principles adopt legal tender as the unit for measuring transactions. This allows adequate calculation of business income in noninflationary economies. In an inflationary economy, however, the lack of stability of the currency creates serious problems that prevent the correct calculation of real business income.

Distortions generated by inflation in the calculation of business income are caused by two elements: first, the lack of stability of the accounting unit adopted, and, second, the fact that many financial instruments are not indexed.

The loss in purchasing power of the currency gives rise to the following distortions:

- Transactions are registered in a currency that has a different purchasing power at the beginning, middle, and end of the financial year.
- Deductions for depreciation of fixed assets and the cost of goods sold are based on historic costs, and therefore do not represent the true cost of their contribution to the production process.

In the case of financial transactions, inflation forces interest rates up in order to reflect the loss in the principal's real value, so that a portion of the interest rate represents anticipated retirement of outstanding debt. Deductibility of nominal interest payments and taxation of nominal interest received lead to an incorrect calculation of income, underestimating it when nominal interest is deducted and overestimating it when it is taxed.

In developing countries with high inflation rates, the absence of inflation adjustments for business profits tends to reduce tax revenues considerably. Such countries are usually net capital importers and the financial liabilities of companies exceed the financial assets of the savers. This leads to higher deductions for nominal interest by companies than the nominal interest earned by national savers, which causes a negative impact on tax revenues that is not offset by the increased collections arising from underestimated depreciation deductions. Where the interest income of savers in the national financial system is exempt from tax, or is taxed at reduced rates, as is the case in Mexico, Guatemala, Honduras, Venezuela, and Paraguay, the negative revenue impact of nominal interest deductibility is even greater.

The absence of indexation, aside from the above-mentioned revenue effects, increases or decreases the tax burden of companies according to the nature of their assets and liabilities and their degree of indebtedness. Small and medium-sized companies that do not have access to financial markets suffer disproportionate increases in their tax burdens, whereas large companies can take action to reduce them considerably. The frequent use of "back-to-back" operations has been detected in several Latin American countries. Shareholders of large companies place their funds in national or foreign banks in order to guarantee credit for their companies, instead of financing them with equity capital, thereby managing to reduce company profits to a minimum.

To summarize, the absence of indexation causes serious problems with respect to the economic decisions of enterprises. It encourages indebtedness instead of equity financing and favors short-term assets as opposed to those with longer useful lives. This implies discrimination against economic activities with high stock levels and low turnover, sectors with longer-lived fixed assets, and enterprises with high equity ratios.

Given this situation, experts currently tend to agree on the advisability of introducing inflation adjustments for business profits. The main question is at what level of inflation are such adjustments justified, bearing in mind the greater complexity they introduce in the tax system. It is likely that with an inflation rate exceeding 20 percent or 30 percent per annum, these adjustments are justifiable.

Most countries that have introduced such adjustments have initially done so partially, generally permitting revaluation of fixed assets with the aim of adjusting depreciation. These partial adjustment mechanisms, besides reducing tax revenues, generate imbalances that favor financial strategies aimed at tax avoidance. An army of tax consultants emerges to provide advice on how to take advantage of these regulations. The complexities of partial adjustment systems, and the possibilities of tax evasion and avoidance that they create, make control practically impossible. These difficulties are caused principally by the lack of symmetry in these partial adjustment schemes. For example, in a system of partial adjustment, the taxpayer has an incentive to "inflate" his revaluation of assets to the maximum, since it will be reflected only in greater depreciation allowances (unless there is a separate tax on assets or net wealth). In an integrated or comprehensive adjustment system, such as that of Chile, asset revaluation also gives rise to an entry in the enterprise's profit account, which curbs such taxpayer maneuvers and facilitates the task of control.

The distortions, complexities, and revenue losses created by partial adjustment systems have led several countries, among them Argentina, Brazil, Chile, Colombia, Israel, Mexico, and Uruguay, to introduce more or less integrated or comprehensive systems of profit adjustment.

The Chilean method is considered one of the more technically appropriate. This method consists of the following:

(1) The revaluation of fixed assets according to CPI variations. Inventories are adjusted to the value of the last purchase while nonmonetary assets (indexed credits or credits in foreign currency) are adjusted in accordance with the variation of the agreed index or the value of the foreign currency. These revaluations are considered taxable income. Assets acquired during the assessment period are only adjusted for the fraction of the period since their purchase.

(2) The revaluation of the firm's net worth according to the CPI variation and of nonmonetary liabilities (indexed debts or debts in foreign currency) in the way indicated in (1) for similar assets. The sum of these adjustments is deducted as a loss.

(3) Depreciation is calculated using the adjusted asset figures for the beginning of the assessment period.

(4) The cost of sales is calculated using the adjusted value of the initial inventory of the reference period.

(5) When nonmonetary assets or liabilities are sold, the revalued figure is considered as cost for the purpose of determining capital gains.

The index used is generally the CPI, except when dealing with nonmonetary assets or liabilities expressed in foreign currencies or those subject to indexing. Such assets and liabilities are adjusted according to the variation in the value of the foreign currency or the index agreed upon. Inventories are adjusted, in general, to the value of the last purchase.[2]

The method described above shows the loss or gain that the firm has derived from inflation. In practice, this system has proved to be less complex to administer than previous partial systems. This is mainly because it is a comprehensive system, whose symmetry hinders tax evasion. It is interesting to note that in Chile the system, introduced in a year when inflation exceeded 300 percent (1975), is still in force, in spite of inflation having declined since 1975 to figures that fluctuate between 10 percent and 25 percent. This shows that both taxpayers and the administration have become accustomed to the system, which does not cause any real problems in application. One "technological" reason for the preservation of the system is that large and medium-sized companies have incorporated the monetary adjustment program in their computerized accounting systems and complications would arise were it to be eliminated.

Although large and medium-sized companies have adapted to the comprehensive adjustment system, this has not been easy for small companies. A senior civil servant of a country in which a comprehensive adjustment system is applied stated that he "prefers not to know what small companies do with the monetary adjustment system and especially with inventory valuation." For small businesses, an appropriate solution might be the cash flow system recently introduced in Mexico.

---

[2]The main conceptual defect of the Chilean system is that it bases adjustments for inventories on replacement costs and adjustments for assets and liabilities denominated in foreign currencies on individual exchange rates. For a full discussion of the criteria for valuation of inventories and assets and liabilities in foreign currency, see McLure and others (1990).

V. Personal Income Tax

Most countries tax the income of private individuals at progressive rates, exempting those whose income is below a certain level. When the tax brackets are measured in monetary units, inflation distorts these parameters. People who were previously exempt begin to be liable and taxpayers move up into higher tax brackets simply because of a nominal increase in their income. This "bracket creep" has led many countries to take corrective measures.

The decision of whether or not to introduce an automatic indexing system depends, among other factors, on the desired income policy. As regards tax administration, it is necessary to bear in mind the following:

- Automatic indexation of exemptions and tax brackets in accordance with a pre-established index is very easy to administer. If exemptions and brackets are expressed in an indexed unit, as is the tax unit of Chile (which is adjusted according to CPI variations), it is not necessary to modify tax forms or instructions to take account of the periodic adjustment. All that is required is the regular periodic announcement of the monetary value of the new tax unit.
- Adjustment of the exempt minimum is necessary to avoid an excessive increase in the number of taxpayers and consequently in the tax administration's work load. If wage earners without other sources of income are not required to file a tax return, the adjustment of the exempt minimum is not as important from an administrative point of view.
- Discretionary adjustments of tax brackets and exemptions are the least advisable because their predictability obliges the administration to make changes in tax forms, instructions, and programs, which increase administrative costs.

Another feature of income taxation that is distorted by inflation is the calculation of capital gains and losses. Many countries tax these gains while others exempt them. In the case of capital gains, distortions arise when comparing historic costs with current sale prices. Countries with high inflation levels that tax these gains generally permit indexation of historic costs according to a general index. In Chile, for example, in the period when occasional capital gains from the sale of real estate were taxed,[3] the CPI was used to index the original cost. Chile's experience was interesting because the indexation of capital gains was not

[3]This levy was introduced in 1964 and abolished in 1974.

difficult to apply; one of the reasons for eliminating this tax, however, was that most of the transactions, once indexed, resulted in capital losses.

VI. Taxes on Interest and Dividends

Capital markets are very sensitive to taxes on dividends and interest. When inflation accelerates, this is one of the areas in which tax treatment needs to be redesigned.

In addition to ensuring better compliance, withholding taxes on interest and dividends decreases the impact of inflationary erosion on revenue from these sources. The tax withheld may be an advance payment on account of the income tax or a final (definitive) payment. From an administrative point of view, a final tax is obviously preferable because it makes it easier to eliminate filing requirements for wage earners, including those who, in addition to a salary, receive interest income or dividends. Moreover, making the withholding tax a final tax eliminates the need to index the withheld amounts for purposes of crediting them against the final payment.

Although withholding makes it easier to tax interest, it does not solve the problem of how to establish a "real" tax base with respect to interest received. When an indexation clause has been included in the loan agreement, the tax law may exempt the indexation (monetary adjustment in Brazil) and tax only the real interest. If the loan is not indexed, nominal interest includes a portion that is an adjustment of the principal and another that is the "real" interest. Some countries have chosen to reduce the tax rate applicable to interest payments during periods of inflation in order to indirectly avoid taxing debt repayment. Chile applies a more technical solution: for tax purposes, loans are expressed in development units[4] and only amounts received by creditors that exceed the adjusted value of the loan are taxed as interest. Chile's experience has shown that such adjustments are workable.

VII. Types of Rates

One obvious result of inflation is the loss of revenue from taxes levied with specific rates. The classic recommendation in this case is to replace

[4]The development unit is an amount fixed by law that is adjusted daily from the tenth of each month until the ninth of the following month, according to the geometric average rate corresponding to the variation of the CPI in the calendar month immediately prior to the month being adjusted. The value of the development unit is published daily.

specific rates with ad valorem rates. From an administrative point of view, this measure makes control of such taxes more complicated, since it requires controlling sales prices, financial accounts, and so forth. An alternative is to keep the specific rates and legislate to establish their periodic adjustment in accordance with a specified index. The index chosen should relate to general price level changes (for example, the CPI) and not to changes in the prices of the goods taxed.

VIII. Fiscal Assessments

As regards property taxes, and especially taxes on real property, inflation reduces tax revenues because property values become outdated. In countries with high inflation rates it is impossible for periodic reassessments to keep values up to date. One practical solution, such as that applied in Chile for example, is to index assessments. At present, fiscal assessments are adjusted biannually in accordance with the CPI variation during the previous six months. This solution, although administratively simple, does not eliminate the distortions among assessments caused by changes in relative property values; on the contrary, it aggravates them. To reduce these distortions, periodic assessments are needed; however, given the chronic lack of resources in the tax administrations of developing countries, they are not usually possible.[5]

IX. Lessons from Experience with Inflation Adjustment Systems

It is generally accepted that when inflation exceeds certain limits, it is necessary to adjust the tax system to protect tax revenues and reduce inequities and distortions produced by inflation. Experience shows that such adjustments are also necessary for reasons related to tax administration. Indeed, if obvious inequities are not corrected, compliance levels will fall because of the perceived unfairness of the system. An example of unequal treatment is the advantage enjoyed by taxpayers who pay with a lag vis-à-vis wage earners whose taxes are withheld. Equally, if delinquent taxes and penalties for noncompliance are not indexed, the administration will be faced with a wave of delinquent taxpayers and tax evaders.

---

[5]In Chile, for example, a process of reassessment of all real estate has ended and will take effect in the second half of 1991. Current assessments derive from assessments performed in 1977 with respect to nonagricultural property and in 1980 with respect to agricultural property, indexed periodically in accordance with the property tax statute.

Experience has shown that ad hoc measures designed to maintain collection levels during inflationary periods—such as increases in rates—increase economic distortions and reduce tax compliance. For this reason, they are not a suitable substitute for a rational system of adjustments for inflation. The question is not, therefore, whether adjustments for inflation are advisable or not, but rather how they should be designed in order to meet their objective effectively.

From a tax administration point of view, certain methods of adjustment for inflation are less cumbersome to manage than others. However, most of them imply an additional cost for the taxpayer as well as for the administration.

Some of the lessons learned from experience with adjustments for inflation follow:

- Positive effects on revenues can be produced by shortening payment periods, increasing the number of provisional payments, and indexing payments. In order to achieve this, it is necessary to have a well-designed system of return filing and tax payment that permits adequate control. Collection through banks and the use of a single form for filing and paying the main business taxes have eased the implementation of measures to decrease collection lags.
- Comprehensive profits adjustments seem to cause fewer problems for tax administration than partial adjustments. The mechanics of comprehensive adjustments frustrate attempts to increase deductions by artificially inflating certain items (for example, indexation of assets and "back-to-back operations"), since they will show up as a profit in the profit and loss accounts.
- Automatic indexation of individual income tax brackets and exemptions gives rise to lower administrative costs than discretionary adjustments.
- Indexation of interest earned is feasible and does not cause major administrative problems, as long as there is a well-publicized daily index.

To conclude, we must emphasize that, despite the administrative costs involved in adjustments for inflation, once inflation exceeds certain limits these costs must be faced, as the alternative is the collapse of the tax system. The most that tax officials (and taxpayers) can demand is that the design of adjustment methods take into consideration the difficulties involved in applying them and that mechanisms that cause the fewest complications are chosen.

REFERENCES

Casanegra de Jantscher, Milka, "Taxing Business Profits During Inflation: The Latin American Experience," *International Tax Journal* (Winter 1976), pp. 128–46.

______, "Inflation Adjustment in Chile," in *Taxation in Developing Countries*, ed. by Richard M. Bird and Oliver Oldman (Baltimore: Johns Hopkins University Press, 4th ed., 1990).

Centro de Perfeccionamiento y Extensión Tributaria, "Corrección Monetaria 1984," Cartilla Técnica, No. 29 (Santiago, January 1984).

Hoerner, J. Andrew, "Indexing the Tax System for Inflation: Lessons from the British and Chilean Experiences," *Tax Notes International* (June 1990), pp. 552–56.

International Fiscal Association, "Inflation and Taxation," Proceedings of the Thirty-First International Congress of Financial and Fiscal Law, *Cahiers de Droit Fiscal International*, Vol. 62-a (Vienna, 1977).

______, "Adjustments for Tax Purposes in Highly Inflationary Economies," Proceedings of a Seminar held in Buenos Aires in 1984 During the Thirty-Eighth Congress of the International Fiscal Association (Antwerp: Kluwer, 1985).

______, "Administration and Compliance Costs of Taxation," Proceedings of the Forty-Third International Congress of Financial and Fiscal Law held in Rio de Janeiro in 1988, *Cahiers de Droit Fiscal International*, Vol. 74-b, 1989.

McLure, Charles, E., Jr., John Mutti, Victor Thuronyi, and George R. Zodrow, *The Taxation of Income from Business and Capital in Colombia* (Durham: North Carolina: Duke University Press, 1990).

Organization of American States, *Inflación y tributación*, Documentos Ocasionales, Programa del Sector Público (Washington, 1978).

Sadka, Efraim, "An Inflation-Proof Tax System? Some Lessons from Israel," IMF Working Paper No. 90/46 (Washington: International Monetary Fund, May 1990).

Tanzi, Vito, *Inflation and the Personal Income Tax: An International Perspective* (Cambridge, England: Cambridge University Press, 1980).

______, "Inflation, Real Tax Revenue, and the Case for Inflationary Finance: Theory with an Application to Argentina," *Staff Papers*, International Monetary Fund, Vol. 25 (September 1978), pp. 417–51.

Weaver, R. Kent, *Automatic Government: The Politics of Indexation* (Washington: Brookings Institution, 1988).

Comments

Renato Botaro

In the little more than twenty years since a major tax reform was implemented in Brazil at the three levels of government (municipal, state, and federal), many changes have occurred in the tax system without adequate harmonization among them. In the last twenty years, the inflation rate in Brazil has always been high. Five economic plans, or shock treatments, were adopted from 1986 to 1991.

The profound changes that the new federal constitution introduced in the fiscal area in 1988 resulted more from political than from technical considerations. Consequently, a new tax reform is necessary despite the relatively short time that has elapsed since the last one, and the Brazilian Government has begun work on this task.

Methods for Diminishing the Effects of Inflation—The Brazilian Experience

Some aspects of the Brazilian experience are important when considering methods for diminishing the negative impact on revenue of high inflation. It must be remembered that the Brazilian tax system has been subjected to adjustments for inflation for more than twenty years. They can be summarized as follows:

Provisional Payments

For large legal entities, an advance monthly payment of one twelfth of the income tax is required, based on the updated value of the previous year's tax.

The following are used for individuals: (1) withholding at source for employees; (2) mandatory monthly payments for professionals, rents from house leasing, and so on; and (3) monthly adjustment option for employees with more than one job. All prepayments are adjusted in the annual return, which can show a positive or negative balance (refund or amount owed).

Reduction of Payment Periods

The reduction of payment periods is a practice much used by the Brazilian tax authorities, notwithstanding the opposition from business and political circles.

Indexation of Payments

For many years, the value of adjustable obligations of the national treasury (ORTN) was adopted as an index to adjust tax payments. In 1986 these were replaced by national treasury obligations (OTN). In 1989 the index was changed again, this time to the value of the national treasury bonus (BTN), set monthly for general use and updated daily for tax purposes.

In February 1991 the total deindexation of the economy was decided on as a means of combating inflation, and a charge named the daily reference rate (TRD) was imposed on overdue tax payments. Although this charge is not an index, people insist on calling it one.

Thus, the last five years have seen five economic stabilization plans and three new indexes (ORTN, OTN, and BTN), before the whole approach was jettisoned in February 1991. At present, with inflation at some 9 percent a month, a new index is already felt to be necessary.

Brazilian reality thus confirms what was said in the paper: after a time, the adjustments caused by inflation become part and parcel of the tax culture and society can no longer get along without them.

Nevertheless, although in the Brazilian case the tax culture has already absorbed adjustments for inflation through the use of the appropriate indexes, it is difficult to count on the full understanding of the taxpayers. During the 1991 filing period, for example, the fact that the individual income tax return was filed at a time when inflation was slowed by a new economic plan made it difficult for people to understand that a correction of only 270 percent was being made on taxes withheld or paid provisionally in the previous year, when inflation had been over 300 percent. Subsequently, the Federal Supreme Court ordered application of that correction index suspended. We now face the problem of having to extend for the second time the deadline for submitting 1991 returns based on incomes of 1990.

Reasons for Adopting an Inflation Adjustment System

The rationale that may lead lawmakers to introduce an inflation adjustment system into tax legislation generally springs from the urge to reduce the effects of inflation on society. In that context the function of tax indexation is to avert the loss of real value from the moment the clock starts running until the tax payment is legally due.

In countries where inflation remains at a high level for many years, the adoption of tax indexation is primarily a means of fiscal justice, inasmuch as those who benefit most from its absence are those best able to pay higher taxes.

As for the mechanism of adjusting business profits for inflation, it has the advantage of presenting a picture that is closer to reality. In financial terms, the analysis of the assets of corporations reveals the existence of some assets whose value shrinks as inflation erodes the currency's purchasing power, and others that maintain their intrinsic value in spite of inflation. The former are monetary assets and the latter are nonmonetary assets. Only the nonmonetary assets should be subject to a monetary correction, because a new monetary expression is necessary for assets that keep their value unaltered despite changes in the currency's purchasing power.

Other Considerations

Inflation adjustments are necessary in a country experiencing chronic inflation or inflation above a reasonable degree. Without adjustments such a society's wealth can be virtually wiped out in a few years or reduced to merely symbolic worth. With respect to tax indexation, the inflation adjustment mechanism is also justified because it prevents the loss of tax revenue.

Meanwhile, it must be recalled that a tax indexing system can lead to general indexation of the economy through the adoption by businesses of the correction indexes used in the system. In such cases, indexation can represent a perverse form of inflation feedback.

In line with this thinking we must bear in mind that the monetary discounting indexes used by the adjustment system can turn into a psychological component of the inflationary process, interfering in price formation.

A problem that arises when the adjustments are made by using price indices is the lag due to the time needed for collection and processing of those indices. The price index used in a month thus usually measures the mean variation in the previous month's prices. In cases where the monetary correction index is announced at the beginning of the month, this will probably cause a lag of more than a month. That is how the inflationary feedback occurs.

Sometimes correcting for expected inflation is preferable to indexing on the basis of past inflation. In one way or another, indexing keeps inflation at levels where it is difficult to overcome.

The introduction of a system of inflation adjustment into tax legislation is complex and entails profound changes in the way businesses keep their accounts. Tax administration also suffers the effects of having to regulate procedures and guide businesses in applying the legislation correctly.

To prevent problems stemming from incorrect interpretations and inadequate tax planning, it is important that the system adopted should be perfectly understood in its structure, function, and effects, not only by the tax authorities but also by businesses and tax consultants.

Charles E. McLure, Jr.

Inflation creates problems in essentially three areas: measurement of income from business and capital, reduction in the real value of amounts stated in nominal (monetary) terms, and evaporation of real tax revenues because of collection lags. Inflation adjustment, or some ad hoc surrogate for it, is required for three reasons: to preserve the real value of tax revenues, to prevent economic distortions, and to prevent inequities. Administrative goals and compliance problems constrain what can be done to achieve these goals. It should be recognized, however, as the authors do, that inflation adjustment may reduce administrative problems, as well as cause them.

The authors devote about half of the paper to collection lags and similar issues—matters that affect primarily the preservation of real revenues—and the rest to other issues: the calculation of the taxable business income, indexing in the personal income tax, taxation of interest income, inflation and excise taxes, and fiscal valuation, issues where income measurement, equity, and neutrality figure more heavily. Reflecting my background as an economist, I would have preferred more emphasis on the second half of the paper; I will emphasize it in my comments. I have little to say about indexation of nominal amounts, which is simple and straightforward.

Collection Lags and Related Problems

Inflation, combined with lags in collections, can cause tax revenues to fall in real terms. The conceptually correct way to deal with this problem is to index payments. There may be problems in knowing the change in the relevant price index on a timely basis, but subsequent adjustments could be made in a final setting of accounts.

Such techniques as increasing the frequency of payments and consolidating tax return and payment forms are poor substitutes for indexing payments. If payments are made too frequently, administration and compliance problems inevitably arise. I am surprised that Mexico chose to rely so heavily on increasing the frequency of payments, which could have been seen in advance to swamp the tax administration system.

Income Measurement

The Haig-Simons definition of income—consumption plus the change in net wealth—is a useful point to begin in discussing the need for inflation adjustment in the measurement of income. Once inflation exceeds a relatively low threshold, it is meaningless to speak of implementing Haig-Simons, unless there is a comprehensive adjustment for inflation.[1] Inflation that is not anticipated undermines the fairness of an unindexed tax system. Anticipated inflation causes such a system to distort the allocation of resources. More commonly, both distortions and inequities occur. In addition, the opportunities for tax avoidance created by an unindexed system are likely to increase compliance and administrative burdens.

The authors' statement that "experts currently tend to agree on the advisability of introducing inflation adjustments for business profits" stands in sharp contrast to the conventional wisdom of a quarter century ago. The Taylor Mission to Colombia (see Joint Tax Program of the Organization of American States and the Inter-American Development Bank (1965, p. 84)) wrote:

> If inflationary pressure is to be contained, certainly *it is not desirable economic policy, in general, to remove its penalties through automatic adjustments*. A more therapeutic method is to permit the painful effects of inflation to be manifested for whatever beneficial effects these will have as a restraint on inflationary pressures. (emphasis added)

The Musgrave Commission (Musgrave (1971, p. 82)) reached the following similar conclusion:

> The Commission. . .believes that the proper solution for Colombia lies in a well-designed stabilization policy. . ., rather than a general and automatic adjustment for inflation provided through the tax system. Such an adjustment would tend to encourage inflation and have detrimental effects on economic development.

Inflation causes mismeasurement of income in four areas: depreciation (and similar) allowances, cost of goods sold from inventories,

[1] It is interesting to note, however, that Henry Simons, in his *Federal Tax Reform* (1950, p. 136), wrote derisively about the possibility of inflation adjustment in the measurement of income, "Does anyone really propose that we correct all tax bases for price-level changes?"

capital gains, and indebtedness (divergence between nominal and real interest income and expense).[2] It is common for business people to propose inflation adjustment (or ad hoc surrogates for it) for the first three of these; they hardly ever want adjustment for interest expense. Such partial steps to compensate for inflation, the authors rightfully note, "generate imbalances that favor financial strategies aimed at tax avoidance." I wish those responsible for tax policy in the United States—and even some of my academic colleagues—realized the problems caused by asymmetric or inconsistent treatment of similar or related transactions.

Despite this discussion of partial steps and asymmetrical treatment, the paper does not indicate clearly how the various forms of inflation adjustment in the measurement of income are related. In particular, how are the integrated systems of income measurement for companies in Chile and Colombia tied in with the taxation of interest received by individuals? Also, in countries that have inflation adjustment of the measurement of income from business and capital and deductions for interest on home mortgages, how is the latter treated?

Similarly, I was somewhat surprised to see the endorsement of a cash-flow tax for small business. It would seem that there are possibilities for game-playing in a system in which part of the economy is taxed under a cash-flow tax and other parts are not. My own proposal for avoiding the problems of income measurement addressed in the second half of the paper is what I call the simplified alternative tax or SAT.[3] Under the SAT, interest and dividends are neither deductible nor taxable and all business expenditures are deducted in the year in which they are incurred. This system avoids all the problems of inflation adjustment (as well as timing issues). In addition, it automatically takes care of another problem the authors address—the need to impose a final withholding tax on interest and dividends; these are taxed by disallowing a deduction for them.

Inflation has impacts on tax liabilities and incentives that depend in complicated ways on debt-equity ratios, types of investment, and provisions of the tax law. The marginal effective tax rate (METR) usefully summarizes the effects of these factors.[4]

[2]For further discussion, see McLure and others (1990, Chapter 7). Some might add exchange rate gains and losses to this list. I do not, because debts denominated in foreign currencies are just a special case of indebtedness.

[3]See McLure and others (1990, Chapter 9), or Zodrow and McLure (1991).

[4]See, for example, McLure and others (1990) for calculations of METRs under the Colombian tax system.

The Case for Specific Excises

Part of the conventional wisdom of public finance has been the superiority of ad valorem taxes, including excises, over specific excises, because the latter are vulnerable to inflation. I believe this view is fundamentally wrong. There are good reasons to prefer specific excises to ad valorem ones in many cases.

I would guess that in almost no case are the social costs connected with private consumption related directly to the value of the consumption; it is far more likely to be related to the quantity of consumption. For example, are the social costs (alcoholism, family dysfunction, traffic accidents) greater from drinking expensive Scotch whiskey than from drinking cheap rum? How about the costs of caring for those with lung disease caused by smoking cheap or expensive cigarettes? Do expensive pesticides necessarily cause more damage than cheap ones? What sense does it make to speak of using ad valorem effluent charges to combat pollution? Specific excises are clearly better in all these cases.

The point about vulnerability to inflation is at best a red herring. Specific excises can be indexed for inflation. They can be reviewed periodically and adjusted on the basis of the best and most recent knowledge about social costs—something that seems less likely to occur under an ad valorem tax system.

REFERENCES

Joint Tax Program of the Organization of American States and the Inter-American Development Bank, *Fiscal Survey of Colombia* (Baltimore: Johns Hopkins Press, 1965).

McLure, Charles E., Jr., John Mutti, Victor Thuronyi, and George R. Zodrow, *The Taxation of Business and Capital in Colombia* (Durham, North Carolina: Duke University Press, 1990).

Musgrave, Richard A., *Fiscal Reform for Colombia: Final Report and Staff Papers of the Colombian Commission on Tax Reform*, ed. by Malcolm Gillis (Cambridge, Massachusetts: Law School of Harvard University, International Tax Program, 1971).

Simons, Henry C., *Federal Tax Reform* (Chicago: University of Chicago Press, 1950).

Zodrow, George R., and Charles E. McLure, Jr., "Implementing Direct Consumption Taxes in Developing Countries," *Tax Law Review*, Vol. 46, No. 4 (1991), pp. 405–87.

8

Improving Tax Compliance

Carlos A. Silvani

This paper comments on the experiences of several countries with regard to tax compliance and suggests certain general guidelines for improving it, particularly in countries where there is a relatively high level of noncompliance.

The goal of tax administration is to foster voluntary tax compliance. Penalizing tax evaders or going after delinquent taxpayers are not in themselves the object of tax administration. Voluntary compliance may be encouraged, however, if the administration is successful in establishing a strong prospect that noncompliance will be detected and effectively punished.

Tax compliance will thus be furthered if there is an effective tax administration. An *effective* tax administration should not be confused with an *efficient* tax administration. An administration may be efficient in that its tax collection costs are very low, yet at the same time it may be ineffective if it is unable to enforce compliance. The effectiveness of the administration is not the only determinant of the level of voluntary compliance, but it is likely to be the key factor, especially in countries in which there is a high level of noncompliance. Many reasons contribute to evasive behavior, including the degree to which the community supports the government and its economic policies.[1] All the same, taxpayers will comply better if they believe that failure to do so will mean assuming a substantial risk of being penalized in a relatively severe fashion. Were this not so, there would be no way of explaining how it is that in Chile, in the late 1970s, with a military government that had limited popular support, there was nevertheless a marked rise in tax compliance. In Argentina, on the other hand, the late 1980s and early 1990s registered the lowest rates of tax compliance in that country's history, even though the government holding office at that time had the fullest support of the community. In Bolivia, with the

---

The author wishes to thank Leif Mutén and Angel Boccia for their comments on an earlier version of this paper.

[1]See Estela Calello, Susana Rovner, and Aldo Schlemenson, "Motivaciones de la evasión en el IVA" (Buenos Aires: Dirección General Impositiva, 1971).

advent of a democratic government, tax administration improved. In Colombia, the change is absolutely independent of popular support for the government, and the same could be said of Spain and Portugal. In other words, the level of tax compliance seems relatively independent of the taxpayers' degree of acceptance of their government and its policies.

The effectiveness of the tax administration is of course not the only determinant of tax compliance. It is enough to note in this connection the negative influence that macroeconomic variables such as the rate of interest and inflation may exert on tax compliance. Nor can it be doubted that a lower cost to taxpayers of complying with the system, its fairness, the simplicity of its laws and procedures, and the services that the tax administration provides to taxpayers are all important factors in expediting and stimulating voluntary compliance. Nevertheless, in countries with a very high degree of noncompliance, the ability of the tax administration to impose effective penalties is perhaps the key to shaping the behavior of taxpayers.

If this is so, then the problem is that of making tax administration effective. Tax administration will be effective if it is able to deal with the following key shortfalls:

(1) Unregistered taxpayers: The first shortfall originates in the gap between potential taxpayers and registered taxpayers.

(2) Stopfiling taxpayers: The second shortfall reflects the difference between registered taxpayers and those who file returns.

(3) Tax evaders: The third is the difference between the tax reported by taxpayers and the potential tax according to the law.

(4) Delinquent taxpayers: The fourth and last gap is the one between the amount of taxes that taxpayers report owing, or that the tax administration may eventually assess, and the tax actually paid by taxpayers.

If tax compliance is to improve, the tax administration must take effective action to deal with these shortfalls. Accordingly, when evaluating a tax administration, objective data must be looked at in order to estimate the degree of effectiveness displayed by the administration in dealing with each of these gaps. And important as it is to learn how effective the administration is in dealing with each gap, the truly key point is to determine the overall degree of effectiveness of the administration. If the administration is able to effectively control only one of these gaps, noncompliance will shift to the gap where the administration exercises weaker control. It is not enough, for instance, to make strong efforts to eliminate the informal economy and register all potential taxpayers if registered taxpayers cannot then be made to file returns and to report and pay the proper amount of tax. This point is particularly important in designing tax policy as well as in allocating tax administration resources.

I. Monitoring Tax Compliance

This section outlines some ideas for narrowing the gaps described above.

Unregistered Taxpayers

Obviously, one prerequisite for learning whether a taxpayer is registered is to have a reliable and efficient single register of taxpayers (SRT). Such a register is needed not only to control this gap but also to provide the basic hinge on which will turn many of the activities to be carried out in order to narrow the other gaps.

Single Register of Taxpayers

The single register of taxpayers should consist of a taxpayer identification number (TIN) and of information associated with each TIN. The data that should be associated with each TIN are name, surnames (distinguishing between paternal and maternal surnames), commercial business name, address, business activity, and type of tax payable by the taxpayer. For control purposes, and depending on the characteristics of the tax system, it will be important in some countries to establish a connection between the TIN of a partnership or a corporation and the TIN of its members, indicating their percentage interest in the entity. Also connected with the TIN of companies (whether sole proprietorships or legal entities) should be the location of branches, if there are any.

Taxpayer Identification Number (TIN)

Ideally, there should be a single TIN capable of identifying the taxpayer in connection with every tax. In some countries, this would not be a realistic solution over the short term, but it should remain a desirable long-term goal. The TIN should be the same number assigned to individuals for purposes of civilian identification—the identity card number, for instance—so long as this number is consistent with all the requirements of a highly reliable TIN. If the TIN is the same as the identity card number, it is easier to cross-check information when monitoring taxpayer compliance. But even where the TIN is the same as, say, the number on the identity card, the tax administration will still have to make sure that (1) no more than one TIN is assigned to any one taxpayer and (2) each TIN is assigned to only one taxpayer. This means that the assignment of TINs, or at least its control, should be centralized.

The TIN should not include any taxpayer characteristic likely to change over time, such as the business activity or the location of the taxpayer's domicile. Otherwise, a problem might arise because the TIN would need to change along with any of those circumstances. In principle, the best TIN is simply sequential. However, if the TIN is not sequential and some of its digits reflect important information, that information should be permanent and unchanging: the date or place of birth of the individual, for example. As for the TIN of companies, only one TIN should be assigned to each company; branches of the company, therefore, should not have a different TIN from that of the head office.

Keeping Domiciles Current

As with any dynamic data base, keeping the single register of taxpayers current is as important as constructing it. Out of all the data in the register the key piece of information to keep current is domicile, because the administration will lose touch with the taxpayer whose domicile is not known with precision. In Colombia in 1986, for instance, before the revamping of the tax administration, computer printouts of value-added tax (VAT) forms mailed out to taxpayers had to be suspended because more than 20 percent of the forms were being returned by the post office for having the wrong address.

Experience has shown that requiring taxpayers to report a change of address and establishing penalties for those who fail to do so is not enough. In some cases, the most practical solution is to record once a year all addresses reported on, say, tax returns, even though the percentage of taxpayers filing returns with a different address than the one registered in the single register of taxpayers is likely to be under 10 percent. An alternative solution is to require tax returns (VAT or income tax) to be filed with identification labels preprinted by the tax administration. In this case, all that needs to be done is to pick out the corrections made by taxpayers on the preprinted labels. Having the tax administration make available preprinted identification labels is a highly recommended practice not only because it helps to update domiciles but also because it guarantees that the taxpayer will correctly use the TIN assigned under the single register of taxpayers.

Business Activity Code

A business activity code should be connected with each taxpayer. This code should preferably follow the structure of the Uniform International Industrial Code (UIIC) to make it easier to draw comparisons with the country's national accounts and with international statistics. To begin with, some three hundred different economic activities ought to be enough.[2]

From time to time, the code of business activity assigned to each major taxpayer should be reviewed. An error resulting from an improper code being assigned to a major taxpayer may cause substantial statistical distortions. Tax returns should ask for (and every so often pick out) the alphabetical description of the business activity to facilitate such review.

Detecting Unregistered Taxpayers

As for detecting unregistered taxpayers, the problem lies primarily in finding the relatively small taxpayers. In countries such as Peru, however, where the informal economy is very large, unregistered taxpayers may also be of medium size. Unregistered taxpayers may be detected chiefly by two means:

(1) The first option involves searches or inspections (*batidas*) in which a group of officials goes door-to-door within a particular geographical area, checking that all persons or establishments engaged in a taxable business activity in that area are properly registered (see Silvani and Radano, Chapter 2 in this volume).

(2) The second option is to go through registered taxpayers in order to detect their suppliers or customers who are not registered taxpayers. This may be done by checking whether purchase invoices being deducted and sales invoices being issued show TINs for taxpayers registered in the single register of taxpayers. If withholding systems are in place, unregistered taxpayers may also be detected by cross-checking the data against the information supplied by withholding agents with respect to transactions in which taxes have been withheld.

On the other hand, problems arise in some cases because the tax administration massively registers persons who are not, and should not, be taxpayers. In these cases, the problem created by "overregistration" of taxpayers is as bad as, or worse than, that of locating unregis-

[2]See Alan A. Tait, ed., *Value-Added Tax: Administrative and Policy Issues*, IMF Occasional Paper No. 88 (Washington: International Monetary Fund, October 1991).

tered taxpayers. Examples of this situation were observed some years ago in Argentina, Brazil, Peru, and Portugal.

Registering a person and assigning that person a TIN is not too heavy a burden for the tax administration, as long as the tax obligations incumbent on such persons are precisely defined. Persons who are not active taxpayers and are therefore under no obligation to file tax returns should not be confused with active taxpayers. Otherwise, a large number of taxpayers will appear to have filed no tax returns, even though they have no obligation to do so, and this will needlessly hamper the work of the tax administration.

Taxpayers Filing No Returns

In many countries, the ratio of stopfiling taxpayers to total registered taxpayers is higher than 20 percent. Some examples are noted in Table 1.

The ratios set out in Table 1 are far higher than desirable. This is usually due to three factors: (1) the single register of taxpayers is out of date and includes many taxpayers who are no longer in business; (2) some returns are filed with errors in the TIN and, accordingly, persons who have filed show up as stopfiling taxpayers; and (3) the tax administration does not deal systematically with stopfiling taxpayers.

The first two problems may be solved by properly updating the register and distributing preprinted identification labels to taxpayers, as described in the preceding section. As for the third problem, it is important that the administration should take steps to exert its control over

Table 1. Ratio of Stopfiling VAT Taxpayers to Total Registered Taxpayers

Country	Year	Percentage of Stopfiling VAT Taxpayers
Sri Lanka	1990	40[1]
Philippines	1987	39[1]
Mexico	1984	33[2]
Colombia	1986	30
Bolivia	1989	23
Portugal	1987	17
Chile	1987	15

Source: IMF, Fiscal Affairs Department.
[1]Relates to the tax on business turnover.
[2]Relates to income tax.

Table 2. Chile: Percentage of Stopfiling VAT Taxpayers, 1987

Taxpayer Size	Annual Sales (*In thousands of U.S. dollars*)		Percentage of Stopfiling Taxpayers[1]			
	More than	Up to	Agriculture	Industry	Commerce	All activities
T1	13,217 or more		0	0	4.4	1.9
T2	2,233	13,217	4.1	2.3	2.7	2.8
T3	852	2,233	5.9	3.9	3.9	4.1
T4	299	852	5.6	5.5	3.6	4.7
T5	80	299	5.6	5.9	5.5	6.1
T6	28	80	6.9	8.4	6.8	7.7
T7	0	28	10.7	18.6	15.8	16.7
T8	Sales equal to zero		16.2	23.7	17.5	15.6
All taxpayers			10.2	13.9	13.9	14.9

Source: IMF, Fiscal Affairs Department.

[1]Stopfiling taxpayers mean those who did not file at least one monthly VAT return in 1987.

major stopfiling taxpayers. In this connection, and in order to define an adequate strategy for monitoring stopfiling taxpayers, it is advisable to rank stopfiling taxpayers by size and by business activity. This is illustrated in Table 2.

Obviously, priority must be given to monitoring stopfiling taxpayers whose sales volume is highest. Control of these taxpayers must be monthly and should be directed in particular to monitoring major taxes, which are generally the VAT (or sales tax), excises, and taxes withheld by the taxpayer, if these taxes are monthly. Deferring action on these taxpayers may mean that the taxes owed to the treasury will be used by them for financing their own business activities. Such a situation should be detected and immediately corrected, because the accumulation of past due and unpaid taxes may climb to very high figures (particularly where withholding is involved) which may mean that after some time the taxpayer may no longer be able to pay even if he wishes to do so. If this should happen, the problem of delinquency may cease to be the company's problem and may become, for the most part, the tax administration's problem.

As for smaller stopfiling taxpayers, control over them could be exercised every six months or every year. Thus, once or twice a year, taxpayers would be required to file any returns that have been omitted and to pay the relevant fines. Imposing and collecting fines is essential in combating this kind of tax delinquency, for it is virtually the only enforcement tool available as a rule to tax administrations in this situation.[3]

In many countries, interest and penalties must be paid before or simultaneously with the filing of overdue tax returns. This makes it difficult to regularize delinquent taxpayers and diminishes the effectiveness of tax administration. The proper policy is to accept the amount of money that the taxpayer is in each instance ready to pay, billing him later on for any balance that might result from a review of the figures. In any event, whether or not payment of the penalties is demanded as a prerequisite for letting taxpayers file overdue returns, the information system should always monitor the penalties imposed. To require as a condition for accepting an overdue tax return that the taxpayer pay all interest and penalties in full merely causes the taxpayer (1) to lower the tax reported or (2) to remain as a stopfiling taxpayer. Tax returns should include two special boxes for the taxpayer himself to settle the interest and penalties due. This would be consistent with the general

[3]In some countries the tax administration is also able, if no tax return has been filed for a particular year, to assess the tax owed by reference to the tax reported in the preceding year.

principle of self-assessment and the information system could check whether the taxpayer has correctly paid the penalties.

Delinquent Taxpayers

In a manner similar to the above suggestion, the tax administration should take swift and effective action on delinquent taxes, in order to make it clear that tax delinquency is a very expensive source of financing. As a rule, tax delinquency is very concentrated, that is to say, a small percentage of delinquent taxpayers accounts for a high percentage of unpaid taxes. Collection priorities should therefore be set consistently with the amount owed. In addition, priority should be accorded to collecting newer debts because usually it is easier to collect on newer debts. For this reason, every effort should be made to collect before the amount outstanding becomes uncollectible. Furthermore, in order to evaluate the effectiveness of collection, it is advisable that uncollectible debts be written off or at least set apart from files on collectible amounts. Concentrating on collecting the newer and more substantial debts will make it possible over time to reduce the ratio of delinquent debt to total collection.

Consideration should be given to assigning collection of small amounts—say under US$10,000—to private collection agencies. The reason is twofold: (1) private agencies would be paid only if they collect the amount owed, which ought to make them more effective than the tax agency; and (2) tax administrations are always short of resources and, in general, rarely collect small delinquent amounts.

To begin with, the tax administration could delegate to the private sector all out-of-court collection entailing completion of all steps preceding executory process and the enforced collection of the amount due. Second, judicial collection might be delegated—which in some countries would require legislative changes. Be that as it may, it would be advisable to have private sector companies deal with collecting minor delinquent amounts, even if it means paying out in commissions the full proceeds from penalties and even part of the tax collected. The idea is to change the behavior of taxpayers, because they will know that if they fail to pay on time they will inexorably have to pay surcharges on top of the tax.

Delegating to the private sector the collection of minor amounts of delinquent taxes also would save the tax administration money. Just as it is often advisable to turn tax collection over to banks, so it would be worthwhile to place collection of minor delinquent taxes in the hands of specialized agencies. The same idea is behind both propositions: to free up resources in order that the tax administration may concentrate on its basic functions.

As for large delinquent amounts, collection of these should not be left to the private sector. If the fee for collecting the amount is set as a percentage of the taxes recovered, large amounts of delinquent taxes could drive up the cost excessively. Besides, in many countries the largest tax debts are owed by government companies or large companies, and collection of the debt may be connected with the settlement of economic and social problems that lie beyond the scope of tax administration.

Control of Tax Evasion

As with any complex system, the effectiveness of a tax administration is determined by its weakest subsystem. Even if a tax administration is very effective in detecting stopfiling or delinquent taxpayers, the overall effectiveness of the administration will be low if it is unable to control evasion. Noncompliance will then take the form of evasion and will widen the existing gap between the amount of reported taxes and the potential tax foreseen by the law.

In order to gauge the effectiveness of the monitoring function and to determine the best strategy to follow, it is advisable to (1) analyze the data in tax returns filed by taxpayers and (2) compare actual tax receipts with the estimated potential tax receipts.

Analyzing the Data in Tax Returns

Depending on the data processing capacity of the tax administration, it may be possible to obtain statistical data that will provide some idea of taxpayer compliance and, in line with that information, guide the enforcement policy. Below, to illustrate, are some income tax and VAT statistics.

Corporate income tax

Table 3 shows the ratio between profits and reported sales in tax year 1985 in a selected European country for all economic activities.

Table 4 shows the percentage of taxpayers who in tax year 1985 reported profits lower than 3 percent of sales in the same European country, for selected business activities. By analyzing these data, the tax administration can gauge whether they reflect evasive behavior

Table 3. Percentage of Taxpayers According to Profits/Sales Ratio Reported for Income Tax, in a European Country, Tax Year 1985

	All Economic Activities	
Profits/Sales	Percentage of taxpayers	Accumulated percentage of taxpayers
Losses	25.3	25.3
From 0 to 1 percent	12.5	37.8
From 1 to 2 percent	11.4	49.2
From 2 to 3 percent	16.1	65.3
From 3 to 4 percent	13.4	78.7

Source: IMF, Fiscal Affairs Department.

Table 4. Percentage of Taxpayers According to Profits Reported for Income Tax in a European Country, Tax Year 1985

Business Activity Code	Selected Business Activity	Percentage of Taxpayers Reporting Profits Lower Than 3 Percent of Sales
3220	Manufacture of wearing apparel, except footwear	70.08
3311	Sawmills and woodworking by mechanical means	72.69
3320	Manufacture of furniture, except metal and molded plastic furniture	75.43
3699	Manufacture of other nonmetal mineral products	70.97
6105	Wholesale trade in tools, hardware, and electrical appliances	74.46
6205	Retail trade in construction materials, metals, and tools	71.77
6206	Retail trade in automobiles, motorcycles, and bicycles	76.76

Source: IMF, Fiscal Affairs Department.

in any particular business activity, and direct its enforcement action accordingly.

Tables 5 and 6 show income tax data from a selected Latin American country for the tax year 1989.

Tables 3 through 6 are meant merely to illustrate, and no comparison of the data set out in them is intended. In the countries taken as examples, however, this information was used as the basis for selecting the business activities and the taxpayers to be monitored, and in both instances the results were highly positive.

Table 5. Percentage of Taxpayers According to Profits/Sales Ratio Reported for Income Tax, in a Latin American Country, Tax Year 1989[1]

Profits/Sales	Percentage of Taxpayers	Accumulated Percentage of Taxpayers	Profits/Sales Average Ratio
Losses	50.0	50.0	0.0
From 0 to 1 percent	6.2	56.2	0.4
From 1 to 2 percent	6.0	62.2	1.1
From 2 to 3 percent	5.0	67.2	2.4
From 3 to 4 percent	3.7	70.9	3.4

Source: IMF, Fiscal Affairs Department.
[1]Covers only 7 percent of taxpayers contributing 87 percent of total tax revenues. Banking and insurance activities were not included.

Table 6. Percentage of Taxpayers According to Profits/Assets Ratio Reported for Income Tax, in a Latin American Country, Tax Year 1989[1]

Profits/Assets	Percentage of Taxpayers	Accumulated Percentage of Taxpayers	Profits/Assets Average Ratio
Losses	50.0	50.0	0.0
From 0 to 1 percent	3.5	53.5	0.3
From 1 to 2 percent	3.1	56.6	1.5
From 2 to 3 percent	2.7	59.3	2.5
From 3 to 4 percent	2.8	62.1	3.4

Source: IMF, Fiscal Affairs Department.
[1]Covers only 7 percent of taxpayers contributing 87 percent of total tax revenues. Banking and insurance activities were not included.

VAT

One piece of information frequently used to analyze compliance with the VAT is the markup reported. Markup is the ratio of all sales to all purchases reported for the VAT during a specific period—one year, for instance. A ratio or coefficient equal to or lower than 1 indicates that the taxpayer is reporting taxable annual sales equal to or lower than his taxable annual purchases. In other words, he is saying that he does not have a positive markup or "profit margin" between sales and purchases sufficient to defray the cost of salaries, financial costs, and other expenses not covered by the VAT.

Table 7 shows the markup reported by VAT taxpayers for all business activities in a selected European and in a selected Latin American country.

As indicated earlier with respect to income tax, Table 7 is intended merely to illustrate the point by using as a specific example the statistical data which in some countries have proved very useful in defining enforcement strategies and guidelines for selecting taxpayers to be audited.

Experience has shown that taxpayers who report a low markup (under 1.10, for instance) have a strong likelihood of turning out to be tax evaders. Experience also indicates, however, that taxpayers with a very low markup (lower than 0.50, for example), can usually furnish reasonable explanations (such as being engaged in the export trade or in making large investments) and the low markup reported cannot necessarily be accounted for as tax evasion.

Estimating Tax Evasion

In some cases, estimating tax evasion may be important because choosing the correct enforcement strategy may depend on the level of evasion prevailing in a particular country. Annex I includes an outline

Table 7. Taxpayer Distribution According to Markup Reported for VAT

Markup Reported for VAT[1]	Percentage of Taxpayers			
	Latin American country		European country	
	Percentage	Accumulated percentage	Percentage	Accumulated percentage
0.01 to 0.50	4.6	4.6	8.6	8.6
0.5 to 1.00	24.3	28.9	16.1	24.7
1.0 to 1.10	19.1	48.0	9.5	34.2
1.1 to 1.20	10.6	58.6	9.4	43.6
1.2 to 1.30	6.4	65.0	7.2	50.8
1.3 to 1.40	4.3	69.3	5.8	56.6
1.4 to 1.50	3.1	72.4	4.7	61.3
1.5 to 1.60	2.4	74.8	3.9	65.2
1.6 to 1.70	1.9	76.7	3.2	68.4
1.7 to 1.80	1.7	78.4	2.7	71.1
1.8 to 1.90	1.4	79.8	2.3	73.4
1.9 to 2.00	1.2	81.0	2.0	75.4
2.0 to 2.10	1.1	82.1	1.6	77.0
Higher than 2.10	17.9	100.0	23.0	100.0

Source: IMF, Fiscal Affairs Department.

[1]Total yearly sales reported, divided by reported purchases for the same year.

of a methodology that has been used several times to estimate evasion of the VAT.

At one end of the scale are countries that have very low levels of evasion—below 10 percent, for instance. In these cases, the enforcement strategy and the system of penalties ought to be steered toward preserving the existing order, so that taxpayers who are complying do not change their behavior as a result of observing those who evade. The most advisable course of action in these cases is to impose drastic penalties and make an example of tax evaders. "Society must punish the bad in order that the good may remain good."[4]

At the other end of the scale may be found those countries with tax evasion levels close to 50 percent. Here, both the problem and the strategy must be totally different, because it is a question of reversing the existing situation. We will deal with this topic below.

II. Guidelines for Tax Audit

This section discusses some general ideas which, taken as a frame of reference, are useful in establishing priorities and planning the allocation of audit resources.[5] The audit function is of crucial importance to a tax administration; if it is not reasonably effective, tax administration will not be reasonably effective either.

To narrow the gap between the tax reported by taxpayers and the potential tax defined by law, an adequate audit plan must be put into practice. The plan must provide for broad coverage of the universe of taxpayers and must encompass diverse economic activities and taxpayers of various sizes. As described below, the various forms of noncompliance must be combated in the manner most suitable to each. In addition, a good audit plan requires special programs to prevent noncompliance. To implement such a plan, an adequate share of the tax administration's manpower must be allocated to this task, but the reality is that many countries devote to tax audit only a small percentage of their tax administration personnel. Many tax administrations assign only 10 percent or 15 percent of their staff to audit. In countries where there is a low level of evasion, on the other hand, the percentage of personnel generally assigned to tax audit is about 40 percent.

---

[4]L. Illanes and L. McArthur, *El control de los impuestos en los países en desarrollo* (Santo Domingo, Dominican Republic, 1981).

[5]Based on Milka Casanegra de Jantscher and Carlos Silvani, "Guidelines for Administering a VAT," *International VAT Monitor* (December 1990), pp. 2–19.

The effectiveness of the audit function should not be measured in terms of straight tax receipts derived from additional assessment; what should be gauged is rather to what extent this function contributes to improving tax compliance. Measuring the effectiveness of tax audit by the amount of taxes collected through audits is like evaluating the authorities responsible for enforcing traffic laws on the basis of how much money they collect in fines from drivers. For both the tax administration and the traffic authorities the objective is to secure maximum voluntary compliance (that is, to minimize noncompliance) without regard to the revenues that may be directly obtained through control. It follows from this line of reasoning that the preferred course of action may be to make the presence of a traffic or a tax inspector conspicuous so as to forestall any breach of the law, even if this action is expected to yield no direct collection of revenue.

The audit function should preferably be evaluated in terms of the quantity and quality of audits carried out and the revenues "voluntarily" paid.[6] It is advisable to encourage the filing of amended returns (corrections) in which the taxpayer acknowledges the mistakes or omissions made by him and detected through tax audit. Amended returns, being returns filed by the taxpayers themselves, are not subject to the costly and lengthy proceedings involved in tax disputes. Even if the taxpayer is not willing to acknowledge the full amount of the tax claimed by the administration, it is preferable in some cases to accept the filing of "voluntary" amended returns in which the taxpayer acknowledges part of the unpaid tax, rather than to pursue an official assessment reflecting what the tax administration believes to be the full amount of the underpaid tax. Official assessments usually involve a legal dispute and it is often better to reach a reasonable compromise accepted by the taxpayer than to obtain a favorable judgment in a court of law.

Typical Forms of Evasion

Adequate planning of the audit function requires definition of the general guidelines for combating the various forms of tax evasion. Some of the most common forms are described below.

Evasion with Fraud

A taxpayer guilty of evasion with fraud commits tax evasion through fraudulent actions such as forging or falsifying records. Accordingly,

[6]Voluntary collection is revenue obtained from the amended returns (corrections) filed by taxpayers after they have been audited.

such actions go beyond the scope of taxation and into the area of criminal offenses. Fraud should be punished even where no harm is done to the treasury.

In order to combat fraud, special programs should be put in place for the thorough examination of a small number of cases. Taxpayers to be audited are those whose characteristics make it reasonable to suppose, in light of earlier auditing, that they have committed fraud. For evasion with fraud, the strategy should rely on the imposition of very stiff penalties; some countries impose prison terms. The penalty should be very severe and should be made public because it must serve as a deterrent. The chief goal of this strategy is not to punish the person guilty of committing fraud in order that he should not do it again but to make an example of that person.

Evasion Without Fraud

To combat those who qualify only as tax evaders—because they have underreported their taxes without committing fraud in the process—the strategy should be different. The evader should be dissuaded from engaging in this behavior again. Here the purpose is not to punish the tax evader in order to make an example of him to others but to prevent repeat offenses. The evader will change his behavior if he learns, or if he believes, that tax evasion does not pay.

In areas where there is a high level of noncompliance, evasion basically hinges on two variables: (1) the probability of being caught and (2) the penalty for evasion. The way to increase the probability of detecting and punishing tax evaders (that is, to increase the risk inherent in tax evasion) is by developing a strategy based on massive and speedy control. The idea is to take action on some of the specific violations committed by the taxpayer, without looking into whether he may have committed others. This would broaden the audit coverage (the ratio between taxpayers and number of audits), thereby raising the risk implicit in evasion. In countries where the tax compliance level is low, the object of enforcement should be to bring about not perfect compliance by a few taxpayers but better compliance by most taxpayers.

If the penalty structure is reasonably adequate, priority should be given to increasing the likelihood of "effectively" punishing the tax evader. Effectively means that the taxpayer should actually pay the penalty, not that he should be punished on paper through an official tax assessment that will never be paid or that will be paid only in very small part. Furthermore, if the likelihood of effectively punishing evasive behavior is very low, taxpayers will take the risk even if the penalty is very severe.

Tax Avoidance

Tax avoidance is the behavior of those taxpayers who take advantage of legal loopholes in order to underreport their taxes. In other words, they take advantage of circumstances not clearly provided for in the legislation, or deficiently construed, in order to lighten their tax burden. If tax avoidance is to be detected, audit programs must be carried out with that specific end in view. Once having detected the manner in which taxes are being avoided, the problem may be overcome by refining the legal provisions and their interpretation, in other words, by amending the legislation. This kind of underpayment of taxes is sometimes engaged in by large taxpayers who have trained professionals to advise them on the interpretation of legal provisions.

Preventive Action

An audit plan should also provide for preventive action, the aim of which should be to persuade taxpayers that evasion does not pay. This is achieved if the tax administration can show the taxpayer that it has the information and the operational ability to punish him if he evades taxes.

It is advisable to devise enforcement programs whose chief purpose is to let the taxpayer know that the tax administration has information on certain economic transactions such as imports, leases, purchases, sales, and payments for professional services. Here the purpose of a visit by an inspector, or of a letter mailed to the taxpayer, is to show the latter that the tax administration has information which, after the tax becomes due, will be compared with his tax returns in order to detect possible inconsistencies. It is obviously not necessary to give the taxpayer a detailed account of all the information the agency has or does not have. The point is to demonstrate to a significant number of taxpayers, before they commit tax evasion, that the tax administration processes data on their economic transactions and that this information will be used in detecting evasion.

Auditing Large Taxpayers

In general, auditing of large taxpayers should be steered primarily toward detecting the tax avoidance practices they engage in through legal interpretations or transactions with related parties. The likelihood is small that major taxpayers would engage in gross instances of tax evasion as not issuing invoices for their sales or falsifying inventory figures, because their own organization and accounting systems do not allow it.

It needs to be kept in mind that the comments below refer only to the audit of large taxpayers and are not applicable to other enforcement actions of the tax administration such as those aimed at detecting stopfiling and delinquent taxpayers.

It is not a good idea to concentrate on auditing large taxpayers. Some countries fall into the error of overdoing the allocation of resources to auditing large taxpayers because it is presumed that this is where the largest tax payoff is to be found. Although this assumption may be correct, and the productivity for each audited case (the potential additional tax to be collected) may be raised by auditing large taxpayers, total tax receipts from all taxpayers may turn out to be lower if auditing of medium or small taxpayers is neglected. This is so because total tax receipts may grow more by focusing audit on medium and small taxpayers, owing to the persuasive effect that this policy has on all taxpayers as a whole.

In some countries almost the entire audit staff is devoted to auditing large taxpayers. The reasoning behind this is that economic concentration is very high and audit activities should therefore be highly concentrated as well. For instance, because as much as 70 percent of tax revenues are accounted for by 5 percent of taxpayers it is presumed that audit should focus mainly on this 5 percent. Such a policy can lead to the absurdity of concentrating tax receipts even more. Thus, in this example, if the tax administration takes no action with respect to the medium and small taxpayers that make up the remaining 95 percent, a situation may develop where 5 percent of all taxpayers will account for 100 percent of all tax revenues.

Concentration of tax receipts in large taxpayers has two causes: (1) income and production are often concentrated and (2) the high rate of tax evasion by medium and small taxpayers, who for this very reason should be especially targeted for audit.

It has been shown in certain cases that a change in audit strategy intended to tighten control over medium and small taxpayers' compliance leads to an increase in total tax receipts and that, notwithstanding the high degree of concentration, this rise in total tax revenues originates primarily in medium and small taxpayers. As shown in Table 8, in Chile, for instance, with the improved effectiveness of tax administration that was partly due to a change in audit strategy, there was a real increase of 55.5 percent in VAT receipts during 1979–82. This growth was due

Table 8. Chile: Increase in VAT Receipts, 1979–82

Taxpayer Size[1]	Percentage Increase
Large	16.5
Medium	86.9
Small	185.6
All taxpayers	55.5

Source: Chile, Internal Revenue Service.

[1]Large taxpayers were defined as those with annual sales of more than US$6 million; medium, between US$6 million and US$600,000; and small, under US$600,000.

to an increase in tax receipts of 16.5 percent from large taxpayers, 86.9 percent from medium taxpayers, and 185.6 per cent from small taxpayers. (See Table 9 for the change in the concentration of VAT receipts in Chile, caused by the improved compliance of medium and small taxpayers.)

Encouraging Future Voluntary Compliance

When the goal is to raise the prevailing level of tax compliance significantly and permanently, promoting compliance is as important as punishing noncompliance. In this connection it is always self-defeating to declare tax amnesties "for the last time," because amnesties actually amount to a reward granted to the tax evader. It is desirable, on the other hand, to encourage future voluntary compliance by concentrating audit activities on the current tax year and blocking off previous years from review. If any significant violations are found while going over the current year, then all preceding periods not barred by the statute of limitations would be looked into. Those taxpayers who have evaded taxes will find it in their interest to have a good future perfor-

Table 9. Chile: Concentration of VAT Receipts

	Percentage of Receipts	
Taxpayer Size[1]	1979	1982
Large	63.4	47.5
Medium	23.2	27.8
Small	13.4	24.6
	100.0	100.0

Source: Chile, Internal Revenue Service.

[1]Large taxpayers were defined as those with annual sales of more than US$6 million; medium, between US$6 million and US$600,000; and small, under US$600,000.

mance if by doing so they are able to block off the past. It goes without saying that this behavioral change will come about only if truly effective auditing is established successfully. Systems similar to the above have been used in Argentina, Chile, and Mexico and have been found useful during a transition period, until a reasonable level of compliance can be assured.

The Withholding Problem

In several countries where tax compliance levels are low, various kinds of withholding systems have been introduced in an effort to reverse the prevailing situation. In very broad terms, the premise is that large taxpayers must withhold the tax when they do business with medium or small taxpayers. Thus, for instance, some countries prescribe that if the government or a large company buys from a medium or small taxpayer, the former must not pay to the latter the full amount of the VAT due on the transaction, but must instead withhold a portion of it. Likewise, if a large company sells to a "nonmajor" taxpayer, that company must collect a surcharge which will be a partial payment against the tax payable by the medium or small taxpayer. Although countries such as Argentina, Chile, Colombia, and Ecuador have successfully implemented various withholding systems, it needs to be stressed that withholding should not be looked at as a cure-all for the problem of tax evasion. It is well to remember that every time a tax is withheld it becomes necessary to monitor not only the withholding agent to make sure that the amounts withheld are actually turned over to the treasury but also the "withholdee" to verify that *only* the amount withheld, and no more, was deducted from the tax owed.

In short, tax administrations that use withholding systems in a general way should evaluate the effectiveness of each kind of withholding. To do this it is necessary to establish at least at the aggregate level (considering all taxpayers) whether the amount collected for each type of withholding is the same, higher, or lower than the amount of deductions taken by taxpayers for each tax withheld. This analysis is crucial because one of the problems observed is that, over time, if withholding is not effectively controlled by the tax administration, the amounts withheld are not turned in by the withholding agents at the proper time and, in addition, taxpayers deduct as amounts withheld larger than those actually withheld.

III. Information Systems

To implement the suggestions made above, an adequate information system is essential. The key is to diagnose properly the situation prevailing in each country and to devise a strategy for introducing an adequate information system. As shown by the experience of many countries, buying computers alone is not enough to improve the effectiveness of tax administration. Table 10 shows the performance of some general indicators in a Latin American country. The situation described below is representative, broadly speaking, of conditions frequently observed in many countries throughout the world, particularly in Latin America and Asia.

The figures in Table 10 show rather consistent behavior in such areas as receipts, returns filed, budgeted expenses, and staff of the tax administration. One item, however, stands out clearly: computer equipment.

Because of changing technology and the priority assigned by the authorities to the purchase of computer equipment, computing capacity grew remarkably in the period under consideration. In 1985 the memory of the computer equipment was 1,500 times larger than in 1965 and nearly 10 times larger than in 1975. This comparison, however, underestimates the computing capacity for 1985 because processing speed has risen significantly over the same period. In addition, the tax administration had no teleprocessing screens in 1965, whereas in 1975 it had 35 and by 1985 it had 1,000. Furthermore, in 1985 the administration had

Table 10. A Latin American Country: Performance of Some Indicators

	1965	1975	1985	1985 in Relation to 1965
Tax receipts (*in constant currency*)	3,106	8,202	10,879	3.50
Returns filed	551,000	1,837,000	2,112,086	3.80
Total administration expenditure (*in constant currency*)	40.2	62.2	219.7	5.42
Number of tax administration personnel	2,313	5,983	6,951	2.96
Memory of central computer	0.61MB	2.5MB	24MB	1,500.0
Number of computer screens	0	35	1,000	—
Memory of peripheral computers	0	0	3MB	—

Source: IMF, Fiscal Affairs Department.

peripheral computers whose capacity was larger than that of the central computer in service in 1975.

Unfortunately, despite the growing computing capacity and the modernization efforts made by the tax administration, the latter did not significantly improve its effectiveness in monitoring tax compliance. This may be deduced from the frequency of tax amnesties declared in that country and from the fact that it was still not possible by 1985 to exercise timely control over registered taxpayers who filed no returns or over delinquent taxpayers—situations that are generally easier to control than tax evasion (that is, the failure to report taxes in the tax return). An increase in computing capacity is not in itself enough to guarantee an increase in the effectiveness of the tax administration.

Problems Connected with Information Systems

One common problem is that the information systems in use yield data with errors and are therefore not very reliable. The immediate consequence of this is that the information produced by the computer is not taken seriously either by the tax administration or by taxpayers. To overcome the problems posed by these errors, solutions are sometimes devised that turn out to be inadvisable. These include duplicating procedures, developing parallel manual processes, and retrieving the same data from different computers for different purposes. All this does is aggravate the problem, because such duplications only serve to make the ever-scarce manpower of tax administrations even scarcer. Besides, such systems are divergent, and in the absence of timely correction of errors even more mistakes will be made. Ultimately, the computing system may be rendered totally useless and may be finally disconnected, which is what happened in Uruguay in the early 1980s, or it may be completely redesigned, as in Colombia and Bolivia beginning in 1985.

Another difficulty frequently observed is the rigidity of systems. In many instances systems do not lend themselves easily to legislative changes because they were designed on the assumption that the tax system is unchangeable. Obviously this is not true, and it is therefore necessary to establish systems capable of handling abstract concepts such as debts, credits, rates, forms, interest, fines, and so on. These concepts will always apply regardless of the type of tax being dealt with, and consequently, if the computing system is designed to operate with these concepts, all that will be required when an existing tax is changed or a new one is established will be to change the rules under which these concepts are processed.

In sum, then, the chief problems connected with information systems are as follows:

- The systems are not very reliable (they produce a considerable number of errors).
- Control of stopfiling taxpayers is done manually.
- Control of delinquent taxpayers is done manually.
- There is no adequate control and procedural follow-up for collecting delinquent taxes.
- The TIN is not reliable enough.
- An independent manual system is used to keep record of payments.
- Processes are duplicated because the same piece of information is transcribed over and over again for different purposes.
- There are duplicate files for documents.
- The systems are too rigid and incapable of swiftly adjusting to changes in tax legislation.
- Statistics are not timely.
- There are no systems to support enforcement activities.

General Guidelines for Developing Information Systems

In developing an information system, the first priority is to design the frame of reference describing the general characteristics of the systems and procedures used by the tax administration. The key is to define an adequate strategy, setting out with precision the course to be followed. In other words, what is the goal going to be? To avoid the seesawing that sets back the progress of tax administration, charting the direction of that progress is more important than its speed. The frame of reference to be used in developing the information system should be defined before taking other decisions, particularly those connected with the purchase of computing equipment. Otherwise serious errors may be made, as demonstrated in some Eastern European countries that have recently introduced structural reforms in their tax administrations. If there is no frame of reference for developing these systems, a situation may arise where the administration becomes the servant of the computer instead of the other way around.

The frame of reference of the tax administration should answer specific questions such as the following:

- Should taxpayers send their tax returns to the offices of the tax administration, to banks, to the post office, or to any of these three?
- Should taxpayers pay their taxes at the offices of the tax administration, at banks, at post offices, or at any one of these three?

- Should separate forms be required for tax returns and for payments or should a single tax return be designed in such a way as to render a separate payment form unnecessary?
- Should banks accept a tax return filed without an accompanying payment in cases where no payment is due or there is a tax credit?
- Should banks accept a tax return unaccompanied by full payment of the taxes due?
- Should the data be retrieved at the tax administration, at banks, or at private data-entry companies?
- Where should the data be validated and what should be the general requirements for validation?
- What is the most adequate level of centralization or decentralization for data entry and processing?
- What sort of TIN should be used? Should the same TIN be used for all taxes at the same time or should its application be gradually extended to different taxes?
- Is teleprocessing necessary? In what applications?
- Is it better to post the data on-line to the current account of taxpayers or to retrieve the data from tax returns in a separate process and then post them to the current account in a subsequent operation?
- Should a different system be established for monitoring large taxpayers?
- How should files be organized to keep the returns filed by taxpayers?
- What information should be asked for in tax returns?
- What systems should be developed as a first priority?
- What systems should be developed to support control activities?
- Should the production of statistics be an independent process or a natural by-product of the information system?
- What sort of controls should be put in place in order to make certain that the systems are secure? In other words, how to prevent the recorded data from being falsified or becoming known to unauthorized persons?

These questions are merely examples from a much longer list of questions to be appropriately answered by the frame of reference established to guide the development of tax administration systems and procedures.

Audit Support Systems

Systems must be developed to support auditors in the field.[7] When visiting a taxpayer, for instance, the auditor should have with him a

[7]This section draws on Milka Casanegra de Jantscher and Carlos Silvani, "Guidelines for Administering a VAT," *International VAT Monitor* (December 1990), pp. 2–19.

computer printout showing the data from tax returns filed by the taxpayer. The visit, furthermore, should be based on very specific presumptions of noncompliance: for example, when it has been detected that purchases made from the taxpayer by certain companies exceed the sales or revenue he reported. This can be detected only by developing systems that cross-check data on the economic transactions carried on by taxpayers.

Below are some examples of enforcement support systems that may be profitably developed.

Abstract of Reported Taxes

The abstract of reported taxes should be a computer printout showing the data reported by the taxpayer when filing his tax return. The purpose of this system is to enable the auditor to conduct the audit using the information in the abstract. To guide the auditor, the computer should highlight on the abstract any inconsistencies such as incorrect deductions and arithmetical errors. The abstract should also include ratios such as sales/purchases, earnings/sales, and the modal value (the most frequent value) that these indicators register for homogenous taxpayers.[8] Basically, the abstract should include three groups of data.

(1) Data reported by the taxpayer in different tax periods, such as the amount of reported sales, the amount of reported purchases, credit carryforwards, and refunds requested. Here, calculation errors detected by the computer should be highlighted.

(2) Statistical data, such as modal value of the markup reported by taxpayers similar to the taxpayer to be audited.

(3) Data on the taxpayer's economic transactions, collected from external sources. Details on value, date, and type of operation for transactions such as imports, sales made to the taxpayer by his suppliers, and purchases made by its customers should be included.

Sales to the Government

It is a good idea to process the purchases made by government companies and state agencies for establishing whether such purchases have been reported as sales by taxpayers who acted as suppliers. In some countries, tax evasion under this heading is frequent. Indeed, there are cases of sales made to tax administrations that have gone unreported by the suppliers.

---

[8]Taxpayers in a similar business activity and with a similar sales volume.

Company Purchases and Sales

It is important to process the purchases of large and medium-sized companies for the same reason given in the preceding item, namely, to try to detect tax evasion on the part of suppliers. It is also important to process the data on sales made by large and medium-sized companies. In this case the objective is to detect those buyers who, over a considerable length of time, report sales figures lower than the amounts of their own purchases from large or medium-sized companies.

Cross-checking of data on purchases and sales should be selective. Only the data on large and medium-sized companies should be processed. In addition, the sales and purchases to be processed should be selected according to guidelines on such points as the minimum amount of operations to be looked at and the type of goods or services being transacted. These criteria should be defined bearing in mind the computer resources needed to enter the data in a timely fashion.

Some have argued that the cost-benefit ratio of these cross-checking systems is unfavorable. The argument is based on two premises: (1) that generating a magnetic-medium recording of the data on sales or purchases is very costly and (2) that the sales or purchases recorded would reflect "above-board" transactions, making this type of information useless in detecting operations "under the counter."

As to the first argument, it would not be very costly to generate purchases or sales files if large and medium-sized companies are asked to supply these data to the tax administration on magnetic media. All that is needed is to ask companies to report, in connection with their sales and purchases, the date, the amount, and the TIN of the taxpayer buying or selling, as the case may be.[9] Producing magnetic files with these data would be an insignificant cost to companies that have computerized invoicing and accounting systems, which is increasingly the case among large and medium-sized companies.

As for the second argument, experience indicates that large companies seldom make "under-the-counter" sales. Small companies, on the other hand, are far more likely to buy from large ones and make backroom sales. This activity could be detected with the proposed cross-checking system. Furthermore, the system could also pick up purchases deducted by large taxpayers that pertain to suppliers who are not registered with the tax administration or who, if registered, are not reporting their sales fully.

[9]It would also be advisable to ask for the invoice number and a description of the goods transacted, as long as this does not entail an excessive cost to the taxpayer.

Imports

In order to detect the unreported sales or revenues of importers, it is important to process data on imports. By comparing the imports made by taxpayers with the sales or revenues they report, it is possible to deduce whether they are underreporting sales in connection with the VAT or revenues for income tax purposes. When dealing with the income tax of individuals, it is also useful to test the income reported by taxpayers against any imports of luxury articles they may have made.

IV. Determinants of Change in Tax Administration

Why do changes occur at a particular time? What are the circumstances that make it possible for a structural and permanent change to take place and significantly improve the effectiveness of a tax administration? We know very little about this. We do know that technology is necessary but not sufficient to ensure progress in tax administration. That it is not sufficient is something to be regretted, because it is, relatively speaking, the easiest part of the puzzle. Simply allocating in the budget of the tax administration a specific amount of money will guarantee the purchase of the most modern technology as far as the equipment is concerned. Many countries, however, have spent many millions on computer equipment without being able to improve the effectiveness of their tax administration—that is, without seeing any drop in the high ratios of tax evasion and delinquency.

Experience leads me to believe that the key ingredient in bringing about change is having a team of men and women with the will and the political authority needed to see the changes through. If significant success is to be achieved, it is essential to have a group of officials with an iron will and even obsessed by the idea of modernizing. This group of officials must have the courage to risk the unknown and must take all necessary precautions against failure.

The task of making a tax administration more effective is obviously neither a simple nor a short-term job, especially because it usually requires introducing reforms in many other areas directly connected with tax administration.

To begin with, it is very often essential to reform the tax laws to simplify the tax system. It is not news nowadays to say that tax policy and tax administration are intimately linked and that it is very difficult to draw the dividing line between these two areas. Nor is it a revelation that a tax system which on paper may seem fair and economically efficient may in fact be exceedingly unjust and inefficient because the tax administration is unable to enforce the law. Achieving substantial improvement in the effectiveness of tax administration also requires a bold simplification of the tax system, as the more successful examples of the 1980s have taught us.

Second, many administrative practices that have been followed for many years need to be changed. Simplification of tax returns, for instance, is likely to run into a great deal of opposition because there will always be ample reasons to justify asking for this or that piece of information or requiring this or that attachment. In response, tax administrators committed to change will be called upon to explain over and over again what history has shown, namely, that taxpayers are not awed by mere requests for information. The behavior of taxpayers will change only when the tax administration can count on timely and reliable information enabling it to detect noncompliance. For this, all that needs to be asked for are a few pieces of information because that is all that the tax administration can process with the degree of quality and timeliness required for effective administration of taxes.

V. Outlook

In my view of the foreseeable future and the prospects held out by technology in the area of tax administration, two predictable and desirable developments stand out: (1) the gradual disappearance of paper as the cornerstone of tax data, and (2) operational decentralization.

The gradual disappearance of paper as the cornerstone of tax data will bring about a profound structural transformation, which, perhaps, will be more important than the one that took place in the 1960s when computers were introduced in the area of tax administration. Even now, many administrations surrender at once before the majesty of paper. At present, in many countries, if the computer tells us that a particular taxpayer cannot be given a tax clearance certificate (*paz y salvo*) because he has not filed a tax return or has a tax debt outstanding, and if that taxpayer in turn proves by means of a copy of a form that he has filed a return or paid the tax, the tax administration gives up straight away and issues the certification applied for, without even checking whether the copy of the form made available by the taxpayer is authentic or a forgery. In tax administration, in principle, paper has the last word, and the information stored in the computer takes a back seat.

In the private sector, by contrast, just the opposite is true. What counts is the information stored in the computer, not the information on paper. Credit card operations, banking operations, and many other similar examples can be found in day-to-day activities where the information stored in the computer takes precedence, in principle, over the data on paper. This is so, of course, because the computers that support these activities produce timely and reliable information, which is often not true of tax administration.

What needs to change before tax administrations can catch up? The first issue to be resolved is the problem of data entry, so that within a short period of time the computer may record in an absolutely reliable way the data set out in tax returns and the payments made by taxpayers. For this reason, tax administrations in the more developed countries have as one of their basic objectives to encourage the transmission of data between the taxpayer and the tax administration without going through paper. This is known as "electronic filing." The data filed by taxpayers in this way reaches the computers of the tax agency almost instantaneously and with a high degree of quality. Much remains to be done, to be sure, and many problems need to be resolved, particularly in the legal area, but the final objective is plain: to maximize the collection of data by electronic means or through magnetic devices in order to guarantee the timeliness and quality of the data processed by the tax administration.

The obstacles that remain now are more of a legal than a technical nature. For example, in the United States, where several million tax returns are already being filed electronically, the problem of the signature as the mark attesting to the intent of the taxpayer remains to be resolved. The taxpayer, besides sending in the data electronically, must also send in a signed paper confirming that he has filed his return. Curiously enough, in other areas of daily life the problem of the signature as validation of the intent of an individual has already been obviated. One may withdraw money from machines known as "automatic tellers," check the balance in a bank account, play the stock market, and buy or sell millions in wheat, oil, or other commodities, merely by providing a secret code: the PIN (personal identification number). Why is it not possible to use a similar system in tax administration? Why is it not possible to assign a PIN to taxpayers who wish to file their tax returns electronically, thereby avoiding the duplication of mailing a signed statement to confirm the electronically transmitted data? Why should taxpayers have to also send in bulky paper records to confirm the data they have submitted in the form of a computer disk? These questions are for the legal profession to answer.

The second development mentioned as predictable and desirable within the near future is that of operational decentralization. More and more, technology is making it possible to use modern computer devices in small units at a reasonable cost. The economy-of-scale reasons that formerly justified the centralized processing of information have vanished. These days operational units located near the taxpayer and in locations where he carries on his economic activities are capable of processing the data and producing the information needed for a more effective control. Furthermore, one of the effects of decentralization is to make operational units increasingly responsible for producing information of the proper quality with the necessary speed.

ANNEX I
Methodology for Estimating VAT Evasion

To estimate VAT evasion, taxable sales, purchases generating tax credits, and investments generating tax credits should be estimated. Using these figures the theoretical tax base can be estimated. Then the amount of potential receipts is calculated by applying the general rate to the theoretical tax base.[10]

Estimating Taxable Sales

Taxable sales are estimated from total supply. Total supply is equal to gross production plus imports. Taxable sales (which generate VAT debits) are calculated by deducting exemptions, exports, and inventory changes from total supply.

Estimating Net Purchases

Total purchases are defined as the intermediate consumption computed in national accounts. Net purchases (which generate VAT credits) are calculated by deducting from total purchases the purchases of exempted inputs (which generate no credits) and purchases of taxable inputs for the production of exempted goods and services (because these goods and services are not taxable and, therefore, the taxpayer cannot recover the VAT paid out for these inputs).

[10]This methodology is for a VAT with a single rate. If there is more than one rate, the tax base estimate must be broken down for each rate.

Estimating Net Investments

Net investments in fixed capital (which generate VAT credits) are estimated from the figures for gross formation of fixed capital in national accounts. To calculate net investments, from gross formation of fixed capital are deducted the exempted capital goods (because these goods are not taxable and, therefore, generate no VAT credits) and the taxable capital goods for the production of exempted goods and services (because these goods or services are not taxable and, therefore, the VAT content of these capital goods cannot be recovered).

Estimating the Tax Base

Deduction of net purchases and net investments from taxable sales yields the theoretical tax base plus the VAT collected. By deducting from this figure the VAT collected, the theoretical tax base (net of VAT) is calculated.

Calculating Theoretical Receipts

The potential or theoretical collection is calculated by applying the VAT rate to the theoretical tax base.

Calculating Collection Losses

Lost collection is calculated by deducting from potential receipts the VAT actually collected.

Outline of Methodology

Sales
  \+ gross production
  \+ imports
= total supply
  − exemptions
  − exports
  − inventory variation
= Taxable sales (1)

Purchases

\+ total purchases (intermediate consumption)
− purchases of exempted inputs
− purchases of taxable inputs for production of exempted goods and services
= Net purchases (2)

Investments

\+ total investments
− exempted investments
− taxable investments for production of exempted goods and services
= Net investments (3)

Theoretical tax base (includes VAT collected)

(1) − (2) − (3) (4)
VAT collected[11] (5)
Theoretical tax base (net of VAT) (4) − (5) (6)
Potential collection = VAT rate x (6) (7)
Collection loss (7) − (5) (8)
Collection loss as a percentage (8) / (7) x 100.

[11]The VAT collected is the net collection remaining after deducting refunds to exporters.

Comments

Javier Etcheberry

As my main comment, I would like to state that the paper presented by Mr. Silvani is exceptionally thorough and covers all aspects of tax administration and tax legislation that should be examined to improve tax compliance in Latin America. The author's classification of taxpayers according to their tax behavior is very useful and facilitates the formulation of enforcement policies. This classification and the comments, data, and specific strategies presented in the paper demonstrate the author's experience—both theoretical and practical—in the field. His paper will help improve audit strategies and the effectiveness of tax administration in Latin America. Indeed, this seminar has demonstrated that the problems of tax administration and the economic and social situation of our countries have many common elements.

It should be noted that breaking down taxpayers as unregistered, stopfiling, evaders, and delinquent is not the only classification that can be used to formulate enforcement policies. Taxpayers can also be classified according to the economic activity they perform, the geographic area in which they are active, or perhaps by their size or legal status, and so forth.

Choosing one of the above-mentioned criteria for a basic taxpayer classification requires determining which criteria can most effectively be used to formulate an enforcement policy appropriate to the tax characteristics of a given country. These criteria may or may not coincide with the author's recommendation. Once the basic classification is established, one of the other criteria can be used to further classify taxpayers in each of the main categories.

In Chile, current efforts are aimed at improving tax audit by stressing classification by sector, because the tax characteristics of the agricultural sector differ from those of the mining sector and these, in turn, differ from those of the industrial sector, and so on. For this reason, working groups have been set up to study audit policy for each of our economy's major sectors.

As the author notes, these classifications are very useful for distributing among the various groups of taxpayers the scarce audit resources available to make tax administration more effective. It is also necessary to quantify the impact of audit on each of the groups within the classification used.

With regard to unregistered taxpayers, who frequently are part of the informal economy, I believe that it is not desirable to enact legislation that would reward these taxpayers with simplified tax requirements. If too many concessions are granted, the informal sector could, over time, tend to grow; moreover, formal sector taxpayers might increasingly use persons belonging to the informal sector for the production or marketing of their goods. It is preferable to have uniform tax legislation despite the fact that smaller taxpayers tend to be tax evaders, because as they become larger, it will be easier to monitor them and to enforce compliance.

Another comment refers to the author's claim that tax evasion depends on the odds of being detected and the size of the penalty imposed. In my view, another element that should be included in the analysis is ethics. If people believe that tax evasion is unethical, tax compliance will be high despite low odds of being detected or low penalties. For this reason, governments, as well as social, religious, and political organizations, should take it upon themselves to ensure that tax evasion is considered unethical in our countries.

As an example, in Chile, during the military government of General Pinochet, the opposition never attempted to send the general population the message that not paying taxes was a way of defying the Government because, as in other Chilean organizations, there was relative consensus that contributing to undermine the Chilean taxpayer's behavior would be unethical and hence undesirable.

Robert A. LeBaube

Carlos Silvani has had a long and impressive association with the subject of taxes. He has taken the opportunity to indicate those points that are of utmost importance to tax administrators in improving compliance with tax laws. I was further impressed with the connection he makes between effectiveness and efficiency in administration. Often governments fall into the attractive trap of efficiency and do not know whether their efforts are truly effective.

My comments fall into two categories, efforts to increase compliance and efforts to increase effectiveness.

Efforts to Increase Compliance

Mr. Silvani describes four tax gaps that must be narrowed in order to increase effectiveness and decrease noncompliance and they are all valid. A study done several years ago for the Internal Revenue Service (IRS) in the United States indicated a similar scenario. The study divided taxpayers into four groups:

(1) Those who understand and comply willingly with the law.
(2) Those who want to comply but do not understand.
(3) Those who understand but choose not to comply fully.
(4) Those who do not comply deliberately.

The trick is to move taxpayers from one group to another. There are many factors that affect this movement that are beyond the abilities of the tax administrators to influence. Things like confidence in the government, complexity of the law, perceptions of fairness of the tax law, fear of detection, and so on, can affect voluntary compliance in either direction.

I would offer two suggestions to increase compliance from a perspective based on my experience with IRS.

First, the use of informants. The IRS receives many thousands of pieces of correspondence about taxpayers alleging noncompliance with the law. In some cases rewards for such information are paid, but the informant must apply for a reward and payment procedures are complex. Much of the information has little or no value and is discarded quickly, but enough is valid to make such a system worthwhile. Public knowledge of such a system can be an effective deterrent.

The second suggestion is more positive in nature. A strong program involving taxpayer education, information, and access will help those who are disposed to comply to meet their obligations under the law. There are some dangers with such a program. Education must not include government propaganda in support of political issues. The education must be in the nature of why government needs taxes, how the laws are determined, and how a responsible citizen participates in the system.

Efforts to Increase Effectiveness

In the area of effectiveness I would offer the following: Carlos Silvani is quite correct when he warns that countries increasing their use of computers should be wary of the computer system controlling the tax administrator rather than the reverse. This has happened several times in the course of IRS experience over the past thirty years. As Malcolm

Lane indicated in his earlier comments, go slowly and make sure that the system is giving you what you want and that you have the capacity to use what the system gives you. This is one area in which the IRS has not done well. For years the computer system has been able to give much more information than the personnel could use. The interesting point, however, is that the public thought IRS could do much more than it really was capable of.

The paper suggests a number of criteria to be examined in designing computer applications. They are excellent and should be followed.

I note with interest the desire to reduce the number of persons who participate in the tax system though the use of paper documents. The United States has embarked on electronic filing where there is no longer a paper return in the hands of IRS. However, there is a paper return in the hands of the taxpayer and the practitioner, if one is used. Most taxpayers, at least in the United States, want something in their hands that indicates they have fulfilled their obligation. A taxpayer may have little reason blindly to trust either a computer or a tax administrator. Even with a fairly sophisticated system and paper documents the U.S. system operates with approximately 15 percent processing errors, about half caused by the taxpayer and half caused by the IRS. With the advent of electronic filing that error rate, on electronic returns, has fallen to 3 percent. For 1990 returns, about 5 million were filed electronically and about 150,000 had errors. I would caution that mechanisms must be installed early to deal with errors quickly and courteously. Confidence and respect for the system can be increased through simple things such as apologies when the system is in error and sympathetic understanding when the taxpayer is correcting his error.

The paper discusses operational decentralization as one of the means to increase effectiveness. I agree fully on this point but caution that one must have the resources, particularly well-trained personnel, to effectively implement such a program. You must also have adequate security of the system to prevent improper access and manipulation of the system. Audit trails as described in the paper on Spain are essential for this purpose. But one must be committed to regular inspection of those trails to determine if anything improper has occurred.

The information and suggestions offered in the paper can serve administrators well in their efforts to maintain and improve taxpayer compliance.

9

Assisting Taxpayers in Meeting Their Obligations Under the Law

Robert A. LeBaube and Charles L. Vehorn

A judge in a tax dispute once remarked that "the art of taxation consists in so plucking the goose as to get the most feathers with the least hissing."[1] His observation illustrates the basic reason why governments need to assist their citizens in meeting their obligations under their nation's tax laws. Perhaps if the goose understood the need to give up some of its feathers and knew the least painful way to perform the removal, it would not hiss nearly as much.

While some may think that tax administrators are not in a good position to reduce the hissing because of a presumed bias to protect the government's interest, others argue that it is the obligation of the tax administration to provide "taxpayer services"—assistance, information, and education. Important objectives of government in the area of tax administration are (1) to support those citizens who wish to comply with the tax laws by making the burden of compliance and payment as light as possible (Adam Smith's third maxim of convenience of payment); (2) to minimize the amount of public and private resources diverted from other uses to ensure that taxes are collected (Adam Smith's fourth maxim of economy in collection); and (3) to strive through education to increase the number of willing compliers. This education includes explaining how society benefits from the taxes and what will happen to those who fail to pay their fair share. The purpose of this chapter is to discuss various aspects of taxpayer services and the methods employed to meet taxpayers' needs. Section I presents the rationale for taxpayer service programs, after giving a brief history of the cyclical growth in taxpayer service efforts in the U.S. Internal Revenue Service (IRS). Section II primarily describes different types of IRS taxpayer service programs and also attempts to weave into the discussion selected experiences of other countries. Section III identifies

[1]*U.S. Life v. Harbison*, 784 F.2d 1239 (5th Cir. 1986), quoting a Jean Baptiste Colbert attribution.

and discusses the major issues concerning the effectiveness of taxpayer services—improving compliance, improving taxpayer confidence, easing the burden of compliance, and dealing with tax law complexity. Section IV presents conclusions concerning the taxpayer service function.

Oliver Wendell Holmes, the noted U.S. Supreme Court Justice, has been widely quoted as stating that, "Taxes are the price we pay for civilization." If that is the case, and we believe it is, then assisting citizens to understand their responsibility and to meet their portion of that cost will engender a more knowledgeable society capable of contributing to the general welfare and to the development of civilization.

I. Rationale for Taxpayer Assistance

All too many countries seem to do their best to make it difficult for taxpayers to comply with the law. The law is complex, contradictory, hard to interpret, and even hard to find; the necessary forms are hard to locate and sometimes they even have to be purchased; forms and payments have to be submitted at inconvenient times and places; and many who become involved with tax officials feel annoyed or harassed. In other words, most countries need to improve their administrative performance, particularly in the areas of clarity, access, and education. Tax administrations that understand taxpayers' problems face the difficult task of finding resources within their budgets to improve taxpayer services. They then face another layer of complicated decision making concerning the level and variety of potential programs. New Zealand, for example, proceeded logically from the purpose of taxpayer services, to goals, and then to programs that would ensure attainment of the goals. For New Zealand's Inland Revenue Department, the purpose of taxpayer services is to ensure that it is as easy as possible for people to comply with the legislation. Two goals follow from this purpose: (1) to inform people of their rights and obligations and (2) to provide people with consistent, impartial, courteous, and prompt service.[2] While good planning by tax officials is important in designing taxpayer service programs, the decision-making authority may not rest solely with tax officials. An examination of the evolution of the taxpayer service func-

[2]See New Zealand (1990).

tion in the United States may help to illustrate the various forces that affect the decision-making process.[3]

Historical Background

The income tax became a reality for most Americans during the war years of 1944 and 1945. Prior to that time, the income tax, which was established by the Sixteenth Amendment to the U.S. Constitution, affected only the wealthy. The war created a great need for revenue, so the tax base was expanded by requiring for the first time that the vast majority of citizens be responsible for filing income tax returns. Assistance was available only to those who were willing to visit a local IRS office either to get help or to have their return prepared by a government employee. Such assistance prevented tax administration staff from performing their normal duties and was not provided at uniform levels throughout the country.

It was not until the mid-1950s that the IRS instituted a formal program for assisting taxpayers. In addition to providing help in the preparation of returns, the IRS extended office hours in some areas and allowed personnel to speak before local groups, on the radio, and on the television.

Over the next two decades, the assistance programs expanded in quality and range of services offered. By the mid-1970s, a centralized telephone service was available to all residents within the United States. For the cost of a local phone call, taxpayers could reach knowledgeable staff to answer their questions. Volunteer programs had begun, and taxes were being taught in most high schools. Even though expenditures for these programs were escalating, the Congress of the United States consistently looked favorably on the function. Between 1972 and 1980, IRS staff years devoted to taxpayer service grew by 140 percent, and the taxpayer service share of total IRS staff years grew from 3.1 percent to 5.8 percent (Steuerle (1986)). Also during this period, compliance rates were at their highest levels.[4]

In the early 1980s, however, taxpayer services were de-emphasized for a number of reasons. Between 1980 and 1986, taxpayer service staff years actually dropped by 8 percent and the taxpayer service share of

---

[3]This paper focuses on taxpayer service programs at the national level, but these programs are just as important at state and local levels. It has been suggested (see Oldman's comments to this paper) that administration of the local property tax could be improved if more information and assistance were provided to taxpayers.

[4]In subsequent sections, the relationship between taxpayer services and compliance is explored in more depth.

total IRS staff years fell to 4.9 percent (Steuerle (1986)). Factors outside the control of tax administrators, such as budget deficits and an increasingly more complex tax law due to major tax legislation almost every year, put pressure on the executive and legislative branches to find ways to reduce costs. Since it could not be proved that taxpayer service increased revenues, there was pressure brought to reduce or, in one year (1983), eliminate entirely funding from the budget.

The U.S. Senate's Committee on Governmental Affairs, Subcommittee on Oversight of Government Management held hearings and prepared a report (United States, Senate (1982)) analyzing how the public might be affected if taxpayer service programs were eliminated. One part of the report addressed the question, "Is it the responsibility of the IRS to provide tax assistance to the public?" (p. 2). The subcommittee found, "There is sentiment in Congress and a consensus among former IRS commissioners that the IRS has the responsibility to provide free tax assistance" (p. 10). One former IRS Commissioner, Donald C. Alexander, stated, "Our government has a responsibility to provide assistance to taxpayers, and we should not force them to pay for advice on how to meet their responsibilities" (p. 12). Additional testimony involving the fairness of the tax system and the complexity of the law brought up the role of private practitioners and their relationship to public sector assistance. Ignoring the fact that public assistance (provided equally to all) and private assistance (only provided for a fee) are not perfect substitutes, some suggested that public assistance was not really needed since an adequate cadre of private practitioners was available to those who needed help. In response, another former Commissioner, Jerome Kurtz, said, "We should be concerned about the question of fairness. Our government is financed largely by a self-assessment individual income tax system which is inordinately complex. We require taxpayers to compute and pay their own liabilities. It seems to me the government has an obligation to help taxpayers to fulfill their obligations" (p. 13).

The proposal to eliminate taxpayer service was rejected by Congress, but full funding was not made available for the years 1983–89. Currently, the taxpayer service function in the United States is receiving favorable support; new technology and innovative programs are being developed for deployment in the near term.

This short review of the history of the taxpayer service function illustrates some points that support the case for government to provide assistance to citizens in meeting their obligations under the tax laws. These are as follows:

- A specifically designated taxpayer assistance cadre permits other employees to perform their regularly assigned tasks without interruption.

- Availability of information, such as through toll-free telephone systems, provides service to citizens in a uniform manner without regard to location.
- Broad-based congressional support of assistance programs provides continuity of service no matter which party is in power in the executive branch.

Several elements of tax administration function more smoothly with an effective taxpayer service program. The three most important are compliance, problem resolution, and dissemination of information.

Compliance with the Law

Citizens must have the means to understand what is required of them in order to comply with the law. At a minimum, tax authorities must provide their citizens with appropriate avenues to comply. This may entail such programs as developing clear forms and instructions; providing points of contact to citizens so that they can request and secure information about their duty; and developing educational programs to inform existing and future taxpayers.

Resolution of Problems

No matter how well (or poorly) citizens comply and tax administrators function, errors occur. Tax administrations must have avenues for citizens to contact and deal with the government. A citizen's tax account is generally the area in which most contact with the government occurs. The success or failure of those contacts can determine to some degree the level of confidence a citizen has in his government. So it is important for tax administrators to be responsive, polite, and willing to apologize if the error was on their part.

Dissemination of Information

A primary element of taxpayer services is to inform the public of their duties and responsibilities under the tax laws. It is essential that tax administrators provide information, such as rulings, regulations, decisions, and other notifications, to foster a reasonably high level of compliance and minimize problems. A major objective of this element is to help citizens conform to the needs of the government by sending clear messages to taxpayers. An example of the importance of this element is provided in a survey taken in Colombia. The survey's purpose was to assess the success or failure of the newly implemented value-added tax (VAT). One third of the respondents noted the importance of adequate and timely information (Orozco de Triana (1987)).

Impressions of Tax Administrators in Other Countries

The view that these elements are essential to a smoothly functioning tax administration is shared by tax administrators in many countries. For example, a tax expert from Trinidad and Tobago (Pounder (1989, p. 1)) has argued that, "in many parts of the free world where the self-assessment system of taxation has been introduced, taxpayer assistance, information and education is one of the fundamental concerns of tax administrations in their efforts to achieve the maximum possible level of voluntary compliance by taxpayers."

A tax expert from Argentina (Asorey (1987, p. 4)) also noted the important link between taxpayer services and compliance, when he stated, "Taxpayer information, assistance and education, as activities aimed at improving voluntary compliance with tax obligations, are problems of common importance in developed as well as developing countries, even though the causes of noncompliance are dissimilar."

With respect to the importance and responsibility that governments have to provide taxpayer assistance and information, a former Director of National Taxes of Colombia (Orozco de Triana (1987)) pointed out that if the government makes demands on taxpayers it must also provide adequate assistance in order to protect the citizen-government relationship. The government must realize that a citizen's frustration is more traumatic and negative when the tax administration does not provide him with sufficient elements for complying with his duties.

It is clear that tax administrators and practitioners support the rationale that taxpayer assistance is an important element in the furtherance of good tax administration.

Another Point of View

There is another side, however, to the question of how much, if any, taxpayer assistance should be provided by governments. Some believe that government should not provide or should severely limit such services, particularly where large numbers of competent private tax practitioners are available to serve the needs of the public. We do not think that private tax preparers and public tax officials providing assistance are perfect substitutes. Instead, both can serve a useful function. While the IRS attempts to provide a uniform level of service across the country, the degree of trust that can be expected between taxpayer and government is a fundamental concern. Many people are reluctant to accept everything the tax administrator has to say. Jones (1987, p. 1) argued that, "taxpayers are often hesitant to rely on direct communications with the Internal Revenue Service. As one example, the growth in use of commercial tax return preparer services exceeds what would be expected from the complexity of the Internal Revenue Code as it applies to individuals. Taxpayers are much more ready to accept negative rules and limitations from their tax advisers than they are from even the most articulate government servants."

Klepper and Nagin (1989) argue that private tax preparers play a mixed role. On the one hand, they contribute to noncompliance by interpreting ambiguous tax provisions in favor of their clients. On the other hand, they contribute to compliance by enforcing nonambiguous tax provisions and by communicating the tax administration's enforcement priorities to taxpayers. Without private tax preparers, who have relatively easy access to the tax administration's information bulletins and letter rulings, taxpayers would bear higher search costs to obtain documented answers to their questions. Those taxpayers that rely on private preparers tend to have higher incomes; more income from sources other than wages, interest, and dividends; and higher marginal tax rates (Long and Caudill (1987)). Also, a relatively larger number of these taxpayers tend to be self-employed or over age 65. Dubin, Graetz, Udell, and Wilde (1990) found that the average income of those who used paid preparers was between 1.7 to 4.6 times higher (depending on type of paid preparer) than taxpayers who used nonpaid assistance from the IRS or volunteer organizations.[5]

II. Types of Taxpayer Information Programs

There are many types of taxpayer information programs available to taxpayers throughout the world. The United States, Canada, and Mexico are examples of countries that offer a variety of programs. The IRS, for example, produces a 28-page booklet, publication no. 910, that lists the types, availability, and accessibility of its many programs. This section of the chapter will examine six major types of taxpayer

[5]These data are from the Special Academic Research File of the 1979 Individual Return Taxpayer Compliance Measurement Program.

information programs. Table 1 illustrates what types of programs are available in various selected countries. In addition to these programs, a broader concept of taxpayer services would include such tax administration activities as improving the design of forms and providing information on recent interpretations of the law through tax bulletins or letter rulings. It would also include the services provided by private practitioners.

Publications

Many countries produce special tax publications. Canada produces 14 tax guides and 30 pamphlets on narrowly focused issues.[6] Most of these publications pertain to the income tax with a few describing aspects of other on-going taxes. In order to implement the new goods and services tax, Canada's tax administration produced close to 90 specific publications. It also created a special tax advisory program and a vendors' inquiry group that answers taxpayers' questions over the phone.[7]

The IRS creates and produces 110 separate publications designed to assist citizens in meeting their tax obligations. These publications are in addition to the large array of forms and instructions produced to aid the taxpayer. The documents range from publication no. 1, "Your Rights as a Taxpayer," to publication no. 929, "Tax Rules for Children and Dependents." Many of the more widely used publications are available at IRS offices and public libraries throughout the country. Every effort is made by the IRS to reflect the law, regulations, rulings, and applicable court decisions in an objective manner, so that the taxpayer is informed and is able to relate his situation to the spirit and letter of the law. Some of the publications are available in Spanish. All of these publications are furnished free of direct charge to the taxpayer.

Although it is difficult to conduct a systematic study of the value of various publications for taxpayers, anecdotal evidence suggests that they can be quite helpful. For example, in 1988 the tax administration of India began publishing, in all indigenous languages, a pamphlet entitled *How to Compute Your Taxable Income*. By 1990, two years after the first publication, computational mistakes had dropped from about 22 percent to 3.5 percent.[8] This reduction in computational errors should

---

[6]Canada (1988).

[7]Conversations with Canadian tax officials (Michael Burpee, Director General, Operations, and Stuart Watson, Director General, Research and Development).

[8]Conversations with S.R. Wadhwa, Chief Commissioner of Income Tax, Bhopal, India.

Table 1. Taxpayer Information Programs in Selected Countries

	Argentina	Canada[1]	Chile[2]	Colombia	Jamaica[3]	Mexico	Trinidad	United States
Publications								
Tax guides (instructions)	x	x	x	x	x	x	x	x
Pamphlets and bulletins	x	x		x	x	x	x	x
Technical publications		x		x	x	x	x	x
Audio cassettes for visually impaired		x						
Newspaper tax supplements			x	x	x	x	x	x
Reminders in press			x					
Media								
Radio or television commercials	x	x	x	x	x	x	x	x
Special television programs		x		x	x		x	x
Video cassettes		x				x		x
Press conferences			x			x		x
Telephone contact								
Telephone assistance	x	x	x	x	x	x	x	x
Tele-refund		x				x		x
Tele-info		x						x
Personal contacts								
Walk-in service		x	x	x	x	x	x	x
Correspondence								
Individually drafted letters		x	x		x		x	x
Standardized letters		x	x		x		x	x
Other programs								
Volunteers		x					x	x
High school program	x	x	x		x	x	x	x
Rural tax scene kits		x						x
Native outreach		x						x
Training for new business							x	x
Participation in seminars and conferences		x		x		x		x

Sources: Conversations with various tax officials and publications from various tax departments.

[1]All publications are in two languages (French and English), with some in additional languages (Chinese, Greek, Italian, Polish, Portuguese, and Spanish). Video cassettes are available in eight languages.

[2]To provide additional taxpayer assistance, 10–15 tax office branches are scheduled to be opened.

[3]Telephone assistance is provided, but not in a formal, structured manner. Also, the high school program is planned.

produce a savings in administrative costs, but an estimate of the magnitude was not available.

Media

Print and electronic media are widely used by the IRS to provide information and educational materials to taxpayers. Several of these media programs are worthy of special mention.

Tax Supplement

Each year the IRS contracts with newspapers throughout the country to produce an income tax supplement to be published early in the filing season. In 1990, this supplement was 23 pages in length, appeared in 2,655 newspapers, and reached more than 42 million households. The supplement brought information to readers about income taxes in a journalistic style and was replete with helpful hints, recommendations, and methods to make filing and paying as easy as possible. Chile also publishes a tax supplement in newspapers.

Advertising Council

In 1987 the IRS approached the Advertising Council for assistance in reversing some distressing trends in the relationship between taxpayers and the IRS. A seven-year trend of later and later filing during the filing period was in evidence, and with the 1986 Tax Reform Act about to affect returns, a further slippage would result in serious, if not insurmountable problems for tax administrators.

The IRS turned to the Advertising Council, a nonprofit organization dedicated to using the creativity and talent of the advertising industry to bring messages of public interest to the population. Its success in environmental awareness, personal safety, vehicular safety, and education for the underprivileged has been exceptional over the past forty or so years. The program that was developed used radio, television, and print media to convey a simple message to the American public, "File early, file accurately." As shown in Table 2, the upward trend in filing late during the filing period stopped during the 1988 filing season. In 1989 and 1990 the number of persons filing earlier and more accurately increased. The IRS has continued its relationship with the Advertising Council in these and other areas, most notably in its volunteer income tax assistance efforts.

Table 2. United States: Percentage of Individual Income Tax Returns Filed by April 1

Year	Percentage	Percentage Change from Previous Year
1984	61.5	—
1985	59.9	−1.6
1986	59.7	−0.2
1987	57.7	−2.0
1988	57.8	+0.1
1989	58.5	+0.7
1990	60.1	+1.6

Source: Internal Revenue Service, Returns Processing and Accounting Division.

Note: Each percentage point represents 1.0 million to 1.1 million returns, depending on the year.

Tax Clinic

Each year, in conjunction with a commercial television station, the IRS produces a tax clinic which is broadcast throughout the country on a Sunday in early February on public broadcasting channels and cable networks. In 1991 the show reached 1.4 million households with an audience estimated at 840,000 viewers. The production follows a quiz show format and is interspersed with interviews with tax officials, accountants, and lawyers discussing timely tax topics. The IRS makes a special effort to staff its telephone sites during and after the show, and the public is invited to call if they have questions. In 1991, 23,885 calls were received during and immediately after the show.

Financial News Network

The IRS produces a weekly television show on the Financial News Network, a cable channel that reaches 200,000 households in the United States. The format permits the IRS to inform the public about how the IRS functions, its relationships with other governmental bodies, and interesting tax topics. Based on the response from viewers' telephone calls and Nielsen ratings, this endeavor has been very successful.

Video Cassettes

The IRS has produced video cassettes on various tax issues. These cassettes have been distributed to video cassette stores in the private sector. These stores then rent the cassettes to consumers who view them at their homes. The tax administration of Mexico also makes use of video cassettes by distributing both cassettes and television monitors to local tax offices. Taxpayers can go to their local tax office and view cassettes on various tax issues.

Telephone Contact

Any resident of the United States can telephone the IRS, toll free, in order to receive information about taxes, to order forms or publications, or to seek information about his personal tax account. In 1990, the IRS answered 38 million telephone inquiries. The toll-free telephone system is operated from 32 centralized sites and has up to 4,900 employees answering taxpayers' inquiries at the height of the filing season. Accuracy, courtesy, and accessibility are the three most important features in operating a telephone system for service to taxpayers.

Accuracy

To provide an accurate answer, the person providing assistance must first understand the nature and extent of a taxpayer's inquiry. Next, the person must know where to find the correct information to deliver to the taxpayer. Finally, the person must make sure that the caller understands and can use the information provided. These three steps are essential to the successful completion of a call. The IRS has had problems in achieving an acceptable level of accuracy. In the late 1970s, tests by the General Accounting Office (GAO) of the United States indicated an accuracy level of about 85 percent. By the time the 1986 Tax Reform Act was implemented, the accuracy rate as measured by GAO and the IRS had fallen to about 65 percent. Since that time, improvements, such as increased managerial emphasis, a more experienced work force, and increased emphasis on probing to obtain all the facts needed about a taxpayer's situation, have helped to raise the accuracy rate (United States, General Accounting Office (1990a)). The accuracy rate jumped from 63 percent in 1989 to 77 percent in 1990 (United States, General Accounting Office (1990b)).

In some respects, increased complexity in the law and less than adequate funding contributed to the decline. But improved methods and systems for measuring accuracy instituted in the mid-1980s may have measured accuracy more stringently than previous attempts. Regardless of the reason, a taxpayer can expect a measurably better answer today than four or five years ago because of continuous efforts to improve the program, such as the integrated test call survey system. This system was instituted in 1988, to survey on a random basis the accuracy of answers to prepared questions. Using the results and information gleaned from this survey, training was improved, local monitoring was increased, methods were strengthened, and problem areas were pinpointed. Through careful management attention to this information, significant progress in accuracy has been achieved (United States, General Accounting Office (1990b)).

Accuracy is also an important dimension in minimizing the burden of tax administration. In Sweden, for example, revenue agents are asked to handle telephone calls during the tax filing season. In this way, the Swedish tax authorities attempt to lower the probability of providing inaccurate information by the use of less highly trained personnel. If accurate and complete answers are provided over the telephone during the filing season, then the work load for the rest of the year will be minimized.

Courtesy

The need for civility and courtesy in dealing with taxpayers is essential to maintain trust and confidence in the tax system. A completely correct answer delivered in a surly, rude, or condescending manner will leave a sour taste in the mouth of the caller and not serve to satisfy the mission of the tax administrator. Even in the years when accuracy was at its lowest, staff providing assistance at the IRS got good marks from callers on their politeness and eagerness to help the taxpayer.

In a survey conducted by Perng and Chovonec (1989), 82 percent of the respondents rated politeness on the part of those providing assistance at the IRS as excellent, the highest rating based on a six-point scale. Another 12 percent gave a rating of 5, the next highest level. Less than 1 percent of respondents gave ratings at the lowest two levels. Using the same rating scale on eagerness to help, 76 percent of the respondents gave an excellent rating. Another 14.5 percent of respondents gave a score of 5, for a total of 90.5 percent at the positive end of the scale. Only 2 percent of the respondents gave ratings at the lowest two levels of the scale.

Accessibility

Taxpayer service representatives who are willing and able to give accurate answers in a courteous manner are of limited use if taxpayers cannot reach the tax administration. Enough equipment and lines must be available to serve the public in an efficient and economical manner. Balancing staffing, equipment, and demand for service has evolved into an art, if not a science. The IRS measures the accessibility of its telephone service on an hourly basis. Because of the increase in demand for toll-free service between 1989 and 1990 (a jump from 34 million to 51 million calls, which includes busy signals and those who abandon the attempt before being assisted), IRS' accessibility rate dropped from 90 percent of incoming calls on the first or second attempt to 74 percent (United States, General Accounting Office (1990b)). Part of the reason for what appears to be an increase in demand is in reality a decrease in IRS resources. Reduction in staffing and a longer time to provide a full explanation to a taxpayer's question meant that taxpayers on average had to call more often before getting through to IRS staff.

Personal Contact

Taxpayers in the United States generally have more personal contact with the tax administrator than any agency of the Federal Government with the exception of the post office. The IRS sends forms and instructions annually to each taxpayer identified on the tax rolls. Of the roughly 45 million taxpayer contacts the IRS had through the taxpayer service system, about 7 million were visits to IRS offices for various services. One fifth of these needed additional forms or publications (Cox and Risler (1990)).

A very large number of taxpayers visit IRS offices to obtain information about the law, how it affects them, and the current status of their tax account. The IRS has 597 sites strategically situated throughout the United States and 13 countries in the world where taxpayer assistance is provided throughout the filing season, January through April. In addition to "official" IRS sites, forms and instructions are also available in thousands of post offices, banks, and libraries throughout the United States. Most of the official sites are staffed throughout the year for service to taxpayers. Few taxpayers need to spend more than an hour to reach an IRS office by public or private transportation. Accessibility is excellent. However, the IRS does not provide, like Spain, a service whereby the taxpayer can sit at a computer in the tax office to receive answers to questions.

Correspondence

Less than 0.4 percent of all taxpayer service contacts, about 172,000, arise from correspondence. The taxpayer service function in the IRS is limited in the types and complexity of issues it handles through correspondence. Rulings, technical advice, determinations, and procedural pronouncements are beyond the jurisdiction of the IRS' taxpayer service function. Such items, of which there are many hundreds of thousands, are handled by other IRS functions. The main distinction between the responsibilities of the taxpayer service function and other functions, which provide services under a broader concept of the term, is whether or not the transaction or situation has already occurred. A question during the filing season in 1991 about a situation in tax year 1990 is retrospective in nature and within the purview of the taxpayer service function. If, on the other hand, the item is prospective in nature, for example, a request for a letter ruling, it generally is outside the purview of taxpayer service. While the IRS receives very few letters compared with other types of contacts, surveys of taxpayers who have written for advice give the IRS its lowest marks in this category (Perng and Chovonec (1989)).

Other Sources of Taxpayer Information

There are several other sources from which taxpayers can receive information regarding their tax obligations. About 47 percent of those filing an individual income tax return use the services of paid preparers. While this is a significant number of people, it is their personal choice and, as mentioned earlier in this paper, may be a reflection of distrust in the system, complexity in the law, or just no desire to do it themselves. Fortunately, the United States has a large number of competent, professional tax preparers who can perform these tasks. Their goodwill and cooperation are essential to the efficient operation of the tax system.

The IRS has several other programs that reach many people and serve certain elements of the population who either cannot afford preparers or cannot perform the task of filing returns themselves. In addition, the IRS has a program for educating new entrants into the work force so they can understand and meet their responsibilities under the law.

Volunteer Programs

The IRS sponsors volunteer programs to reach those who cannot do their own tax return and cannot afford or may not choose to pay a professional for the service. Volunteers are recruited from various walks of life, such as accountants, retirees, and other persons interested in helping those unable to help themselves. The volunteer income tax assistance program operates throughout the nation. The IRS trains the volunteers, and they work at the centers for no remuneration from either the Government or the taxpayers. A second volunteer area involves tax counseling for the elderly. Sponsoring organizations have members who visit shut-ins, retirement homes, and nursing homes for helping the elderly meet their tax obligations. The Government reimburses the sponsoring organizations for certain expenses, but neither these organizations nor their workers receive other remuneration. Together these programs and their 79,000 volunteers provided free assistance to 2 million persons in filing their returns in 1990. An internal IRS cost-benefit study conducted in 1989 indicated that the value of the services provided by the volunteers was worth $50 million if the IRS had to pay for their time.

Understanding Taxes

One of the essential tasks of tax administration is to prepare young citizens for the time when they must file tax returns. A good basic knowledge of civic responsibility needs to be learned in the educational system. The United States has a program called "understanding taxes" that is taught in secondary schools to students between the ages of 14 and 18. It is not a mandatory course but more than 4 million students in more than 20,000 schools participated in the program in 1990. The course explains the benefits of government, the need for taxes, and how to prepare a simple tax return. This program has been improved substantially since its initiation more than 20 years ago. A major revamping of the program occurred in 1988. The Joint Council on Economic Education and the Agency for Instructional Technology joined with the IRS to improve the course and its delivery systems. Video tapes, computer diskettes, and a modular approach significantly increased the variety and flexibility of the course. Evaluations submitted by teachers using the program were overwhelmingly positive.

Other countries have similar programs. In Spain, for example, the Ministry of Finance has cleverly designed material in comic book form to make the basic rationale for paying taxes understandable. The book, *El Puente*, describes how one Indian village that has a market is separated by a canyon from another village without a market. The village lacking the market decides to benefit the public by building a bridge over the canyon. The necessary resources for the bridge are obtained through taxation.

One developing country that has shown a long-term interest in taxpayer education is the Philippines. Beginning in 1961, the Joint Legislative-Executive Tax Commission undertook periodic surveys in order to determine the level of tax consciousness, the degree of compliance, the attitude of the taxpayer toward the tax administration, and the common problems of tax administration. Based on these surveys, a long-term program to improve taxpayer education, information, and assistance was established. A major part of the program was an effort to foster tax consciousness through the schools. Currently both elementary schools and high schools have incorporated the teaching of taxation in their curricula (Yoingco and Quintos (1979)). The Bureau of Internal Revenue has gradually expanded the educational effort to reach adults. For example, according to the Bureau's 1987 Annual Report, during that year, it conducted 3,179 seminars, 3,227 symposiums, and 12,007 public forums and made 478,474 house-to-house visits to inform taxpayers of their obligation under the law.

Small Business Tax Seminars

The IRS has had in place for many years a program that provides new business persons the opportunity to attend a seminar where a great deal of information on business tax matters is disseminated. More than 1,000 of these seminars are conducted each year throughout the 50 states and approximately 10,000 people attend. In contrast to these IRS seminars that are not mandatory, some socialist countries use mandatory educational meetings once or twice a year as the major (and sometimes only) program to provide business taxpayers with information and assistance on recent changes in the tax law.

In 1989 a new addition to the IRS program was developed with the help of representatives from educational groups. It had been discovered that many new business persons did not attend seminars conducted by the IRS because of fear of the agency. Through a joint effort a new course was designed to be taught in community colleges and adult education facilities. Although developed by the IRS, it was taught by individuals not connected with the IRS in more than 1,500 schools during 1990. A total of 42,254 students participated in the program. The Mexican tax administration has also developed seminar material that is used by instructors who are not tax officials (Mexico, Undersecretariat of Revenue of Mexico (1991)).

III. Major Issues Concerning the Effectiveness of Taxpayer Assistance

Does Taxpayer Assistance Improve Compliance and Reduce Noncompliance?

Improving compliance and reducing noncompliance are not the same because they apply to different activities of the tax administration that may be targeted to different types of taxpayers. On the one hand, publishing taxpayer guides and explaining the tax system in the media foster compliance—one of the major goals of a tax administration—primarily among those taxpayers who try to follow the law. Enforcement activities, on the other hand, are needed to reduce noncompliance among those taxpayers who try to evade paying their full tax liability. Tax audits, for example, increase the risk that tax evaders will be detected and punished.[9] While taxpayer assistance programs may do little to reduce noncompliance, many tax administrators believe that taxpayer assistance programs can be extremely effective in improving compliance, especially by reducing taxpayer ignorance and confusion. Unfortunately, there are few studies (see subsequent discussion) that provide quantitative evidence on the effects of taxpayer services. Witte and Woodbury (1983), for example, found that IRS educational efforts appeared to raise the level of compliance, but the effect was small.

Does Taxpayer Assistance Improve Taxpayer Confidence in the Tax System?

The answer to this question may appear to be straightforward. Simple logic would seem to dictate that effective, courteous assistance that helps citizens meet their obligations under the tax laws would improve taxpayer confidence in the tax system. If that were the only criterion for establishing confidence in the tax system, one could reasonably deduce that good assistance would raise confidence levels in the tax system. However, there are many other factors that contribute to the degree of taxpayer confidence. Some of these factors are as follows:

- The tax law may be perceived as unfair to some segments of the population.
- The complexity of the law may reduce taxpayers' ability to understand their obligation, and confusion hardly engenders confidence.
- Enforcement policies could be unevenly or harshly applied.
- Taxpayer service personnel may be less than competent or courteous.

Each of these factors can affect the level of confidence taxpayers have in the tax system. It is therefore very difficult to measure with

[9]For an interesting discussion of how the IRS audit function has changed by placing greater reliance on information reporting, conducting fewer audits of taxpayers, and increasing the severity of punishment, see Dubin, Graetz, and Wilde (1990).

any high degree of precision whether taxpayer assistance improves confidence in the tax system.

Even with these limitations, some researchers have attempted to ascertain whether taxpayer assistance improves taxpayer confidence. Two studies have been conducted involving surveys of taxpayers that may shed some light on the question. In response to questions dealing with assistance, Hendricks (1990) found that 75 percent of the respondents agreed that the IRS assistance program was "very helpful" or "somewhat helpful." While this is encouraging, it shows that 25 percent of the taxpayers dealing with the IRS were not favorably impressed with the help offered.[10] Hendricks observed that good people, training, and a simpler, fairer tax law could improve the credibility of the system. His survey also showed that 86 percent of the respondents answered "not sure" or "no" to the question: "Do we have a self-assessment federal tax system?" This response suggests that a large portion of the population does not understand one of the basic tenets of U.S. tax administration. However, Hendricks expressed the belief that the taxpayer assistance and compliance programs are important vehicles to remedy this lack of awareness. He also argued that taxpayer confidence in the Federal Government is not at the appropriate level, but continued emphasis on taxpayer education, tax simplification, and fairness would help to raise that level.

Another study, by Cox and Risler (1990), reported the results of a 19-week survey conducted from February 22 to June 30, 1988. More than 9,000 taxpayers were asked to participate and more than 6,000 responses were tallied. The study measured the participants' perceptions about how the assistance they received would affect their behavior and their taxes. The actual performance could not be measured because this would violate taxpayer confidentiality, so to the extent that perceptions were different from what taxpayers actually did the results may be overstated or understated. The data strongly suggest that assistance does affect confidence by improving compliance with the law. More than 80 percent of the requests for assistance provide individuals with information that will help them meet their obligation under the law.

The paper concluded: "From the responses given by individuals surveyed about their contacts with Taxpayer Service, it appears that Taxpayer Service provides individuals with the type of assistance they need to comply with the tax laws and that these individuals plan to follow the advice they receive." One generally does not follow the

[10]It would be important to find why these 25 percent were not favorably impressed to evaluate whether this was due to the IRS program or to the taxpayers' disappointment at receiving information that would raise their tax liability.

advice of someone unless there is some confidence in that party. As long as assistance programs and the staff providing the assistance give good information that can be relied upon, it does seem reasonable to conclude that confidence in the tax system will be improved. Conversely, deterioration in the performance of those providing the assistance will hurt confidence in the system.

Does Taxpayer Assistance Ease the Burden of Complying with the Tax Laws?

While it seems reasonable to believe that taxpayer assistance will ease the burden of compliance, there have been few empirical studies performed to test in a systematic fashion the validity of this belief. In a study based on a 1984 taxpayer survey, Smith (1987) found support for the hypothesis that taxpayers' perceptions of the quality of taxpayer assistance have an indirect affect on the level of compliance. Although Smith's study, which relies on a recursive model to produce estimated effects, is one of the few rigorous attempts to address the linkage between taxpayer assistance and compliance, it did not go as far as a more recent study conducted by Price Waterhouse (1989) for the IRS. This study found that most line item errors on tax returns were due to a misunderstanding of the tax forms or the instructions. Taxpayer assistance significantly reduced the line item errors by clarifying for the taxpayer what specifically should be reported.

The study's methodology was to set up a laboratory experiment with four separate groups completing hypothetical tax returns. Three of the groups were allowed to use different types of taxpayer assistance: (1) either telephone or walk-in assistance; (2) only telephone assistance; and (3) only walk-in assistance. The fourth group, the control group, was not allowed to use taxpayer assistance. Taxpayers were recruited in Dallas, Texas, through newspaper advertisements and were administered a screening questionnaire over the phone to determine items such as their age, income, filing status, and whether they prepared their own return. Of those who qualified after the initial screening, 400 were selected to meet different hypothetical tax return situations. An additional 10 percent (or 40) were selected to substitute for participants who failed to show up for the test.

The participants were asked to report to a large meeting hall where they each were given a selected hypothetical return situation, placed randomly into one of the four groups, and asked to fill out the tax return. They were told that if they filled out the return correctly, they would receive additional monetary compensation. Those participants

Table 3. Differences Between Groups in Total Tax Reported
(By Measure of Error)

	Percent Error	Average Error (*In U.S. dollars*)	Absolute Error (*In U.S. dollars*)
Groups with assistance	59	10	297
Group with no assistance	64	−79	482
Difference	5	−69	185
Probability of no statistical difference	0.187	0.446	0.043

Source: Price Waterhouse (1989).
Note: Mathematical mistakes on returns were not counted as errors.

who used taxpayer assistance (65 percent of those in the groups with assistance) were also asked to rate the quality of the IRS assistance.

Price Waterhouse reviewed all the tax returns and computed three measures of tax compliance: (1) the percent of returns with errors; (2) the average error, a measure that does not change the sign of the error so underreporting and overreporting errors tend to offset each other; and (3) the absolute error, a measure of the absolute value of the error. Average error indicated a group's average dollar difference between correct tax liability and tax liability actually reported on the hypothetical returns. Absolute error, on the other hand, indicates the seriousness of errors in completing the tax returns—the higher the magnitude of error, the lower the level of compliance.

Table 3 presents the difference between the groups with assistance and the group with no assistance with respect to the three measures. The percent of returns with an error in reporting the total tax (after removing simple mathematical errors) was 5 percent less for the groups with assistance than the group with no assistance (59 percent versus 64 percent). The statistical probability of no difference between the two groups was less than 19 percent. With respect to the average error measure, the difference was an underreporting of $69 for each return, but the difference is not statistically significant.[11] This, the report argues, can be partially explained by the fact that overreporting and underreporting errors tend to cancel each other out. The difference in absolute error of $185, however, is statistically significant with a low probability of about 4 percent that no difference between the two groups

[11] Even if the evidence does not support a short-run revenue gain from taxpayer services, it seems reasonable that long-run revenue is enhanced when the IRS assists a taxpayer who would have otherwise overreported.

exists. Difference among the three groups with assistance were statistically insignificant for all three measures.

Those participants who consulted with the IRS staff on one or more occasions were asked to complete a questionnaire regarding the quality of the assistance received. Almost 69 percent were "very pleased" with the assistance and another 20 percent were "somewhat pleased." However, some of the tax return errors attributed to those in the groups with assistance were due to incorrect advice from the IRS staff who provided incorrect answers for about 15 percent of the questions and correct, but insufficient answers for another 8 percent of the contacts. Even though incorrect advice was given to 41 taxpayers in 49 separate contacts, only 17 taxpayers made mistakes on their hypothetical returns that affected tax liability. This contributed to 8 percent of the absolute error for the taxpayer groups with assistance.[12]

In a review of the Price Waterhouse laboratory test, Wilt, Perng, and Mannion (1990) concluded that the test demonstrated taxpayer assistance significantly improves the accuracy of returns, thus increasing the level of taxpayer compliance, but left unresolved the question of whether revenues increase, since taxpayer assistance reduces the probability of both underreporting and overreporting errors.

How Does Complexity of the Tax Law Affect Assistance Efforts?

The United States has had a considerable increase in complexity within its tax code over the past decade. Almost every year the Congress has passed major tax legislation that has added to the complexity of tax administration. Paradoxically, a general objective of the legislation was tax simplification (for example, removing taxpayers from the tax rolls), but complexity for certain sets of taxpayers increased (for example, calculating the allowable deduction for nonmortgage interest payment). These numerous changes have had a serious impact on taxpayer assistance programs. The most notable, of course, is the increased budgetary requirements to provide adequate levels of assistance, forms, publications, and information to taxpayers. In real dollars, adjusted for inflation, the budgetary requirements of taxpayer service have more than tripled since 1973 when the program was formally recognized as

[12]The reasons given why some taxpayers did not follow the incorrect advice were that some felt they received the wrong advice and some realized that the incorrect advice conflicted with other information. Also, some may have followed the advice, but it had no effect on their actual tax liability. In one example a taxpayer was advised to fill out Schedule B (report of interest income) when it was not required.

a functional entity with a status equal to the other major functions within IRS such as examination and collection.

Some of the reasons that led to the tremendous increase in budgetary requirements that are directly related to increased complexity of the law are as follows:

- The time required to answer taxpayers' questions on telephone calls has almost doubled in the past five years.
- Forms and publications have increased in number and complexity. New methods to test the adequacy of forms prior to issuance are very costly.
- The development of programs for volunteer groups to help those who cannot prepare their own returns is costly, but benefits to the public far outweigh the costs.
- Time spent in training and development of staff who assist taxpayers has risen twofold to threefold.
- The development of programs for educational institutions for high school students and new businesses has been expensive.
- The initiation of quality control and measurement systems to determine the effectiveness of service has cost a considerable amount in investment and maintenance.

These and other items have largely been due to increased complexity. As the law became more complex in the 1980s and budgets became tighter, the accuracy of information given to taxpayers began to diminish.

Complexity of the tax law is of great concern to the IRS, tax practitioners, academicians, as well as the taxpayer who must comply with the law. Many tax experts believe that if the rate of complexity continues to escalate, the U.S. tax code may become unadministrable. These same experts, however, are pessimistic about efforts to reduce complexity. For example, Deborah Schenk (1990) argued, with respect to the personal income tax, that there is little likelihood of significant simplification being achieved in the Internal Revenue Code because there is no constituency that is focused enough to overcome the hurdles that stand in the way. Her premise points out the problems of maintaining revenue neutrality while achieving fairness in the application of the law, particularly to low-income taxpayers. In the area of simplification for the preparers of returns, she suggested that the Congress may not be ready to trade off some time-honored concepts such as vertical and horizontal equity. In addition, she suggested that there is little likelihood of Congress ending the use of the tax system to provide incentives for nontax-related national objectives.

Some countries, however, have been able to reduce complexity. Colombia's tax reform in 1983–88 kept simplification of the tax system as a major objective, even to the point of sacrificing some provisions for horizontal equity if they could not be administered effectively. One concrete example of Colombia's success is in the design of new tax forms. The number of lines on the corporate income tax return was reduced from 420 to 55, and the number of lines on the individual income tax return was reduced from 210 to 41 (Vázquez-Caro, Reid, and Bird (1992)). Another example is the United Kingdom's value-added tax return: over the years this form has been reduced to a single page with only seven blocks to fill out.

IV. Conclusions

This paper has attempted to examine some of the elements required to assist taxpayers in meeting their obligations under the law, describe various types of taxpayer information programs, and assess the effectiveness of the taxpayer service function. While the U.S. Congress has debated the question of government-provided taxpayer services, most researchers and practitioners agree that IRS programs to assist, inform, and educate taxpayers achieve higher levels of tax compliance than would otherwise be the case, particularly when taxpayers are in general agreement with the policies of the Government and perceive that the tax laws are being fairly administered. Unfortunately, there is no evidence to assess the effort of the taxpayer service function on revenue-raising capacity. Nevertheless, there are bits and pieces of evidence showing that in the face of rising tax law complexity, taxpayer services increase compliance levels, improve taxpayer confidence, and ease the burden of compliance. This evidence is compelling enough, even without a bottom line on revenue-raising capacity, to dictate that tax administrators should actively pursue a program of assistance, information, and education. The evidence also indicates that such programs are enhanced to the extent that administrators constantly examine themselves to ensure that fairness and equity are practiced to the limit permitted under the laws.

REFERENCES

American Bar Association, Tax Section, "Professional and Trade Associations as Instruments of Taxpayer Assistance and Information," *Tax Administration Review*, No. 6 (July 1989), pp. 87–96.

Asorey, Rubén O., "Treasury-Taxpayer Relations," paper presented at the Twenty-First General Assembly of the Inter-American Center of Tax Administrators (Ottawa, May 1987).

Bergherm, Donald E., "The Future Is Only as Bright as We Are Willing to Make It," *Tax Administration Review*, No. 6 (July 1989), pp. 71–85.

Canada, Revenue Canada, *Inside Taxation, 1987* (Ottawa, 1988).

Chaplin, Ken, "Taxpayer Assistance, Information and Education," *Tax Administration Review*, No. 6 (July 1989), pp. 149–62.

Cox, Dennis, and Mary Helen Risler, "The Effect of Taxpayer Service on Compliance," paper presented at the IRS Research Conference on Taxpayer Behavior (Washington, November 15, 1990).

Dubin, Jeffrey A., Michael A. Graetz, Michael A. Udell, and Louis L. Wilde, "The Demand for Tax Return Preparation Services," California Institute of Technology, Social Science Working Paper No. 714, May 1990.

Dubin, Jeffrey A., Michael A. Graetz, and Louis L. Wilde, "The Changing Face of Tax Enforcement, 1978–1988," *Tax Lawyer*, Vol. 43, No. 4 (Summer 1990), pp. 893–914.

Fullarton, Shirley, "Taxpayer Assistance, Information and Education in Canada," *Tax Administration Review*, No. 6 (July 1989), pp. 163–84.

Hendricks, Norman H., "Taxpayer Perception of the IRS: Assistance, Enforcement, and Positive Incentives," paper presented at the IRS Research Conference on Taxpayer Behavior (Washington, November 15, 1990).

Jones, John B., Jr., "Treasury-Taxpayer Relations," paper presented at the Twenty-First General Assembly of the Inter-American Center of Tax Administrators (Ottawa, May 1987).

Klepper, Steven, and Daniel Nagin, "The Role of Tax Preparers in Tax Compliance," *Policy Sciences*, Vol. 22 (1989), pp. 167–94.

Long, James, and Steven Caudill, "The Usage and Benefits of Paid Tax Return Preparation," *National Tax Journal*, Vol. 40 (March 1987), pp. 35–46.

Mexico, Undersecretariat of Revenue of Mexico, "Improvement of Tax Authorities-Taxpayer Relations Through Modern Taxpayer Information, Education and Assistance Programs," paper presented at the Twenty-Fifth General Assembly of the Inter-American Center of Tax Administrators (Washington, May 1991).

New Zealand, Inland Revenue Department, *The 1990/1991 Corporate Plan* (Auckland: Government Printer, 1990).

Orozco de Triana, Alba Lucia, "Taxpayer Assistance, Information, and Education," paper presented at the Twenty-First General Assembly of the Inter-American Center of Tax Administrators (Ottawa, May 1987).

Perng, Shien, and Mike Chovonec, "Taxpayer Perceptions About the Quality of Taxpayer Service," in *Trend Analysis and Related Statistics: 1989 Update* (Washington: Internal Revenue Service, Office of the Assistant Commissioner for Planning, Finance, and Research, Document No. 6011, 1989).

Philippines, Bureau of Internal Revenue, *Annual Report, 1987* (Manila, 1988).

Pounder, Joseph D., "Taxpayer Assistance, Information and Education for Promotion of Voluntary Compliance," *Tax Administration Review*, No. 6 (July 1989), pp. 1–21.

Price Waterhouse, *A Laboratory Test on the Effect of Taxpayer Assistance on Compliance: Final Report*, No. TIR-86-0258 (July 10, 1989).

Russo, Philip, P., "Innovations in Taxpayer Service," in *Trend Analysis and Related Statistics* (Washington: Internal Revenue Service, Office of the Assistant Commissioner for Planning, Finance, and Research, Document No. 6011, 1987), pp. 19–20.

Schenk, Deborah H., "Eliminating Complexity for Individual Taxpayers: A Revenue Loser Without a Constituency," in *Proceedings of the Invitational Conference on the Reduction of Income Tax Complexity*, sponsored by the American Institute of Certified Public Accountants and the American Bar Association (Washington: Tax Management Institute, 1990).

Smith, Adam, *An Inquiry into the Nature and Causes of the Wealth of Nations* (London: Methuen & Company, 1904).

Smith, Kent W., "Quality Service by the Internal Revenue Service and Compliance: A Structural Equation Model" (unpublished, July 1987).

Steuerle, C. Eugene, *Who Should Pay for Collecting Taxes? Financing the IRS* (Washington: American Enterprise Institute, 1986).

United States, General Accounting Office (1990a), "IRS' Budget Request for Fiscal Year 1991 and Status of the 1990 Tax Return Filing Season," Statement by Jennie S. Stathis before the Subcommittee on Oversight, Committee on Ways and Means, House of Representatives (Washington: General Accounting Office, GAO/T-GGD-90-26, March 22, 1990).

_____ (1990b), *Tax Administration: IRS' 1990 Filing Season Performance Continued Recent Positive Trends* (Washington: General Accounting Office, GAO/GGD-91-23, December 1990).

United States, Senate, Hearing Before the Subcommittee on Oversight of Government Management of the Committee on Governmental Affairs, *Oversight of IRS Taxpayer Assistance Programs*, 97th Congress, 2nd Session, March 24, 1982 (Washington: Government Printing Office, 1982).

Vázquez-Caro, Jaime, Gary Reid, and Richard Bird, "Tax Administration Assessment in Latin America," Latin America and the Caribbean Technical Department, Regional Studies Program, Report No. 13 (Washington: World Bank, January 1992).

Walker, Kenneth I., "Remarks at Conference on Taxpayer Enquiries and Office Examination," September 24, 1987.

Wilt, Don, Shien Perng, and Jack Mannion, "The Effect of Taxpayer Assistance on Compliance: A Laboratory Test," paper presented at the IRS Research Conference on Taxpayer Behavior (Washington, November 15, 1990).

Witte, Ann D., and Diane F. Woodbury, "What We Know About the Factors Affecting Compliance with the Tax Laws," in *Income Tax Compliance: A Report of the ABA Section of Taxation Invitational Conference on Income Tax Compliance* (Reston, Virginia: American Bar Association, 1983).

Yoingco, Angel Q., and Vicente G. Quintos, *Philippine Tax System Under the New Society* (Manila: GIC Enterprises Co., 1979).

Comments

María Corina Arocha

I shall comment on the paper presented by Robert LeBaube and Charles L. Vehorn from the standpoint of the specific situation of Venezuela, a country with considerable problems in its tax system and a low level of compliance which is currently designing a far-reaching tax reform.

Since 1989, the new economic strategy based on the correction of macroeconomic imbalances and promotion of domestic and external efficiency and competitiveness has underscored the need for an in-depth fiscal reform.

The Venezuelan economy has been characterized in recent years by a significant decline in per capita GNP. From 1981 to 1990 that figure fell by 20 percent, more than twice the average drop for Latin America (9.4 percent). Services such as public safety, education, health, water, and electricity demonstrably deteriorated in that period. A return to the per capita income of 1981 will require a growth rate of 5 percent over five years, which in turn will require a sustained process of structural changes and investment in human capital, infrastructure, and services.

This ambitious effort to achieve structural change cannot be sustained by traditional financing schemes. Oil continues to be important, but it is no longer sufficient. Consequently, neither oil nor borrowing, nor certainly inflation, can provide the basis of public funding. The tax system must therefore become the primary source for financing public activities. However, the tax system is not equipped for that important job and must therefore be modernized.

The Venezuelan tax system is characterized by excessive dependence on oil revenue. By 1989, non-oil taxes together represented only about 3.3 percent of GDP, while oil revenues accounted for 15 percent. Of the former, 2.2 percent came from business income taxes, less than 0.4 percent from individual income taxes, and the rest from taxes on cigarettes, liquor, official stamps, and other items.

The development of the country on the basis of oil revenues has contributed to the underdevelopment of the rest of the tax system. Paying taxes is, to many Venezuelans, a rather strange notion. We are talking about a country with very little in the way of a tax culture.

The Venezuelan tax system is highly distortionary. On the one hand, it applies a top rate of 50 percent, while on the other hand it offers a lavish system of tax incentives: exemptions, credits, and rebates.

Similarly, businesses pay taxes on inflationary earnings, and if they distribute dividends the shareholder is subject to the individual income tax.

The legal structure is complex: it includes a great many tax-related laws, decrees, and rulings, and the law contains elements that unnecessarily complicate tax administration without offering any benefit in terms of revenue.

In addition, legislation pertaining to fines and penalties is out of date. To give an example, the interest for late payment is 18 percent when the market rate of interest is about 40 percent. These inconsistencies result in low revenues, reduce the system's equity, and make it hard to administer.

Venezuela's tax administration can be described as ineffective, and its credibility among taxpayers is not such as to ensure adequate compliance. Of the many reasons for this situation, the most important is that tax officials lack motivation or are not properly trained; in extreme cases, they leave something to be desired where honesty is concerned. An inadequate staffing policy has produced a continuous decline in the quality of tax administration personnel. Furthermore, systems and procedures are complex, there is no appropriate information system, accounting is done manually and its results are inconsistent with the data of the automated system, and the filing systems are very poor.

In the area of serving and informing the public, the organization is in place and the functions are established, but the staff and material resources with which to fulfill the aim of "serving and offering efficient and timely information and advice to the taxpayer" are lacking. Staff are assigned from the personnel roster, or work mostly in other units or are shared with other agencies, so that they are distracted from their primary function.

The only useful response to this dismal state of the Venezuelan tax system is a comprehensive reform with changes to the tax structure, procedures, and administration. To that end, three main courses of action were adopted starting in 1989.

- Rationalize the tax system by broadening its base and establishing rates compatible with international models.
- Simplify taxes by eliminating or reformulating those that are unproductive, difficult to administer, or both, and creating a tax structure based on few taxes and effective collection.
- Modernize the tax administration by improving procedures and systems, introducing modern automated systems, improving the physical infrastructure, and raising the quality of staff.

To implement its strategy for modernizing the tax system, the Ministry of Finance submitted two bills to the Congress of the Republic in December 1989: an amendment to the Income Tax Law, including the introduction of a comprehensive system of adjustment for inflation, and a law establishing the VAT. Also submitted to Congress in the course of 1990 were partial amendments to the Organic Tax Code and a Draft Law on Public Credit to finance the modernization of tax administration.

A tax system reform of the magnitude proposed in Venezuela naturally entails a broad program of taxpayer education, information, and assistance. It does not pay to skimp on such a program, and the Government has therefore committed itself to investing substantial resources in this area.

Once the need for a system to provide service to taxpayers was established, the Ministry of Finance was confronted with the difficulty, as LeBaube and Vehorn point out, of defining the level and kind of programs to be developed, while taking into account the severe constraints imposed by the scarcity of resources, especially that of qualified staff, facing the Venezuelan tax administration.

With regard to developing the taxpayer service system, the first decision has been to set up public information and counseling offices. These are being run jointly with the Presidential Commission for State Reform, which, acting on an executive order, has prepared some basic guidelines for the organization and operation of the public outreach offices that must be included in all state agencies.

The creation of those offices is intended first and foremost to establish a direct relationship between the tax authority and the taxpayer in an attempt to diminish the importance of the "intermediary," whose actions have been proved to be damaging to the interests of both the taxpayers and the tax administration. Another purpose of these offices is to start rebuilding taxpayers' confidence in the administration—a confidence which was being lost because of the low quality of that administration.

Success in the pursuit of these objectives will hinge largely on the personnel working in the offices. For that reason clear guidelines have been laid down for the selection, training, and upgrading of the staff that will be taking part in these programs. In addition to knowledge of tax matters, officials must be ready to provide information and seek solutions to the problems that arise. They must be able to communicate both orally and in writing, and to analyze and condense. Most important from the standpoint of re-establishing confidence in the tax administration, they must have a clear sense of dedication.

Work with the private sector has proceeded vigorously. The focus has been on joint efforts with associations of manufacturers, merchants, developers, and so on, as well as accountants, lawyers, economists, and other professionals active in the tax field, to devise taxpayer information and education programs covering the new VAT and the inflation adjustment system. Without the cooperation of those groups, the implementation of these two instruments in the near future would not be feasible. The following are some of the efforts being carried out with the private sector, the universities, and the National School of Finance:

- Information: (1) meetings, seminars, and discussions; (2) publications, including technical documents explaining the reasons for the reform and its effects, pamphlets describing new legal provisions and procedures, and fiscal supplements in press; (3) media, including announcements on radio and television and publicity through special programs and video cassettes; and (4) correspondence.
- Education and training: (1) training, consisting of courses, workshops, and other programs at the basic, technical, and university levels; (2) publications, including guides and manuals; and (3) media, including special programs on VAT, video cassettes, and tax education programs.

Given the changes to be introduced in Venezuela, there is no doubt that these taxpayer information and education programs will go forward. The question that arises in the case of less developed and poorly funded systems, as resources allocated to such efforts are usually modest, is whether the services will reach the taxpayer and what their levels and range will be.

I would therefore urge that, bearing in mind the resource constraints, these taxpayer services programs be so designed technically that they produce the best results possible and continue to do so over time.

Oliver Oldman

This is a fine paper bringing together a lot of useful information and experience about taxpayer assistance as well as the authors' ideas. They are to be complimented in advancing the state of the art of thinking about this topic.

It is a nice coincidence that the paper on taxpayer assistance at this conference was assigned to me. I played a small role in the development of the U.S. Internal Revenue Service programs to use volunteers to provide taxpayer assistance, now called VITA (Volunteer Income Tax Assistance), and in bringing together the IRS and law student volunteers some thirty years ago. Also, for some years now my wife has served in the VITA program and in Tax Counselling for the Elderly. Each year now the IRS and the American Association for Retired Persons coordinate training for new volunteers and updating for regular volunteers. There is no question from my discussions with my wife and from students who have participated in volunteer assistance work that taxpayers are most grateful and appreciative of this effort made by volunteers with official logistical support. Those discussions also lead to a picture of numerous ordinary persons who desire to comply with the tax laws but whose understanding of them is extremely limited. Volunteer programs should probably be expanded, at least in American society, by exerting the effort to identify groups of taxpayers who would like to have available to them a volunteer trained by the IRS. One example that comes to mind is a wide range of clubs and other informal organizations devoted to everything from sports to music whose members consist of lower-middle-income persons. Official outreach to such groups to seek and train volunteers could have a handsome payoff in terms of the development of taxpayer attitudes and understanding.

In order to make further progress in understanding the use of taxpayer assistance programs, useful additional research might be carried out not only on the volunteer programs discussed above but also on the full range and variety of officially manned programs. I have in mind in particular the desirability of conducting interviews both with the people who directly provide the assistance to the taxpayers, that is IRS employees and volunteers, and also their bosses. Similarly, a significant sample of taxpayers who receive assistance ought to be interviewed. The idea here is of course to conduct qualitative in-depth studies to supplement quantitative studies in order to gain new insights about taxpayer assistance generally.

The paper provides a comprehensive list of officially provided sources of information for taxpayers. To be added to that list is the extensive participation by IRS officials in tax seminars and conferences the agendas for which are primarily set by the private organizers of those meetings. IRS cooperation and its supplying of speakers is highly regarded by those who attend the meetings.

The paper stated that in Spain taxpayers already have access to a computer which answers the taxpayer's questions. It is surprising that the United States does not now do this even though it has already installed a highly successful interactive video program for the automatic training of IRS employees. The IRS is actively developing a plan for taxpayer access to computers and thereby to official information.

The paper states that 25 percent of assisted taxpayers were not favorably impressed by the assistance rendered to them. I wonder whether or not those are the persons with the more difficult problems and also those who had high expectations of receiving particular answers which they did not get. In short, the 25 percent figure may be misleading.

The paper contains a useful discussion of the revenue impact of overreporting and underreporting resulting from the taxpayer assistance program. Averaging together overreporting and underreporting has the effect of canceling one out to the extent of the other. Perhaps these should not be averaged. A taxpayer who might have overreported and thereby increased revenue but through assistance files correctly and thereby reduces revenue is a happy taxpayer. The increase in the taxpayer's level of confidence with respect to the IRS (and perhaps government generally) is also an important form of revenue increase in the long run. The asset value one might attach to a satisfied taxpayer goes up. In short, correcting overreporting is not a net revenue loss but a sound expenditure of funds to improve compliance and attitudes and the national wealth in the sense of satisfied taxpayers.

The discussion in the paper with respect to complexity as the cause of a decline in the accuracy of information given to assisted taxpayers needs a qualification. During the 1980s in the United States the number and frequency of legislative changes was probably far more important than increasing technical complexity in terms of impact on accuracy. Indeed, as a whole, legislators thought that they were simplifying the law. Mere change is a complicating factor in that people—both officials and taxpayers—have to change their ways. During periods of change we can expect a decline in accuracy but one that ought to be reversed if change stops.

While the present conference did not focus on administrative aspects of the property tax, it might be useful to include a few words comparing taxpayer assistance under a property tax with that under income taxes. By a property tax I mean a tax levied annually on the current capital value (but it could also be on the rental value) of real estate at a percentage of the value. Under the property tax the government does all the work of administration with little or no input from the taxpayer at all. Taxpayers are not "assisted" because they do not generally have to file declarations or provide other information directly to the tax administration. Nevertheless taxpayers do a great deal of complaining about property taxation and property tax administration. Only in the most recent years have property tax administrators begun to provide adequate outreach and information to taxpayers about the way the property tax works and why the amounts paid by taxpayers differ one from the other. Among the approaches increasingly used around the United States is to publish information about tax values of property and current sales values of property and to make such information available in a manner that enables taxpayers readily to compare the tax burden on their own parcels of property with those of other comparable parcels. Perhaps taxpayers ought to be given more access to people in property tax administration in order better to understand and compare the valuation data. This would be analogous to taxpayer assistance under income tax programs.

Conversely, some thought might be given in income tax administration to providing taxpayers with comparative income information for a variety of different types of activities so that taxpayers have a handle on what other taxpayers are reporting and paying. In the case of the property tax a taxpayer can identify particular parcels of property with which he is familiar and compare their tax values with his own because that information is public information. The practical issue for the property taxpayer is the ready accessibility of the information so that he can use and compare it. Should more information similarly be available to income taxpayers about other taxpayers? Different countries have different practices here. My own judgment is that the increasing trend in recent years toward further and further privacy of tax information is a trend in the wrong direction. Figuring out ways to open up and make accessible more income tax information that is not necessary to be kept private is a task which ought to be faced now.

Finally, a couple of comments about the literature. The 1983 American Bar Association Tax Section Conference on Income Tax Compliance dealt with a variety of issues some of which relate to taxpayer assistance. The resulting volume published by the Tax Section contains information useful to those concerned with the topic of this paper. Similarly, *Readings on Income Tax Administration*, edited by Patrick L. Kelley and Oliver Oldman, was published in 1973 by the Foundation Press. It, too, contains writings and comments relevant to the paper. Looking back at that volume reminded me of how properly fashionable it now is to quote a statement by Milka Casanegra de Jantscher that "tax administration *is* tax policy." We should keep quoting that statement because it is a step beyond what Carl Shoup said at the first CIAT General Assembly on May 5, 1967 in Panama, that "tax administration is the key to tax policy." It is that phrase which is repeated on the cover of the *Readings* volume just cited.

10

Organizational Structure and Human Resources in Tax Administration

Aldo Schlemenson

Achieving good tax compliance involves a variety of factors such as the tax administration's image, its employees' credibility, their readiness to serve, and so on, many of which have already been discussed in this volume. In this paper we emphasize two fundamental factors that affect the efficiency and effectiveness of any organization: (1) organizational structure and (2) human resources. These factors are the pillars of any organizational development strategy.

Organizational structure is the formal framework required for an organization to operate as an integrated system that processes information and solves problems. Delineating the responsibilities of each area and its constituent roles and correctly defining the interrelationships among these roles facilitates harmonious operation and allows the entire organization to work toward a common goal. The confusion generated when the responsibilities of the various roles are poorly defined impairs the functioning of the organization. Designing an appropriate organizational structure therefore helps to reduce ambiguity and increase productivity. Employees benefit from a coherent set of rules because they know exactly what is expected of them and what objectives they are supposed to meet. This makes it possible to channel constructively the internal creative energies needed to do a job effectively.

With respect to staffing, placing people in the appropriate positions should be a basic concern of management. However, this is a difficult goal to reach. People seek not only fair wages but also the opportunity to work at a level that allows them to use their abilities fully. Evaluating and correctly placing personnel is a necessary requirement for the proper functioning of any organization. The challenge faced by management staff—and this is a central aspect of their operational responsibilities—is to promote and continuously monitor, at the level of each employee, equilibrium among three basic variables: (1) each employee's individual ability; (2) the nature of the work he has to do; and (3) the compensation he receives. Proper exercise of this management responsibility will make it possible to increase job satisfaction and, as a result, the productivity of the entire organization.

The problems involved in organizational structures and human resources are essential aspects of any organization, and a considerable amount of literature is devoted to them. However, only in rare instances has this knowledge been applied to the field of tax administration.

I. Organizational Structure

Overview

The term "organizational structure" varies in scope. It encompasses the definition of (1) an organizational chart; (2) the mission and functions of the organization and of its various constituent areas and roles; (3) the formal mechanisms linking these areas and roles; (4) the scope of the authority of each role; and (5) the hierarchical levels. All this requires a simple organizational design that integrates the various areas.

Our examination of this topic is based on a study made in 1975 in the General Tax Directorate of Argentina and subsequently revised in 1988. Through analysis and detailed description of the roles that make up the functioning structure, four fundamental aspects of the organization and its structure were examined:

(1) Formal organization—as illustrated and explained in official documents.

(2) Presumed organization—as assumed by the members of the organization.

(3) Existing organization—the one actually applied.

(4) Required organization—as it should be to meet current and future tax administration requirements.

The field work consisted of two parts. In the first, 50 senior officials of the organization were interviewed. The second involved interviewing regional, section, and agency managers: a total of over 150 officials.

In the following pages, we will touch specifically on some organizational dysfunctions that are clear examples of structural anomalies that affect an administration's operational performance. Further on, we will present a proposed organization and structure.

Existing Organization

Vertical Fragmentation

This section deals with organizational problems that affect the line of command. The line of command is composed of the higher levels, which plan and direct, and the operating levels, which are responsible for implementing the plans. In the Argentine tax administration, the highest level corresponds to the role of general director. Immediately subordinate to that role are the specialized directorates: collection, audit, technical and legal affairs, internal inspection, computing systems, research, and administration (Figure 1). In official documents, these directorates are termed advisory areas in order to differentiate them from the operating areas. We will call this the "strategic planning" level, since the plans this level is responsible for formulating presuppose a thorough understanding of general policies and involve the administration's overall goals.

Since 1983, under the organizational structure of the Argentine General Tax Directorate, functions assigned to the audit directorate include "coordinating and directing the elaboration and preparation of internal and external audit procedures and programs to be applied by inspection personnel." Among the functions assigned to the collection directorate are "directing and coordinating the plans, regulations and procedures established and applied by the various offices that perform collection tasks."

The "operating area," or area of implementation, is composed of "zones" which, according once again to official documents, have a management function and are directly subordinate to the general director. The zones have the task of "coordinating, supervising and directing, within the limits of the regions for which they are responsible, the plans, regulations and procedures established by the higher authority."[1]

The "regions," which, according to the formal structure, are subordinate to the zones, are the operating units and are established according to geographic criteria. They are responsible for implementing the objectives set by the programs and procedures issued by the advisory areas, particularly the audit and collection areas.

As can be seen from Figure 1, the zones are at the same hierarchical level (decision-making level) as the directorates or advisory areas. In practice, there is also a very close relationship between the planning areas (especially collection and audit) and the regions (Figure 2). This relationship, indicated in the figure by a broken line, is in addition to the link between the regions and zones. This creates a dual formal and functional connection that leads in practice to virtual "dual subordination."

---

[1]See General Tax Directorate, Estructura Orgánico Funcional; Decree No. 453 of February 28, 1980; Ministry of Economy Resolution No. 243 of March 2, 1981, and Decree No. 641 of March 26, 1982.

Figure 1. Argentina: Formal Organization of Tax Administration

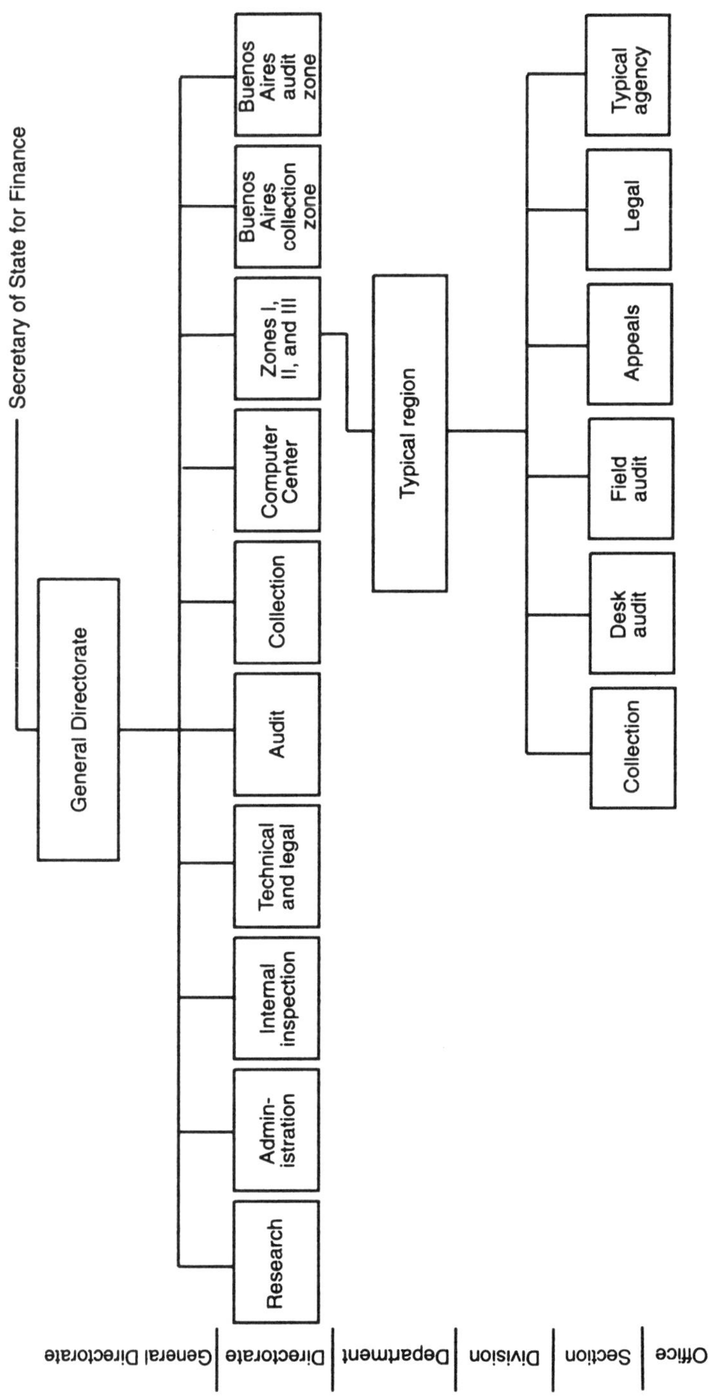

Figure 2. Argentina: Existing Organization

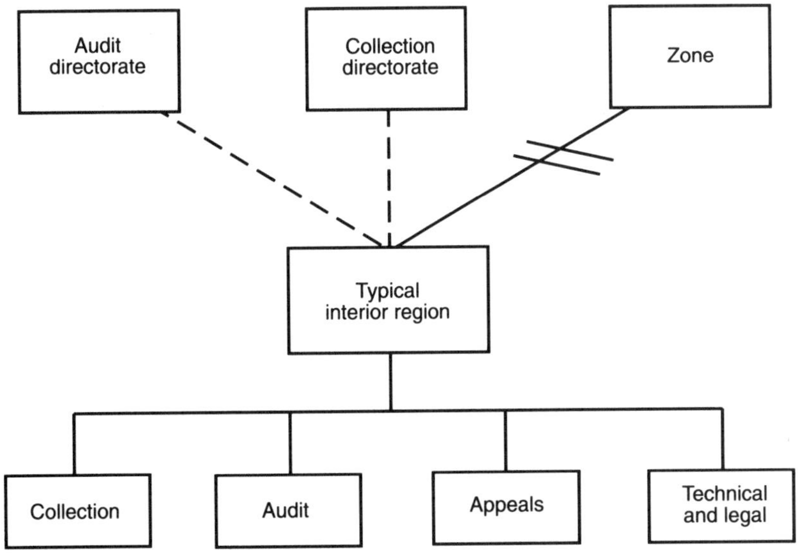

Note: Broken lines indicate informal functional subordination. Unbroken lines indicate formal subordination.

Discrepancies between what is officially postulated and what actually happens create problems, some of which are described below.

Relationships between the "advisory or regulatory" areas (such as collection and audit), on the one hand, and the "operating or line" areas, on the other, are subject to imprecisions and contradictions with respect to the authority of each area, the power of command of the former over the latter areas, the exercise of control, and so forth. The relationships of subordination are unclear. Because there is a significant degree of ambiguity in the boundaries that separate the areas, their actions are less effective. For example, according to official documents, the collection and audit directorates are responsible for formulating plans and procedures that must then be implemented by the regions. These plans involve objectives in the form of instructions, and these same regulatory areas are responsible for evaluating the execution of the plans at a later date. In any organization, both the responsibility for issuing instructions and that of evaluation are the prerogative of the higher level of authority. Consequently, the advisory area directorates informally assume these powers of higher executive authority with respect to the regions (operating areas). We say "informally" because, formally speaking, the regions are subordinate to the zones. As there is no clear line of command, relationships between the directorates and the regions are not backed by the degree of authority necessary to enforce compliance with the instructions, and, as a result, the regions do not recognize a relationship of subordination. In practice, moreover, the zones lose their real authority. This situation is summarized in Figure 2.

Because it is not clear that issuing instructions to the operating areas (regions) constitutes an act of delegation of objectives and responsibilities for which these areas will be held accountable, the organizational structure itself creates a significant degree of ambiguity in its line of command. This ambiguity is supported by the above-mentioned formal contradiction, which provides a basis for possible resistance to or partial implementation of plans. In both the interviews with regional managers and the interviews with section and agency managers in the interior of the country, officials mentioned this formal contradiction and indicated the various forms of organizational dysfunction it causes. First, they pointed to the phenomenon generally referred to as "multiple subordination." The regions receive plans from various sources, for example, the collection and audit directorates, that imply mutually incompatible objectives. This can create priority conflicts or various regulatory contradictions.

In some cases, the aforementioned directorates (advisory areas) do not restrict themselves to their planning functions. Instead, they, too, carry out operations with their own staff and, in doing so, intervene in the regions' geographic and jurisdictional areas. The regions express dissatisfaction with procedures that in some instances mean that the same taxpayer is contacted repeatedly. As for the zones, as has already been mentioned and judging by what actually occurs, it is not clear specifically what this level contributes as a center of authority. The surveys point repeatedly to the marginal position of the zone in contrast to the direct relationship between the directorates—in particular, collection and audit—and the regions. The result is a vacuum of real power in the zones. Nevertheless, they still interfere with the establishment of a clear system of accountability (delegated responsibility). In this case, the regions' formal and informal multiple subordination to the directorates and the zones creates bureaucratic interference that affects operational efficiency.

As may be gathered from these comments, to function coherently, the strategic command and the operating area should be part of the same line of command. Between these two levels, there should be a clear, functional relationship of subordination in which predetermined responsibilities are backed by authority, and which unequivocally allows the higher level to take responsibility for results. All the officials interviewed called for this definitional transparency. Regional managers would like these relationships clearly defined. Furthermore, heads of directorates, whose authority also appears confused, are equally unable to assume responsibility for the results of what they delegate.

The need to define a clear line of command presents us with a new problem. While at the higher level the principle of specialization predominates (collection, audit, technical and legal affairs, and so on are specialized areas), at the regional level these functions are integrated under a common authority. The regional manager is thus a generalist; he is responsible for bringing together the various functions performed by the sections. What we have here is a contradiction between organizational principles at two distinct levels of the institution. When surveyed, regional and section managers unhesitatingly stated their preference for the integrated regional model, since interdependency solves the problems of overspecialization. It simplifies paperwork and procedures, allows employees to perform multiple functions, and avoids duplication of requests to taxpayers.

With regard to their participation in planning, the managers interviewed said that this participation was slight and should be greater, since they have first-hand information about the taxpayers. Consequently, the people who plan the administration's actions do so without adequate information concerning regional realities in the broad sense. In general terms, a gap is perceived between the planners and the executors. In the opinion of those interviewed, this leads to unrealistic plans that fail to take regional characteristics into account.

To summarize, in the case analyzed, there is a gap between the advisory and operating areas. This discontinuity creates problems in implementing plans established at the higher level. Strategic planning is too far removed from concrete operations. This isolation produces a break in the line of command, which causes difficulties in enforcing the principle of delegated responsibility and, as a result, reduces managerial effectiveness.

The break in the line of command is basically due to two reasons:

(1) The operating unit managers do not officially report to the advisory and planning areas, from which they nevertheless indirectly receive instructions.

(2) The advisory areas are divided by specialization, while the operating sector is integrated under a single, versatile role: the "regional manager," who, through his subordinates, takes responsibility for all functions. This contradiction gives rise to situations of multiple authority and multiple subordination that are further complicated by the existence of an additional authority above the regional managers: the zone manager.

Horizontal Fragmentation

Horizontal fragmentation is defined as the lack of integration among offices or regulatory areas at the organization's higher levels. Although lack of integration is more prominent in the three basic areas—collection, audit, and technical and legal—it affects all of the directorates. Thus, the areas behave internally as if they were independent, isolated organizations. Each has its own systems, its own organizational forms, its own operations technology, and its own "organizational culture." In turn, each has developed a fragmentary relationship with the taxpayer.

When queried on the subject, 76 percent of regional and section managers advocated greater integration among the different higher level areas. This integration would make it easier to meet the various objectives emanating from the different areas and entrusted to a single management role: that of regional manager. To achieve this, integration must take place at the directorate level. The structure proposed further on reflects this necessity.

Organizational Cultures

The tax administration is marked by the existence of two cultural groups with shared orientations. These groups are strongly conditioned by the structure, that is, the existence of two very different areas: collection and audit.

The organizational culture and orientation fostered by the collection function is based on mass processing and impersonal methods with strong reliance on automated data processing. The collection culture is based on the following values: management efficiency, centralized information, and data objectivity.

The culture or orientation fostered by the audit function is based on personal actions vis-à-vis individual taxpayers. To operate, it requires a large number of employees who are given a wide margin of discretionary power and who are highly specialized and trained in the technical aspects of taxation. The work methodology consists of analyzing the tax compliance of selected taxpayers in order to detect tax evasion and establish corrective measures. This orientation gives auditors a strong sense of identity and pride in belonging. Because of the discretionary power enjoyed by these officials, their ethical conduct is of great importance. This fact makes it necessary to encourage moral values, which have an important impact on the organization's image.

In the Argentine case, one of these organizational "cultures" has been dominant over time. The results of a survey on job satisfaction among collection and audit employees show that cultural differences are encouraged by the prestige of belonging to one or the other group. Employees indicate a preference for the audit area, which would appear to be confirmed by the number of requests for transfer. This prestige derives from the greater experience and specialized technical knowledge required in this area. Furthermore, greater autonomy and discretionary power is associated with work in this area. Finally, training and experience gained in the area of audit is very highly valued outside the organization, which makes it easier for its employees to make the transition to the private sector.

In brief, the consequences of horizontal fragmentation at the top of the executive pyramid are manifested in the following:

(1) Lack of horizontal coordination.
(2) Lack of unified criteria among plans.
(3) Multiple functional subordination, which is a source of conflict for regions when various directorates formulate plans without prior agreement.
(4) Problems in determining work priorities in the regions.
(5) Power struggles at the upper levels that can lead to disarray at the top. The different organizational cultures behave like power groups fighting to impose their orientations. The resulting internal politics focus attention away from the real problems of productivity and efficiency.

All these stumbling blocks affect the necessary unity of focus and criteria that should prevail in elaborating plans and dealing with taxpayers. As a result, the organization presents an incoherent image that tends to confuse the taxpayers.

Required Organization

The following sections present organizational proposals aimed at solving the problems described above.

The Principle of Delegated Responsibility

Establishing the concept of responsibility and delegation as a principle of internal organization is essential to managerial efficiency. According to this concept, each level of the organization should be managerial. In other words, it should base its operations on the delegation of explicit objectives in terms of quantity, quality, and time required for compliance. An officer at that level must be accountable for these objectives to the higher authority that delegated them to him. Therefore, the managers of the operating units—in this case, the regional managers—must have a single superior authority to which they are accountable for results. To achieve this it is necessary to create a single directorate of operations to solve the problem of multiple subordination. This proposal is clarified below.

It is also necessary to establish, at every level, systems to evaluate compliance with objectives, taking into account not only the quantitative results for the period but also the quality of the work done and of relations with the taxpayer.

In the operations area, the levels might be structured as shown in Figure 3. Each of the levels in Figure 3 represents a distinct authority, has its own profile, and performs a clearly differentiated function in terms of the responsibilities exercised at that level. Levels IV and V are what we refer to as ''strategic''; they deal with the definition of plans and development projects, as well as the organization's policies. Levels III and II (regional managers and section managers) work directly with the operational level. The regional manager has direct access to both taxpayers and employees. Although he does not handle all the information, he maintains broad personal control over all of the problems specific to his area of responsibility. Note that in this proposal the zones do not constitute an intermediate level between the director-

Figure 3. Operational Responsibilities

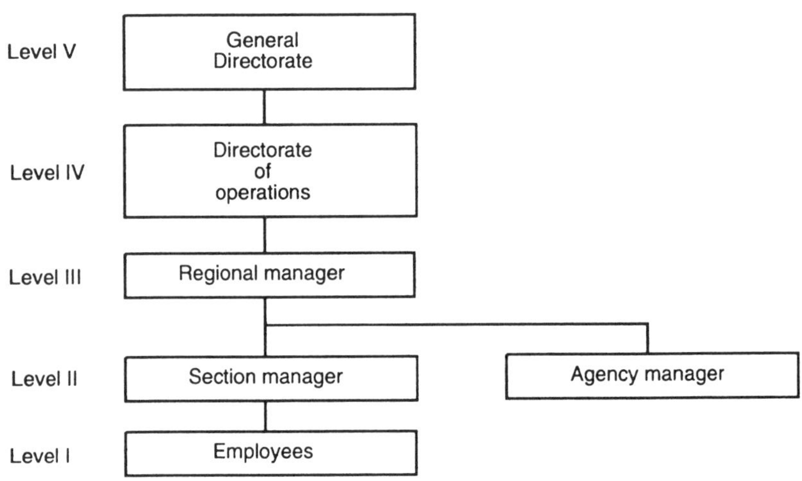

ate of operations and the regional manager. Differentiation of this level is considered unnecessary, since it could result in bureaucratic interference.

Integration at the Top

The directorates would constitute the strategic command. As outlined in the following paragraphs, this level would be made up of the directorates of administration, internal inspection, technical and legal affairs, computerization and systems, and operations, with the directorate of operations integrating the functions of the collection and audit areas.

Integration of this wide range of functions should be approached through a system of coordination and strategic planning, ultimately administered by the general director. His mission would be to facilitate horizontal relationships and the development of shared responsibilities by putting together a team with the goal of elaborating integrated plans for the entire administration.

According to Goldberg and Frost (1985), strategic planning should be formalized and should be a high-level management tool. Its objective is to define a desired future and to establish a process, with defined steps and stages, to make that future happen. Planning allows the organization as a whole to discuss and agree on a basic set of desired orientations, as well as on the collection objectives it wishes to achieve.

Second, the strategic plan would give rise to one or more integrated operational plans. These plans would establish the actions needed to reach objectives, agreed by all the directorates, in a period of about one year. Each of the directorates would be responsible for the development of more detailed programs for implementation in their areas, within the framework of the general plan and on the basis of quantity, quality, and time objectives coordinated with the other areas. The plan should include a centralized system of tracking, evaluation, and management supervision, which would be in addition to the tracking and evaluation carried out by the head of each area.

The Directorate of Operations

As suggested in the preceding section, the conflicts of multiple subordination could be resolved by creating a directorate of operations. This directorate would be implementation-oriented and would work through the decentralized operating units (regions) to achieve the objectives set by the plan. Thus, the director of operations would be responsible to the general director for the results of the plans delegated to the operating areas. The collection and audit functions would be attached to this directorate, to which the collection and audit specialists would be subordinate as advisors.

Establishing and strengthening the advisory nature of the positions in charge of developing collection and audit regulations, procedures, and systems means limiting the powers of these positions to delegate work or objectives to the regions or operating units. Thus, the power of delegation would remain in the hands of a single authority: the director of operations. Creating a directorate of operations not only solves the problem of multiple subordination of regions or decentralized operating units but also makes it possible to unify the criteria used to design the systems.

The desirability of functional interdependence between the two areas makes it necessary to have a single, integrated system of collection and audit. From the standpoint of data processing, the systems are mutually supportive, which means that when conceived as a whole, they acquire functional interdependence. When the functions are integrated at the strategic level, it is easier to create versatile roles at the operational levels, filled by employees who can handle the two aspects of tax administration. Both the ability to substitute and mobility are encouraged, since these foster employee satisfaction and consequently improve productivity.

Creating a unified directorate of operations to which the regional managers are directly subordinate would make it possible to achieve clear, basic linkage between three levels in the line of command: general director, director of operations, and regional manager. As this linkage should be governed by the principle of delegated responsibility, exactly what is expected of each level should be specified in terms of results and which procedures and policies should be followed.

The Region as Basic Operating Unit

The proposal that the region should be the basic operating unit emphasizes the function of the regional administrator or manager as the administration's representative to the taxpayers and defines his position in the hierarchy (see Figure 4). He is seen as a true manager—entrusted with the required discretionary powers—of a complex operating unit concentrating all the basic functions. He must be responsible for the pace and quality of the work and for meeting the goals set for him in the plans. To increase operational performance, the region headed by the regional manager must be compatible in size with the maintenance of personal ties with both employees and taxpayers. Compatibility of

Figure 4. Proposed Regional Structure

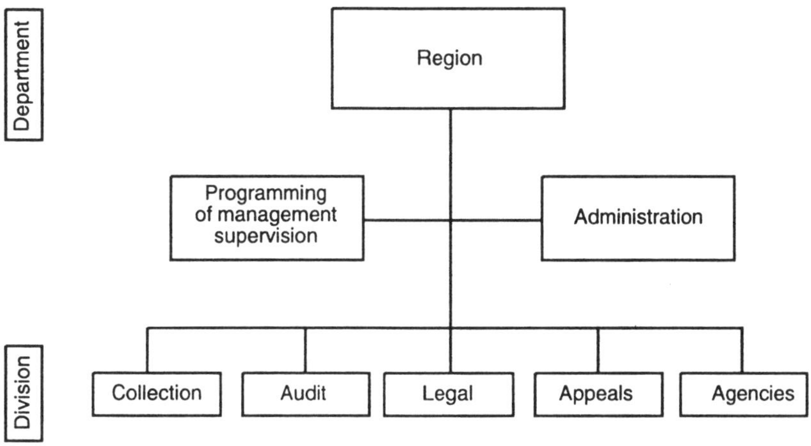

size is a requisite for good structural design. Thus, the regions should have a limited number of employees—between 150 and 200 in all—who work with a limited number of taxpayers—around 50,000, hypothetically—whom they serve and monitor.

Regions or operating units that are too big should be split up. A large number of taxpayers registered with a small number of operating units prevents good contact and personalized, efficient taxpayer monitoring. Big regions can hinder the development of effective taxpayer information and assistance programs.

The surveys conducted point to the need to give greater autonomy to the regional manager. First, as has already been mentioned, the regional manager should participate in plan design so that the plans will take actual local social and economic conditions into account. The information contributed by the regional manager is of fundamental importance for the planning level. Periodic meetings for consultation should be scheduled between regional managers and their immediate superior.

The tendency toward centralization in the existing systems must be reversed. Overcentralization accentuates internal rigidity and lessens the effectiveness of monitoring. Reversing this centralizing tendency is a way of bringing the administration closer to the taxpayer. This requires giving the officials in charge of regional units a certain degree of autonomy to monitor operations personally and to bring their ability and experience to bear in dealings with the taxpayers.

Table 1. Proposed Levels of Responsibility for Tax Administration

Level and Role	Work	Incumbent Profile	Discretionary Decisions
Level V General director (Plans work over a horizon exceeding five years.)	Manages a unified system in constant interaction with the economic and political environment; establishes general framework; highest level in line of command.	Capacity for abstract and conceptual thinking; long-range, broad vision; political flexibility; moral leadership.	Defines policies and objectives; determines long-term overall goals and their appropriateness to the situation; coordinates strategic plan.
Level IV Director of operations Director of legal affairs Director of administration Director of systems and computing Director of internal inspection (Plans work over a two-year horizon.)	Strategic planning; specialized general management; medium-range development projects; defines general work systems; shapes the work culture in his area; generates rules and procedures.	Capacity for abstraction and generalization; able to see the whole picture; manages various projects simultaneously; ability to integrate smaller groups; selective perception of relevant information.	Supervises broad secondary units; handles emergency situations; provides examples; defines objectives and oversees their fulfillment.
Level III Regional managers Department managers (Plans work over a one-year horizon.)	Manages broad operating units; generalist; manages smaller groups (various sections performing specialized tasks, such as step-by-step systems); critical path area; manages a program.	Direct leadership ability; ability to use relevant information; anticipation of consequences; extrapolation; broad knowledge and experience; management of broad groups; imaginative and step-by-step control; public relations aptitude.	Defines a program of work; supervises; implements changes to handle emerging problems; participates in the elaboration of plans.
Level II Section managers Agency managers (Plans work over a six-month to one-year horizon.)	Manages a set of tasks and objectives; specialist; operational management within a specified set of rules, regulations, and procedures; manages a group of employees.	Able to identify significant information and problems; ability to analyze and draw conclusions; acceptance of authority; specific knowledge; face-to-face management of group.	Defines priorities; administers simple resources (material and staff) on the basis of a given program.
Level I Supervisor Employees	Simple tasks; few variables; solves one problem at a time; physical manipulation.	Good psychomotor coordination; ability to concentrate; good memory, perception.	Decisions affecting work quantity and quality.

While the various divisions that make up the region would be organized according to the principle of specialization, the unit administrator or manager is by training and ability a "generalist," which means that he can visualize the entire task in an integrated fashion. Furthermore, the administrator should have sufficient autonomy to pursue the objectives set for him by the tax administration's plan, without bureaucratic hindrance.

Required Hierarchical Levels

The number of hierarchical levels and their proper delimitation and definition is a fundamental aspect of organizational structure.

Generally speaking, tax administration requires about five hierarchical levels, as can be seen from Table 1. Too many hierarchical levels, or imprecise definition of these levels, creates bureaucratic interference and unnecessary supervisory bodies. Table 1 represents a general scheme based on the levels of abstraction of the tasks involved. For a more detailed profile of each level, it would be necessary to define the required technical knowledge, skills, experience, and so forth. Our definition of these levels is based on the proposal by Jaques (1989).

Summary of Proposals

At the beginning of this section, we defined simplicity and clarity of structure as required qualities. These qualities are achieved by properly defining roles and by clearly differentiating responsibilities, beginning with the role of the general director. Table 1 shows the added value contributed by each level of the organization.

Clarity is also needed in the relationships of subordination between the various management levels in the line of command: who reports to whom, who decides what, who plans, who executes, who supervises, controls, or evaluates; who formulates plans, what is the level of participation of the others, who advises whom, who provides services, and so forth.

Understandably, relationships among tax administration roles are not limited to the relationship of hierarchical subordination. The various specialized areas (such as collection and audit) should have a strictly advisory function, that is, one accomplished by the staff of an implementation-oriented director, termed a director of operations in this paper. The advisory function is in fact the result of a director's need for specialists to help him in his own planning. Thus, the advisor has the authority to study and propose options and to define standards and procedures within certain limits relative to his field of specialization. He does not have management authority, that is, authority actually to delegate responsibility for tasks and objectives.

Structural simplification is linked to the number of required hierarchical levels. As has already been said, a typical tax administration probably needs five hierarchical levels. The description of these levels makes clear the levels of authority needed to manage the organization's operations. Each of these levels is managerial, since the occupant of a given level has the authority to decide on specific questions autonomously and also manages a number of employees who have been assigned to him.

II. Human Resources

The administration of human resources is a fundamental pillar of tax administration. As indicated in Table 1, there are different degrees of complexity in the tasks associated with the various posts or hierarchical levels. The occupants of these posts require a certain level of ability, knowledge, skill, and experience. The descriptions given provide profiles of the roles or posts and of the abilities required to fill them.

States of Disequilibrium

To establish a consistent human resources policy, it is necessary to differentiate three basic variables that should be in equilibrium, as well as to understand the importance of interrelationships among them in the dynamics of the organization. These three variables are (1) the complexity of the role and the tasks performed at a given level; (2) the individual ability required to do the job; and (3) differential compensation.

In practice, the above-mentioned variables are usually not in equilibrium. Experience in tax administration points to three principal factors that can affect worker satisfaction:

- Compensation.
- The work itself and the opportunities it affords for the exercise of individual ability and judgment.
- Development, advancement, and career opportunities.

Some studies (for instance, Calello and Rovner (1975)) show high levels of worker dissatisfaction in relation to these factors—particularly on the lower rungs of the ladder (levels I and II in Table 1). Excessive, centralized prescription of systems, regulations, and procedures restricts autonomy of action and can for this reason produce dissatisfaction.

The studies reveal significant differences in job satisfaction between collection and audit employees, associated with the tasks specific to the two areas. Because the tasks in the collection area are more highly regulated—owing to the centralized nature of the systems and regulations—they are also simpler, more elementary, and more routine, and, as a result, duller and more tedious for the employees. In contrast, audit tasks offer a chance to observe broader, more complete processes requiring analysis, collection, and interpretation of data—mental operations that suppose greater autonomy and therefore provide a higher degree of satisfaction.

Dissatisfaction is greater among collection employees who have completed a college-level course of study (those with a masters degree in business administration, as well as accountants, and lawyers), specifically because they do not see any opportunity to put their professional abilities to use in the foreseeable future.

On the other hand, professionals in the audit area find opportunities there for training in the technical aspects of taxation that will allow them to opt for well-paid jobs in the private sector at a later date.

Tax administration requires a large number of employees with good college backgrounds, and it invests considerable effort in training them. However, the difficulties of administering these human resources result in a steady flow of talented employees to the private sector, where they find greater opportunities to increase the value and level of their abilities. These factors explain the modest results of programs to attract and develop young professionals. It is necessary for these programs to be based on real possibilities of motivating work and for applicants to be placed in positions in keeping with their current and potential abilities.

Even at the higher levels of the tax administration structure—such as the roles associated with level III—the abilities, experience, and judgment of officials are underutilized, which reduces their autonomy and the amount and quality of what they contribute. Take for example the previously mentioned case of the regional managers, who are limited in their participation in developing collection and audit plans and in providing their local knowledge of taxpayers in their area. This affects the realism and feasibility of the plans and restricts the authority and freedom of decision of the regional managers. The result is a considerable degree of dissatisfaction.

Given the importance of this role—which we consider managerial—it is necessary clearly to establish the required profile, which must include not only knowledge and experience but also ethical values and an impartial attitude toward the taxpayer. These managers must also have the ability to handle different functions in an integrated fashion, since the role in question is that of a "generalist."

When perspectives for the full development of employee abilities, knowledge, and experience are limited, or when compensation is not commensurate with the individual's abilities, conflicts arise. Because such situations discourage employee commitment and motivation, they affect the general climate of the organization.

There are also situations in which officials occupy positions that are beyond their abilities, knowledge, or experience. In such cases, there is a decline not only in general management quality but also in the productivity of the area managed and the motivation of the employees.

In government service, the placement of officials frequently is not based on merit. Often promotions are given because of seniority or political influence, which generally brings the supposedly favored officials up against their "level of incompetence." This situation gives rise to feelings of frustration and dissatisfaction.

The area manager's ability is the determining factor in successful leadership. A well-qualified director is in a position to handle critical situations successfully, motivate his superiors and employees, and inspire taxpayer confidence. To achieve this, he must have a highly capable and committed operational management staff, trained to deal effectively with the critical situations usually faced.

The organization has a series of managerial tools for ensuring that employees are placed in roles whose levels of responsibility match their individual abilities. One of these is the evaluation of employee performance, efficiency, and effectiveness. This function, which is generally performed routinely without really discriminating among the personal attributes assessed, should ensure and regulate this match. To do so, it must be part of a broader system that includes periodic meetings to evaluate directors and managers. These periodic meetings could support employee promotions and career development and ensure consistency in that regard. Holding periodic competitions also helps to rescue hidden talents from anonymity and is always seen as a guarantee of equity. In short, these procedures help to re-establish the principle of "merit" that should govern job placement.

Wage Policy

Many tax administrations experience problems in connection with salary levels. These problems are usually the main reason why the best employees are lost to the private sector, which provides better compensation. In many cases, wage policy discourages the most able, who become frustrated and dissatisfied with their jobs. When internal competitions are held for management level positions, a significant lack of interest has been noted in some instances. Motivational analysis has demonstrated that the salary difference between the management position in question and, for example, an advisory position at more or less the same level did not compensate for the increased responsibility associated with the position vied for. This fact was the main reason for employee disinterest.

In the Argentine case, surveys on job satisfaction demonstrate that the "incentive fund" does not function as such—it is not a real incentive to productivity—much less as an award for merit. Employees assimilate it with the general concept of compensation, and it is expected as part of salary. Because it does not discriminate individual performance, it does not act as a motivating factor to stimulate individual productivity.

If the tax administration is to be made more effective, its wage policy must be revised. Accurate analysis of individual performance cannot be side-stepped. The opinion of the employee's immediate superior, corroborated in turn by the area manager, must be given special weight in promotions and pay increases. Unfortunately, under the current system the opinion of the immediate superior has little or no impact, and the area manager is not required to participate in the evaluation of all the employees who report to him indirectly.

It is necessary to define a salary scale that establishes pay differences in keeping with the various levels. To do this, all posts must be adequately categorized. For each level, it should be possible to identify about four wage categories, which would make it possible to reward differences in performance among employees at the same level. The tax administration salary scale should be in accord with the national earnings indices for equivalent positions, both in public administration and in the private sector. Otherwise the desired efficiency and effectiveness cannot be hoped for.

III. Conclusions

These conclusions derive from the study on Argentina referred to in Section I above, but many of them are applicable to tax administrations in other countries.

Structure

There are two kinds of basic organizational dysfunction:

(1) Vertical fragmentation

This dysfunction affects the clarity of the line of command. Operationally speaking, fuzziness about the type and degree of authority is evident in some planning areas. There are problems of multiple subordination: different directorates supervising or giving instructions to the same operational manager.

(2) Horizontal fragmentation

Horizontal fragmentation is defined as the lack of interdependence or integration among directorates or regulatory areas (the strategic level) that should constitute a single planning unit.

Another problem is excessive separation between the collection and audit areas, which have different organizational cultures. These two functions need to be structured into integrated systems.

The proposed changes are as follows:

(1) Integration at the top

The first suggestion is to increase integration mechanisms through a unified strategic planning system that ensures the participation of the various areas and tends to establish convergent models and criteria.

The second is to link the collection and audit functions in a single directorate of operations to which specialists working in each of these systems report in the capacity of advisors.

(2) Vertical integration

It is suggested that the lines of command should be clarified. The director of operations would be the immediate superior of the regional manager, to whom the latter would be accountable. The role of regional manager would continue to be that of a versatile generalist.

(3) Hierarchical levels

There should be only five hierarchical levels. Table 1 described the roles that make up each level and the work performed—in terms of complexity and the required abilities.

Human Resources

(1) The conceptual framework defines a desired equilibrium between three variables: ability, complexity of task, and compensation.

(2) The level of compensation is vitally important to job satisfaction. It is followed, in order of importance, by the opportunities the work provides to exercise one's abilities, motivation, and individual autonomy. Finally, development and career opportunities have considerable impact on employee expectations. Professionals who feel that they have limited career opportunities in the organization tend to go elsewhere.

(3) There are mismatches between employees and positions. Highly complex posts—such as those of director or regional manager—demand a high level of abstract and conceptual thinking, as well as leadership abilities and ethical values. When individuals are not qualified for the position they occupy, the general functioning of the organizational system suffers, as does employee motivation.

(4) This proposal highlights the need to strengthen the position of regional manager. This post is conceived as managerial in nature. Its occupant is a true representative of the administration who exercises dual leadership: outside, in relation to the taxpayers, and inside, in relation to the employees in his area of command.

It is essential to establish a hierarchy of the officials who will occupy these posts. To do so, they must be identified and correctly placed.

(5) Given the characteristics of the work system, there is a tendency to underutilize employees at levels I and II of the organization. The work is routine and promotes a low level of autonomy. Employee mobility and work enrichment systems should be encouraged. It is desirable to increase team work.

(6) The institution must develop mechanisms and systems for correctly evaluating the organization and employee performance. Responsibility for evaluating employees should lie with their immediate superior, assisted in turn by his own superior (the head of the area in question). Mechanisms of this kind would help to re-establish the principle of merit and to reward good employee performance with raises or adequate promotions.

(7) Revision of the wage policy is indispensable. However, this does not necessarily imply higher salary costs, since the current inequitable distribution of pay makes the salary scale more expensive. When the internal system pays the most productive and penalizes the most unproductive, output will increase. This is why a salary scale that establishes equitable differences in pay based on the different levels of task complexity should be adopted. There should be about four categories for each hierarchical level, for a total of 20 groups.

BIBLIOGRAPHY

Calello, Estela, and Susana Rovner, *Encuesta de Satisfacción Laboral en Empleados de Recaudación y Fiscalización* (Buenos Aires: Dirección de Estudios, Dirección General Impositiva, 1975).

Calello, Estela, J. Colombo, M. Rosales Creo, and I. Scocco, "Análisis Sociológico de la Evasión Fiscal," *Boletín de la Dirección General Impositiva,* No. 398 (Buenos Aires), February 1987.

Casanegra de Jantscher, Milka, Carlos Silvani, and Charles L. Vehorn, "Modernizing Tax Administration," in *Fiscal Policies in Economies in Transition*, ed. by Vito Tanzi (Washington: International Monetary Fund, 1992).

Goldberg, Gerald H., and Lorraine Frost, "Towards a Simplified Organic and Functional Structure of Tax Administration" (New York, 1985).

Jaques, Elliott, *Requisite Organization* (Arlington, Virginia: Cason Hall, 1989).

Rovner, Susana, and Estela Calello, "Encuesta a Funcionarios de Regiones" (unpublished; Buenos Aires: Dirección de Estudios, Dirección General Impositiva, 1975; updated 1987).

Silvani, Carlos, and Aldo Schlemenson, "Análisis Organizacional y Cambio Planificado," Cuaderno No. 16 (Panama: Inter-American Center of Tax Administrators, 1975).

Schlemenson, Aldo, "Lineamientos Generales para el Cambio de Estructura" (unpublished; Buenos Aires: Dirección General Impositiva, January 1987).

Comments

Francis P. Greaney

Mr. Schlemenson's paper focuses on the organizational aspects of a tax department. He divides his discussion into two parts: (1) organizational structure; and (2) human resources.

His discussion of the organizational structure focuses on the differing roles of the various levels of the organization and the characteristics or abilities of the people assigned to these positions. He also makes the important point that the organization must strive to achieve a balance between the complexity of the work, the capacity of the individual, and the level of compensation, for each employee in the organization in order to establish an environment where the staff will flourish.

While Mr. Schlemenson's points are all very valid, the discussion is somewhat abstract. Most of the points that he makes can be applied to almost any organization.

More emphasis needs to be placed on the specific characteristics and constraints facing a tax department. In addition, while he outlines the requirements of organizational structure and staffing, he provides little indication of how a tax department suffering from deficiencies in these areas can effect changes. While each organization may take a somewhat different approach to change, it would be useful to provide some examples of how various countries have successfully or unsuccessfully undertaken changes in their organizational structure and personnel.

I would like to emphasize the philosophy of the organization. I believe this point is of primary importance. The structure of the organization and the personnel within it are the means to fulfilling the organization's objectives.

The first part of my discussion deals with the philosophy of the organization and the image that it attempts to project to the public. The second part deals with the personnel and the methods used to achieve a balance in the staff. The third part deals with the structure of the organization and how changes can be effected in the organization.

Philosophy

In discussing the philosophy of the organization, we should first start by noting the special characteristics of a tax administration organization and how it fits within the context of overall government policies and organization. First of all, the tax department deals with only half of government policy. It is the revenue-gathering arm of the government. As such it has little if any role in providing services and benefits to the citizens. This is the domain of other arms of the government. Being relegated to one sphere, particularly the revenue-gathering one, severely limits what the organization can do to improve its image and profoundly affects how it must deal with the public.

A common complaint heard throughout the world is that "people do not want to pay taxes because they do not believe that the government spends the money wisely" or worse, "the money is lost due to inefficiency and corruption." While there is often skepticism about these remarks among the international community, I believe that the overall perception of government policies does play an important role in the general public's willingness to comply with taxes. Carlos Silvani points out in his paper that there is no evidence that changes in governments and government policies result in significant changes in tax compliance. However, I would contend that the effect that government spending policies have on tax compliance can only be seen over the long run. A change in government policies must be given time to take effect, and the public must realize the results of the new policies before they react and more willingly comply with taxes.

The tax department's unique position as the revenue-gathering arm of the government greatly influences the department's orientation and philosophy in its dual roles as a producer and as a provider of services. The tax department cannot operate as other organizations, particularly private firms, where the costs and benefits are directly related. By providing quality products and services to its customers, private firms can increase their business as more customers return as a result of satisfaction with the products and service they receive for the money they spend. The tax department, which is in itself unable to provide anything in return for the payments made, cannot follow this approach. It must therefore seek a different balance and emphasis on how it carries out its production functions and its service functions. While this general issue is relevant to all areas of public administration, it is of particular importance in establishing the appropriate philosophy of a tax department.

In the area of tax administration the production function includes collecting tax payments, processing tax returns, undertaking enforcement action against delinquents, and so on, much of which takes on a production-line-like character, as noted by Mr. Schlemenson. (It should be noted however, that Mr. Schlemenson argues that the impersonal, oversystematized and overcentralized processes present in many countries should be changed to place the tax department in closer personal contact with the taxpayers.) The service function, in many ways the more difficult function to appropriately define and provide, includes not only the important functions of taxpayer assistance, as noted in the paper by Robert LeBaube and Charles Vehorn (Chapter 9 in this volume), but also governs all the department's interactions with the taxpayers.

It is the service function of the tax department that is most restricted by the role of the tax department as the revenue-gathering arm of government. While it is extremely important that the tax department provide quality services to taxpayers to assist them in fulfilling their tax obligations, the effect of quality service in developing "repeat customers" is limited precisely because the tax department cannot provide taxpayers with much, if any, direct benefit in return for their tax payments. Therefore the most that the service function can hope for is to make it as easy and painless as possible for the taxpayer to fulfill his obligations and to project a positive image of the department in all its interactions with the public.

Given the constraints placed on the tax department in terms of providing services to taxpayers, much of the task of establishing and projecting the image of the tax department falls to the production functions. The production functions must establish the department's image as an efficient and effective operation that is capable of enforcing compliance with the tax system on those that do not voluntary comply. I would therefore place considerable emphasis on improving the department's ability to promptly identify those that do not comply, establish how much they owe in tax, and enforce compliance through a combination of penalties and legal action.

Personnel

Another important issue relating to the philosophy of the tax department is: How can the department instill within its employees the philosophy and objectives of the organization? As Mr. Schlemenson pointed out, the employees are an important factor in determining the effectiveness of the organization. I would put it even more strongly and say that "the organization is only as good as its people." As mentioned above, often important restrictions are placed on the tax department by general government policies. The tax department is often required to conform to broader government policies, in hiring, firing, compensation, and promotion. While the department often has more flexibility in structuring the organization, its ability to appropriately staff the new (or even the current) organizational structure is often very limited. This again highlights the importance of how the tax department relates to the rest of the government.

Mr. Schlemenson's discussion of the factors concerning personnel, the complexity of the work, the capacity of the employee, and the level of compensation are well laid out. However, the important operational issue of how to achieve a balance between these three factors was neglected. There are several alternatives, but again, they must fit into the context of the overall civil service. The three primary alternatives are (1) hiring new staff; (2) reassigning staff; and (3) training current staff.

The first approach is generally a viable option only if the organization as a whole is understaffed. If the problem is strictly having inappropriate staff, civil service regulations generally would make it impossible, or at least extremely difficult, to hire new people to replace current staff. The paper by Silvani and Radano (Chapter 2 in this volume) mentions that Bolivia contemplated creating an entirely new tax department to operate alongside the current department, in an attempt to get appropriate staff and to instill the desired spirit within the department. This did not prove feasible, but the tax authorities nevertheless were able to reform the department through extensive use of newly hired staff with new attitudes and orientations.

The second approach, reassigning staff, is almost as difficult as the first. In many countries more emphasis is placed on seniority than on ability. In other cases, there are restrictions on how fast a person may be promoted or what academic background he must have to qualify for a particular position. While these restrictions are often an attempt to ensure a certain level of competence and quality in the government service, they severely restrict the tax department's ability to achieve the proper balance of personnel at the various levels. Mrs. Christian mentioned this as an important constraint in Trinidad and Tobago in her efforts to staff the new VAT Administration Center for the introduction of the value-added tax (VAT). (See Comments to Chapter 5 in this volume.)

Mrs. Christian was able to assemble an exceptional core staff for the VAT because of her firsthand knowledge of individuals and the special attention she placed on establishing a new environment and philosophy by which the VAT would operate. New facilities, approaches, and procedures for the VAT administration helped to effect a significant change in attitude, particularly in the initial stages of the VAT. Unfortunately the most fundamental changes were not possible due to the bureaucratic links with other parts of Inland Revenue and the requirements to assume many senior staff steeped in the traditional modes of operations into the VAT. Greater attention to modernizing the operation of the entire Board of Inland Revenue may have helped to effect a more complete change.

Because of the limitations in the first two approaches, the third approach is almost always used—training. The importance of training is well recognized, though the emphasis tends to focus more on the technical aspects than on the managerial aspects. There are often great deficiencies in staff's technical capabilities, particularly in developing countries, and such training can be an important step toward achieving a balance between the complexity of the job and the capabilities of the staff at the technical level. However, isolating the training efforts to technical issues limits the effects that the training efforts have on the overall operation of the organization and tends to fall well short of providing the necessary backgrounds and skills to those who manage the department. Fortunately, recent training efforts in Costa Rica and Guatemala have recognized this problem and placed a heavier emphasis on managerial and supervisory training. It will take some time before the success of these programs can be evaluated.

The three approaches mentioned above tend to focus on providing a balance between the complexities of the job and the capabilities of the personnel. In order to achieve a true balance, the issue of compensation must also be addressed. This, more so than any other, is greatly influenced by overall government policies. Limitations in compensation seem to affect tax departments more severely than any other area of government. This is no doubt due to the technical nature of many of the positions and the fact that in many cases the very companies that the tax department is trying to control are competing for the department's most talented personnel. Although the problem of employee compensation is well recognized, and some efforts have been made to provide pay supplements for some categories of personnel (particularly computer personnel), I am unfamiliar with any country that has successfully solved this problem.

Organizational Reforms

Closely related to the issue of personnel is the establishment of an appropriate organizational structure. The two must be complementary. In order to establish the appropriate divisions and hierarchy as outlined by Mr. Schlemenson, it is critically important that appropriate personnel be assigned to the relevant positions. Without the proper staffing, the organization will not function properly. In addition, care must be taken to ensure that the design of the organizational structure is effectively converted into actual operation. While there must be sufficient flexibility in the organization to allow it to adapt to varying needs, too often the actual operation of the organization is quite different from the design on paper.

The differences can be attributed to two factors. The first factor, as mentioned by Mr. Schlemenson and with which I wholeheartedly agree, is that there is often a breach between the advisory and the operational sectors of the department. Great care needs to be taken to ensure that the advisory sectors are adequately in tune with the realities of the tax department, just as the design of tax policies must be in tune with tax administration. The second factor, somewhat related to the first, is that insufficient attention is given to overcoming bureaucratic inertia. This is an area that requires great attention in order to successfully implement reforms and modernization of a tax department.

In some ways it may seem easier to establish a new organizational structure within the institution, for example, establishing a new department to administer a new tax (much like was done in Trinidad for the VAT), than to change the current organization. The preparations can begin with a clean slate and establish a well-designed and coherent structure. However, this approach presents a huge undertaking and is very costly in terms of time, energy, and resources. This approach is probably only possible in conjunction with a significant overall tax reform effort where the political support is strong enough to marshal the required resources.

The importance of linking tax policy and tax administration reforms is not adequately recognized in this regard. Most people in the taxation community recognize the importance of balancing tax policies with administrative realities to ensure that they can successfully achieve policy goals (whether or not they actually succeed in coordinating the two in practice). However, not enough attention has been placed on the importance of linking administrative reforms with policy reforms as a means of providing adequate access and support from the policymakers in terms of resources and commitment to administrative reform. I think reflection on the successful administrative reform efforts presented at this conference supports this view.

Conclusion

In conclusion, I would like to encourage more emphasis and work to be placed on precisely *how* countries have successfully and unsuccessfully implemented reforms in tax administration. I am interested specifically in how a tax department can instill the proper philosophy and orientation within its organization; how a tax department should approach implementing structural changes; and how a tax department should go about trying to achieve the proper balance between the technical requirements, capabilities, and compensation among its staff.

Edgar Gutiérrez

My thoughts on the subject treated by Aldo Schlemenson are based on my experience of many years as a tax administrator in Costa Rica. Mr. Schlemenson's conclusions are distilled from consulting experiences in three countries—Argentina, Peru, and Venezuela—and may point to an organizational strategy applicable to tax administration in general.

The first issue is whether this strategy is valid in countries whose size and population are different, as are Costa Rica's, where socioeconomic indicators are also different (for instance with respect to literacy and public services), and where the state is a small, concentrated geographical entity.

In my view, Mr. Schlemenson's strategy is applicable even under those conditions. Of course a few adaptations or adjustments would probably be necessary, especially because public administration in countries such as my own is highly centralized, and the tax authority assumes an excessively distant attitude in its dealings with taxpayers.

The following comments concern the approaches, policies, and objectives outlined by Mr. Schlemenson.

The administration of a tax system can, like the administration of any endeavor, be planned and executed in very different ways, all of which may be more or less efficient. By and large the organization of a tax authority evolves in response to various and complex causes, some historical, some legal, some political, and, of course, some that are purely technical. When we examine the entity responsible for administering taxes in a given country, we must keep in mind that the institutions of that country—not only socioeconomic but also legal and administrative—constitute a mirror image of the country. The tax authority is and always will be a reflection of the country's overall public administration, which in turn is influenced by the general state of education and the level of development of the economic and social institutions, whether public or private.

According to Mr. Schlemenson, tax administration exists because the taxpayer exists. The latter is the epicenter around which all administration activity revolves, either to persuade him or to compel him. In this model, an effective tax administration eschews coercion in favor of seeking voluntary compliance with tax obligations. It stresses the limitations of legal coercion to induce desirable tax conduct, and the need to provide the tax authorities with modern methods, developed in other technical or scientific fields (areas), for persuading the taxpayer to comply voluntarily.

Changing the emphasis from coercion to persuasion implies the abandonment of an administrative style that prevails in almost all areas of public administration, which probably has strong legal backing and which, in the fiscal realm, is extremely rigid. Many difficulties arise in putting this strategy into practice in the context of an essentially coercive tradition.

The Perception of Government and Its Efficiency

Taxpayers will be more willing to pay taxes if they have a reasonably favorable view of government. This has to do in large measure with the problem of the legitimacy of governments, that is, with the extent to which they are acknowledged to have the authority to give orders that should be obeyed. Regardless of whether a tax system relies on coercion or persuasion, it is imperative for the system's effectiveness that it be legitimate. Orders from a legitimate authority are more persuasive than those from one whose legitimacy is disputed. In some countries of Latin America this has been an important factor for a long time.

Another issue is whether people are generally in agreement with the government's spending policy. The image that the taxpayer has of the government is determined by elements ranging from the personality of its leaders to the treatment the taxpayer receives when he has to go to a tax collection office. Although it is true that many factors that lead to a less than favorable image of the government are outside the tax administrator's control, the administrator's activities do offer considerable scope for improving that image. Tax administration is actually one of the most important public services, a service which by its nature, quality, efficiency, and cost has a major influence on the attitude of the taxpayer.

Unfair Tax Systems

When the tax system is not designed to work in a just and equitable manner, or administrative weakness allows important sectors of the population not to pay the taxes they owe, nagging irritation is added to the image of an inefficient government. Tax equity must be measured not only in terms of the ability to pay taxes but also by whether most taxpayers pay what they owe.

Conditions making for inequities in the tax system are apt, all too often, to spring from the very heart of that system: tax law. More specifically, they spring from two features of the law: exemptions created by the legislature and the quality of the legal text.

In countries such as Costa Rica, the exemption regime has grown in an arbitrary and haphazard fashion. Exemptions of the type found in Costa Rica distort forecasts regarding the productivity of the taxes, because they are not based on consideration of their economic and revenue impact but are blindly passed into law. At the same time, they create the impression of a system whose components can be removed at will, thus inciting taxpayers to evasion by raising doubt as to the need for any taxes.

The poor quality of tax legislation does the tax system further disservice and makes the taxpayer even less inclined to abide by the law. This problem stems from several factors: in general, the low level of legislative skill found in our countries and, in particular, inconsistencies written into the law as a result of the political wrangling that usually accompanies attempts to create new taxes or modify existing ones. The resulting poor quality of the law can confuse the tax authority with ambiguities that make evasion or avoidance possible, which again creates the impression of an irrelevant system subject to endless manipulation.

My experience of many years in Costa Rican tax administration allows me to state that tax administration in developing countries is not geared, as one would wish, to voluntary compliance; it is not designed to offer taxpayers the best possible service. Efforts to boost revenues by reorganizing tax administration have often been postponed. Instead, increased revenues have been sought by raising tax rates and adding new elements to the tax base. A revision of administrative strategies is seen as a medium- or long-term process, whereas fiscal needs are immediate. The short-term view predominates in political circles, and the tax authority has scant power to persuade politicians to undertake changes in strategy.

Making tax administration more efficient and maximizing voluntary compliance is a very difficult task. In Costa Rica at the present time there are 165 different taxes, which makes the system very complex and inefficient. Earlier I said the administration of any endeavor could be defined and pursued in different ways, all more or less efficient, but what really matters is that the means used be reasonable and produce useful results at the lowest cost. Tax administration is no exception to this general rule.

Taxpayers should be able to fulfill their obligations without excessive compliance costs. For this purpose it is necessary to offer taxpayers considerable assistance, especially in dealing with new taxes or substantial tax reforms. Such assistance will take many forms—counseling, distribution of information, preparation of simple forms, and so forth, as well as offices where they can make their payments with a minimum of inconvenience and delay. All those items should be part of a system that encourages voluntary compliance. However, while furthering voluntary compliance, the authorities must make sure that delinquent or manifestly dishonest taxpayers are not given the opportunity to circumvent the law with impunity. To do otherwise would be to discourage voluntary compliance and consequently increase the administrative burden and costs.

To bring about the restructuring of tax administration according to the model designed by Mr. Schlemenson, coordination between tax policy and the country's political system is very desirable. In countries with developing economies such coordination does not always exist. What happens is that as social objectives and economic aspirations expand, tax policy fails to keep up and the tax system no longer reflects the country's social and economic objectives. A study by the IMF on Costa Rica notes, "In Costa Rica, for instance, and the same may be true of other developing countries, public finances are surprisingly complex considering the nation's small size. That complexity arises from the high number of taxes as well as an elaborate system of very specific incentives, combined with a formidable number of public sector activities. Many of the public sector activities seem to be guided not by clear objectives but by political pressures exerted by special interest groups, or else by a sort of inertia that develops over the years and is reflected in legislation."

Important consequences derive from this complexity. First, it becomes very difficult to evaluate the tax system or public expenditure in terms of the traditional criteria of public finance, such as equity and efficiency. For example, it would be almost impossible to estimate the impact of public expenditure and taxes on the various types of income. Who gains and who loses because of this expenditure or that tax cannot be determined. Consequently, it is impossible to ascertain the extent to which the current structure of public finances works for or against the goal of equity. What appears likely is that the finances of the public sector affect different people in different ways, depending on the incentives to which they have access, the pension scheme to which they belong, and so on down the line. Inevitably, differences in treatment generate pressures by groups to improve their relative positions. It is equally important to note that it is not clear how much commitment there is to the goal of neutrality in resource allocation. In sum, what impact does the public sector, given all its activities, have on the allocation of resources?

Second, it is difficult to determine whether fiscal policy measures (for example, a change in the tax rate, or a public spending cut) bring the system closer to meeting the government's objectives. The lack of transparency obscures the relationship between changes in approach and changes in policy objectives.

Third, and largely as a consequence of the previous two points, it is politically difficult to reach a consensus on the necessary tax measures. Policy changes cannot be sold to the electorate purely on the basis of their technical virtues. The thrust of the debate shifts from technical to political issues.

The foregoing considerations would make it highly desirable, in the case of Costa Rica, for the national authorities to initiate a process aimed at eventually bringing about a simpler and more open public sector. Among the steps taken in such a process—which would undoubtedly take several years—would be the elimination of many taxes and special treatments (such as tax incentives) and of many expenditure programs, and the consolidation of others. The fiscal objective would be a more efficient public sector, whose impact, in terms of equity and efficiency, would be easier to measure.

While in the more advanced countries a mere handful of taxes are used to produce the necessary revenue, in Costa Rica—and no doubt the same is true in other developing countries—the system spawns large numbers of taxes. Many of them produce very little revenue, and some taxes actually cost more to administer than they bring in. Add the expenses incurred by taxpayers in the course of fulfilling their tax obligations, and the cost of generating revenue through these low-performance taxes rises further. An excessive number of taxes absorbs administrative resources, creates confusion in the tax system, increases opportunities for tax evasion, and leaves taxpayers with the impression that the tax burden is greater than it really is.

When a tax system is based on poorly conceived taxes it is useless to speak of neutrality or equity. A system of this kind does not provide an appropriate foundation for an administrative strategy based on voluntary compliance. It is impossible to know, moreover, the impact of such a tax system on income distribution or resource allocation.

The first step that a country must take under those circumstances is to reform its tax system and rationalize its taxes. This will enable policymakers, the tax administration, and taxpayers to concentrate their attention on a smaller number of more productive taxes. The government should undertake the task of trimming the tax system, ridding it of unproductive levies. The country would then have a more rational, better administered tax system. This would be a gradual process requiring a few years for completion, but it should commence without delay.

The organizational structure model set out by Mr. Schlemenson should prove very useful for the reorganization and design of tax administration, but it will be impossible to attain the hoped-for efficiency if the complexity of public finance systems is not attacked first.

11

Privatization of Tax Administration

Luis Fernando Ramírez Acuña

To speak of privatizing tax administration is risky, despite the winds of reform blowing in that direction in this early part of the 1990s. At first sight, the title of this study may possibly suggest a major contradiction in terms. The administration of a country's tax system, along with the administration of justice and national defense, are probably the most frequent examples of what ought not to be privatized. Or at least they ought not to be privatized in the sense that, being functions inherent to the state, there should be no loss or delegation of autonomy. However, this does not mean that certain administrative tasks should not be contracted out to the private sector where this can be clearly shown to improve efficiency or effectiveness. The difference is that the state loses no autonomy if certain administrative activities are delegated. A company or a person is not free to establish a tax; this must be done by law or by a government decision.

Consequently, the topic is approached from the standpoint that the tax laws are within the sole purview of the state and come into being as a result of actions taken by the competent authorities. Even so, it is worth noting that countries are increasingly entrusting the construction of certain public works to private sector entities and authorizing them to collect certain taxes on that account. Thus, for instance, it is common now for the construction of a highway or a harbor to be awarded through public bidding to private entities (national or foreign) on condition that they make the initial investment and then collect the tolls, taxes, or improvement charges needed to pay for building the project.

Looked at from this angle, government divests itself of (privatizes) certain functions related not only with collecting taxes but also with building public works. To some extent, these are examples of privatization of tax and budget execution at one and the same time. The important point to note is that these arrangements are always made without the state losing its power of supervision. In other words, the private sector

I am grateful for comments from Richard Bird, Jorge Martinez-Vazquez, and Teodoro Nichtawitz.

cannot decide on its own that it is going to build a highway and collect tolls. It is the state that adopts the decision and awards a concession to the private sector, under certain conditions and usually for a predetermined length of time.

One of the most important lessons we have learned in recent years may be that in order to have a strong state we do not necessarily need a large state. Indeed, in some cases a large state cannot be a strong state. It is for this very reason that, in the area of tax administration, having government entrust some tasks to the private sector instead of directly discharging them may lead to higher efficiency and effectiveness. In other words, such a measure may help build a smaller but stronger tax administration.

I. Tasks That May Be Assigned to the Private Sector

To examine the feasibility of contracting out certain tasks to the private sector, it may be helpful to classify each task under one of the three basic types of work performed by a tax administration, namely: (1) collection of tax receipts; (2) audit; and (3) collection of delinquent taxes.

Collection of Tax Receipts

The possibility of subcontracting some tasks involved in tax collection depends on the type of tax being administered, for example, whether it is a mass tax or one applicable only to a few taxpayers, whether it operates under a self-assessment system or must be assessed by the tax authority.

When dealing with a system of taxes massively applied and based on self-assessment, the following tasks may be contracted out to the private sector to a greater or a lesser degree, as has in fact been done in several countries.

Printing Tax Return Forms

The forms used for tax returns are frequently changed—nearly every year in some countries—either because the laws change or simply because an effort is made to streamline procedures. Some tax administrations purchase the equipment needed to set up their own printing shop directly within the tax agency. Other countries have a government printing house where all printing by government agencies must be done.

Some—Bolivia, Argentina, and Colombia, for example—have their own official printing houses but turn to private companies in order to print their tax forms.

Experience suggests that the tax department should be permitted either to print its forms in its own printing shops or contract the work out to the private sector. As a rule, private companies have more flexibility than public ones when it comes to printing and designing the layout of forms, as well as making last-minute changes in them, always according to the instructions received from the tax authorities.

Distribution and Sale of Forms

In most countries, distribution of tax return forms takes place as follows: (1) the forms are picked up by taxpayers at tax administration offices, as in Argentina and Bolivia; (2) the forms are mailed to known taxpayers, as in the United States and Uruguay; (3) a specialized company is hired, usually the same company that prints the forms, to take care of their distribution, as in Colombia (although these specialized companies may in turn use the mail); (4) the forms are available at banks or may be purchased in stationery shops and bookstores. There are also combinations of these options. Another way, which has been used sporadically in Peru and other countries, is to distribute the forms in dailies or other newspapers.

Another issue related to tax forms is deciding whether the taxpayer should pay for them or not. Most countries have chosen not to charge for the form because this delays the distribution process, and have instead absorbed the total cost as an expense of tax administration. In Peru, however, the taxpayer is charged for the cost of the form. In Brazil, banks must bear the printing cost of forms used for payment of taxes through the banking system.

The option of distributing the forms to each taxpayer by mail, or of using for that purpose the services of a specialized company, makes it possible to send out each form with the data on the taxpayer preprinted on self-adhesive labels, thereby making it more likely that the "inputting" of the data after the taxpayer has filled in the information will include fewer identification errors capable of hindering subsequent data processing. If the preprinted form is sent out showing the name, the address, and the identification number of the taxpayer, a lower margin of error is guaranteed when the data are later recorded and faster data entry can be achieved.

Receipt of Forms Filled Out by Taxpayers

The receipt of tax returns filled out by taxpayers is one of the most delicate areas of tax administration. However, private companies have recently been entrusted with this task in some countries.

In countries such as the United States or Canada taxpayers usually mail their tax returns to the tax administration. In nearly all Latin American countries, however, taxpayers deliver completed tax forms directly to the offices of the tax administration, basically for two reasons: (1) there is a generalized perception that the mail does not work properly and (2) there is also the legal tradition of letting the taxpayer have a stamped copy of the form or a special receipt to show that the return has been filed.

In practice, accepting delivery of the forms at the offices of the tax administration has been a difficult business because it is a cyclical event for which the tax administration does not have the proper infrastructure. In recent years this task has been increasingly delegated, especially to banks, which are accustomed to receiving documents, waiting on the public, and engaging in a large volume of transactions every day. This has been the case in the last five years in Bolivia, Chile, Colombia, and Ecuador. As a rule, banks have been authorized to do this work. In principle, not only banks but also other entities in the financial sector can be enlisted for this purpose.

The receipt of tax returns is a delicate task because it sets in motion the process that will lead to accounting entries, collection, assessment of penalties, audit, rulings on appeals or claims filed by the taxpayer, and so on.

A first obstacle to be surmounted if a decision is made to have the private sector (banks) receive tax returns is the requirement of confidentiality.

In most tax systems the information set out in tax returns is confidential and may not be used for purposes other than tax determination. In some countries the information provided by the taxpayer may not even be used as evidence against him. Thus, it is conceivable that no penalties might be imposed for illegally obtained income so long as that income has been reported by the taxpayer.

Confidentiality of the information reported on tax returns is crucial for the success of a self-assessment system. However, when banks are placed under a duty to preserve the confidentiality of the data disclosed by the taxpayer and are barred from using that information for other purposes, the taxpayer usually finds that his banker is someone who, in view of their credit and commercial relationship, may be trusted with the information set out in the tax return.

Another major point to be addressed if the receipt of tax returns is to be contracted out is that banks must be under an obligation to receive returns submitted either with or without an accompanying payment. Filing of the tax return is an act wholly separable from payment, though the two may take place simultaneously. It is desirable to induce the taxpayer to report and pay taxes at the same time, so as to reduce the volume of operations; however, if the taxpayer wishes only to file a return and pay the tax later on, he should have that option and banks should have to accept his tax return.

It is important to specify in the contract with banks their obligation to receive from taxpayers tax returns and payments of all kinds, irrespective of the amount of taxes reported or paid (large or small taxpayers) and of whether they are or are not customers of the particular bank. This will give the taxpayer more options when filing his returns and will encourage competition among banks to provide better service.

Also advisable, as will be seen later, is that the compensation paid to banks should reflect the number of tax returns received by each bank and not merely the amount of taxes collected, so that banks may not be tempted to accept tax returns and payments only from "large" taxpayers.

When banks are given the task of receiving tax returns, one point that should be amply clear to the tax administration, to the banks, and to the taxpayers, is that the stage of filing returns should not involve any verification activities. In other words, the bank should not be given the authority to challenge the data submitted by the taxpayer; it should make no review other than to check the identification number and other information needed to make certain that each taxpayer's payment will be posted correctly.

Processing Tax Return Data on Magnetic Media

It is not conceivable now that a system of taxes massively applied and based on self-assessment can be administered without the aid of computers.

One of the most serious difficulties faced by tax administrations in recent years has been their limited understanding of strategies in the area of automatic data processing. At first, most countries designed a centralized system with large data processing centers, the center being sometimes a unit of the tax administration and other times an independent agency. Later, decentralized systems were attempted, and more recently three countries, Colombia, Bolivia, and, later, Ecuador, have chosen to assign the "data entry" function to the banking system, reserving for themselves the processing of the data. In other cases, Chile for instance, a specialized agency (a service company) is employed to enter the data.

The availability of good, systematized, and timely information does not depend on who does this work but on the fulfillment of certain requirements. These are (1) a tax identification number that works properly and includes, insofar as possible, a check digit; (2) forms that are simple to complete and that call for relatively few data to be entered into the computer; and (3) a computer system within the tax administration that is capable of interacting with the system in banks or other entities commissioned to do the work. Needless to say, the banking system must have an infrastructure suited to the efficient performance of this work.

One of the advantages of commissioning banks to transcribe the data onto magnetic media is that it helps to unclog the bottleneck usually experienced by the data processing centers of tax administrations; each bank is responsible for processing only the tax returns received by it. This advantage should translate into a requirement of timeliness for banks transcribing the data and sending the magnetic media to the tax administration along with the tax returns. A time frame not exceeding 15 days after the tax return has been filed is a reasonable time for a payment or a tax return to have found its way into the computer of the tax administration.

Some basic quality control over the transcription of data by banks is imperative. Banks should be required to transcribe data twice, or to use some other system that guarantees a low margin of errors. Furthermore, a system of penalties must be devised for deficiencies in the quality of the data transcribed; banks should be penalized by means of monetary charges or a lowered compensation when they make mistakes beyond a certain margin of tolerance. It is also essential for the tax administration itself to design its own data entry system, which ought to set the standard and be open to no changes on the part of any bank. Only the tax administration should be authorized to change it.

One of the disadvantages of entrusting the task of data entry to banks may be that, over time, the ability of the tax administration to make structural changes in the design of forms or in the procedures for receiving tax returns is reduced, inasmuch as any such changes would entail not only retraining the staff of the administration itself but retraining or requiring the retraining of bank personnel.

As in the stage of filing returns, in the transcription stage the bank should not be authorized to engage in any verification activities. The bank should transcribe the data as submitted by the taxpayer even if it detects errors by the taxpayer. In some cases, to gain time, data entry programs have been designed jointly by banks and the tax administration, with a view to detecting arithmetical errors (addition, subtraction, multiplication, division, percentages, and so on) to be able to ask the taxpayer to correct them, but without any coercive power being exercised in the process. In practice, this could be an "ex ante" control offered by the bank as a service to customers.

Receipt of Cash, Checks, Securities, or Other Means of Payment Allowed for Payment of Taxes

Although many tax administrations still have their own infrastructure for receiving tax payments, the trend is clearly in the direction of transferring this function to banks, which do such work routinely and have the installed capacity needed to perform it.

If this function is entrusted to the banking system it may be discharged simultaneously with the receipt of tax returns, or separately. In some countries, payment may be made at the banks but returns must be filed at the tax offices.

Some administrations have chosen to receive payments from large taxpayers directly at their offices (as in Peru and Uruguay) or at an official bank or a national bank (as in Argentina and Bolivia); payments from other taxpayers are usually received throughout the banking system. All manner of combinations are now being used. However, if compensation paid to banks is linked to the amount of tax payments they receive, then banks would not be interested in joining the system if payments from large taxpayers are excluded from the system of payment through the banks.

When a tax administration that has been collecting taxes directly at its offices decides to let banks do this work, there is a strong tendency to give the taxpayer the option of paying at one or the other location. This, however, is seldom advisable for two reasons: (1) for an administration to preserve its collection infrastructure while it lets banks take over this function means forfeiting the possibility of using the personnel from that infrastructure for more pressing or important business, such as enforcement activities, and (2) if "input" problems arise in the processing of data it becomes hard to tell with any degree of certainty in which system they originate. For this reason, once the decision is made to let collection take place through banks, this work should be entrusted to them exclusively; in other words, the tax administration should relinquish this function and should redefine the duties of staff formerly assigned to do that work.

Thought should be given to the possibility of letting banks accept cash or other widely used means of payment. Insofar as possible, no additional requirements should be placed on personal checks—such as prior clearance or certification of funds—because these hinder the work considerably. If a personal check is returned because of insufficient funds, the payment is simply regarded as never having been made, aside from any penalties that may apply. The tendency to place additional requirements on personal checks is typical of countries where there are mechanisms such as the *paz y salvo* (tax clearance certificate), which is issued against the tendering of a check, even though the check may later bounce.

In designing procedures for filing tax returns and making tax payments in banks, one key element to be considered is the control that must be exercised over banks with respect to their turning tax receipts over to the tax administration (or the treasury). An important lesson is that there must be penalties (interest on arrears) for the late surrender of tax monies collected. This control must obviously be coupled with control of the tax returns filed.

Furthermore, timely updating of taxpayer data in the computers of the tax administration is essential if bank errors are to be detected in time. Most bank errors can be detected when the tax administration sends a notice to the taxpayer advising him that his tax return or tax payment has not been received. When dealing with taxes for which the administration has no single register of taxpayers, the system for monitoring banks must be different: for instance, asking certain taxpayers to check their tax payments, as recorded by the tax administration, against what they have actually paid, based on their own records.

Withholding at Source as a Way of Privatizing Payments

Withholding at source has been one of the most revolutionary steps taken by tax administrations in their efforts to privatize, by making agents in the private sector responsible for withholding taxes and turning them over to the government. It has turned into an assignment given to the private sector to collect taxes in advance.

Although the advantages of withholding as a form of privatization of tax administration tasks are countless, I have excluded this topic from this review because it deserves a separate study. However, attention should be drawn to a side effect caused by the increasingly widespread use of withholding at source, namely, the additional simplification inherent in reducing the number of persons who file taxes without reducing the number of taxpayers. In some countries, the number of tax returns to be processed fell by as much as 50 percent after salaried employees were excluded from the obligation of filing returns, thanks to a legal provision under which the tax they owe is equal to the amounts withheld from their salaries.

Furthermore, it is evident that withholding at source has been generally effective in reducing tax evasion. Some experts have nevertheless voiced the concern that this tool is being used as a cure-all without full awareness of the fact that a widespread system of withholding at source requires monitoring of withholding agents as well.

Tax Refunds

As withholding at source becomes the rule, the volume of tax refunds tends to rise, which is not bad in itself so long as there is an efficient tax refund system in place. A speedy system of tax refunds is conceivable provided the data on taxpayers are reliable. Thus, banks themselves could refund the surplus or balance in favor of taxpayers after the tax returns of, say, large taxpayers, have been filed. Banks would turn over to the tax administration the net tax receipts after deducting the amount of tax refunds. This, of course, would not be in the nature of a definitive reimbursement and would not bar the tax administration from subsequently looking into whether the tax refund was properly made.

This sort of swift, direct refund is conceivable only for large taxpayers or for other taxpayers who take out a bond or insurance policy from the same bank or from an insurance company in order to guarantee to the tax administration that the proper amounts will be reimbursed to it if, upon review, it is shown that the taxpayer was not entitled to the refund.

When it comes to tax refunds, however, most administrations prefer to be cautious and in most cases make a review to establish the amount of the refund. In some countries, however, the taxpayer has to wait longer than a reasonable length of time for his tax refund, while the matter is being reviewed. This is more serious when the amounts to be refunded are used by the treasury to finance its own operations, and there are no provisions allowing indexing of late refunds or payment of interest on them.

Audit

The most controversial side of private sector involvement relates to tax audit, with good reason. Deciding which taxpayers are to be audited, for how long, and in what ways, is properly the responsibility of the tax administration, for the fulfillment of which it is granted discretionary authority, the power to impose penalties and the power to enforce the law.

The most significant step taken to privatize the audit function may well have been the introduction of self-assessment. From a historical perspective this was an enormous innovation, the changeover from a system in which the tax and the taxable base were established by the tax authorities, to one in which both are calculated by the taxpayer himself. Under this system the taxpayer must not only pay the tax but must determine it, compute it, and report it himself; if he should fail to do so, penalties will be applied. The tax authorities confine themselves to reviewing the reported data and, of course, computing and collecting underpayments as well as any applicable penalties.

Some taxes, though they may be massively applied, require that the tax base be computed by the tax administration, as in the case of real estate taxes for which an official valuation of the property is made in order to calculate the tax. Some administrations are assigning private companies the task of measuring the tax base by using objective means, such as aerial photography, to determine the size of properties; others are trying out self-assessment by the taxpayer himself, and a trend toward self-assessment of property values is beginning to emerge in countries such as Bolivia and Colombia. Such self-assessment and reporting by the taxpayer may have positive results where the law provides (as in the case of Colombia, for example) that any entity in the public sector may, by a unilateral decision, acquire any piece of real estate for the value reported by the taxpayer plus 25 percent to cover any underassessment on the part of the taxpayer. The possibility that the government can buy the property at the price reported by the taxpayer cannot be regarded as confiscation because the price is set by the owner. So long as this possibility is considered credible, the outcome may be that self-assessment of real estate will approach real values in order to forestall the possibility of having to sell for a lower price.

In the area of customs duties, some countries such as Bolivia and Indonesia have hired specialized companies to check the value of imports, owing usually to the absence of proper control systems at customs. This type of service basically involves checking the value reported by the importer against reference prices in order to establish the duty payable. Countries wishing to embark on such schemes should weigh the costs of the service against the benefits provided.

The audit function, when dealing with massively applied taxes based on self-assessment, may include certain features intended to encourage compliance or to simplify administration, which cannot strictly speaking be considered "privatization," but which reflect a private sector mentality. Some countries have introduced legislation regulating such features, which merit discussion because they aim at decreasing the audit work load by introducing some elements of a private sector approach to tax administration. Below we discuss some of them.

The Signature of an Accountant on Tax Returns

By requiring the signature of an accountant on tax returns, a good deal of the responsibility for the veracity of the information reported is placed on a professional accountant, thereby making the task of audit easier and improving at the same time the quality of the data reported by the taxpayer.

The obligation to have the tax return signed by a public accountant is usually mandatory for larger taxpayers (companies, businesses, and so on), because they are commonly under an obligation to keep books of account and consequently have an accountant or a tax advisor. The fact that the signature of an accountant is required to file a tax return does not mean that the return will not be looked at by the tax administration. The idea is merely that having an accountant check the return raises the odds against tax evasion. Of course, this requirement is usually accompanied by severe penalties when violations attributable to the accountant or tax advisor are detected, so that he may be said to share to some extent the responsibility of the taxpayer.

Audit Insurance

Audit insurance guarantees to taxpayers who increase their tax payments by more than a certain percentage over the immediately preceding tax period that they will not be audited. This device is usually resorted to on a purely temporary basis (a particular tax period or tax year) when there is an awareness that the tax administration does not have even the minimum audit capacity for reasonable enforcement. Accordingly, the administration makes a first selection and excludes from audit procedures all those taxpayers who register a substantial increase in their tax payments. This policy is announced beforehand, so as to encourage taxpayers to increase their payments by the established minimum and thereby win immunity from audit. To illustrate this mechanism, let us take a country with an annual inflation rate of 20 percent, real economic growth equal to 5 percent (which means that nominal economic growth is 26 percent), and a tax system with unitary elasticity (which would imply that nominal tax revenues should increase by 26 percent). The audit insurance would then be guaranteed to taxpayers who increase their tax payments by, say, 36 percent as a minimum. Actually, audit insurance may—and insofar as possible should—be set up on a differential basis, that is to say, in line with the behavior of relatively homogeneous economic sectors.

The problem with this procedure is that taxpayers whose potential tax increase is higher than what is required for giving them insurance against audit will tend to keep their tax payment to the minimum needed for immunity from control. Even so, the idea is that the administration should tolerate these possible violations for the sake of being able to devote its limited resources to auditing those taxpayers who fall short of the minimum required for audit insurance.

Expert Certification

Certification by an expert is used, for example, in Mexico, and goes farther than requiring the signature of a public accountant on tax returns. The taxpayer who files a return with a tax certification from a public accountant has, in the eyes of the tax administration, a "guarantee" that his return meets current tax regulations. Accordingly, any liability for inconsistencies found in the return rests with the accountant who signed the tax certification, the taxpayer escaping any penalty for mistakes that can be laid to the former.

Two essential characteristics are noteworthy in this procedure: (1) the system is voluntary; in other words, it applies only to taxpayers who wish to avail themselves of it, in which case they must bear the cost of tax certification; and (2) besides being voluntary, the system allows the taxpayer to choose his own accountant, which is meant to ensure the confidentiality of the information.

Legitimizing Previous Tax Returns

A mechanism that has already been introduced in the legislation of several countries—the Dominican Republic being probably the first—guarantees to the taxpayer that his tax returns for earlier tax periods will not be audited so long as his most recent return is correct. It is certainly attractive for the taxpayer to have the option of barring audits for earlier tax periods. For this option to operate properly and protect him from audits, however, he will in practice always have to file correctly in the future. Otherwise, the possibility of auditing him will apply once again. If the goal of having the taxpayer file accurate returns is attained, the tax administration will have gained, because ensuring proper future compliance is more important than preserving the possibility of reviewing the past.

Reducing Penalties if the Taxpayer Does Not Appeal

In line with the idea of simplifying the work of tax administration and improving compliance by taxpayers, legislation has been enacted in some countries to discourage controversies between the government and the taxpayer, without, however, disregarding due process if the taxpayer believes he is entitled to challenge a decision of the tax administration. The taxpayer is given the right to a gradual reduction of his penalty in proportion to the reduction in the work that the tax administration or the courts have to do in connection with his case.

The idea of gradually reducing penalties may be illustrated by the following example:

(1) Let us suppose that a taxpayer has underreported certain incomes and thus underpaid $1,000 in taxes.

(2) Let us further suppose that the tax administration is able to detect 25 percent of all unreported income, which in this case would mean $250 in taxes (in many tax administrations this ratio is substantially lower).

(3) Finally, let us suppose that the penalty applicable to the taxpayer is 200 percent of the amount of the unreported tax detected, in other words, $500 ($250 x 200 percent).

In the end, the administration would be able to collect a total of $750 ($250 in taxes and $500 as the penalty). Of course, after imposing the penalty the tax administration would probably have to institute proceedings for collection, particularly in view of the stiff penalty involved.

A system that substantially reduces penalties might succeed in collecting a higher amount. The outcome will naturally depend on the assumptions made in the example set out below. The purpose of that example is to illustrate what kind of results might be expected from a strategy of reducing penalties while increasing the resources devoted to audit.

(1) Once the unreported income is detected by the tax administration, instead of imposing the penalty described above the administration allows the taxpayer to correct all his errors, holding out the possibility of reducing the penalty to, say, 20 percent in lieu of 200 percent. The condition for reducing the penalty is that the taxpayer must actually *pay* the unpaid tax, along with the reduced penalty.

(2) If the taxpayer calculates the odds and does not know exactly how much of his unreported income has been detected by the tax

administration, he will probably correct his tax return provided the penalty is reduced considerably. It is important to point out that at this stage the administration should let the taxpayer know that it has evidence regarding the unreported income, without, of course, telling him what sort of evidence.

(3) If we assume that the taxpayer declares the entire unreported income, the penalty will have been reduced to only $200 (20 percent of the unreported $1,000), but on the other hand, a tax of $1,000 will have been recovered. In other words, the tax administration will actually collect $1,200 and will save itself collection and litigation proceedings against the taxpayer.

(4) If we assume that the taxpayer does not—as is likely—declare all of the income initially unreported, the tax administration will nevertheless collect the portion accepted by the taxpayer, plus the reduced penalty, but in this case it will retain the option of imposing the 200 percent penalty on the tax payable on the income that the taxpayer has failed to include in his amended return. In other words, it is preferable to give the taxpayer the opportunity of correcting his return and of changing his behavior, with the least possible expenditure of resources on the part of the tax administration.

(5) On the penalty imposed by the administration (for the uncorrected portion of the taxpayer's return) a smaller reduction should be offered—say a 40 percent penalty instead of the 20 percent penalty mentioned above—against the taxpayer's commitment not to challenge the administration's version of the facts and to pay the tax due plus the penalty thus reduced. This would discourage litigation and would show taxpayers that the longer they persist in trying to put off the penalty through evasion or litigation, the costlier it will be for them.

Through this type of measure, combined with broader audit coverage, some countries have successfully put in practice the notion that pursuing improvements in compliance by all taxpayers is better than achieving perfect compliance by a few or exhaustively auditing a handful. From a different standpoint, this policy reflects a private sector attitude in that the less litigation there is the more resources will be freed for the administration to reinforce audit work.

For the policy of reducing penalties to be successful, however, the coverage of audit (ratio of taxpayers audited to total taxpayers) must be expanded; in other words, the likelihood of detecting tax evasion will need to increase.

Requesting Information from Third Parties

The attempt to control tax evasion has led tax administrations to require from taxpayers additional information concerning their financial or commercial dealings, in order to make sure that taxes have been correctly assessed. In addition, both taxpayers and nontaxpayers must provide the administration with information intended for checking the accounts of other taxpayers. This is a way of privatizing control, by relying on third parties for information used for audit purposes. To expedite the process of matching the information received with information reported by taxpayers, it is advisable that the data be supplied on magnetic media.

In the last two decades tax administrations have tended to ask for too much information, especially when they began to use computers. At present, many administrations are rethinking this strategy, after learning that having the computers and asking for the information was not enough to control tax evasion. In fact, taxpayers themselves were the first to realize that by giving the administration information "indigestion," its attention would be distracted over purely formal matters and it would never get to the heart of the problems.

Recently, there has been a widespread trend toward simplifying forms and asking only for such information as the computer is able to process, but providing in the law that the taxpayer is required to keep records and to make them available to the tax administration on request.

Collection of Delinquent Taxes

In principle, it should not be very difficult to turn over to companies or persons (preferably lawyers) the task of collecting the delinquent tax portfolio of a tax administration. The practice is not very widespread, but tax administrations are increasingly considering a move in this direction.

If this task is to be successfully accomplished by the private sector, the tax administration must provide reliable data on delinquent taxes; the legal system must provide for administrative collection procedures instead of always requiring involvement of the courts; the interest charged on delinquent taxes must be higher than the prevailing market rate, so that taxpayers will not be tempted to use their delinquent taxes as working capital; and/or collection costs must be paid by the taxpayer on whose account the collection proceedings had to be undertaken.

Other key points to be considered include the system itself for turning listings of taxpayers over to companies or persons charged with collecting delinquent taxes, the compensation arrangements, and the incentives established to encourage speedy collection. Care must be taken not to turn over the portfolio of large taxpayers exclusively to private companies (in fact, the tax administration should begin by commissioning the collection of delinquent taxes owed by small taxpayers), and care should be taken to evaluating the number of cases of successful collection as well as the geographical location of delinquent taxpayers.

The choice between turning collection over to private companies and paying a commission (a variable salary) to the tax administration's own officials engaged in collecting delinquent taxes is an interesting one, because in the first case the task is privatized and in the second a private sector attitude is applied. In Argentina, for example, the officials of the tax administration engaged in this work have a variable salary, determined by the results obtained.

Assigning a variable salary to tax administration employees according to the amount of delinquent taxes they recover does, of course, generate debate. Kept within reasonable bounds, however, this policy is beginning to make inroads in a good many tax administrations.

II. Remuneration for Work Assigned to the Private Sector

How to pay for the services of the private sector once a function of the tax administration has been privatized may be even more controversial than the decision to privatize.

Probably the first question that needs to be answered is whether the service can be simultaneously entrusted to several persons or entities or whether it requires exclusivity. In either case, but especially in the latter, the most advisable course of action is to award the contract after calling for bids. In both cases, competition should be stimulated among the various entities providing the service.

When the private sector is called upon to perform a task previously discharged by the public sector, compensation for that service will in some cases be a fixed amount payable by the tax administration under a contract; but in other cases it will be necessary to regulate the amount that may be charged directly by the entities newly responsible for providing the service.

When it comes to receipt of tax payments, and collection of delinquent taxes by the private sector, tax administrations use different remuneration methods. These range from paying for each staff hour of work involved to paying a percentage of the amount of taxes collected.

In the case of collection through the banks, one way to remunerate them is to let the banks keep the taxes collected for a reasonable length of time that will cover their costs. Of course, compensation systems may have some more sophisticated features aimed at stimulating competition among the banks themselves, in order to provide better service to the taxpayer, handle the largest number of persons, and reward processing of good quality performed by the banks.

In some countries, competition has meant that the profitability of these operations has fallen off over time, because banks, in their effort to attract large taxpayers, have opted for sharing their profit with the customer (the taxpayer) by offering him loans at preferential interest rates to pay his taxes, thereby sharing with him the profit derived from the tax collection work.

When the choice is made to compensate banks by letting them use the tax receipts for a certain period, the time specified varies across countries. In Bolivia, Colombia, and Ecuador, for example, this period is about 15 days. In other words, the compensation received by the banks is equal to the rate of interest they are able to obtain for 15 days on the amount of taxes collected. In the countries mentioned, the service provided by the banks includes receiving tax returns, processing the data onto magnetic media, accepting payments, and ultimately turning over, within an equally brief time frame, properly filed copies of the forms received, copies of the magnetic tapes, and the money collected.

Penalties are usually provided for banks that fail to meet their obligations. Aside from the interest applied when tax receipts are not turned over on time, the systems in force in Bolivia, Colombia, and Ecuador impose separate penalties based on the frequency of delay in submitting documents and the number of mistakes made in transcribing the data onto magnetic media. It is advisable to have a penalty-free margin of tolerance and, in particular, more flexible regulations during the early months of implementation of the system, when banks do not yet have enough experience with it. Another useful feature is to reward, through temporary monetary incentives, the bank that registers the highest degree of compliance.

Finally, it is important to underscore that banks should be compensated in such a way as to encourage each one to handle the largest number of taxpayers. In other words, the factors to be considered for setting their remuneration should be not only the amount of money collected but also the number of documents received and transcribed onto magnetic media. Absent this, banks may concentrate on receiving only payments from large taxpayers that involve few documents and large amounts of taxes.

As for the compensation of agents withholding taxes at source, attempts have been made to give them a tax credit or a tax discount, but in practice the normal procedure in countries where the rate of inflation is not very high is to give the withholding agent a reasonable length of time before he must turn over the money withheld, which is the equivalent of paying the agent the rate of interest prevailing during that period.

Turning now to what might be called "taxpayer assistance" or "taxpayer services," an enormous field opens up for private sector participation. Data base systems that make it possible to make computer inquiries about current tax legislation; software designed for preparation of tax returns; private audits before filing returns; publication of specialized literature; and training seminars on tax matters; these are all examples of private sector activities aimed at assisting the taxpayer in his dealings with the tax administration. Of course, the tax administration will need to step in and provide these services, or share in their provision, where they have not yet been developed by the private sector.

III. The Private Sector Approach to Tax Administration

One aspect that has been stressed in this study is that privatization is not always a way to improve a service that is being provided poorly by the tax administration. Indeed, many tasks are better performed by the tax administration itself acting with private sector mentality, which means investing resources to train employees, improving job conditions, devising financial and other incentives to encourage the best employees, and so on.

It is better to have fewer well-paid employees than a larger number who are poorly paid. The tax administration must pay a competitive salary in order to keep its best employees.

Happily, this private sector managerial approach has begun to be accepted by many tax administrations. It is now common to observe specialized units devoted to large taxpayers, "red carpet" treatment for the largest taxpayers, different management and audit strategies for various types of taxpayers—all of which should not be viewed as a form of discrimination. In fact, discrimination could be said to exist if taxpayers who are different are treated in the same way.

IV. Conclusions

Privatization of tax administration does not mean giving up government control over tax policy in a particular country. Quite the contrary, it means letting the private sector perform certain tasks under the supervision of the tax administration, in order to improve efficiency or effectiveness.

When a tax administration delegates certain logistical functions to the private sector it must have a firm hold on its managerial ranks to enable it to monitor, to introduce any necessary changes in the delegated services, and to react adequately to any problems that may arise. This reaction may include reclaiming for the tax administration any functions that the private sector may be performing poorly at a particular time.

Experiences in privatizing tax administration functions have not necessarily followed a sequence by starting out with tax collection, then moving on to audit, and finally dealing with collection of delinquent taxes. Instead, some of these functions have been turned over to the private sector whenever this was thought advisable in order to improve efficiency or effectiveness.

A policy of gradually reducing penalties while substantially raising the likelihood of detecting tax evaders is preferable to a policy of imposing stiff penalties and exhaustively auditing only a few cases. Stiff penalties encourage litigation and make it necessary to devote resources to fighting the taxpayer in court, rather than to exercising better enforcement.

Differential treatment of large taxpayers has enabled tax administrations to set better priorities in the area of services to the taxpayer and to improve their control over tax compliance.

Imposing penalties on taxpayers, issuing final interpretations of tax legislation, auditing returns to ascertain the true tax base, and reaching settlements with taxpayers in an effort to change their behavior in the area of tax compliance are all functions that should remain in the hands of tax administrations. Even so, certain penalties are beginning to be entrusted to the private sector when they involve a low degree of subjectivity, as when private sector agents collect not only the delinquent taxes but also the interest or penalty owed for late payment, which is standard for all taxpayers.

Most tax administrators complain that they do not have enough inspectors or resources to adequately discharge the audit function. Recently, the possibility has emerged of letting the private sector (basically banks) do a large part of the logistical work involved in processing payments and returns, thereby freeing resources to strengthen audit activities, where the administration is called upon to play a more important role.

Privatizing does not always mean greater efficiency, but delegating certain tasks to the private sector, as some countries have successfully done, offers an attractive alternative for tax administration in the decade ahead of us.

Comments

Jorge Martinez-Vazquez

Ramírez Acuña's paper is interesting and innovative. The advanced state of the privatization of tax administration in Latin America surprises me. Ramírez Acuña has performed a valuable task in guiding us through the current privatization efforts in a number of countries in several areas of tax administration.

My comments are designed as a supplement to Ramírez Acuña's work and are divided into two parts. I shall start by taking a little more time to frame the privatization process in tax administration within the wider movement to privatize the public sector in the last decade. The fundamental idea here is to see that there are lessons for tax administration in the experience with privatization in the rest of the public sector. The second part of my comments will examine some of the propositions and experiences described by Ramírez Acuña. For reasons of space I shall refer specifically to cases I think should be emphasized or require further study before definitive conclusions can be offered on them. I shall also refer to some other areas of tax administration, in addition to those mentioned by Ramírez Acuña, which I think are suitable for privatization.

Lessons for Tax Administration from the Experience with Privatization in the Public Sector

The nature of the process of privatizing tax administration differs in important aspects from the process of privatizing the rest of the public sector. Analysis of some of these differences leads us to some interesting conclusions regarding the nature, objectives, limitations, and problems of privatizing tax administration.

The impetus for the privatization of the public sector in the past decade, in both developed and developing countries, sprang largely from ideological opposition to the growth of the public sector and to the general belief that the private sector may be more efficient than the public sector, especially with respect to organization and incentives. This privatization of the public sector has taken three distinct forms: complete devolution of the public function, maintenance of control of the public function while turning over implementation or production to the private sector, and deregulation. Only the second form of privatization is relevant for purposes of tax administration. But even here the differences between tax administration and the rest of the public sector are important. The government can in principle transfer to the private sector any kind of activity that represents a quid pro quo or compensation for services. Only the state, however, has the right to collect taxes. This coercive power to require the surrender of income without a direct payback is the characteristic which perhaps best defines the state and as such is inalienable.

These premises provide an appropriate guideline for what should and should not be privatized in tax administration. Tax administration involves a number of functions such as tax collection, audit, and investigation of taxpayers (if they fail to file or have ceased to file), and action in legal procedures and administrative appeals. All these functions include, in one form or another, an information component and a decision component. The latter contains the principle of public authority and must therefore not be privatized. Examples include the (administrative) interpretation of the law in an audit or the execution of an eviction. But all the information components, including the collection of data, documents, and the like, may, from a constitutional or legal point of view, be privatized.

Naturally, some aspects of tax administration could legally be privatized but should not be for reasons of efficiency. For example, from the theory of business organization we know it is more efficient to keep certain activities within the organization and not subcontract them, when the costs of recontracting with third parties—because of, for instance, lack of information or a very changeable context—are high.

Another important difference between privatization of tax administration and of the rest of the public sector is the political element. Often the privatization of certain public sector activities is a result of pressures of a political nature, for example, for the containment or reduction of public spending. Frequently, such proposals enjoy the support of a majority of the population and are promoted by politicians seeking election or re-election. In contrast, we would expect only in very special cases to find the average citizen exerting political pressure in favor of more efficient tax administration or political parties making improved compliance with tax requirements a central theme of their election campaigns. On the contrary, many taxpayers may be more satisfied with tax systems that permit a certain amount of evasion, provided it does not pose a serious threat to basic services. Politicians may favor less tax evasion because they see evasion as working against equitable taxation and they want the revenue. But it can also be argued that politicians prefer systems with more administrative discretion. An interesting conclusion from these observations is that, contrary to the situation in the rest of the public sector, the impetus for the privatization of tax administration has to come from within the public administration itself.

What are or ought to be the goals in privatizing tax administration? In the light of the Latin American experience so far, the most fundamental of these goals seems to have been that of raising the tax authority's operational capacity to a level which had proved unattainable in the public sector. The need to turn to the private sector in basic aspects of administration seems to be linked to rigidities and other problems in the recruitment and compensation of civil service personnel. From this perspective, privatization can be interpreted as a substitute for an adequate personnel policy. An assumption to be verified empirically is that an inverse ratio exists between the degree of privatization of tax administration and personnel problems in the public sector.

However, it may also be that even when the public sector can recruit and retain employees of the same caliber as the private sector, the latter is more efficient than the private sector. The greater efficiency may derive from better use of resources owing to such factors as incentives and organization. Other goals in addition to efficiency may be considered when evaluating the privatization of a particular tax function. An example of another important goal is that of lessening the taxpayer's cost of compliance. It might be, for instance, that the cost of collecting the tax internally through its own agencies would be the same for the government as collecting through the private banking system. However, the latter route would be considered superior if it is more convenient to the taxpayer, that is to say, if it makes the process of compliance less costly.

What are the most significant problems we can expect in the process of privatizing tax administration given the experience with privatization in the rest of the public sector? First, where public sector employees are organized in unions and reports of planned privatization emerge, labor opposition to privatization can be expected, especially if privatization actually threatens to cut the number of jobs in the public sector. A second problem may be the low quality of services performed by the private sector following privatization. One way to tackle this problem is to invite bids from service providers or use other means that might increase competition among them and protect the quality of service offered by the private sector.

An additional obstacle to the privatization of certain facets of tax administration may arise from a faulty cost-benefit calculation by the public sector. For example, methodologies frequently used in cost-benefit analysis do not internalize all the costs of the public sector. While most public sector agencies, including the tax authority, receive subsidies of many kinds, private firms typically have to pay all their own costs. Often the costs of buildings, furnishings, and equipment, as well as employee pensions, are ignored in cost-benefit calculations in the public sector.

Corruption can also be an important problem accompanying the privatization of tax administration. This problem may be greater for small countries where the number of businesses capable of performing the privatized tasks is small and those businesses are more likely to be controlled by or have some kind of link to government officials. The history of tax administration, with the practice of awarding the right to collect taxes to the highest bidder—common in the old civilizations of the Mediterranean basin and current in Europe up to the Age of Enlightenment—clearly shows that privatization of tax administration and corruption and abuse of power can go hand in hand. The most important lesson to learn from this historical experience is that the government must not lose control, whether direct or indirect, of the private enterprise providing the tax services. An indirect way of exercising this control is to ensure a certain degree of competition within the private sector. A good example is competition among banks to have taxpayers pay their taxes at bank branches.

An important alternative to the privatization of tax administration mentioned by Ramírez Acuña—and which has also been experimented with in other areas of the public sector—is individual incentive systems. On this I would like to inject one note of caution. Incentive systems might be an effective weapon in attacking the problem of efficiency in the public sector, but only if the public sector is able to attract and retain the same quality of personnel as the private sector. Such systems would be less effective if salaries in the public sector are markedly below those of the private sector. In this case the most fundamental problem is the lack of qualified personnel and not the lack of incentives.

Privatization of Tax Administration in Latin America

Ramírez Acuña's paper emphasizes, and rightly so, areas of administration that already have experience with privatization. The bulk of the privatization of tax administration in Latin America seems to have taken place in the area of collection. It seems that almost nothing has been privatized in the audit area and nothing in the legal and inspection areas (inspection of nonfilers and of those who have ceased to file). These last two areas are not even mentioned in Ramírez Acuña's paper. But even with respect to collection, almost all privatization experiments have been in a narrower area, the collection of current taxes. Much less has been done with the privatization of the collection of delinquent accounts. It is not surprising that privatization began in the areas of tax administration that are easier to privatize or less apt to compromise the principle of *patria potestas* embodied in public administration.

Although a good many aspects of tax collection have been privatized, the giant step taken in recent years in this area has been to transfer to the private banking system the receipt of returns and payment of taxes. Given the unreliable mail service in many Latin American countries, the return and payment traditionally had to be completed in person in offices of the ministry of finance. Frequently, this practice meant a significant increase in compliance cost for the taxpayer. An irony of many Latin American tax systems is still that the refrain "in this country everyone is a tax evader" can be heard while long lines of taxpayers patiently wait their turn for hours to pay their taxes in finance ministry offices. The transfer to private banks of the receipt of the return and collection of the tax has cleared one of the greatest tax administration bottlenecks in many countries. El Salvador, Guatemala, and Panama can be added to the countries mentioned by Ramírez Acuña.

Given the high probability that other countries will adopt similar privatization measures, one lesson to be learned from experience is the need to ensure that the tax authority retains personnel qualified in data processing and has the equipment necessary to verify the tapes of data sent by the private banks. An independent system for checking payments is also important to eliminate the possibility of abuse on the banks' part. As Ramírez Acuña points out, the banks' omissions would come to light if the tax authorities were to send taxpayers a notice of failure to pay. However, for this procedure to function properly, a system providing an up-to-date list of taxpayers and their current accounts would be necessary. Unfortunately, this is a problem area for many Latin American tax administrations. In spite of international technical assistance in this area during the last decade, several Latin American countries still do not have an operational individual register or current account system.

Should the treasury turn all tax collection activities over to the private sector? Transferring them to the private banking system, as Ramírez Acuña notes, could free resources for other areas of tax administration. Nevertheless, it may be desirable to keep personnel qualified and experienced in tax collection within the administration.

Another big step in the privatization of tax collection is, as Ramírez Acuña indicates, withholding at source. In addition to making the task of the administration easier, withholding of tax at source has other advantages, for example, decreased tax evasion. Although reporting systems are not perfect substitutes for withholding systems, they have also contributed indirectly to the privatization and simplification of tax administration in some countries. However, reporting systems have seen much less development in Latin America and are not mentioned in the paper. Ramírez Acuña highlights another effect of withholding systems that he considers very important: the possibility of reducing the number of filers without reducing the number of taxpayers. He mentions the example of some countries in which the number of returns was cut 50 percent following exclusion of wage-earners subject to withholding. For these taxpayers the amount withheld is the final tax.

This subject—the waiver of the requirement to file a return for taxpayers subject to withholding at source—merits a little more discussion, given its swift acceptance in Latin American countries. The advantages inherent in the elimination of a universal filing requirement are clear; the most important is that it simplified tax administration. However, there are also disadvantages to this procedure. Aside from the political and philosophical appeal of the universal return and citizen participation, the possibility of increased evasion is perhaps the most important disadvantage. For example, in countries where the personal income tax system leaves it up to the taxpayer to identify and claim various types of deductions and rebates, the elimination of universal filing is an open invitation to falsify deductions. Elimination of the filing requirement also makes it possible for the withholder to defraud the treasury, since there is no independent proof that the tax was paid and that this was done in the amount later filed by the withholding agent. The rejoinder to this line of reasoning has been that, after all, Latin American tax authorities do not have the ability to audit all the returns of wage-earners subject to withholding and that it is unrealistic to pretend otherwise. However, no tax administration is able to audit all taxpayers. It is a known fact that even in the most advanced countries the tax authorities audit only a tiny percentage of the taxpayers and clearly lack the capacity to audit all of them. However, the possibility of being audited appears to play an important role in the "voluntary" compliance of taxpayers. The same logic applies to withholding. One way in which eliminating requirements for filing returns with respect to wages earned may not lead to tax evasion is if the law allows the taxpayer absolutely no discretion: for example, if it grants the taxpayer the right only to a single overall rebate. However, the problem of controlling the withholding agents remains.

In the audit area, Ramírez Acuña correctly points to the self-assessment system as an important step in privatizing this function. The author also notes that some countries have begun to use self-valuation for property taxes. One form of property self-assessment was actually used in Guatemala in the 1987 tax reform, but with little success. The amounts filed represented a very low increase over the real estate values established decades earlier, and a large number of private businesses boycotted the registration and self-valuation process.

Ramírez Acuña also mentions several measures that tax authorities have adopted to facilitate audit activities. These include the signature of the accountant or professional preparer of the return and the fiscal certificate (the preparer not only signs but also assumes responsibility before the treasury for his own errors in computing the tax and interpretation of the legal provisions). Three other measures described by Ramírez Acuña as simplifying inspection—audit insurance, the acceptance of the preceding years if the last tax period is filed correctly, and the reduction of sanctions if the taxpayer does not challenge or appeal the audit—bear similarity to tax amnesties and for that reason are more controversial. It is true that these three types of measures can be more effective than the traditional tax amnesties because they try to change future taxpayer behavior. For example, in the case of audit insurance, the tax authority guarantees to taxpayers that they will not be audited if taxes filed in the current year exceed those filed in the preceding year by a certain percentage. This offer to accept previous years is revoked in the event of failure to meet tax requirements in subsequent years.

Even so, the three types of measures share certain disadvantages with tax amnesties. Their worst feature is that they undermine the public's confidence in the tax authority. Taxpayers grow accustomed to expecting a new form of amnesty or negotiation with the authority. Another serious objection is that those who have paid their taxes may resent that other individuals with the same or higher incomes are officially permitted not to pay their fair share. It is essential to respect the principle of equity and the perception that everyone must pay his or her "fair" share when attempting to secure a high degree of taxpayer compliance. For this reason, the tax authority must take pains to cultivate an image of impartiality in its dealings with taxpayers. From this perspective I do not believe it is a good idea to give special or "red carpet" treatment to large taxpayers as Ramírez Acuña suggests.

I would like to end these comments with a brief summary of other functions of tax administration that lend themselves to privatization and with which one could experiment. Something mentioned at the beginning of these comments should be recalled here: all functions of tax administration have, in different proportions, a decision-making component and an information or implementation component. Only the first component, decision making, involves the principle of *patria potestas* wielded by the state as embodied in the tax authority and as such cannot be privatized. That leaves a number of activities in the area of audit which could be privatized. The tax authority could engage domestic or foreign experts to document areas that require technical expertise not possessed by the authority. For example, the authority could engage private actuaries to analyze the finances of insurance companies and prepare a file prior to an audit of such companies. Later, a decision on all legal interpretations, the application of fines, and the like would be carried out solely by the tax authority.

The same logic could be applied to two other important functions of tax administration: the monitoring of taxpayers and legal action. The tax authority could, for instance, contract with the private sector for a survey designed to identify nonfilers. The survey could be limited to certain groups of professionals. Once the nonfilers were identified, the authority, using its own resources, could act with respect to those taxpayers or subject them to a presumptive tax. In the legal area the public authority could engage private attorneys to represent the authority in court cases involving appeals by taxpayers. These two examples provide a glimpse of what a more imaginative view of the privatization process might lead to in the realm of tax administration.